Advances in Offshore Wind and Wave Energies—2nd Edition

Advances in Offshore Wind and Wave Energies—2nd Edition

Guest Editors

Pedro Beirão
Mário J. G. C. Mendes

MDPI

Basel • Beijing • Wuhan • Barcelona • Belgrade • Novi Sad • Cluj • Manchester

Guest Editors
Pedro Beirão
Mechanical Engineering
Department
Coimbra Institute of
Engineering
Coimbra
Portugal

Mário J. G. C. Mendes
Mechanical Engineering
Department
Instituto Superior de
Engenharia de Lisboa (ISEL)
Lisbon
Portugal

Editorial Office
MDPI AG
Grosspeteranlage 5
4052 Basel, Switzerland

This is a reprint of the Special Issue, published open access by the journal *Journal of Marine Science and Engineering* (ISSN 2077-1312), freely accessible at: https://www.mdpi.com/journal/jmse/special_issues/3R0BMQ68G7.

For citation purposes, cite each article independently as indicated on the article page online and as indicated below:

Lastname, A.A.; Lastname, B.B. Article Title. *Journal Name* **Year**, *Volume Number*, Page Range.

ISBN 978-3-7258-6560-4 (Hbk)
ISBN 978-3-7258-6561-1 (PDF)
https://doi.org/10.3390/books978-3-7258-6561-1

Contents

About the Editors

Pedro Beirão

Pedro Beirão has been affiliated with the Mechanical Engineering Department of the Coimbra Institute of Engineering, Polytechnic Institute of Coimbra, Portugal, since November 1996, and has been an Assistant Professor since 2004. He obtained his Ph.D. in Mechanical Engineering from Instituto Superior Técnico (IST) in 2007 and his M.Sc. and Bachelor's degrees in Mechanical Engineering from the Faculty of Science and Technology of the University of Coimbra in 1999 and 1996, respectively. Since 2004, he has been collaborating with the IST Center of Intelligent Systems in the Institute of Mechanical Engineering as a researcher. His main research areas are wave energy and wave energy converters, modelling, control, PLCs, pneumatics, and oil hydraulics. He has co-authored several scientific publications, including articles, book chapters, and proceedings of peer-reviewed international scientific conferences. He is also the co-author of several national and international patents and utility models. In 2015, he received an honorable mention in the New Generation | 15 contest, sponsored by Siemens® to recognize national young engineering talents in technical and higher education.

Mário J. G. C. Mendes

Mário J. G. C. Mendes is an Associate Professor in the Mechanical Engineering Department, Instituto Superior de Engenharia de Lisboa (ISEL), Polytechnic University of Lisbon, Portugal, where he is the current coordinator of the master's degree in mechanical engineering. He is a member of CENTEC—Centre for Marine Technology and Ocean Engineering (Group of Marine Dynamics and Hydrodynamics) and a member of CIMOSM—Centro de Investigação em Modelação e Optimização de Sistemas Multifuncionais. He obtained his PhD (2008) from the Instituto Superior Técnico (IST), Technical University of Lisbon, Portugal, with a thesis titled "Multi-agent Approach to Fault Tolerant Control Systems", his MSc degree in Mechanical Engineering (2001) in the area of Control Systems, and his Engineering degree (5-year course, after BSc) in Mechanical Engineering (1998) in the area of Automation and Robotics, all from at the same institute (IST). He has published work on his research interests: Design and control systems for renewable energies and energetic efficiency, Offshore wind and wave energy, Industry 5.0—Digital factories, multi-agent system approaches in Fault-Tolerant Control systems, Safety–Fault Detection and Isolation Systems, and Soft Robotics. He has also recently started working in the areas of onboard decision support systems and smart and sustainable cities. He won second place in the H-INNOVA Award 2022 (3rd edition) with the project TOUCH REHAB: Soft Robotic Glove for Hand Rehabilitation. This award was the result of teamwork between two ISEL Master's students in Biomedical Engineering and two Professors. He also won, in 2015, the teacher award of the New Generation | 15 by Siemens® with a proposal for industry 4.0. The New Generation award is an innovative ideas contest, designed for technical and higher education, to recognize young national talents in engineering.

Journal of
Marine Science and Engineering

MDPI

Editorial

Advances in Offshore Wind and Wave Energies—2nd Edition

Pedro Beirão [1,2,*] and Mário J. G. C. Mendes [3,4,*]

1 Mechanical Engineering Department, Coimbra Institute of Engineering, Polytechnic of Coimbra, Rua Pedro Nunes—Quinta da Nora, 3030-199 Coimbra, Portugal
2 IDMEC—Mechanical Engineering Institute, Avenida Rovisco Pais, 1049-001 Lisbon, Portugal
3 Mechanical Engineering Department, Instituto Superior de Engenharia de Lisboa (ISEL), Polytechnic Institute of Lisbon, Rua Conselheiro Emídio Navarro 1, 1959-007 Lisbon, Portugal
4 CENTEC—Centre for Marine Technology and Ocean Engineering, Instituto Superior Técnico (IST), University of Lisbon, Avenida Rovisco Pais, 1049-001 Lisbon, Portugal
* Correspondence: pbeirao@isec.pt (P.B.); mario.mendes@isel.pt (M.J.G.C.M.)

The urgent need to mitigate the severe environmental impacts of climate change urges for a global transition to low-carbon energy technologies, crucial for achieving global sustainability goals. Renewable energies arise as the most advantageous technologies to mitigate climate change, contributing to the necessary emission reductions [1]. Offshore renewables like offshore wind and wave energy are emerging as two of the most promising candidates for delivering clean, scalable, and secure energy. While offshore wind is already a mature industry, wave energy faces more challenges, progressing slowly toward commercial readiness. Despite the impressive advances of the past decade, there are technical, economic, and environmental issues that must be surpassed.

This Special Issue, Advances in Offshore Wind and Wave Energies—2nd Edition, provides an updated overview of progress in these areas and highlights promising directions for future research.

Over the past two decades, offshore wind has evolved from an experimental technology to the principal source of renewable energy generation. By 2023, global offshore wind capacity exceeded 64 GW, with projections exceeding 260 GW by 2030 and potentially 460 GW by 2050 if aligned with the Paris Agreement goals [2]. Floating offshore wind platforms allow access to high-quality wind resources far from shore, making them essential to offshore wind projects' success [3]. Offshore wind is now among the most cost-effective large-scale renewable sources [4].

Presently, global energy demand increases dramatically. Therefore, turbine upscaling becomes a solution to optimize power generation and decreasing the Levelized Cost of Energy (LCoE), which represents the average cost of electricity over a project's lifetime. Turbines started from 2 to 3 MW in the early 2000s, recently increasing above 15 MW prototypes, with rotor diameters exceeding 250 m [5]. Particularly in offshore wind systems, larger turbines create new engineering challenges in the design of supporting substructures (below seawater level) and structures (above seawater level). Regarding the substructures, monopiles dominate shallow waters (<40 m), jacket-frames are widely applied in intermediate depths, and floating platforms (spar, semi-submersible, tension-leg) extend feasibility to >60 m water depth [3]. Towers must support increased loads while maintaining structural integrity, cost-efficiency, and transportability [5].

Wave energy has an immense theoretical potential—estimated at more than 29,000 TWh/year globally [6]. Although due to well-known harsh challenges—severe environment conditions, survivability and reliability, huge economic costs, low energy conversion efficiency, and lack of standardization [7]—its development evolved slowly when compared with wind energy [6]. However, wave energy is gradually progressing to commercial demonstration projects. The availability of large-scale test sites promotes its development by providing real-sea validation of WEC prototypes [8].

Regarding the last drawback pointed above, the variety of wave energy converters (WECs) designs was gradually narrowed to promising categories such as oscillating water columns (OWCs), point absorbers, and overtopping devices [6,9]. OWCs are particularly attractive due to their simplicity and potential for hybridization with offshore wind systems. Advances include variable-geometry chambers, L-shaped ducts, and adaptive skirts that improve energy capture across wave conditions [9]. Improvements in OWC air turbines (especially self-rectifying turbines) and power take off (PTO) damping strategies contribute to an increase in reliability and energy conversion efficiency [6] which are also two of the disadvantages previously referred.

Currently, the combination of wind and wave renewable technologies into hybrid multipurpose offshore platforms offers several benefits, promising efficiency gains, cost reduction, complementarity and marine space optimization. Hybrid systems can achieve important efficiency gains when compared with independent WEC and wind turbine devices, especially when device geometry and PTO systems are optimized for varying sea states [10]. By sharing infrastructures, placing WECs on wind turbine substructures, foundations, electrical cabling, and maintenance logistics are shared, lowering costs [5]. Since wind and wave often reach its peak at different times, they create smoother combined outputs, thus reducing variability [11]. Hybrid wind–wave platforms decrease the seabed footprint, avoiding spatial conflicts with fisheries, shipping, or wildlife conservation [12].

Beyond wind–wave integration, the concept of multi-use ocean platforms is expanding to include aquaculture, hydrogen production, and maritime logistics. These synergies align with the European Union's strategies for sustainable ocean space management [12].

However, this wind–wave synergy requires continuous investment in innovative R&D, policy support, and interdisciplinary collaboration between academia and industry. Important barriers still remain not only for standalone offshore wind (e.g., grid integration, environmental impacts on marine ecosystems) and wave energy (e.g., WEC survivability in extreme conditions, cost reduction, standardization), but also for hybrid wind–wave systems (e.g., structural design, dynamic load management).

Offshore wind has already reached a mature level, while wave energy demonstrates a sustainable progress. Consequently, the future of renewable energy may rely on synergies between offshore wind and wave systems. They can share infrastructures and complement each other to supply stable, reliable, cost-competitive, and large-scale renewable power, contributing to the reduction of fossil fuel dependency. Additionally, interdisciplinary collaboration between researchers, engineers, climate experts, and politics is essential to assure offshore renewable energy sustainability in the next future.

The manuscripts collected in this Special Issue reflect a broad spectrum of themes, ranging from fundamental modeling and control strategies to integrated energy system design and long-term resource assessment.

The first and last contributions of this Special Issue, from Liu et al. (Contribution 1) and Palma et al. (Contribution 8) address the control and operational resilience of floating offshore wind turbines, emphasizing the importance of developing fault-tolerant approaches and advanced forecasting methodologies. Those researchers are aware that the development of reliable and cost-effective floating technologies will be crucial for to take advantage of deep-water resources. Therefore, developed control strategies will contribute to improve efficiency and increase reliability in severe marine environments, where operational costs cannot be neglected.

https://doi.org/10.3390/jmse14010025

Hybrid systems, combining wind and wave energy conversion, also receive attention in this Special Issue. Research from Pérez-Collazo et al. (Contribution 2) and Ahmad et al. (Contribution 4) demonstrate that integrated configurations can deliver smoother power outputs, improved capacity factors, and enhanced grid compatibility. Artificial intelligence and advanced control methods further reinforce the potential of these systems to become viable, scalable solutions in offshore renewable energy.

Another important area represented in the Special Issue is foundation stability and protection. Fixed-bottom offshore wind structures, which are the pillar of offshore deployment, suffer from scouring and seabed erosion. The review and design principles presented by Gao et al. (Contribution 3) provide valuable guidance for engineers and developers, supporting the safe and sustainable expansion of offshore wind systems.

Wave energy research is also represented through novel approaches to conversion and integration. WEC optimization and control methods investigated by Huang et al. (Contribution 5) and the development of energy storage and hydrogen production systems studied by Fayek et al. (Contribution 6), show that wave energy can contribute to future multipurpose energy systems, demonstrating the ability of offshore renewable energy to provide electricity combined with hydrogen supply solutions.

Tong et al. (Contribution 7) presents the long-term assessment of wave climate and resource variability for the South China Sea, supported by artificial intelligence and data-driven modeling, highlight the importance of understanding regional dynamics to the design of resilient systems. This research contributes to diminish the uncertainty in project planning and increase the predictability of offshore renewable production over extended periods.

Overall, contributions included in this Special Issue, ranging from the integration of novel control strategies, hybrid systems, to wave climate resource assessment, emphasize the multidimensional nature of offshore renewable energy research.

Funding: This research received no external funding.

Acknowledgments: The Guest Editors of the Special Issue "Advances in Offshore Wind and Wave Energies—2nd Edition" are deeply grateful to all authors for their valuable contributions. We wish to extend our sincere gratitude to the reviewers for their constructive comments and suggestions, not to mention all the editorial team of *JMSE* for their continuous support in the preparation of this Special Issue. We hope that this Special Issue serve as a valuable resource for researchers, practitioners, and decision makers working toward advancing offshore wind and wave energy technologies.

Conflicts of Interest: The authors declare no conflicts of interest.

List of Contributions:

1. Liu, S.; Han, Y.; Ma, R.; Hou, M.; Kang, C. A Novel Composite Pitch Control Scheme for Floating Offshore Wind Turbines with Actuator Fault Consideration. *J. Mar. Sci. Eng.* **2023**, *11*, 2272. https://doi.org/10.3390/jmse11122272.
2. Pérez-Collazo, C.; Greaves, D.M.; Iglesias, G. A Jacket-Frame Mounted Oscillating Water Column with a Variable Aperture Skirt. *J. Mar. Sci. Eng.* **2023**, *11*, 2383. https://doi.org/10.3390/jmse11122383.
3. Gao, D.; Pan, X.; Liang, B.; Yang, B.; Wu, G.; Wang, Z. A Review and Design Principle of Fixed-Bottom Foundation Scour Protection Schemes for Offshore Wind Energy. *J. Mar. Sci. Eng.* **2024**, *12*, 660. https://doi.org/10.3390/jmse12040660.
4. Ahmad, I.; M'zoughi, F.; Aboutalebi, P.; Garrido, A.J.; Garrido, I. Advancing Offshore Renewable Energy: Integrative Approaches in Floating Offshore Wind Turbine-Oscillating Water Column Systems Using Artificial Intelligence-Driven Regressive Modeling and Proportional-Integral-Derivative Control. *J. Mar. Sci. Eng.* **2024**, *12*, 1292. https://doi.org/10.3390/jmse12081292.
5. Huang, L.; Wang, S.; Pan, B.; Liu, H.; Zhang, J.; Wu, S. Research on Decoupling Duty Cycle Optimization Control Method of a Multiport Converter for Dual-Port Direct Drive Wave Power Generation System. *J. Mar. Sci. Eng.* **2024**, *12*, 1811. https://doi.org/10.3390/jmse12101811.

https://doi.org/10.3390/jmse14010025

6. Fayek, H.H.; Fayek, F.H.; Rusu, E. Quantum-Inspired MoE-Based Optimal Operation of a Wave Hydrogen Microgrid for Integrated Water, Hydrogen, and Electricity Supply and Trade. *J. Mar. Sci. Eng.* **2025**, *13*, 461. https://doi.org/10.3390/jmse13030461.
7. Tong, Y.; Li, J.; Chen, W.; Li, B. Long-Term (1979–2024) Variation Trend in Wave Power in the South China Sea. *J. Mar. Sci. Eng.* **2025**, *13*, 524. https://doi.org/10.3390/jmse13030524.
8. Palma, G.; Bardazzi, A.; Lucarelli, A.; Pilloton, C.; Serani, A.; Lugni, C.; Diez, M. Analysis, Forecasting, and System Identification of a Floating Offshore Wind Turbine Using Dynamic Mode Decomposition. *J. Mar. Sci. Eng.* **2025**, *13*, 656. https://doi.org/10.3390/jmse13040656.

References

1. Obiora, S.; Olusola, B.; Hu, Y.; Ozsahin, D.; Adun, H. Assessing the decarbonization of electricity generation in major emitting countries by 2030 and 2050: Transition to a high share renewable energy mix. *Heliyon* **2024**, *10*, e28770. [CrossRef] [PubMed]
2. GWEC. *Global Offshore Wind Report 2023*; Global Wind Energy Council: Brussels, Belgium, 2023. Available online: https://www.apren.pt/contents/publicationsothers/gwec-global-offshore-wind-report-2023.pdf (accessed on 27 September 2025).
3. Wang, X.; Zeng, X.; Li, J.; Yang, X.; Wang, H. A review on recent advancements of substructures for offshore wind turbines. *Energy Convers. Manag.* **2018**, *158*, 103–119. [CrossRef]
4. IRENA. *Floating Offshore Wind Outlook*; International Renewable Energy Agency: Abu Dhabi, United Arab Emirates, 2024. Available online: https://www.irena.org/-/media/Files/IRENA/Agency/Publication/2024/Jul/IRENA_G7_Floating_offshore_wind_outlook_2024.pdf (accessed on 27 September 2025).
5. Ribeiro, J.; Ribeiro, B.; Pimenta, F.; Tavares, S.; Zhang, J.; Ahmeda, F. Offshore wind turbine tower design and optimization: A review and AI-driven future directions. *Appl. Energy* **2025**, *397*, 126294. [CrossRef]
6. Falcão, A.F.O.; Henriques, J.C.C. Oscillating-water-column wave energy converters and air turbines: A review. *Renew. Energy* **2016**, *85*, 1391–1424. [CrossRef]
7. Ringwood, J.; Zhan, S.; Faedo, N. Empowering wave energy with control technology: Possibilities and pitfalls. *Annu. Rev. Control.* **2024**, *55*, 18–44. [CrossRef]
8. Neill, S.; Fairley, I.; Rowlands, S.; Young, S.; Hill, Y.; Unsworth, C.; King, N.; Roberts, M.; Austin, M.; Hughes, P.; et al. Characterizing the Marine Energy Test Area (META) in Wales, UK. *Renew. Energy* **2023**, *205*, 447–460. [CrossRef]
9. Rezanejad, K.; Souto-Iglesias, A.; Guedes Soares, C. Experimental investigation on the hydrodynamic performance of an L-shaped duct oscillating water column wave energy converter. *Ocean. Eng.* **2019**, *173*, 388–398. [CrossRef]
10. Simonetti, I.; Cappietti, L.; Elsafti, H.; Oumeraci, H. Optimization of the geometry and the turbine induced damping for fixed detached and asymmetric OWC devices: A numerical study. *Energy* **2017**, *139*, 1197–1209. [CrossRef]
11. Fusco, F.; Nolan, G.; Ringwood, J.V. Variability reduction through optimal combination of wind/wave resources—An Irish case study. *Energy* **2010**, *35*, 314–325. [CrossRef]
12. Stuiver, M.; Soma, K.; Koundouri, P.; Van den Burg, S.; Gerritsen, A.; Harkamp, T.; Dalsgaard, N.; Zagonari, F.; Guanche, R.; Schouten, J.-J.; et al. The governance of multi-use platforms at sea for energy production and aquaculture: Challenges for policy makers in European seas. *Sustainability* **2016**, *8*, 333. [CrossRef]

https://doi.org/10.3390/jmse14010025

Journal of
Marine Science and Engineering

MDPI

Article

A Novel Composite Pitch Control Scheme for Floating Offshore Wind Turbines with Actuator Fault Consideration

Shuang Liu [1], Yaozhen Han [1,*], Ronglin Ma [2], Mingdong Hou [1] and Chao Kang [1]

1 School of Information Science and Electrical Engineering, Shandong Jiaotong University, Jinan 250357, China; ls_0823@163.com (S.L.); houmingdong@sdjtu.edu.cn (M.H.); kangchao@sdjtu.edu.cn (C.K.)
2 School of International Education, Shandong Jiaotong University, Jinan 250357, China; maronglin@sdjtu.edu.cn
* Correspondence: hanyz@sdjtu.edu.cn

Abstract: It is of great importance to simultaneously stabilize output power and suppress platform motion and fatigue loads in floating offshore wind turbine control systems. In this paper, a novel composite blade pitch control scheme considering actuator fault is proposed based on an augmented linear quadratic regulator (LQR), a fuzzy proportional integral (PI) and an adaptive second-order sliding-mode observer. Collective pitch control was achieved via the fuzzy PI, while individual pitch control was based on the augmented LQR. In the case of actuator fault, an adaptive second-order sliding-mode observer was constructed to effectively eliminate the need for the upper bound of unknown fault derivatives and suppress the chattering effect. This paper conducted co-simulations based on FAST (Fatigue, Aerodynamics, Structures, and Turbulence) and MATLAB/Simulink to verify the effectiveness and superiority of the proposed scheme under different environmental conditions. It is shown that platform roll was reduced by approximately 54% compared to that under PI control. For the tower fore–aft moment, load reductions of 45% or more were achievable. The proposed scheme can greatly reduce the pitch and roll of the floating platform and loads in the windward direction of the wind turbine.

Keywords: floating offshore wind turbine; adaptive second-order sliding-mode observer; linear quadratic regulator; fuzzy proportional integral; actuator fault

1. Introduction

Due to the increasing physical size of floating offshore wind turbines (FOWTs) and the strong coupling of wind turbine structures, advanced pitch control methods are urgently needed to maintain a stable output power, restrain platform motion and reduce the fatigue loads [1].

Wind turbine pitch control is classified into collective pitch control (CPC) and individual pitch control (IPC). The CPC algorithms mainly include nonlinear proportional–integral derivative (PID) [2], adaptive control [3], sliding-mode control [4], etc. However, for CPC, it is assumed that all blades have similar structural characteristics and bear similar aerodynamic loads, which rarely happens in practical applications [5]. As we know, maintaining a stable output power is contradictory to reducing platform motion and fatigue loads [6]. IPC can effectively reduce the unbalanced loads caused by disturbance, tower shadow effect and wind shear effect while maintaining a stable output power and has drawn strong attention from wind turbine control engineers and scholars [7,8]. Bossanyi performed IPC-related work [9]. Roh et al. [10] proposed a PI-based IPC scheme. The bending moment at the blade root defined by the rotating coordinate reference frame is converted into the tilt bending moment and yaw bending moment at the hub under the fixed coordinate reference frame through Coleman transformation, and two parallel PI controllers are used to control the hub load. Yet, this control method is based on two independent single-input–single-output (SISO) controllers, and multiple SISO control loops may be coupled to each other and affect FOWT performance.

Considering the structural complexity and multiple control objectives of FOWTs, many advanced control methods for FOWTs, based on modern control theory, have been applied [11]. Raach et al. [12] proposed an IPC method based on nonlinear model predictive control, which adjusts three blade pitch angles to achieve multiple-input–multiple-output (MIMO) control of FOWTs. Blade loads can be further reduced by this method, but platform roll, yaw and tower loads were not analyzed. Tong et al. [13] proposed a linear variable-parameter MIMO control method by adjusting blade pitch angle and rotor speed. It can simultaneously adjust output power and reduce pitching motion, but the authors did not pay attention to the in-plane motion of the blade and the sideway motion of the tower.

As one of the advanced control methods of modern control theory, linear quadratic regulator (LQR) can easily achieve closed-loop optimal control for MIMO systems and has the advantages of simple construction and convenient physical implementation. Hence, it is expected to become the control method for commercial FOWTs and has been widely studied [14]. Namik and Stol [15] proposed a multi-objective control algorithm based on LQR and applied it to CPC and IPC. Under different weighting matrix weights for IPC, the simulation results were compared and showed that if greater weighting matrix weight is assigned to power regulation, the platform motion will increase. On the contrary, if greater weight is assigned to reducing the platform motion, the output power fluctuation will increase. It can be seen that the choice of the LQR weighting matrix plays an important role in the stability of the FOWT. Thus, for the LQR control of FOWTs, the selection of the two penalty matrices (the state weight matrix (Q) and the control weight matrix (R)) is very important and also determines the control performance. Wang et al. [16] proposed an LQR scheme based on the Pareto multi-objective binary probability optimization algorithm, which expresses the expected control performances as multi-objective fitness functions to design a set of Pareto LQR controllers and find the optimal Q and R matrices. In addition, intelligent algorithms such as genetic algorithm [17], ant colony algorithm [18] and particle swarm optimization (PSO) [19] were also adopted to optimize the Q and R matrices. Subsequently, Namik and Stol [20] applied an LQR controller based on disturbance-regulated control to a spar-type FOWT. The fluctuation of the output power was improved. However, this method increased the pitch drive, which adversely affected the floating platform. Kim et al. [21] proposed a method to introduce the LQR as a feedforward term into PI control. Their goal was to improve the performance of traditional PI control using a method different from the optimal control method. Sarkar et al. [22] proposed an IPC method based on a wavelet LQR to reduce FOWT loads, but this method increased the fluctuation of the rotor speed and affected the power generation efficiency. The authors of [22] continued their study by combining CPC and IPC [23]. CPC was obtained by controlling the generator rotor speed error via integral control to maintain a stable output power, and IPC was achieved by an LQ controller to improve the platform motion and reduce the blade 1P load. The simulation results showed that this method achieved better results than the PI control and seemed to have advantages. To sum up, there are still difficulties in the design of a pitch control system that can simultaneously meet the requirements of output power stabilization, platform motion suppression and blade and tower fatigue loads reduction for FOWT control.

The above studies were conducted under the assumption that the sensors and the pitch actuators were reliable. In actual operation, the hydraulic pitch system may suffer from faults such as hydraulic leakage, pump wear, high air content in the hydraulic oil, valve blockage and pump blockage, resulting in slow pitch action and negatively affecting the stable operation of the wind turbine. Therefore, actuator faults in blade pitch control systems have the greatest impact on wind turbines. The detection and diagnosis methods of actuator faults include signal-based, data-driven and model-based methods; Gao et al. [24] reviewed them. Effective model-based methods utilize an observer. Shi et al. [25] proposed an adaptive observer to estimate actuator fault, but in this method, the adaptive law needs to be calculated by linear matrix inequality and linear variable parameter technology, which increases the complexity of the observer design. Sun et al. [26] proposed an unknown input observer to estimate the actuator fault. This method can minimize the influence of sensor noise on the observer to estimate the fault; yet, it is necessary to use fault correction to transform the multiplicative fault into an additive fault form, which reduces the model accuracy.

The sliding-mode observer (SMO) is widely used due to its simple structure and strong robustness [27]. Georg et al. [28] proposed a method based on a Takagi–Sugeno SMO to estimate and reconstruct a pitch system's actuator fault. This method can quickly detect faults, but the reconstruction accuracy needs to be improved. Cascaded SMOs were adopted to estimate the state and fault of the pitch system in [29]. The estimation errors were almost zero, which allowed reconstructing the pitch system fault in finite time, but the errors increased when the fault occurred. Lan et al. [30] proposed an adaptive SMO to estimate the states of the pitch system and verified it with a CPC method. Liu et al. [31] extended the scheme in [30] using an adaptive SMO to observe faults, combined with two IPC methods based on PI and H∞. However, the simulation results showed that the IPC methods increased the standard deviation of the output power and the observation fault error compared with the CPC method. To conclude, the observer accuracy of the pitch actuator state and its fault determines the fault compensator performance. Improving fault diagnosis capability can greatly reduce the economic cost of FOWTs.

Therefore, considering the above-mentioned difficulties in the control and fault reconstruction of spar-type FOWTs, a novel pitch control scheme considering actuator fault is proposed in this paper. These are the main novelties of this method: (1) The scheme combines CPC and IPC to achieve blade pitch control. Fuzzy PI was adopted in CPC to mainly stabilize the output power, and an augmented LQR was constructed in IPC to reduce the fatigue loads of the blades and tower and simultaneously suppress platform motion and maintain output power stability. The presented augmented LQR allowed for the introduction of the blade rotor speed error into the performance index function to achieve accurate tracking of the output power; a particle swarm optimization algorithm (PSO) algorithm was used to optimize the Q and R matrices. (2) Considering the influence of actuator hydraulic leakage fault on FOWTs, an adaptive super-twisting sliding-mode (ASTSM) observer is proposed to observe the state and fault of the pitch system for fault reconstruction. The adaptive gains of this observer were used to deal with the uncertainty of actuator fault and disturbance and were adjusted dynamically according to the uncertain values. This method could effectively suppress chattering and increase the observation accuracy.

The rest of this paper is organized as follows: in Section 2, the structure and characteristics of the spar-type FOWT, as well as its complex dynamic and reduced-order model are described; Section 3 introduces the pitch control strategy and the ASTSM observer design; Section 4 describes the simulation environment and simulation settings and verifies the effectiveness of the proposed scheme on a 5 MW spar-type FOWT; and finally, conclusions are drawn in Section 5.

Table 1 shows the acronyms used in this paper for better understanding.

Table 1. Acronyms used.

ASTSM	Adaptive super-twisting sliding mode
CPC	Collective pitch control
CSM	Classical sliding mode
DOF	Degree of freedom
DEL	Damage-equivalent load
FTC	Fault-tolerant control
FOWT	Floating offshore wind turbine
IPC	Individual pitch control
LQR	Linear quadratic regulator
MIMO	Multiple input–multiple output

Table 1. *Cont.*

|MAX|	Maximum absolute value
PID	Proportional integral derivative
PSO	Particle swarm optimization
RMS	Root mean square
SISO	Single input–single output
SMO	Sliding-mode observer
STSM	Super-twisting sliding mode
STD	Standard deviation

2. FOWT Modeling

2.1. The Studied Spar-Type FOWT

The foundation of a spar-type FOWT is a slender column loaded at the bottom. Its ballast weight can balance the center of gravity and thus guarantee the overall stability of the wind turbine. This work considered the 5 MW OC3-Hywind spar-type FOWT as the study object and conducted co-simulations based on FAST and MATLAB/Simulink [32]. The overall structure of the spar-type FOWT and its platform's degree of freedoms (DOFs) are shown in Figure 1. It includes a wind turbine, a floating platform, and a mooring line. Table 2 reports the relevant parameters of the wind turbine. The main parameters of the spar-type floating platform are shown in Table 3.

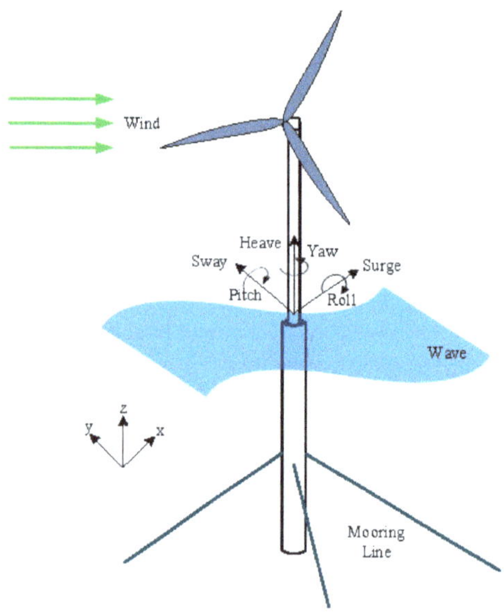

Figure 1. Spar-type FOWT.

Table 2. NREL 5 MW wind turbine parameters.

Parameter	Value
Rated power	5 MW
Number of blades	3
Rotor, hub diameter	126 m, 3 m
Hub height	90 m
Cut-in, rated, cut-out wind speed	3 m/s, 11.4 m/s, 25 m/s
Cut-in, rated rotor speed	6.9 rpm, 12.1 rpm
Rotor mass	110,000 kg

Table 2. *Cont.*

Parameter	Value
Nacelle mass	240,000 kg
Tower mass	347,460 kg
Generator inertia	534.116 kg·m^2
Nacelle inertia	2607.89 × 10^3 kg·m^2
Hub inertia	115.926 × 10^3 kg·m^2

Table 3. Spar-type platform parameters.

Parameter	Value
Draft	120 m
Center of gravity	89.92 m
Displacement	8029 m^3
Total mass of the floating platform	7.466 × 10^6 kg
Roll Inertia	4.229 × 10^9 kg·m^2
Pitch Inertia	4.229 × 10^9 kg·m^2
Yaw Inertia	1.642 × 10^8 kg·m^2
Number of mooring lines	3
Cable stiffness	3.842 × 10^8 N

2.2. Dynamics Modeling

The spar-type FOWT is a complex dynamic system with strong nonlinearity and coupling, which suffers from fatigue loads caused by wind, waves and platform motion. In general, aerodynamic loads are estimated by the blade element momentum theory, and hydrodynamic loads are calculated via the Morrison equation [11].

2.2.1. Aerodynamic Model

The FOWT power depends on the interaction of its rotor with the wind. The rotor converts the kinetic energy of the wind into mechanical energy. The aerodynamic torque T_a, the power P_a, and the thrust F_t acting on the rotor are [6]

$$\begin{cases} T_a(t) = \frac{1}{2\omega_r(t)}\rho A {v_r}^3(t) C_p(\lambda(t),\beta(t)) \\ P_a(t) = \frac{1}{2}\rho A {v_r}^3(t) C_p(\lambda(t),\beta(t)) \\ F_t(t) = \frac{1}{2}\rho A {v_r}^2(t) C_t(\lambda(t),\beta(t)) \end{cases} \quad (1)$$

where $\omega_r(t)$ is the rotor angular velocity; ρ is the air density; A is the rotor swept area; $v_r(t)$ is the effective wind speed on the rotor plane; $C_p(\lambda(t),\beta(t)), C_t(\lambda(t),\beta(t))$ are a power coefficient and a thrust coefficient, respectively; $\lambda(t)$ is the tip speed ratio; and $\beta(t)$ is the pitch angle, where $\lambda(t) = (\omega_r(t)\cdot R)/v_r(t)$, and R is the rotor radius.

2.2.2. Pitch Actuator System and Its Fault

The pitch system consists of three identical hydraulic pitch actuators, each of which can be modeled as a second-order system

$$\ddot{\beta}(t) = -2\zeta\omega_n\dot{\beta}(t) - {\omega_n}^2\beta(t) + {\omega_n}^2\beta_{ref}(t) \quad (2)$$

where $\beta_{ref}(t)$ is the pitch angle reference value, and ω_n, ζ are the natural frequency and the damping ratio of the pitch actuator model.

Hydraulic leakage is a potential fault that affects the system more than pump wear. It can cause changes in pitch system parameters

$$\begin{cases} \zeta(t) = (1 - f_{hl}(t))\zeta_0 + f_{hl}(t)\zeta_{hl} \\ \omega_n(t) = (1 - f_{hl}(t))\omega_{n_0} + f_{hl}(t)\omega_{n_{hl}} \end{cases} \quad (3)$$

where $f_{hl}(t)$ is the fault indicator, with $f_{hl}(t) \in [0,1]$, for all t, $\dot{f}_{hl}(t) \geq 0$. The leakage is irreversible if the system is not repaired. It should be noted that the pressure is only 50% of the rated pressure at $f_{hl}(t) = 1$. ζ_0, ω_{n_0} are the standard parameters under normal pressure, with values of 0.6 and 11.11 rad/s; $\zeta_{hl}, \omega_{n_{hl}}$ are the parameters under low pressure, with values of 0.9 and 3.42 rad/s, respectively.

Substitute (3) into (2) and rewrite it in the form of state space

$$\begin{cases} \dot{x}_1 = x_2 \\ \dot{x}_2 = -\omega_{n_0}{}^2 x_1 - 2\zeta_0\omega_{n_0} x_2 + \omega_{n_0}{}^2 u + \eta_{hl}(x) f_{hl} \\ y = x_1 \end{cases} \quad (4)$$

where $[x_1, x_2]^T = [\beta, \dot{\beta}]^T$ is the system state, and $u = \beta_{ref}$ is the reference input of the pitch system. The fault distribution function is $\eta_{hl}(x) = (\omega_{n_0}{}^2 - \omega_{n_{hl}}{}^2)(x_1 - u) + 2(\zeta_0\omega_{n_0} - \zeta_{hl}\omega_{n_{hl}})x_2$. The unit step response of the pitch system with different values of f_{hl} is shown in Figure 2. It can be observed that hydraulic leakage is characterized by gradual faults and affects the control performance of the FOWT.

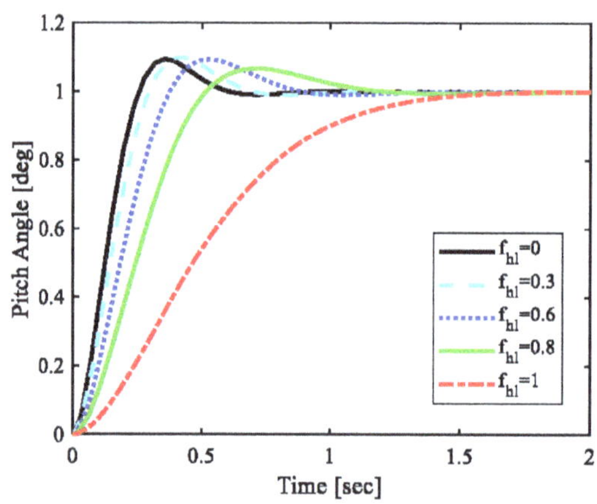

Figure 2. Step response of the pitch actuator system with different values of f_{hl}.

2.2.3. Drivetrain Model

In order to increase the rotational speed of the rotor, the aerodynamic torque was converted into a generator torque through a drivetrain to achieve the high speed required by the generator. A drivetrain can be described by the following three first-order differential equations [21].

$$\begin{cases} J_r\dot{\omega}_r(t) = T_a(t) - K_{dt}\theta_\Delta(t) - (B_{dt} + B_r)\omega_r(t) + \frac{B_{dt}}{N_g}\omega_g(t) \\ J_g\dot{\omega}_g(t) = \frac{K_{dt}}{N_g}\theta_\Delta(t) + \frac{B_{dt}}{N_g}\omega_r(t) - (\frac{B_{dt}}{N_g^2} + B_g)\omega_g(t) - T_g(t) \\ \dot{\theta}_\Delta(t) = \omega_r(t) - \frac{1}{N_g}\omega_g(t) \end{cases} \quad (5)$$

where J_r, J_g indicate the rotational inertia of the low-speed shaft and high-speed shaft, B_r, B_g are the viscous friction coefficients of the low-speed shaft and high-speed shaft, B_{dt} is the attenuation coefficient of the drivetrain, K_{dt} is the torque hardness of the drivetrain, $\theta_\Delta(t)$ is the torsion angle, N_g is the gear ratio, $T_g(t)$ is the generator torque, and $\omega_g(t)$ is the generator speed.

2.2.4. Generator Model

The generator coupled to the drivetrain performs the conversion of mechanical energy to electrical energy. The generator torque $T_g(t)$ is regulated according to its reference value $T_{g_{ref}}(t)$, and its dynamics are approximated by a first-order model

$$\dot{T}_g(t) = -\frac{T_g(t)}{\tau_g} + \frac{T_{g_{ref}}(t)}{\tau_g} \tag{6}$$

where τ_g is the time parameter for the generator system. The generator power depends on the generator rotor speed and the applied loads and is expressed as

$$P_g(t) = \eta_g \omega_g(t) T_g(t) \tag{7}$$

where η_g is the generator efficiency.

2.3. *Reduced-Order Model of the FOWT*

A strongly coupled dynamics system can accurately represent the FOWT behavior, but it also makes the controller design rather complicated. In this paper, the complex dynamic system of the FOWT was linearized, and a linear quadratic optimal pitch control was designed. Because the wind turbine bears most of the aerodynamic load in the downwind direction, the five DOFs in this direction were selected to deduce the reduced-order model of the FOWT.

For the purpose of optimal controller design, the linear state space equation of the FOWT is expressed as

$$\begin{cases} \dot{x} = Ax + Bu + Ew \\ y = Cx \end{cases} \tag{8}$$

where $x = [x_1{}^T, \dot{x}_1{}^T]$, and $x_1 = [x_p, x_{tfa1}, x_{b1f1}, x_{b2f1}, x_{b3f1}]$; x_p is the pitch of the floating platform, x_{tfa1} is the fore–aft movement displacement of the tower, x_{bif1}, $i = 1,2,3$ is the displacement of the blades 1, 2 and 3 in the flapwise tip, $u = [\beta_1, \beta_2, \beta_3]^T$ is the three blades' pitch angle, and $w = \tau_{wind} + \tau_{wave}$ is the environmental disturbance vector due to wind and wave loads. In order to simplify the LQR controller design, the matrix A is described by the second-order motion equation for the selected FOWT DOFs in the case of ignoring external disturbances [6,8]. It is expressed as

$$M\ddot{x}_1 + D\dot{x}_1 + Kx_1 = 0 \tag{9}$$

where the matrix M and matrix K are the mass coefficient and the stiffness coefficient of the FOWT linearization system, and the matrix D is the damping coefficient term which is usually relatively small [23].

$$M = \begin{bmatrix} m_{pp} & m_{pt} & m_{pb1} & m_{pb2} & m_{pb3} \\ m_{pt} & m_{tt} & m_{tb} & m_{tb} & m_{tb} \\ m_{pb1} & m_{tb} & m_{bb} & 0 & 0 \\ m_{pb2} & m_{tb} & 0 & m_{bb} & 0 \\ m_{pb3} & m_{tb} & 0 & 0 & m_{bb} \end{bmatrix} \tag{10}$$

$$K = \begin{bmatrix} k_p & 0 & 0 & 0 & 0 \\ 0 & k_t & 0 & 0 & 0 \\ 0 & 0 & k_{b1} & 0 & 0 \\ 0 & 0 & 0 & k_{b2} & 0 \\ 0 & 0 & 0 & 0 & k_{b3} \end{bmatrix} \tag{11}$$

$$D = \begin{bmatrix} d_p & 0 & 0 & 0 & 0 \\ 0 & d_t & 0 & 0 & 0 \\ 0 & 0 & d_b & 0 & 0 \\ 0 & 0 & 0 & d_b & 0 \\ 0 & 0 & 0 & 0 & d_b \end{bmatrix} \quad (12)$$

In the matrix M,

$$\begin{cases} m_{pp} = 12H^2\int_0^R \mu_b(r)dr + \sum_{i=1}^{3}\left[4H\int_0^R r\mu_b(r)dr\cos(\varphi_i) + \int_0^R r^2\mu_b(r)dr\cos^2(\varphi_i)\right] \\ +H^2(m_n + m_h) + I_P + I_P{}^{pitch} \\ m_{pt} = 6H\int_0^R \mu_b(r)dr + \int_0^H h\mu_t(h)\phi_t(h)dh \\ m_{pb_i} = 2H\int_0^R \phi_b(r)\mu_b(r)dr + \int_0^R r\phi_b(r)\mu_b(r)dr\cos(\varphi_i), i = 1,2,3 \\ m_{tt} = 3\int_0^R \mu_b(r)dr + \int_0^H \phi_t{}^2(h)\mu_t(h)dh + m_n + m_h \\ m_{tb} = \int_0^R \phi_b(r)\mu_b(r)dr \\ m_{bb} = \int_0^R \phi_b{}^2(r)\mu_b(r)dr \end{cases} \quad (13)$$

where H is the height of the tower; R is the length of the blade; φ_i is the azimuth angle of the ith blade; m_n, m_h are the masses of nacelle and the hub; I_p is the moment of inertia of the platform; $I_p{}^{pitch}$ is the hydrodynamic additional mass factor associated with the selected pitch DOF of the platform; $\mu_b(r)$ and $\mu_t(h)$ are the mass per unit length of blade and tower; and $\phi_b(r)$ and $\phi_t(h)$ are the normalized, basic model shapes in the blade flapwise direction and the fore–aft displacement direction of the tower.

In the matrix K,

$$\begin{cases} k_p = F_{pitch}^{Hydrostatic} + k_{mooring}^{Lines} \\ k_t = \int_0^H EI_{tfa}(h)\left(\frac{d^2\phi_t(h)}{dh^2}\right)^2 dh \\ k_{bi} = \int_0^R EI_{bf}(r)\left(\frac{d^2\phi_b(r)}{dr^2}\right)^2 dr + \omega_r{}^2\int_0^R\int_r^R \mu_b(\xi)\xi d\xi \phi_b'^2(r)dr \\ -g\int_0^R\int_r^R \mu_b(\xi)\xi d\xi\phi_b'^2(r)dr\cos(\varphi_i) \;\; i = 1,2,3 \end{cases} \quad (14)$$

where $F_{pitch}^{Hydrostatic}$ is the hydrostatic force associated with the selected pitch DOF of the platform, $k_{mooring}^{Lines}$ is the stiffness of the linearized ropes of the mooring system, k_t is the elastic stiffness of the tower, k_{bi} is the sum of the elastic stiffnesses of the blades, and $EI_{tfa}(h), EI_{bf}(r)$ are the section stiffnesses in the fore–aft displacement direction of the tower and in the flapwise direction of the blade.

In the matrix D,

$$\begin{cases} d_t = \frac{2\zeta_t}{\omega_t}k_t \\ d_b = \frac{2\zeta_b}{\omega_b}k_b \end{cases} \quad (15)$$

where d_p is the linear hydrodynamic damping coefficient associated with the selected pitch DOFs of the platform, d_t and d_b are the structural damping coefficients of the tower and blade, ω_t and ω_b are the intrinsic frequencies of the tower and blade, and ζ_t and ζ_b are the damping ratios of the tower and blade, respectively.

We have

$$\text{Matrix } A = \begin{bmatrix} 0_{5*5} & I_{5*5} \\ -M^{-1}K & -M^{-1}D \end{bmatrix}, \text{ Matrix } C = \begin{bmatrix} I_{5*5} & 0_{5*5} \\ 0_{5*5} & 0_{5*5} \end{bmatrix};$$

the matrix B is obtained by a Taylor series expansion of the second equation in (1) around the full-load operating point (o.p.) (the operating point is considered to be the nominal wind speed of 18 m/s, corresponding to a nominal blade pitch angle equal to 15°)

$$F_t = F_t|_{o.p.} + \frac{\partial F_t}{\partial \beta}|_{o.p.}\beta + \frac{\partial F_t}{\partial \omega_r}|_{o.p.}\omega_r + \frac{\partial F_t}{\partial v_r}|_{o.p.}v_r \quad (16)$$

When the external disturbances and torque change relative to the rotor speed are ignored, the matrix B is obtained by

$$B = \frac{\partial F_T}{\partial \beta}|_{o.p.} \tag{17}$$

It is worth noting that although the optimal controller was designed based on the reduced-order model of the FOWT with 5 DOFs, the final proposed controller was tested based on the full-order nonlinear model of the FOWT.

3. Research Methodology

The focus of this study was on the region 3 (above the rated wind speed region) of the FOWT. The proposed pitch controller combines CPC and IPC. The former was used to maintain output power stability by controlling the rotor speed of the generator, and the latter was constructed by the augmented LQR method to effectively reduce the wind turbine loads and maintain the output power at the same time. Considering the pitch actuator fault, the ASTSM observer was built to observe the actuator state and its fault, and the observation result was transmitted to the fault compensator. The fault-tolerant control (FTC) system with the fault compensator restored the pitch system to a fault-free state. The structure diagram of the proposed scheme is shown in Figure 3. The control input for a single blade pitch angle is

$$\beta_i(t) = \beta_{CPC}(t) + \beta_{IPC_i}(t) \quad i = 1,2,3 \tag{18}$$

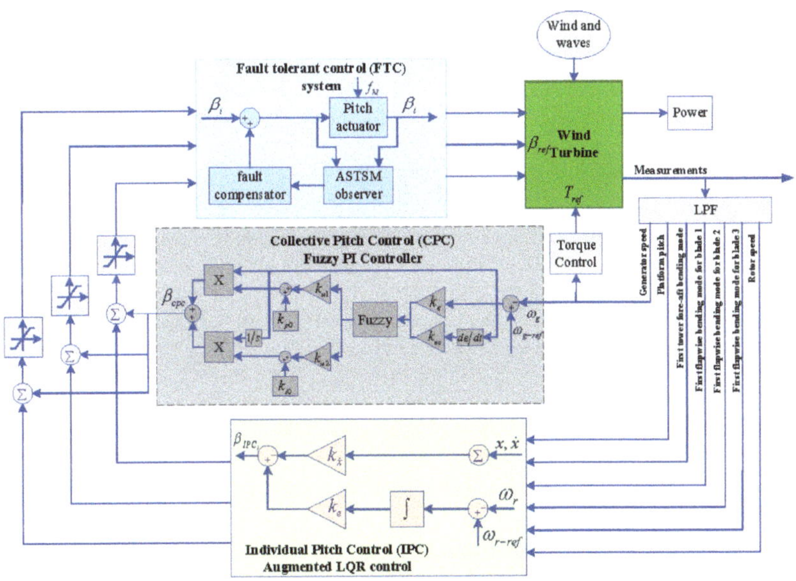

Figure 3. Diagram of the proposed scheme structure.

3.1. CPC Design

To apply PI control to the FOWT, the error signal was chosen as

$$e(t) = \omega_{g_{ref}}(t) - \omega_g(t) \tag{19}$$

where $\omega_{g_{ref}}(t)$ is the rated generator speed, and $\omega_g(t)$ is the actual generator speed.

Then, the control law of the PI pitch controller is

$$u_\beta(t) = k_{P0}e(t) + k_{I0}\int_0^t e(\tau)d\tau \quad (20)$$

where k_{p0}, k_{I0} are proportional gain and integral gain.

However, a practical difficulty is that the loads on a wind turbine are complex and vary when the environmental conditions, such as turbulent wind and sea wave, change. It is difficult to select the optimal gains of the traditional PI controller. A fuzzy PI controller can adjust the control parameters online and has strong adaptability and robustness. This study constructed a fuzzy PI control scheme, which is shown in the "Collective Pitch Control (CPC)" section of Figure 3. In Figure 3, k_e, k_{ec} are proportional factors, and k_{u1}, k_{u2} are quantization factors. The fuzzy PI controller uses the generator rotor speed error *e* and the error rate of change *ec* as inputs, and adopts fuzzy rules to adjust the PI parameters online; the outputs are k_{P1}, k_{I1} which are added to the initial values k_{p0}, k_{I0} to obtain the actual parameters of the PI controller outputs. The fuzzy field is usually selected in the range [−6, 6] for wind turbine pitch control to maintain the variation of the allowable error at about 5% of the rated rotor speed, which is considered reasonable [33]. The indices *e* and *ec* were set as [−6, 6], and k_{P1}, k_{I1} were set as [−1, 1] in this study. A detailed procedure for fuzzy controller design can be found in the authors' previous study [34].

Then, the pitch angle input under CPC is

$$\beta_{CPC}(t) = (k_{P0} + k_{P1})e(t) + (k_{I0} + k_{I1})\int_0^t e(\tau)d\tau \quad (21)$$

3.2. IPC Design

3.2.1. Augmented LQR Controller Design

In this section, the blade rotor speed error is introduced into the performance index function, and the augmented LQR control method is presented.

Rewrite (8) as

$$\begin{cases} \dot{x} = Ax + Bu \\ y = Cx \end{cases} \quad (22)$$

According to (22), the control's objective is to make the blade rotor speed accurately track the given signal *r(t)* = *a* × 1(*t*) (where *a* is a constant vector—here, *a* = 12.1 rpm—and 1(*t*) is a step signal with an amplitude of 1). Then, the error is $e = r - y_1$ (y_1 represents the actual blade rotor speed. Since the state equation of the FOWT under LQR control does not include the blade rotor speed, it is represented by y_1).

Then, the time derivatives of (22) and the tracking error *e* are deduced as

$$\begin{cases} \ddot{x} = A\dot{x} + B\dot{u} \\ \dot{e} = \frac{d(r-y_1)}{dt} = -\dot{y}_1 = -C_1\dot{x}_1 \end{cases} \quad (23)$$

Choose the augmented state vector as $\tilde{x} = [\dot{x}^T, e]^T = [x_p, x_{tfa1}, x_{b1f1}, x_{b2f1}, x_{b3f1}, e]^T$, then the state equation of the augmented system is obtained as

$$\dot{\tilde{x}} = \tilde{A}\tilde{x} + \tilde{B}\tilde{u} \quad (24)$$

where $\tilde{u} = \dot{u}$, $\tilde{A} = \begin{bmatrix} A & 0 \\ 0 & -C_1 \end{bmatrix}$, $\tilde{B} = \begin{bmatrix} B \\ B_1 \end{bmatrix}$, and the corresponding performance index function is

$$J = \frac{1}{2}\int_0^\infty (\tilde{x}^T Q\tilde{x} + \tilde{u}^T R\tilde{u})dt \quad (25)$$

where $Q = \begin{bmatrix} Q_1 & 0 \\ 0 & Q_2 \end{bmatrix}$ is a positive semi-definite symmetric matrix.

The above problem was transformed into a conventional LQR problem, and the optimal control law was obtained by the LQR method

$$\widetilde{u} = \widetilde{K}\widetilde{x} = -R^{-1}\widetilde{B}^T P\widetilde{x} \tag{26}$$

where P satisfies the Riccati Equation (27).

$$P\widetilde{A} + \widetilde{A}^T P - P\widetilde{B}R^{-1}\widetilde{B}^T P + Q = 0 \tag{27}$$

$\widetilde{K}$ is expressed as a block matrix $\widetilde{K} = [K_{\dot{x}}, K_e]$ according to $\dot{x}$ and e. Then,

$$\dot{u} = \widetilde{u} = \widetilde{K}\widetilde{x} = \begin{bmatrix} K_{\dot{x}} & K_e \end{bmatrix} \begin{bmatrix} \dot{x} \\ e \end{bmatrix} = K_{\dot{x}}\dot{x} + K_e e \tag{28}$$

The integral of (28) is obtained as

$$u = K_{\dot{x}}x + K_e \int_0^T e(\tau)d\tau \tag{29}$$

The schematic diagram of this augmented LQR control is shown in the "Individual Pitch Control (IPC)" section in Figure 3. It can be observed that the integral of the wind turbine blade rotor speed error e is fed back to the input of the controller; hence, accurate tracking of the output power can be achieved.

3.2.2. PSO Algorithm

The performance of an LQR controller strongly depends on the weighting matrices (Q, R); therefore, their selection is important. The PSO algorithm, which is based on swarm search to deal with optimization problems in continuous or discrete space, is applied to optimize the weighting matrices. It uses the particles constantly moving in the solution space as the optimization swarm.

Each particle adjusts its speed according to the optimal solution which has been already determined, so as to search for a better solution. Figure 4 illustrates how the PSO algorithm works. The velocity and position update formulas of each iteration particle are

$$v_i^{t+1} = wv_i^t + c_1r_1(pbest_i^t - x_i^t) + c_2r_2(gbest_i^t - x_i^t) \tag{30}$$

$$x_i^{t+1} = x_i^t + v_i^{t+1} \tag{31}$$

where v_i^t is the velocity of the ith particle at the tth iteration; x_i^t is the position of the ith particle at the tth iteration;w is the weight coefficient; c_1, c_2 are acceleration coefficients; r_1, r_2 are random numbers in the interval [0, 1]; and $pbest, gbest$ are the optimal past positions of the particle itself and the particle swarm, respectively.

3.3. ASTSM Observer Design

In this section, considering the influence of the actuator hydraulic leakage fault on the FOWT, the ASTSM observer is proposed to observe the state and fault of the pitch system for fault reconstruction. The "co-design" structure is shown in Figure 3 ("Fault-tolerant control (FTC) system").

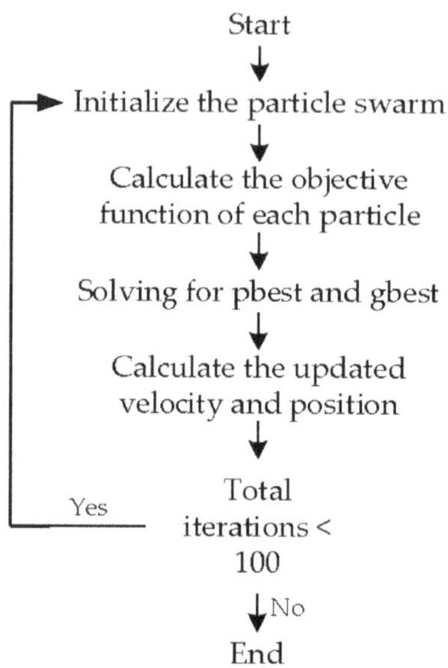

Figure 4. Working principle of the PSO algorithm.

3.3.1. Fault Compensator

A fault compensator with a common design structure [31], which can make the pitch recover to a fault-free state in case of faults, was adopted. The fault compensator is

$$u_\beta(t) = \frac{{\omega_{n_0}}^2}{\hat{\omega}_n{}^2(t)}\beta_{ref}(t) - \frac{\eta_{hl}(\hat{x})\hat{f}_{hl}(t)}{\hat{\omega}_n{}^2(t)} \tag{32}$$

where $\hat{\omega}_n{}^2(t) = (1-\hat{f}_{hl}(t)){\omega_{n_0}}^2 + \hat{f}_{hl}(t){\omega_{n_{hl}}}^2$, $\eta_{hl}(\hat{x}) = ({\omega_{n_0}}^2 - {\omega_{n_{hl}}}^2)\hat{x}_1 + 2(\zeta_0\omega_{n_0} - \zeta_{hl}\omega_{n_{hl}})\hat{x}_2$, and $\hat{x}$ is the observation value of the ASTSM observer. Thus, the observation values of x_1, x_2, f_{hl} are needed, and the observation method will be described next.

3.3.2. The ASTSM Observer

According to (4), the ASTSM observer is constructed as

$$\begin{cases} \dot{\hat{x}}_1 = \hat{x}_2 + k_1 v_1(x_1, \hat{x}_1) \\ \dot{\hat{x}}_2 = -{\omega_{n_0}}^2\hat{x}_1 - 2\zeta_0\omega_{n_0}\hat{x}_2 + {\omega_{n_0}}^2 u + \eta_{hl}(\hat{x})\hat{f}_{hl} + k_2 v_2(x_2, \hat{x}_2) \\ \dot{\hat{f}}_{hl} = v(f_{hl}, \hat{f}_{hl}) \end{cases} \tag{33}$$

For (33), the control law $v(\cdot)$ can be designed by the adaptive super-twisting algorithm [35]

$$\begin{cases} v(s) = k_1(t)v_1(s) + k_2(t)v_2(s) \\ v_1(s) = \sqrt{|s|}sign(s) \\ \dot{v}_2(s) = sign(s) \end{cases} \tag{34}$$

where s represents the sliding variable, and $k_1(t), k_2(t)$ are adaptive gains

$$\begin{cases} \dot{k}_1 = \begin{cases} \alpha_1\sqrt{\frac{\sigma_1}{2}}sign(|s|-\varepsilon) & k_1 > \underline{k} \\ \bar{k} & k_1 \le \underline{k} \end{cases} & (k_1(0) > \underline{k}) \\ k_2 = \beta_1 k_1 \end{cases} \tag{35}$$

where $\alpha_1, \beta_1, \sigma_1, \varepsilon, \bar{k}, \underline{k}$ are arbitrary positive numbers, and $\underline{k}$ can be arbitrarily small.

Defining the observation errors $e_{x_1} = x_1 - \hat{x}_1, e_{x_2} = x_2 - \hat{x}_2, e_{f_{hl}} = f_{hl} - \hat{f}_{hl}$ and then subtracting (33) from (4), the observation error dynamic equation can be obtained

$$\begin{cases} \dot{e}_{x_1} = e_{x_2} - v_1(x_1, \hat{x}_1) \\ \dot{e}_{x_2} = -\omega_{n_0}{}^2 e_{x_1} - 2\zeta_0\omega_{n_0}e_{x_2} + \eta_{hl}(x)f_{hl} - \eta_{hl}(\hat{x})\hat{f}_{hl} - v_2(x_1, \hat{x}_1) \end{cases} \tag{36}$$

$$\dot{e}_{f_{hl}} = \dot{f}_{hl} - v(f_{hl}, \hat{f}_{hl}) \tag{37}$$

Defining $\tilde{\eta}_{hl} = \eta_{hl}(x) - \eta_{hl}(\hat{x})$ and $\eta_{hl}(x)f_{hl} - \eta_{hl}(\hat{x})\hat{f}_{hl} = \tilde{\eta}_{hl}f_{hl} + \eta_{hl}(\hat{x})e_{f_{hl}}$, (36) is rewritten as

$$\begin{cases} \dot{e}_{x_1} = e_{x_2} - v_1(x_1, \hat{x}_1) \\ \dot{e}_{x_2} = -\omega_{n_0}{}^2 e_{x_1} - 2\zeta_0\omega_{n_0} + \tilde{\eta}_{hl}f_{hl} + \eta_{hl}(\hat{x})e_{f_{hl}} - v_2(x_1, \hat{x}_1) \end{cases} \tag{38}$$

From Section 2.2.2, f_{hl} is bounded; then, assume $|f_{hl}| \leq L, \left|\dot{f}_{hl}\right| \leq \overline{L}$ is satisfied.

For (34), the sliding surface is defined as

$$s = \left\{ col(e_{f_{hl}}, e_{x_1}, e_{x_2}) \middle| e_{x_i} = 0, i = 1,2 \right\} \tag{39}$$

For the stability proof, refer to [35].

4. Simulation Results and Discussion

The effectiveness of the proposed scheme was verified. The aerodynamic, mechanical and electrical parts of the FOWT were simulated by FAST code, and the proposed controller and observer were developed in the MATLAB/Simulink environment. A fully nonlinear simulation was executed in FAST, enabling all DOFs of the FOWT. Due to physical limitations, the constraint of the pitch angle and its rate of change for the NREL 5 MW FOWT were $\beta \in [0°, 90°]$, $\dot{\beta} \in [-8, 8](°)/s$.

The simulations were performed under two different wind and wave conditions. Turbulent wind fields were generated by the software TurbSim v2.00 [36], and random waves were simulated by the Pierson–Moskowitz spectrum. For each environmental condition, 600 s simulations were performed using different stochastic seeds based on time series of wind and wave loads. The environmental conditions are shown in Table 4, and the time series are shown in Figure 5.

Table 4. Environmental parameters.

Case No.	Wind Speed (m/s)	Turbulence Intensity (%)	Wave Height Hs (m)	Peak Spectral Period Tp (s)
1	18	12.733	6	10
2	20	12.36	9	13

The fatigue loads for the blades and the tower were analyzed via the NREL's MLife code [37]. MLife is a Matlab-based tool for post-processing results from wind turbine testing and aeroelastic dynamic simulations. The damage-equivalent loads (DELs) were obtained for a life of 20 years and a frequency of 1 Hz.

The time-series data of the first 30 s were removed in the analysis to eliminate the influence of the initial transient process. The effect of faults on the pitch actuator was simulated by modifying the natural frequency and damping ratio of the pitch system dynamics. The superiority of the presented ASTSM observer was verified by comparing it with the classical sliding-mode (CSM) observer [38] and the super-twisting sliding-mode (STSM) observer [39].

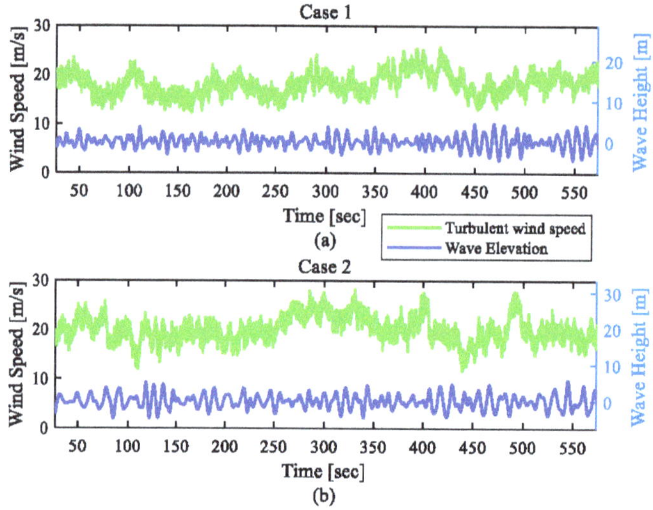

Figure 5. (**a**) Wind speed and waves for Case 1, and (**b**) wind speed and waves for Case 2.

4.1. Control Performance Analysis

The values of the parameters of the CPC–PI control were chosen as $k_{p0} = 0.01$, $k_{i0} = 0.001$. The feedback gain matrix of the augmented LQR controller optimized by the PSO was

$$K_{\dot{x}} = \begin{bmatrix} -0.0205 & 0.0347 & 0.00371 & -0.0358 & 0.0196 & -0.00877 & -0.0188 & -0.0244 & 0.0208 & 0.00568 \\ -0.0283 & -0.0309 & -0.00649 & -0.0228 & -0.0207 & 0.0207 & 0.0117 & -0.00978 & 0.0019 & -0.023 \\ -0.0337 & 0.0323 & -0.00268 & -0.0249 & -0.0635 & -0.00635 & 0.0321 & -0.0189 & -0.0234 & 0.0106 \end{bmatrix},$$

$$K_e = \begin{bmatrix} 0.0191 \\ 0.0321 \\ 0.0176 \end{bmatrix}$$

Figure 6 shows the PSO convergence plot for the performance indicator function mentioned in Section 3.2.1 over 100 iterations.

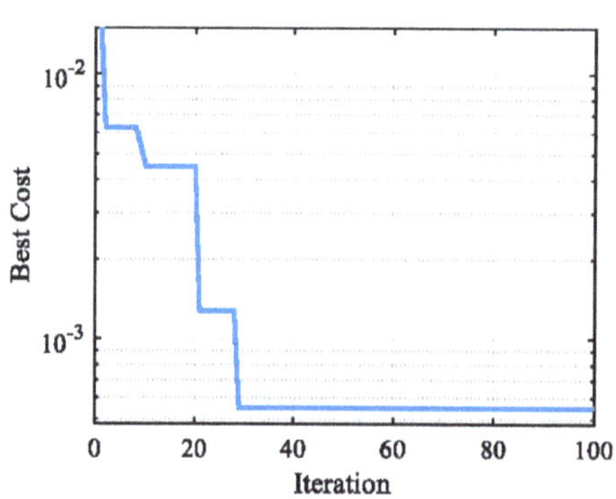

Figure 6. Convergence of the PSO for the performance index function.

The proposed controller performance was investigated in terms of wind turbine output power, platform motion and fatigue DELs. Figure 7a,b shows the output power and rotor speed for case 1, and Figure 7c,d shows the responses for case 2. It can be observed that under the two environmental conditions, the fluctuations of power output and rotor speed under the proposed control method were much smaller than under CPC–PI control. CPC–PI control increased the fluctuation frequency of the output power and the rotor speed when the wind and waves changed, while the proposed method could suppress this fluctuation and maintain the stability of the output power. Figure 8a–c shows the platform pitch, roll and yaw motions for case 1, and Figure 8d–f shows the responses for case 2. It can be observed that the proposed controller significantly reduced the pitch and roll of the platform.

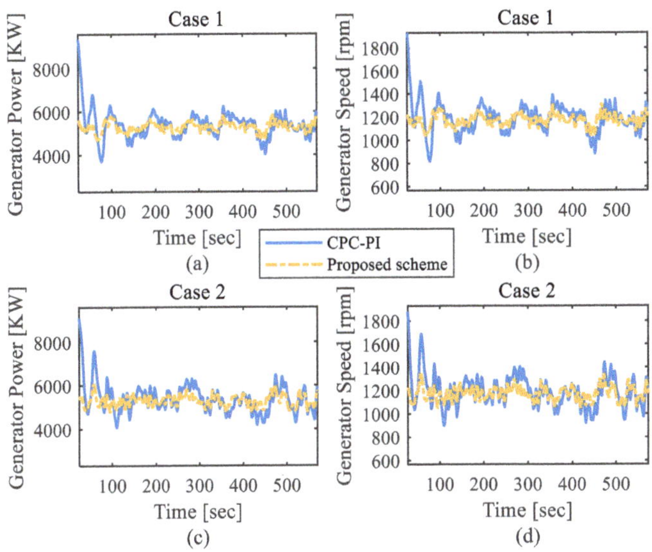

Figure 7. Generator power (**a**) and generator speed response (**b**) on Case 1, Generator power (**c**) and generator speed response (**d**) on Case 2.

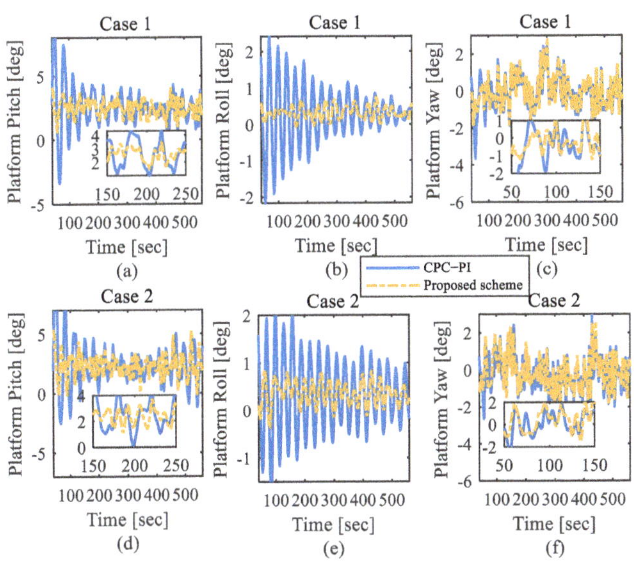

Figure 8. Platform motion response (**a–c**) in Case 1, and platform motion response (**d–f**) in Case 2.

Figure 9 reports the bar graph based on the root mean square (RMS), standard deviation (STD) and maximum absolute value (|MAX|) index, with the CPC–PI control results as the baseline. The comparisons of Figure 9a–j show the advantages of the proposed control scheme. Compared with the CPC–PI method, the RMS value of the rotor speed in case 1 with the proposed scheme could reach 1174.1 rpm, which was closer to the rated value (1173.7 rpm). With respect to platform motion, the RMS values of pitch, roll and yaw were reduced by 15%, 54% and 9%, respectively. Figure 9k–p shows the fatigue DELs of the FOWT. It is shown that the loads were suppressed or remained basically unchanged under the proposed control scheme. Compared with the CPC–PI control, the DELs of the blade out-of-plane moment and in-plane moment were reduced by 10% and 2%, and the DELs of the tower fore–aft moment and side-to-side moment were reduced by 10% and 45% in case 1. To sum up, compared with the PI control, the proposed scheme reduced platform motion and fatigue DELs, while maintaining a stable output power.

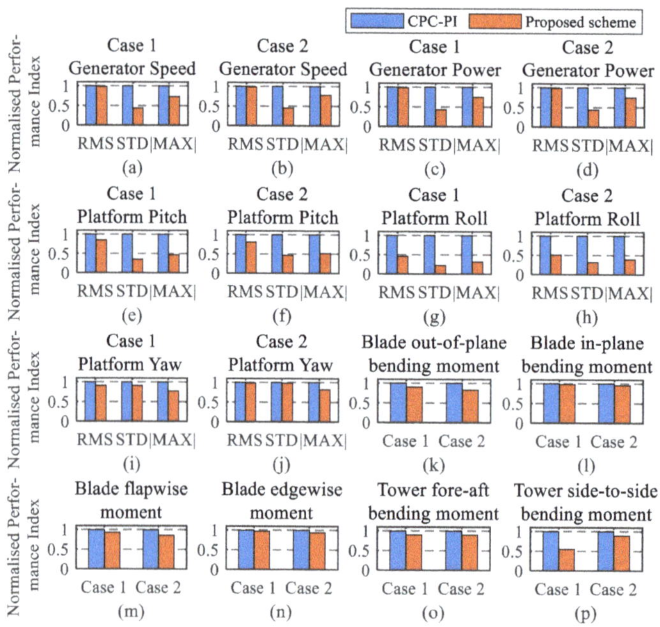

Figure 9. Nominal performance index normalized to the CPC–PI results.

Figure 10 shows the pitch angle change under the proposed controller and the CPC–PI controller in the two random environments. It can be observed that the proposed controller increased the frequency of the blade pitch to achieve the interacting control objectives. However, Figure 11 indicates that the maximum pitch rate was completely within the safety limit of the constraint condition of 8 deg/s.

4.2. Performance in the Presence of Actuator Fault

Although FAST is an effective tool for wind turbine control verification, it does not include the dynamic response of any pitch actuator. To compensate for this defect, an additional pitch actuator dynamics module was added to the existing model. To achieve fault reconstruction for the pitch system, the performance of the proposed ASTSM observer was evaluated with three pitch systems suffering from hydraulic leakage faults. Faults 1, 2 and 3 persisted for the entire simulation time. According to (35), the parameters of the ASTSM observer were chosen as follows

Pitch system 1: $\alpha_1\sqrt{\frac{\sigma_1}{2}} = 0.41,\ \varepsilon = 0.0125,\ \underline{k} = 0.4,\ \overline{k} = 0.41,\ \beta_1 = 0.07.$

Pitch system 2: $\alpha_1\sqrt{\frac{\sigma_1}{2}} = 0.35$, $\varepsilon = 0.0125$, $\underline{k} = 0.3$, $\overline{k} = 0.35$, $\beta_1 = 0.05$.

Pitch system 3: $\alpha_1\sqrt{\frac{\sigma_1}{2}} = 0.45$, $\varepsilon = 0.0125$, $\underline{k} = 0.4$, $\overline{k} = 0.45$, $\beta_1 = 0.08$.

For convenience, only the estimation results of the ASTSM observer for actuator faults in case 1 are shown. Figure 12 shows the three pitch systems faults and the observations from the ASTSM observer. It can be seen that the ASTSM observer could accurately observe the pitch actuator faults, which verified the effectiveness of the ASTSM observer.

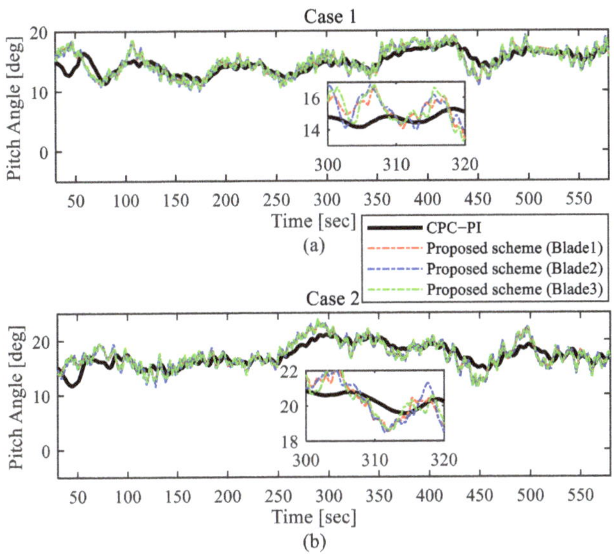

Figure 10. (**a**) Pitch angle change for Case 1, and (**b**) pitch angle change for Case 2.

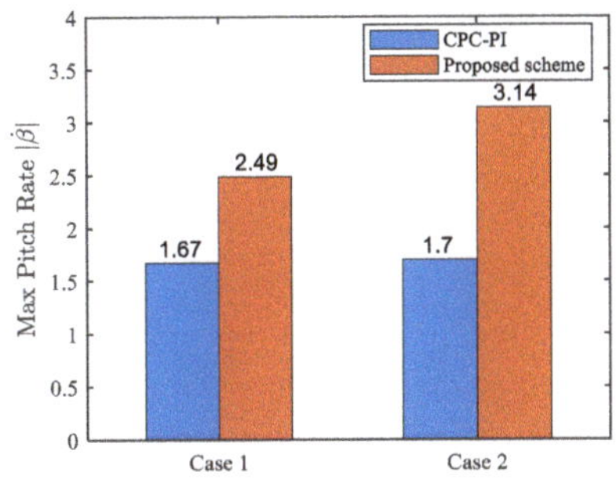

Figure 11. Blade maximum pitch rate.

In order to demonstrate the superiority of the presented ASTSM observer, our model was compared with the CSM observer and the STSM observer. The observation errors of the pitch actuator faults are shown in Figures 13–15. It was observed that with the CSM observer there was obvious chattering and a large observation error. With the STSM observer, chattering was reduced. When the ASTSM observer was adopted, the chattering effect and observation error were greatly reduced. The performance indicators in Table 5 are defined as

$$\left\|e_{f_{hl_i}}\right\|_2 = \sqrt{\int_0^{600} \left|e_{f_{hl_i}}(t)\right|^2 dt}, \ \left\|e_{f_{hl_i}}\right\|_\infty = \max_{t\in 0-600}\left|e_{f_{hl_i}}(t)\right|, \ i = 1,2,3 \tag{40}$$

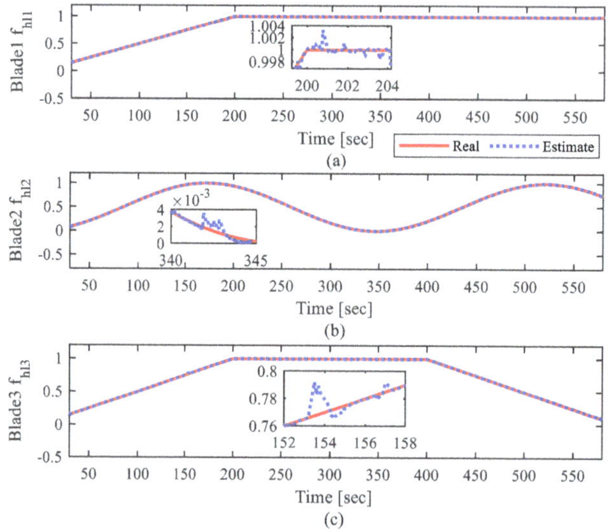

Figure 12. (**a**) Fault estimation of blade 1, (**b**) fault estimation of blade 2, (**c**) fault estimation of blade 3.

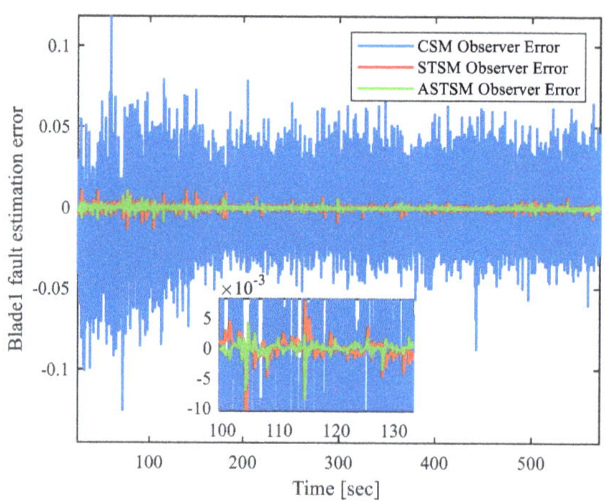

Figure 13. Observation error of different sliding-mode observers for pitch actuator 1 fault.

Table 5. Fault observation error comparison.

Pitch System	Performance Indicators	CSM Observer	STSM Observer	ASTSM Observer
Pitch system 1	$\left\|e_{f_{hl_1}}(t)\right\|_2$	5.64	0.26	0.16
	$\left\|e_{f_{hl_1}}(t)\right\|_\infty$	0.16	0.01	0.01
Pitch system 2	$\left\|e_{f_{hl_2}}(t)\right\|_2$	49.2	0.38	0.02
	$\left\|e_{f_{hl_2}}(t)\right\|_\infty$	13.17	0.11	0.004
Pitch system 3	$\left\|e_{f_{hl_3}}(t)\right\|_2$	6.22	0.39	0.22
	$\left\|e_{f_{hl_3}}(t)\right\|_\infty$	0.15	0.03	0.02

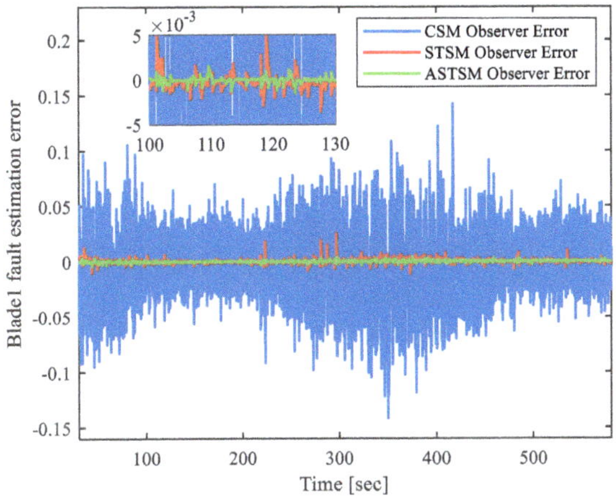

Figure 14. Observation error of different sliding-mode observers for pitch actuator 2 fault.

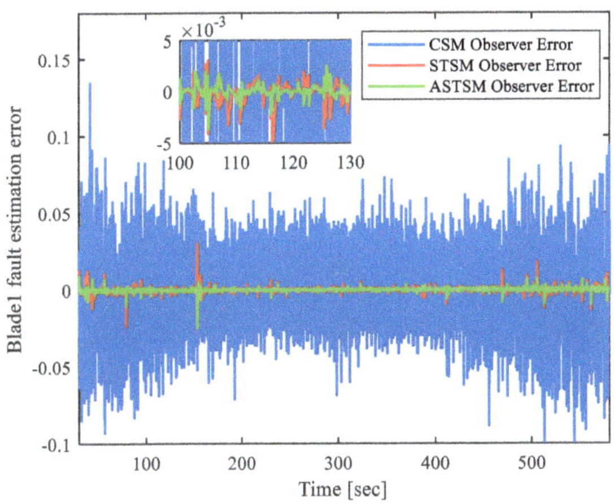

Figure 15. Observation error of different sliding-mode observers for pitch actuator 3 fault.

Table 5 shows a more detailed comparison of the fault observation errors. In the presence of the considered pitch system faults, these performance indexes verified the superiority of the ASTSM observer. This was a consequence of the fact that the observer gain varied according to the effect of the fault on the deviation of the sliding variable from the sliding surface (39). To clarify this, the changes in the ASTSM observer gains are shown in Figure 16. Since the adaptive parameters of the ASTSM observer varied with the tracking error, the sliding surface (39) could be infinitely close to zero, so as to effectively suppress the system chattering.

The accuracy of the ASTSM observer provides a strong guarantee for the fault compensator to restore the pitch system to a fault-free state. Figure 17 shows the bar graph based on the STD and |MAX| index, with the fault-free system as the reference object; all results were normalized based on the fault-free results. In case 1, it was observed that the STD of the rotor speed increased by 43% in the presence of a fault. In terms of platform motion, the STD of pitch, roll and yaw increased by 16%, 128% and 115%, respectively. The DELs of the blade out-of-plane moment and in-plane moment increased by 53% and 4%, and the DELs of the tower fore–aft moment and side-to-side moment increased by 22% and 178% in the presence of a fault. With the help of the ASTSM observer, the fault and state of the pitch system were determined, and the fault compensator could restore the pitch system to a fault-free state and then reduce the impact of the actuator fault on the FOWT.

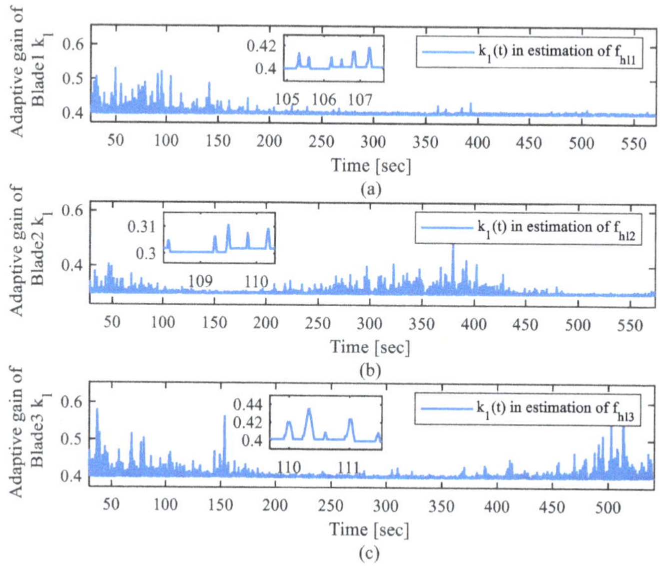

Figure 16. (**a**) Adaptive gain of blade1 $k_1(t)$, (**b**) adaptive gain of blade2 $k_1(t)$, (**c**) adaptive gain of blade3 $k_1(t)$.

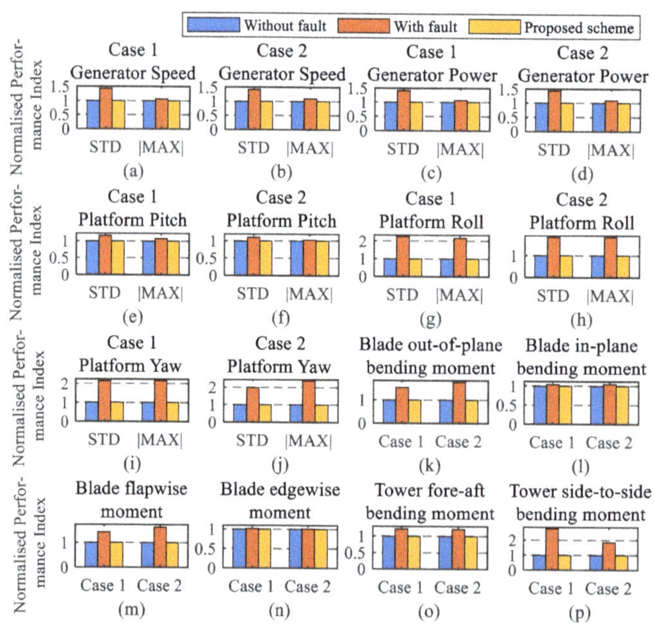

Figure 17. Nominal performance index normalized to the fault-free results.

5. Conclusions

To suppress power output fluctuation, platform motion and fatigue loads in the spar-type FOWT, this paper proposes a novel composite blade pitch control scheme combining CPC and IPC. A fuzzy PI control method was designed for CPC to achieve rated rotor speed tracking and then stabilize the output power. The platform pitching motion displacement, the tower fore–aft movement displacement, the blade displacement in the along-wind direction and the tracking error of the blade rotor speed were chosen as augmented state vectors to design an LQR controller for IPC to suppress loads and platform motion and improve output power stability. The ASTSM observer was adopted in the presence of actuator fault scenarios to facilitate FTC. The simulation results indicated that the proposed scheme performed well in coping with power fluctuation, fatigue load, platform motion and actuator fault simultaneously. Under environmental conditions 1, compared to the traditional PI method, the proposed scheme reduced the root mean square of pitch, roll and yaw in the floating platform by 15%, 54% and 9%, respectively. In terms of the internal and external moments of the blade plane, the DELs were reduced by 2% and 10%, respectively. The DELs were reduced by 10% and 45%, respectively, in the longitudinal and transverse moments of the tower foundation. It should also be noted that the proposed method could significantly suppress the loads in the windward direction of the FOWT; yet, the suppression effect in the crosswind direction (blade in-plane and edgewise direction) was not obvious. Feedforward control compensation based on wind and wave forecasting and simultaneous fault observation in sensors and actuators are the breakthrough objectives of this work in the future.

Author Contributions: Conceptualization, Y.H. and R.M.; methodology, S.L. and M.H.; software, S.L.; validation, C.K.; formal analysis, Y.H.; investigation, R.M.; resources, S.L.; data curation, R.M.; writing—original draft preparation, S.L.; writing—review and editing, Y.H. and R.M.; visualization, C.K.; supervision, M.H.; project administration, Y.H.; funding acquisition, Y.H. All authors have read and agreed to the published version of the manuscript.

Funding: This research was funded by the National Natural Science Foundation of China, grant number 61803230; the Shandong Provincial Natural Science Foundation, grant number ZR2023MF034; and the University Outstanding Youth Innovation Team Development Plan of Shan-dong Province, grant number 2019KJN023. The APC was funded by the Shandong Provincial Natural Science Foundation, grant number ZR2023MF034.

Institutional Review Board Statement: Not applicable.

Informed Consent Statement: Not applicable.

Data Availability Statement: Data sharing not applicable. No new data were created or analyzed in this study.

Conflicts of Interest: The authors declare no conflict of interest.

References

1. Ha, K.; Truong, H.V.A.; Dang, T.D.; Ahn, K.K. Recent Control Technologies for Floating Offshore Wind Energy System: A Review. *Int. J. Precis. Eng. Manuf.-Green Tech.* **2021**, *8*, 281–301. [CrossRef]
2. Gambier, A.; Nazaruddin, Y.Y. Collective pitch control with active tower damping of a wind turbine by using a nonlinear PID approach. *IFAC-Pap.* **2018**, *51*, 238–243. [CrossRef]
3. Lasheen, A.; Elnaggar, M.; Yassin, H. Adaptive control design and implementation for collective pitch in wind energy conversion systems. *ISA Trans.* **2020**, *102*, 251–263. [CrossRef]
4. Li, S.; Han, Y.; Pan, W.; Liu, S.; Hou, M. Variable-Gain Higher-Order Sliding Mode Pitch Control of Floating Offshore Wind Turbine. *J. Mar. Sci. Eng.* **2021**, *9*, 1172. [CrossRef]
5. Jongerius, S.R.; Lentink, D. Structural analysis of a dragonfly wing. *Exp. Mech.* **2010**, *50*, 1323–1334. [CrossRef]
6. da Cunha Barroso Ramos, R.L. Effect of turbulence intensity on the linear quadratic control of spar buoy floating wind turbines. *Mar. Syst. Ocean. Technol.* **2021**, *16*, 84–98. [CrossRef]
7. Collet, D.; Alamir, M.; Di Domenico, D.; Sabiron, G. Data-driven fatigue-oriented MPC applied to wind turbines Individual Pitch Control. *Renew. Energy* **2021**, *170*, 1008–1019. [CrossRef]

8. Sarkar, S.; Fitzgerald, B.; Basu, B. Individual Blade Pitch Control Strategies for Spar-Type Floating Offshore Wind Turbines. Ph.D. Thesis, Trinity College Dublin, Dublin, Ireland, 2020.
9. Bossanyi, E.A. Individual blade pitch control for load reduction. *Wind. Energy Int. J. Prog. Appl. Wind. Power Convers. Technol.* **2003**, *6*, 119–128. [CrossRef]
10. Roh, C.; Ha, Y.J.; Ahn, H.J.; Kim, K.H. A Comparative Analysis of the Characteristics of Platform Motion of a Floating Offshore Wind Turbine Based on Pitch Controllers. *Energies* **2022**, *15*, 716. [CrossRef]
11. Pustina, L.; Lugni, C.; Bernardini, G.; Serafini, J.; Gennaretti, M. Control of power generated by a floating offshore wind turbine perturbed by sea waves. *Renew. Sustain. Energy Rev.* **2020**, *132*, 109984. [CrossRef]
12. Raach, S.; Schlipf, D.; Sandner, F.; Matha, D.; Cheng, P.W. Nonlinear model predictive control of floating wind turbines with individual pitch control. In Proceedings of the 2014 American Control Conference, Portland, OR, USA, 4–6 June 2014; IEEE: Stuttgart, Germany; pp. 4434–4439.
13. Tong, X.; Zhao, X. Vibration and power regulation control of a floating wind turbine with hydrostatic transmission. *Renew. Energy* **2021**, *167*, 899–906. [CrossRef]
14. Ma, Y.; Sclavounos, P.D.; Cross-Whiter, J.; Arora, D. Wave forecast and its application to the optimal control of offshore floating wind turbine for load mitigation. *Renew. Energy* **2018**, *128*, 163–176. [CrossRef]
15. Namik, H.; Stol, K. Individual blade pitch control of floating offshore wind turbines. *Wind. Energy Int. J. Prog. Appl. Wind. Power Convers. Technol.* **2010**, *13*, 74–85. [CrossRef]
16. Wang, L.; Ni, H.; Zhou, W.; Pardalos, P.M.; Fang, J.; Fei, M. MBPOA-based LQR controller and its application to the double-parallel inverted pendulum system. *Eng. Appl. Artif. Intell.* **2014**, *36*, 262–268. [CrossRef]
17. Joelianto, E.; Christian, D.; Samsi, A. Swarm control of an unmanned quadrotor model with LQR weighting matrix optimization using genetic algorithm. *J. Mechatron. Electr. Power Veh. Technol.* **2020**, *11*, 1–10. [CrossRef]
18. Al-Khazraji, H.; Rasheed, L.T. Performance Evaluation of Pole Placement and Linear Quadratic Regulator Strategies Designed for Mass-Spring-Damper System Based on Simulated Annealing and Ant Colony Optimization. *J. Eng.* **2021**, *27*, 15–31. [CrossRef]
19. Murari, A.L.L.F.; Rodrigues, L.L.; Altuna, J.A.T.; Potts, A.S.; Almeida, L.A.L.; Sguarezi Filho, A.J. A LQRI power control for DFIG tuned by a weighted-PSO. *Control. Eng. Pract.* **2019**, *85*, 41–49. [CrossRef]
20. Namik, H.; Stol, K. Individual blade pitch control of a spar-buoy floating wind turbine. *IEEE Trans. Control. Syst. Technol.* **2013**, *22*, 214–223. [CrossRef]
21. Kim, K.; Kim, H.G.; Song, Y.; Paek, I. Design and simulation of an LQR-PI control algorithm for medium wind turbine. *Energies* **2019**, *12*, 2248. [CrossRef]
22. Sarkar, S.; Chen, L.; Fitzgerald, B.; Basu, B. Multi-resolution wavelet pitch controller for spar-type floating offshore wind turbines including wave-current interactions. *J. Sound Vib.* **2020**, *470*, 115170. [CrossRef]
23. Sarkar, S.; Fitzgerald, B.; Basu, B. Individual blade pitch control of floating offshore wind turbines for load mitigation and power regulation. *IEEE Trans. Control. Syst. Technol.* **2020**, *29*, 305–315. [CrossRef]
24. Gao, Z.; Liu, X. An overview on fault diagnosis, prognosis and resilient control for wind turbine systems. *Processes* **2021**, *9*, 300. [CrossRef]
25. Shi, F.; Patton, R.J. A robust adaptive approach to wind turbine pitch actuator component fault estimation. In Proceedings of the 2014 UKACC International Conference on Control (CONTROL), Loughborough, UK, 9–11 July 2014; IEEE: Hull, UK; pp. 468–473.
26. Sun, X.; Patton, R.J. Robust actuator multiplicative fault estimation with unknown input decoupling for a wind turbine system. In Proceedings of the 2013 Conference on Control and Fault-Tolerant Systems (SysTol), Nice, France, 9–11 October 2013; IEEE: Hull, UK; pp. 263–268.
27. Bai, H.; Yu, B.; Gu, W. Research on Position Sensorless Control of RDT Motor Based on Improved SMO with Continuous Hyperbolic Tangent Function and Improved Feedforward PLL. *J. Mar. Sci. Eng.* **2023**, *11*, 642. [CrossRef]
28. Georg, S.; Schulte, H. Diagnosis of actuator parameter faults in wind turbines using a takagi-sugeno sliding mode observer. In *Intelligent Systems in Technical and Medical Diagnostics*; Springer: Berlin/Heidelberg, Germany, 2014; pp. 29–40.
29. Rahnavard, M.; Ayati, M.; Yazdi, M.R.H.; Mousavi, M. Finite time estimation of actuator faults, states, and aerodynamic load of a realistic wind turbine. *Renew. Energy* **2019**, *130*, 256–267. [CrossRef]
30. Lan, J.; Patton, R.J.; Zhu, X. Fault-tolerant wind turbine pitch control using adaptive sliding mode estimation. *Renew. Energy* **2018**, *116*, 219–231. [CrossRef]
31. Liu, Y.; Patton, R.J.; Lan, J. Fault-tolerant individual pitch control using adaptive sliding mode observer. *IFAC-Pap.* **2018**, *51*, 1127–1132. [CrossRef]
32. Jonkman, J.M.; Buhl, M.L. *FAST User's Guide*; National Renewable Energy Laboratory: Golden, CO, USA, 2005.
33. Asgharnia, A.; Shahnazi, R.; Jamali, A. Performance and robustness of optimal fractional fuzzy PID controllers for pitch control of a wind turbine using chaotic optimization algorithms. *ISA Trans.* **2018**, *79*, 27–44. [CrossRef]
34. Liu, S.; Han, Y.; Du, C.; Li, S.; Zhang, H. Fuzzy PI Control for Grid-side Converter of DFIG-based Wind Turbine System. In Proceedings of the 2021 40th Chinese Control Conference (CCC), Shanghai, China, 26–28 July 2021; IEEE: Jinan, China; pp. 5788–5793.
35. Han, Y.; Liu, X. Continuous higher-order sliding mode control with time-varying gain for a class of uncertain nonlinear systems. *ISA Trans.* **2016**, *62*, 193–201. [CrossRef]
36. Jonkman, B.J.; Buhl, M.L., Jr. *TurbSim User's Guide*; National Renewable Energy Laboratory (NREL): Golden, CO, USA, 2006.

37. Hayman, G.J. *MLife Theory Manual for Version 1.00*; National Renewable Energy Laboratory: Golden, CO, USA, 2012; Volume 74, p. 106.
38. Hussain, J.; Mishra, M.K. An efficient wind speed computation method using sliding mode observers in wind energy conversion system control applications. *IEEE Trans. Ind. Appl.* **2019**, *56*, 730–739. [CrossRef]
39. González, J.A.C.; Salas-Peña, O.; De León-Morales, J. Observer-based super twisting design: A comparative study on quadrotor altitude control. *ISA Trans.* **2021**, *109*, 307–314. [CrossRef]

Journal of
Marine Science and Engineering

MDPI

Article

A Jacket-Frame Mounted Oscillating Water Column with a Variable Aperture Skirt

Carlos Pérez-Collazo [1,*], Deborah M. Greaves [2] and Gregorio Iglesias [2,3]

1 Centro Universitario de la Defensa en la Escuela Naval Militar, Plaza de España s/n, 36920 Marín, Spain
2 School of Engineering, Computing and Mathematics, University of Plymouth, Plymouth PL4 7AA, UK
3 MaREI Centre, Environmental Research Institute & School of Engineering, University College Cork, T12AK5 Cork, Ireland
* Correspondence: carlos.perez.collazo@cud.uvigo.es

Abstract: During the last decade jacket-frames have emerged as the main kind of substructure for bottom-mounted offshore wind farms in intermediate water depths. With the offshore wind industry moving towards deeper waters, the predominance of jacket-frames is expected to increase in future years. Multipurpose platforms combining wind and wave energy are proposed as an innovative solution to enhance the sustainability of offshore wind energy. In this research, a multipurpose platform is investigated with a novel feature in its oscillating water column (OWC) wave energy converter—a variable geometry skirt. A comprehensive physical modelling campaign was carried out using a 1:50 scale model. The performance of the OWC and its interaction with the wave field were investigated under four different skirt aperture angles. It was found that the skirt aperture angle plays a significant role in the capture-width ratio and the pneumatic mean power of the OWC. The best performance was obtained with a skirt aperture angle of 140 deg. More generally, these results prove that the variable-geometry skirt is a promising innovation for hybrid wave-wind systems mounted on jacket-frame substructures.

Keywords: hybrid wind-wave energy; oscillating water column (OWC); offshore wind; physical modelling

1. Introduction

In the global effort towards mitigating climate change [1], the adoption of a clean energy system based on harnessing renewable energy resources is fundamental [2]. These efforts have seen exceptional development in the offshore wind industry in recent years [3]. However, if the ambitious objectives of the Paris Agreement [4] are to be achieved, to keep global temperature rise this century below 2 degrees Celsius above pre-industrial levels, the European offshore wind industry should fulfil its ambition of installing 460 GW by 2050 [5].

To foster offshore wind energy while maintain its low impact on other marine resources, it is important to consider its multiuse, combining exploitation with other marine resources such as wave energy [6], aquaculture, seaweed farming [7], and maritime leisure [8]. It is in relation to this and on the various synergies that offshore wind energy and wave energy conversion systems have that the combination of those technologies was proposed [9–11]. Among these synergies, it is worth remarking the increased sustainability that the combined exploitation of two marine resources would have in comparison with independent offshore wind and wave energy projects. This is not only justified for the shared costs due to the combined access to common infrastructures and facilities, but also for the lower seabed footprint of a combined project [9,12]. Increasing the energy yield per area of seabed used is a key parameter to reduce pressure on conventional marine recourses users, such as fisheries [13]. Therefore, combined multiuse energy platforms are expected to contribute to accelerate the deployment of offshore renewable energies and, at the same time, ensure the sustainability of multiple maritime sectors and their respective economic activities.

Previous research on hybrid systems was initially led by some EU funded research projects, including MARINA Platform [14], MERMAID [15], and ORECCA [16]. These projects led to the definition of several hybrid concepts during the last decade. Dong et al. [17] have recently identified more than 39 different hybrid concepts that were proposed to date. Out of these, 27 combined an oscillating body (OB) type of wave energy converter (WEC) into the foundation system of an offshore wind turbine (e.g., [18–21]), while 12 utilised an oscillating water column (OWC) type of WEC (e.g., [22–28]). When it comes to the integration of Wind-OWC (W-OWC) hybrid concepts into intermediate waters offshore wind foundation systems [9], with typically greater than 30–40 m water depth, the jacket-frame substructure is most commonly considered [29,30]. However, jacket-frame substructures are among the most expensive to manufacture; they have a higher load capacity combined with a reduced seabed impact and a larger water depth range of installation (up to 80 m in recent projects) [31,32]. This has raised them among the most common substructure types for these water depth ranges. With the offshore wind industry pushing forward towards deeper water grounds and targeting intermediate and deep-water projects, jacket-frame and floating substructures are the ones expected to pay a leading role in the next couple of decades. This makes jacket-frame substructures a clear candidate when considering a hybrid wind-wave energy system.

Among WEC technologies, OWCs are considered one of the most successful options, partially due to the simplicity of the concept. These are formed by a hollow chamber partially submerged in water with an open bottom and a trapped air volume, which is driven in and out of the chamber through an air turbine by the action of the incoming waves, and also for their low operational and maintenance costs [33]. When it comes to increasing performance of an OWC, it is important to address the air turbine part of the system, as evidenced by the fact that multiple air turbine designs have been investigated in the last few decades, mostly self-rectifying air turbines [34]. The hydrodynamics of the OWC chamber is also known to have a relevant effect on the overall system performance; chambers should be designed to ensure a near-resonant condition for the incident waves while at the same time avoiding energy losses [35,36].

The effects on the OWC geometry on its performance have been widely investigated in previous literature. Boccotti [37] compared the effect of the front wall on an U-OWC with a conventional OWC, finding an increase in the natural period of oscillation. Rezanejad et al. [38] proposed the addition of a step at the front of the OWC chamber, increasing, in this way, an additional resonant mechanism close to the frequency of the incident waves. An L-shaped OWC geometry oriented in the wave propagation direction was proposed by [39,40]. Furthermore, several publications have tackled the effects that specific geometrical variations would have on the performance, for example, effects of the length and the opening angle of harbour walls [41] and the slope of the chamber's front and rear walls [42]. In addition, when it comes to isolated OWC devices, cylindrical chambers are the most often used, so that the wave direction does not affect performance [43], as has been studied for nearshore sites [44,45]. It is in relation to this that the work preceding this publication has proposed a patent application [46] of a variable geometry OWC chamber to be installed as a hybrid wind-wave energy system. Among the different systems proposed in such patent application, there is one proposing a variable aperture skirt, which aims to increase the energy performance of the OWC by orienting the skirt aperture to the incident wave direction.

The work presented in this paper aims to further understand the hydrodynamic response of a jacket-frame mounted OWC (Figure 1), which has a novel skirt system that can adjust its geometry to different aperture angles. This research explores a variable aperture skirt system that extends the hybrid wind-wave energy converter previously introduced in [47]. A thorough test campaign involving a 1:50 scale model of this device was carried out, considering various skirt setups. Following this experimental campaign, the interaction between the OWC skirt aperture and the wave field was studied. The performance of the different skirt aperture angles was assessed and compared with the previous research.

Figure 1. Jacket-frame mounted OWC energy converter (partially reproduced from [47]).

The remaining content of this article has been structured as follows. Section 2 outlines the materials and methods employed in the experimental campaign. Section 3 details the results derived from this campaign, subsequently analysed in Section 4. Ultimately, Section 5 draws conclusions based on the findings.

2. Materials and Methods

2.1. The Model

The physical model used for this research (Figure 2) was built upon that used in [47]. Four different OWC configurations were considered, comprising an individual OWC chamber configuration for each skirt aperture angle. Figure 3 and Table 1 outline the key dimensions and parameters of the jacket-frame foundation, the OWC chamber, and its skirt. Furthermore, the scale model was targeted for a site with a 50-m water depth [43]; geometrical similarity and Froude dynamic similitude criterion were considered for the part of the chamber of the OWC below the mean free surface [48]. The Froude number (Fr) is defined as the ratio between inertia (F_i) and gravity forces (F_g):

$$F_r = \frac{F_i}{F_g} = \frac{v^2}{g\,L}, \tag{1}$$

where, v is a characteristic velocity of the system, g is the gravitational acceleration, and L is a characteristic length of the system.

Air compression forces have a significant role in an OWC system, and this requires a different scaling of the pneumatic section of the chamber, the OWC chamber above the still water level, to account for the air compressibility effects [49,50]. Hence, for this experiment the volume of the pneumatic part of the chamber was scaled using scale ratio equal to λ^2, instead of the λ^3 suggested by Froude, following [51–53]—i.e., this means that the volume of the air part of the OWC chamber should be oversized, in comparison with a Froude geometrical scaled model.

(**a**) (**b**)

Figure 2. Images of the model during tests: (**a**) the experimental set-up view; and (**b**) the model's view from an underwater camera.

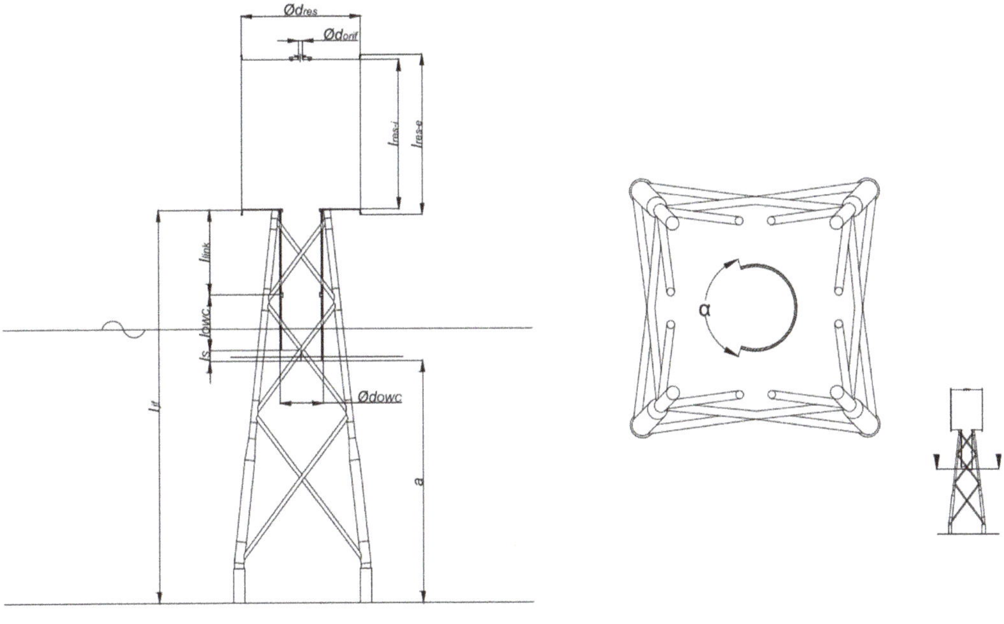

(**a**) (**b**)

Figure 3. The 1:50 scale model: (**a**) a cross-sectional view; and (**b**) a cut view displaying a horizontal plane at the skirt level (partially reproduced from [47]).

Clear acrylic pipe was used to build the four bottom sections of the OWC chamber, including the skirt. Therefore, a bottom part of the model was manufactured for each of the three skirt aperture angles and a fourth one was built without the skirt. The remainder of the model was kept as in the previous research [42]. The induced damping of the power take-off (PTO) system on the OWC at full-scale was simulated by means of an orifice plate [54,55], selecting the diameter of the orifice to match a value of the area coefficient of 1% (i.e., 15 mm) [56].

Table 1. Model main parameters.

Parameter	Symbol	Dimension
OWC air part external diameter	d_{res}	450 mm
OWC air part external length	l_{res-e}	585 mm
OWC air part internal length	l_{res-i}	545 mm
OWC air part wall-thickness	e_{res}	1.5 mm
OWC chamber draught	c	80 mm
OWC chamber external diameter	d_{OWC}	160 mm
OWC chamber length	l_{OWC}	200 mm
OWC chamber-reservoir link length	l_{link}	294 mm
OWC chamber wall-thickness	e_{OWC}	4 mm
OWC orifice diameter	d_{Orif}	15 mm
Jacket-frame length	l_{jf}	1438 mm
Jacket-frame base width	w_{jf}	525 mm
Skirt length	l_S	40 mm
Skirt angle	α	140-180-220 deg
Distance to the floor	a	884 mm
Water depth	H	1000 mm

2.2. Experimental Set-Up and Testing Programme

The characterization of the influence of the skirt angle aperture on the performance of the hybrid wind-wave energy converter was carried out through an experimental campaign at the University of Plymouth's COAST Laboratory, in the ocean basin. This is a 35 m long and 15.5 m wide basin, with a variable floor depth, which was set to match the water depth at the Wave Hub site (1.0 m at the model scale), the North Cornwall test center that was used as reference to set the metocean conditions.

Figure 4 shows the layout of the experimental set-up, including the position of the wave gauges, used to record the free surface displacement along the wave basin, and the hybrid model. Table 2 provides additional details on the exact location of the wave gauges and the model. The analysis of incident and reflected waves in the incoming wave field was conducted using the three front wave gauges (WG1, WG2, and WG3), while the rear wave gauge (WG4) recorded the transmitted wave. Additionally, a differential pressure transducer (Omega PX2300-0.5BDI, Omega Engineering Inc., Manchester, UK) tracked the pneumatic pressure difference at the OWC chamber. A sample rate of 128 Hz was set for the data acquisition.

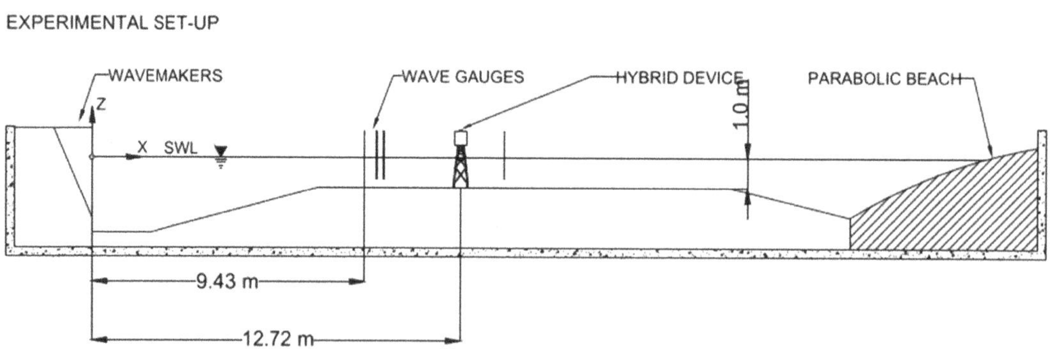

Figure 4. The experimental set-up from a side-view (partially reproduced from [47]).

Table 2. Position of model and the wave gauges (WG).

Parameter	X [m]
WG1	9.430
WG2	9.870
WG3	10.120
WG4	14.100
WG5 (OWC)	12.590
Centre of the model	12.720

A total of 47 wave conditions were used for this experimental campaign. Following [57], three different experimental test series were defined. Table 3 presents the regular waves experimental programme (referend as Series A). Meanwhile, irregular waves experimental programmes are detailed in Table 4 (referred as Series B and Series C). The duration of the tests for Series A was defined for a minimum of 100 waves, while ensuring a minimum of 60 min at prototype scale for the irregular waves test series, following [58], covering between 271 and 571 waves.

Table 3. Wave conditions for regular waves (wave period T and height H data in prototype values).

Series A		T [s]						
		6	7	8	9	10	11	12
H [m]	1.5	SA01	SA06	SA11	SA16	SA21	SA26	SA31
	2.5	SA02	SA07	SA12	SA17	SA22	SA27	SA32
	3.5	SA03	SA08	SA13	SA18	SA23	SA28	SA33
	4.5	SA04	SA09	SA14	SA19	SA24	SA29	SA34
	5.5	SA05	SA10	SA15	SA20	SA25	SA30	SA35

Table 4. Wave conditions for Series B and C, irregular waves (significant wave height H_S and energy T_E, mean T_Z and peak T_P wave period data in prototype values).

Series	Test Number	H_S	T_E	T_Z	T_P
Series B	SB01	0.5 m	6.05 s	5.04 s	7.06 s
	SB02	1.5 m	6.49 s	5.41 s	7.57 s
	SB03	2.5 m	6.98 s	5.82 s	8.14 s
	SB04	3.5 m	8.00 s	6.67 s	9.33 s
	SB05	4.5 m	8.48 s	7.05 s	9.87 s
	SB06	5.5 m	9.10 s	7.58 s	10.62 s
Series C	SC01	3.5 m	6.60 s	5.50 s	7.70 s
	SC02		7.20 s	6.00 s	8.40 s
	SC03		8.40 s	7.00 s	9.80 s
	SC04		9.00 s	7.50 s	10.50 s
	SC05		9.60 s	8.00 s	11.20 s
	SC06		11.40 s	9.50 s	13.30 s

The accuracy of the experimental set-up was ensured by means of a repeatability test series, considering both regular and irregular waves. Four different wave conditions were tested for regular waves, and two sea states were selected in the case of irregular waves. Each one of the tests was repeated four times and data from the wave gauges, the inner free surface oscillation inside the OWC chamber, and the pneumatic pressure were compared by means of the cross-correlation coefficient (R^2) and the normalised root mean square error ($NRMSE$). Table 5 shows the mean values of both statistical indicators.

Table 5. Mean values of the main statistical indicators of the repeatability tests series.

		WG1	WG2	WG3	WG4	OWC	Δp
Regular waves	R^2	0.996	0.996	0.996	0.995	0.996	0.965
	NRMSE	3.30%	3.04%	2.96%	3.27%	3.68%	5.10%
Irregular waves	R^2	0.972	0.971	0.971	0.957	0.957	0.951
	NRMSE	3.28%	3.69%	3.38%	4.55%	4.18%	3.70%

3. Results

3.1. Reflection and Transmission Analysis

Signals recorded from the wave gauges (WG1, WG2, and WG3) were analysed following the method proposed by [59,60] in order to derive the incident and reflected wave data. Furthermore, data from WG4 were also used to determine the transmitted wave. Therefore, by establishing the heights of incident, reflected, and transmitted waves, Equations (2) and (3) were applied for regular waves, while Equations (4) and (5) were utilized for irregular waves, enabling the calculation of reflection and transmission coefficients (K_R and K_T).

$$K_R = \frac{H_R}{H_I}, \tag{2}$$

$$K_T = \frac{H_T}{H_I}, \tag{3}$$

$$K_R = \sqrt{\frac{m_{0R}}{m_{0I}}}, \tag{4}$$

$$K_T = \sqrt{\frac{m_{0T}}{m_{0I}}}, \tag{5}$$

where, H_R, H_I, and H_T refer to the reflected, incident, and transmitted wave height, respectively, and m_{0i} is the generic zero order moment,

$$S_i = \int_{f_{min}}^{f_{max}} S_i(f)df, \tag{6}$$

where, S_i is the generic power spectral density.

Figure 5 illustrates regular waves data (Series A) and the four skirt angle configurations plotted against the non-dimensional wave number (*kh*). Transmission and reflection coefficients data obtained for irregular waves (Series B and Series C) are represented for the four skirt configurations in Figures 6 and 7, respectively. Note that the dataset containing the data from this and the remaining sections can be found in the Supplementary Materials.

It is clear from the results plotted in the figures that neither reflection nor transmission coefficients (K_R and K_T) are affected by the variation of the aperture angle. Therefore, the interaction of the device and the wave field is independent of the variation of the skirt angle. K_R increases, in general, with *kh*, and so decreases with the wave period for both random and regular waves, ranging from around 0.07 to 0.38 for regular waves and between 0.13 and 0.50 for irregular waves. K_T values are shown to be approximately constant at around 0.36 for regular waves, while the transmission coefficient is clearly increasing with *kh* for random waves, ranging from 0.06 to 0.41. This behaviour is consistent with that previously observed in [47].

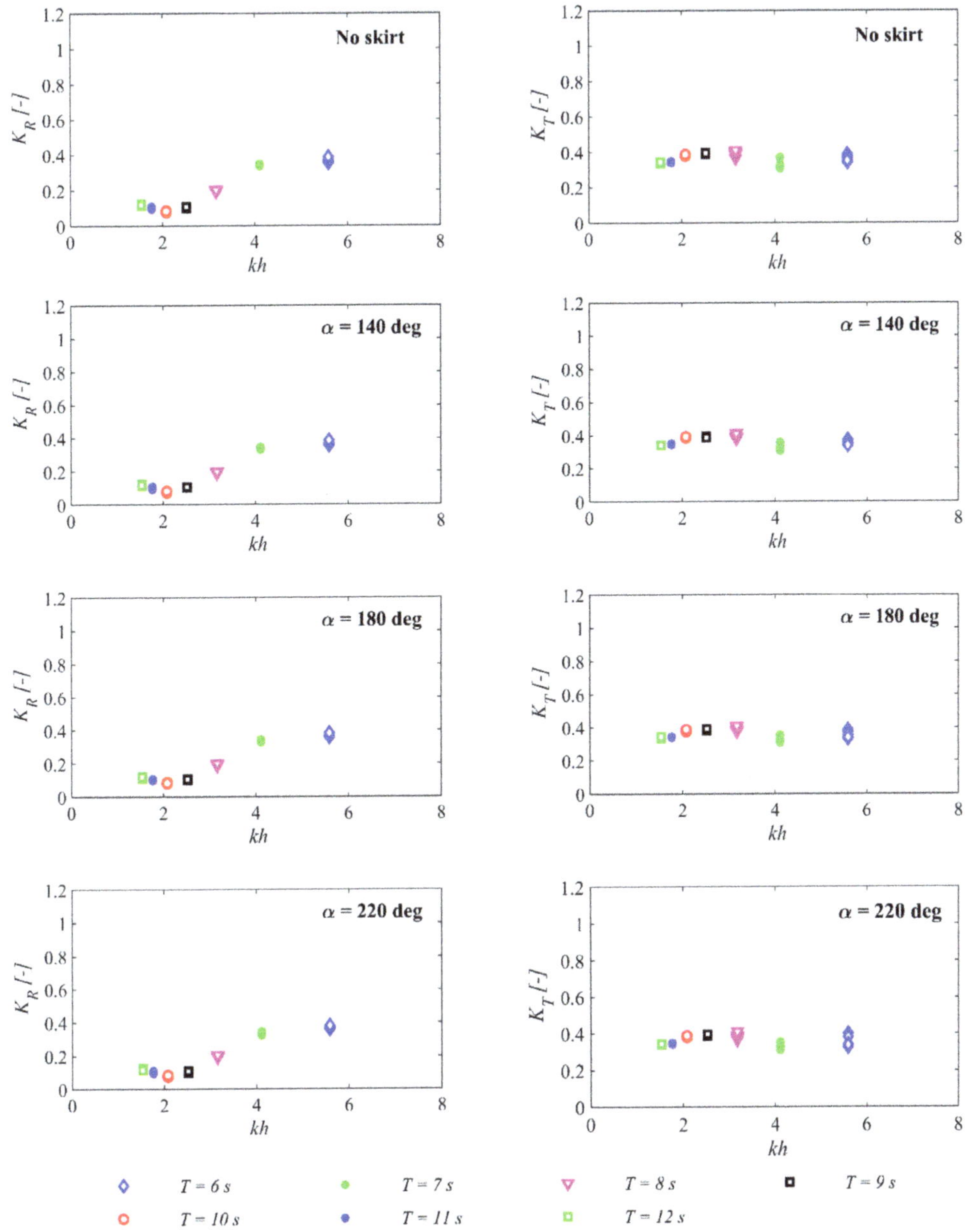

Figure 5. Values of K_R and K_T for the model with and without skirt and tree different skirt aperture angles for regular waves); (data in prototype values).

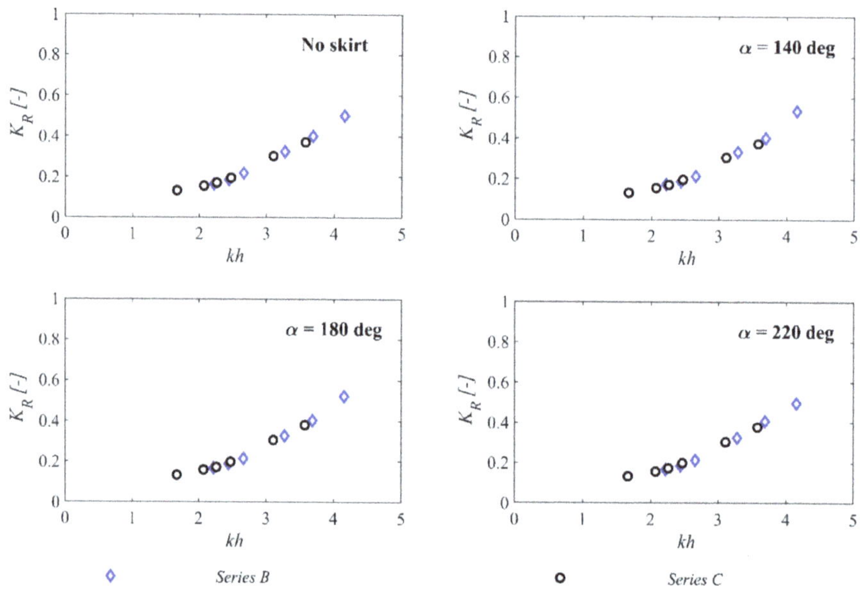

Figure 6. Values of K_R for the model with and without skirt and three different skirt aperture angles for irregular waves; (data in prototype values).

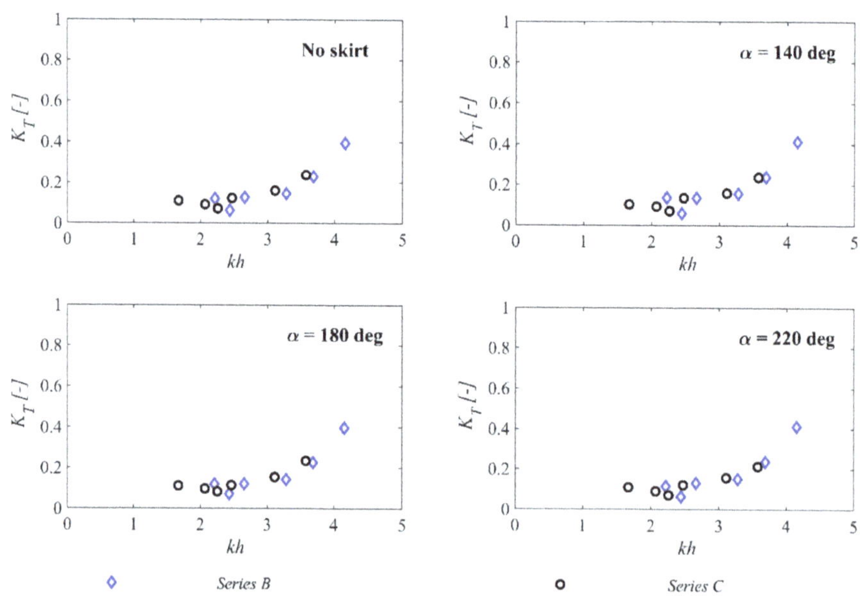

Figure 7. Values of K_T for the model with and without skirt and tree different skirt aperture angles for irregular waves; (data in prototype values).

3.2. Hybrid Wind-Wave Device Performance

The performance of the hybrid wind-wave device can be determined based on the incident wave height obtained from the reflection analysis, described in the section above, and on the data from the free surface oscillation inside the OWC chamber (WG5) and the differential pneumatic pressure between the inner OWC chamber and the atmosphere (Δp). The performance of the device can be then evaluated by using the capture-width ratio (C_{WR}) as defined in Equation (7).

$$C_{WR} = \frac{P_m}{P\,b}, \tag{7}$$

where, P_m is the mean pneumatic power of the OWC chamber defined by Equation (8), P denotes the incident wave power per meter of wave front defined by (9) for regular wave and (10) for random ones, and b is the OWC chamber width.

$$P_m = \frac{1}{t_{max}} \int_0^{t_{max}} \Delta p\; q\; dt \tag{8}$$

where, q is the volumetric air flow rate through the chamber's orifice, t is time, and t_{max} is the time that corresponds to the duration of the test.

$$P = \frac{\rho_W\, g\, H_I^2\, c_g}{8} \tag{9}$$

$$P = \rho_W\, g \sum_{i=1}^{N} S_i (c_g)_i \Delta f \tag{10}$$

where, ρ_W is the density of the water, g stands for the acceleration of the gravity, c_g is the group velocity, H_I is incident wave height, N is the number of frequency components (for each frequency differential Δf), and S_i is the spectral density for the i-th component.

Capture-width ratio values are represented against the non-dimensional wave number (kh), first for regular waves in Figure 8 and then for irregular waves in Figure 9. Overall, C_{WR} data range from 0.5% to 7.0% for regular waves and from 1.2% to 5.4% for irregular waves. Mean values of the C_{WR} are 2.6%, 3.1%, 2.2%, and 2.9%, respectively, for angles of 0-, 140-, 180-, and 220-degrees skirt aperture for regular waves and are, respectively, 2.3%, 3.6%, 2.8%, and 2.8% for random waves.

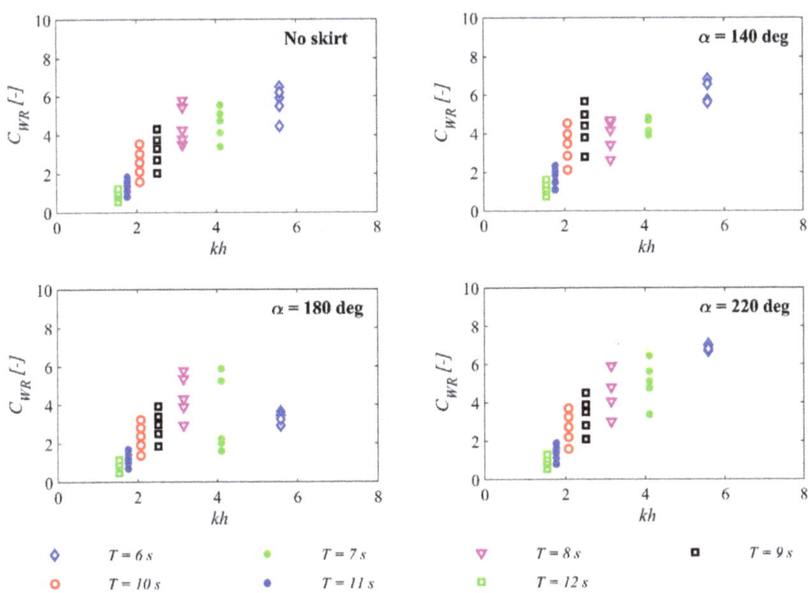

Figure 8. Values of the capture width ratio (C_{WR}) for the model with and without skirt and three different skirt aperture angles for regular waves, and for different values of the wave period (T); (data in prototype values).

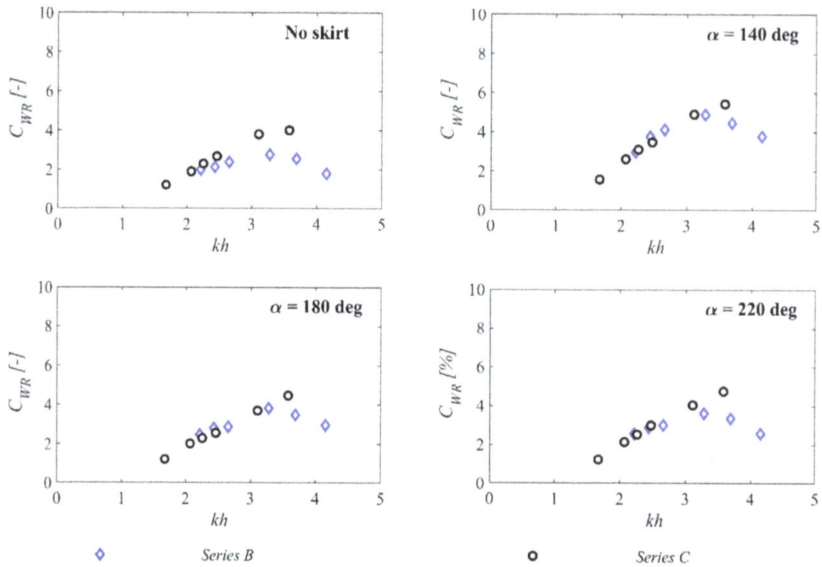

Figure 9. Values of the capture width ratio (C_{WR}) for the model with and without skirt and tree different skirt aperture angles for irregular waves; (data in prototype values).

It is clear from Figures 8 and 9 that the C_{WR} is significantly influenced by the skirt aperture angle. Though the maximum performance is found for the largest aperture, 7.0% at $\alpha = 220$ deg, the device with the smallest skirt aperture, $\alpha = 140$ deg, presents not only the best mean performance (3.1%) but also a broader area of heightened efficiency. Moreover, data from regular waves (Figure 8) and irregular waves (Figure 9) highlight the significant influence of the wave period on device performance. Generally, the C_{WR} tends to increase as the wave period decreases. From the regular waves data, different performance peaks can be identified that clearly change for each aperture angle. For the chamber without a skirt, the best performance is found at the wave periods of $T = 8$ and 6 s, whereas for the 140-degrees aperture angle this is found at $T = 9$ and 6 s; for the 180-degrees aperture angle this is found at $T = 8$ and 7 s, and for the 220-degrees aperture angle this is found at $T = 6$ s.

To delve deeper into how wave height influences the device's performance across various skirt aperture angles, as hinted in Figure 8, the capture-width matrix is defined for regular waves in Figure 10 for each of the three skirt aperture angles alongside the device configuration without a skirt. The different skirt aperture angles notably impact the optimal performance regions observed within each of the four OWC chamber configurations, showing the largest area for the aperture angle of 140-degrees, the second largest area for the angle of 220-degrees, then for the configuration without skirt and finally the smallest area is shown for the 180-degrees configuration. Furthermore, it can be observed that the increase in wave height, generally, implies an increase in the device performance.

Finally, the power matrix for regular waves is presented in Figure 11 in terms of the wave height (H) and period (T) for each one of the three skirt aperture angles and the device configuration without a skirt. The figure shows that the largest mean pneumatic power (P_m) is found at the wave period of $T = 11$ s.

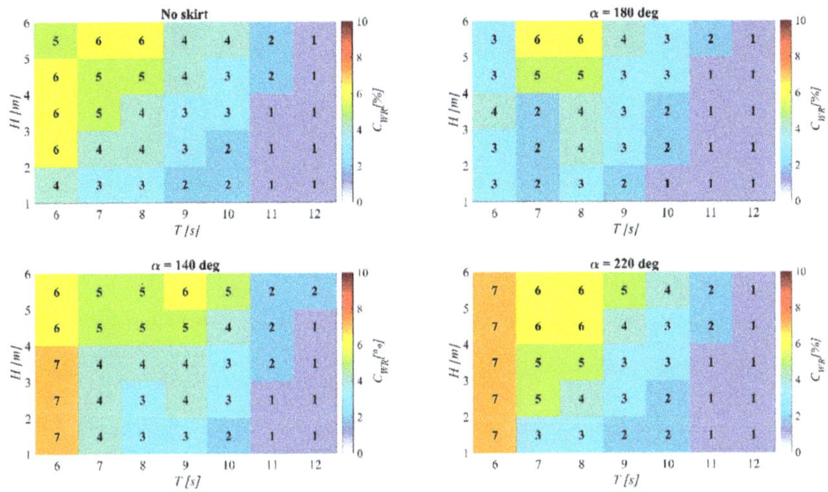

Figure 10. Capture width ratio (C_{WR}) matrices for the model with and without skirt and three different skirt aperture angles, the wave height (H) and period (T) for regular waves; (data in prototype values).

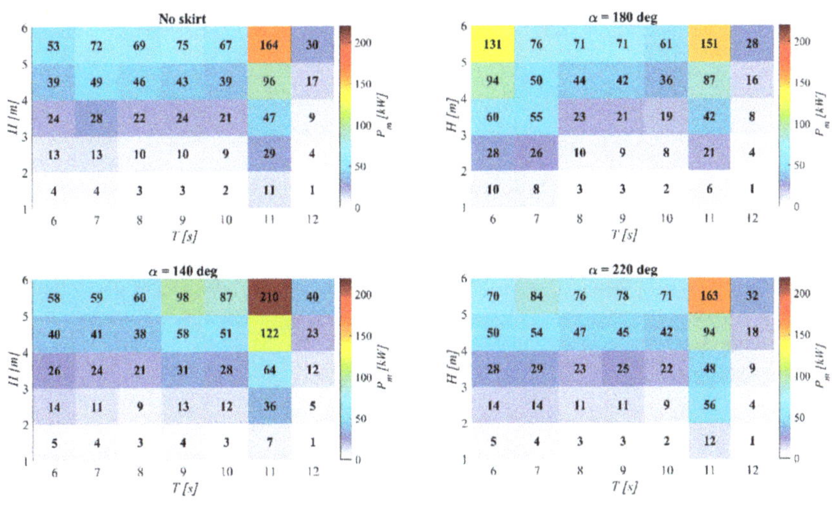

Figure 11. Power matrices for the model and its different skirt configuration, representing the mean pneumatic power for the different regular wave conditions, (data in prototype values).

4. Discussion

In this work, a novel variable aperture skirt system for an OWC WEC was studied when this was mouthed as a hybrid wind-wave energy converter on a jacket-frame offshore wind substructure system. A physical modelling test campaign was carried out on a 1:50 model of a geometrically scaled version of a jacket-frame prototype for a 50 m water depth site. In order to ensure the full-scale application of the experimental data, best practices were following when defining the experimental set-up. For example, by modifying the pneumatic part of the OWC chamber so that air compressibility effects on the aerodynamical damping are considered, the performance of the device is not overestimated. In addition to this, repeatability tests were conducted to estimate the uncertainty on the data.

The effect of the OWC's skirt aperture angle was parametrically studied by defining four different configurations of the hybrid wind-wave device, one chamber with three different exchangeable skirts, each one with a different aperture angle from a smaller to a larger aperture angle (α = 140 degree, 180 degree and 220 degree respectively). In addition, and in order to set a reference, a chamber without skirt was also tested. From the experimental data, it was observed that changes on the skirt configuration were not modifying the interaction between the hybrid device and the wave field, i.e., differences on the reflected and transmitted waves were neglectable for the four model configurations. Furthermore, regarding the device performance, a clear influence of the skirt was observed, identifying the smaller aperture angle (α = 140°) as the best performing one, especially for the larger wave periods (T = 9 to 12 s). This behaviour is observed for both the capture width ratio (C_{WR}) and the mean pneumatic power (P_m). It is worth remarking that the larger aperture angle configuration (α = 220°) has shown the best performance for the shorter wave periods (T = 6 to 8 s).

A straightforward comparison exercise will be to compare the capture width matrices of the model with the three skirt aperture angles, element by element, with the reference model without skirt. Doing this, it can be appreciated that, on average, the best performing skirt aperture angle (α = 140°) increases the efficiency of the OWC by about 13%. One of the characteristics defined by the patent of the skirt systems allows it to self-adapt its aperture angle to better perform for the different wave conditions. Considering this would mean that the device would select the best performing skirt configuration for each incident wave condition. Applying this optimisation to the cases tested in this research would mean that, on average, the variable skirt aperture OWC chamber would increase its efficiency by about 20%, 7% more than the best performing fix-aperture skirt. This increase in performance justifies the use of variable aperture skirt systems on isolated offshore OWC systems.

The results obtained in this research show that multipurpose platforms have a potential to coexist under jacket-frame offshore wind substructure systems. This is especially important as this type of substructure is aimed to be the leading one on the upcoming years, as the industry is moving towards deeper waters. Although it is true that the rated power of the offshore wind turbine is about two orders of magnitude larger than the OWC one (15 to 0.2 MW), when it comes time to analyse the temporal distribution of the energy yield, wave energy production is, generally, delayed and has a lower variability [61]. However, for multipurpose platforms to become a reality, there are still plenty of challenges to address; for example, the structural response of the substructure including the OWC system requires to be further studied, as well as the integration of the OWC generated energy with the offshore wind electric grid.

5. Conclusions

This work further develops a hybrid wind-wave energy converter. In particular, the research carried out here increases the understanding of a particular characteristic of this hybrid device: its variable aperture skirt angle. On the basis of the results obtained from the experimental campaign, two main outcomes can be drawn. First, the four different OWC chamber configurations tested have been shown to produce a negligible effect on both on the wave reflection and on the wave transmission. Then, it was found that the skirt aperture angle of 140-degrees was found to exhibit the best performance in terms of capture width ratio.

Based on the analysis of the performance of the hybrid wind-wave energy converter, the following main conclusions may be drawn:

- The OWC skirt aperture angle configuration was shown to not influence the wave field, meaning that the change in the skirt configuration would influence it.
- The hybrid device reflects between 7% and 50% of the incident waves, while between 6% and 41% is transmitted. It was also found that these values are similar to other WECs and hybrid devices.

- The energy conversion performance of the OWC was improved with a skirt in comparison with that of the device without a skirt.
- The best performance of the hybrid device in terms of capture width ratio occurs for the skirt aperture angle of 140-degrees.
- The region of best performance in the capture-width matrix varies in size significantly with the skirt aperture configuration, with the largest area observed for the 140-degrees aperture angle.

In summary, the variable skirt aperture angle for the jacket-frame mounted OWC hybrid device developed in this work represents a viable approach to increasing performance of OWC devices mounted as hybrid wind-wave energy converters. This work contributes to better understanding the effects of a variable aperture skirt on an OWC device. Further work is required to better understand the implementation of this kind of skirt system in OWC design.

Supplementary Materials: The following supporting information can be downloaded at: https://www.mdpi.com/article/10.3390/jmse11122383/s1.

Author Contributions: Conceptualization, C.P.-C., D.M.G. and G.I.; methodology, C.P.-C., D.M.G. and G.I.; formal analysis, C.P.-C., D.M.G. and G.I.; writing—original draft preparation, C.P.-C.; writing—review and editing, G.I. and D.M.G.; supervision, D.M.G. and G.I.; project administration, C.P.-C.; funding acquisition, D.M.G. All authors have read and agreed to the published version of the manuscript.

Funding: This research was funded by the Higher Education Innovation Fund (HEIF) and the School of Engineering, Computing and Mathematics of the University of Plymouth.

Informed Consent Statement: Not applicable.

Data Availability Statement: The research materials supporting this publication may be accessed at http://-Note: hyperlink will be added once the manuscript is accepted for publication. If you have any question regarding these research materials, please contact the corresponding author of this paper.

Acknowledgments: The authors are grateful to the COAST Lab technical support staff for their help during the experimental campaign. In addition, the authors are also grateful to Johan Skanberg-Tippen, Tim Hatton and James Harvey for all their help during the construction of the model used in this experimental campaign.

Conflicts of Interest: The authors declare no conflict of interest. The funders had no role in the design of the study; in the collection, analyses, or interpretation of data; in the writing of the manuscript, or in the decision to publish the results.

References

1. Weisse, R.; von Storch, H.; Callies, U.; Chrastansky, A.; Feser, F.; Grabemann, I.; Günther, H.; Pluess, A.; Stoye, T.; Tellkamp, J.; et al. Regional Meteorological–Marine Reanalyses and Climate Change Projections. *Bull. Am. Meteorol. Soc.* **2009**, *90*, 849–860. [CrossRef]
2. Kang, J.-N.; Wei, Y.-M.; Liu, L.-C.; Han, R.; Yu, B.-Y.; Wang, J.-W. Energy Systems for Climate Change Mitigation: A Systematic Review. *Appl. Energy* **2020**, *263*, 114602. [CrossRef]
3. Sun, X.; Huang, D.; Wu, G. The Current State of Offshore Wind Energy Technology Development. *Energy* **2012**, *41*, 298–312. [CrossRef]
4. United Nations. Framework Convention on Climate Change Adoption of the Paris Agreement. In Proceedings of the 21st Conference of the Parties, Paris, France, 30 November–13 December 2015.
5. Jeffrey, H.; Sedgwick, J. *ORECCA European Offshore Renewable Energy Roadmap*; ORECCA: Munchen, Germany, 2011; pp. 1–201.
6. Astariz, S.; Perez-Collazo, C.; Abanades, J.; Iglesias, G. Co-Located Wave-Wind Farms: Economic Assessment as a Function of Layout. *Renew. Energy* **2015**, *83*, 837–849. [CrossRef]
7. Stuiver, M.; Soma, K.; Koundouri, P.; van den Burg, S.; Gerritsen, A.; Harkamp, T.; Dalsgaard, N.; Zagonari, F.; Guanche, R.; Schouten, J.J.; et al. The Governance of Multi-Use Platforms at Sea for Energy Production and Aquaculture: Challenges for Policy Makers in European Seas. *Sustainability* **2016**, *8*, 333. [CrossRef]
8. Quevedo, E.; Delory, M.; Castro, A.; Llinas, O.; de Lara, J.; Papandroulakis, N.; Anasrasiadis, P.; Bard, J.; Jeffrey, H.; Ingram, D.; et al. Multi-Use Offshore Platform Configurations in the Scope of the FP7 TROPOS Project. In Proceedings of the 2013 MTS/IEEE OCEANS, Bergen, Norway, 10–14 June 2013; pp. 1–7.

9. Perez-Collazo, C.; Greaves, D.; Iglesias, G. A Review of Combined Wave and Offshore Wind Energy. *Renew. Sustain. Energy Rev.* **2015**, *42*, 141–153. [CrossRef]
10. Perez-Collazo, C.; Jakobsen, M.M.; Buckland, H.; Fernandez Chozas, J. Synergies for a Wave-Wind Energy Concept. In Proceedings of the EWEA Offshore 2013, Frankfurt, Germany, 19–21 November 2013; pp. 1–10.
11. Casale, C.; Serri, L.; Stolk, N.; Yildiz, I.; Cantù, M. Synergies, Innovative Designs and Concepts for Multipurpose Use of Conversion Platforms. In *Results of ORECCA Project—WP4*; ORECCA: Munchen, Germany, 2012; pp. 1–77.
12. Perez-Collazo, C.; Greaves, D.; Iglesias, G. Proof of Concept of a Novel Hybrid Wind-Wave Energy Converter. In Proceedings of the OMAE2018, Madrid, Spain, 17–22 June 2018; Volume 10. Ocean Renewable Energy.
13. Qu, Y.; Swales, J.K.; Hooper, T.; Austen, M.C.; Wang, X.; Papathanasopoulou, E.; Huang, J.; Yan, X. Economic Trade-Offs in Marine Resource Use between Offshore Wind Farms and Fisheries in Scottish Waters. *Energy Econ.* **2023**, *125*, 106811. [CrossRef]
14. Cordis Marina Platform. Available online: https://cordis.europa.eu/project/id/241402/es (accessed on 23 September 2022).
15. Cordis Mermaid. Available online: https://cordis.europa.eu/project/id/288710/reporting/es (accessed on 23 September 2022).
16. Cordis Orecca. Available online: https://cordis.europa.eu/project/id/241421/es (accessed on 23 September 2022).
17. Dong, X.; Li, Y.; Li, D.; Cao, F.; Jiang, X.; Shi, H. A State-of-the-Art Review of the Hybrid Wind-Wave Energy Converter. *Prog. Energy* **2022**, *4*, 042004. [CrossRef]
18. Wei, Y.; Bechlenberg, A.; van Rooij, M.; Jayawardhana, B.; Vakis, A.I. Modelling of a Wave Energy Converter Array with a Nonlinear Power Take-off System in the Frequency Domain. *Appl. Ocean Res.* **2019**, *90*, 101824. [CrossRef]
19. Baudry, V.; Babarit, A. Assessment of the Annual Energy Production of a Heaving Wave Energy Converter Sliding on the Mast of a Fixed Offshore Wind Turbine. In Proceedings of the Renewable Energy Congress XI (WREC XI), Abu Dhabi, United Arab Emirates, 25–30 September 2010.
20. Wan, L.; Gao, Z.; Moan, T.; Lugni, C. Experimental and Numerical Comparisons of Hydrodynamic Responses for a Combined Wind and Wave Energy Converter Concept under Operational Conditions. *Renew. Energy* **2016**, *93*, 87–100. [CrossRef]
21. Li, L.; Gao, Y.; Yuan, Z.; Day, S.; Hu, Z. Dynamic Response and Power Production of a Floating Integrated Wind, Wave and Tidal Energy System. *Renew. Energy* **2018**, *116*, 412–422. [CrossRef]
22. Konispoliatis, D.N.; Katsaounis, G.M.; Manolas, D.I.; Soukissian, T.H.; Polyzos, S.; Mazarakos, T.P.; Voutsinas, S.G.; Mavrakos, S.A. REFOS: A Renewable Energy Multi-Purpose Floating Offshore System. *Energies* **2021**, *14*, 3126. [CrossRef]
23. Iturrioz, A.; Sarmiento, J.; Ayllón, V.; Armesto, J.; Jurado, A.; Guanche, R.; Vidal, C.; Losada, I. *Experimental and Numerical Design of a Combined Wind-Wave Concept*; Taylor & Francis Books Ltd.: London, UK, 2016; pp. 667–673.
24. Aubault, A.; Alves, M.; Sarmento, A.J.N.A.; Roddier, D.; Peiffer, A. Modeling of an Oscillating Water Column on the Floating Foundation Windfloat. In Proceedings of the International Conference on Offshore Mechanics and Arctic Engineering, Rotterdam, The Netherlands, 19–24 June 2011; pp. 235–246.
25. Sarmiento, J.; Iturrioz, A.; Ayllón, V.; Guanche, R.; Losada, I.J. Experimental Modelling of a Multi-Use Floating Platform for Wave and Wind Energy Harvesting. *Ocean Eng.* **2019**, *173*, 761–773. [CrossRef]
26. Zhu, H.; Hu, C.; Sueyoshi, M.; Yoshida, S. Integration of a Semisubmersible Floating Wind Turbine and Wave Energy Converters: An Experimental Study on Motion Reduction. *J. Mar. Sci. Technol.* **2020**, *25*, 667–674. [CrossRef]
27. Zhou, Y.; Ning, D.; Shi, W.; Johanning, L.; Liang, D. Hydrodynamic Investigation on an OWC Wave Energy Converter Integrated into an Offshore Wind Turbine Monopile. *Coast. Eng.* **2020**, *162*, 103731. [CrossRef]
28. Cong, P.; Teng, B.; Bai, W.; Ning, D.; Liu, Y. Wave Power Absorption by an Oscillating Water Column (OWC) Device of Annular Cross-Section in a Combined Wind-Wave Energy System. *Appl. Ocean Res.* **2021**, *107*, 102499. [CrossRef]
29. Dang, T.D.; Phan, C.B.; Truong, H.V.A.; Le, C.D.; Nguyen, M.T.; Ahn, K.-K. A Study on Modeling of a Hybrid Wind Wave Energy Converter System. In Proceedings of the 2016 16th International Conference on Control, Automation and Systems (ICCAS), Gyeongju, Republic of Korea, 16–19 October 2016; pp. 182–187.
30. Chuan, Q.; Ping, J.; Wen, D. Hybrid Offshore Wind, Wave and Tidal Turbine Energy Conversion System: Structure and Electrical Interface. *Proc. CSEE* **2014**, *34*, 2013–2021.
31. Wang, X.; Zeng, X.; Li, J.; Yang, X.; Wang, H. A Review on Recent Advancements of Substructures for Offshore Wind Turbines. *Energy Convers. Manag.* **2018**, *158*, 103–119. [CrossRef]
32. Lozano-Minguez, E.; Kolios, A.J.; Brennan, F.P. Multi-Criteria Assessment of Offshore Wind Turbine Support Structures. *Renew. Energy* **2011**, *36*, 2831–2837. [CrossRef]
33. Falcão, A.F.O.; Henriques, J.C.C. Oscillating-Water-Column Wave Energy Converters and Air Turbines: A Review. *Renew. Energy* **2016**, *85*, 1391–1424. [CrossRef]
34. Falcão, A.F.O.; Henriques, J.C.C.; Gato, L.M.C. Self-Rectifying Air Turbines for Wave Energy Conversion: A Comparative Analysis. *Renew. Sustain. Energy Rev.* **2018**, *91*, 1231–1241. [CrossRef]
35. Simonetti, I.; Cappietti, L.; Elsafti, H.; Oumeraci, H. Optimization of the Geometry and the Turbine Induced Damping for Fixed Detached and Asymmetric OWC Devices: A Numerical Study. *Energy* **2017**, *139*, 1197–1209. [CrossRef]
36. Hayati, M.; Nikseresht, A.H.; Haghighi, A.T. Sequential Optimization of the Geometrical Parameters of an OWC Device Based on the Specific Wave Characteristics. *Renew. Energy* **2020**, *161*, 386–394. [CrossRef]
37. Boccotti, P. Comparison between a U-OWC and a Conventional OWC. *Ocean Eng.* **2007**, *34*, 799–805. [CrossRef]
38. Rezanejad, K.; Bhattacharjee, J.; Guedes Soares, C. Stepped Sea Bottom Effects on the Efficiency of Nearshore Oscillating Water Column Device. *Ocean Eng.* **2013**, *70*, 25–38. [CrossRef]

39. Howe, D.; Nader, J.-R. OWC WEC Integrated within a Breakwater versus Isolated: Experimental and Numerical Theoretical Study. *Int. J. Mar. Energy* **2017**, *20*, 165–182. [CrossRef]
40. Rezanejad, K.; Souto-Iglesias, A.; Guedes Soares, C. Experimental Investigation on the Hydrodynamic Performance of an L-Shaped Duct Oscillating Water Column Wave Energy Converter. *Ocean Eng.* **2019**, *173*, 388–398. [CrossRef]
41. Daniel Raj, D.; Sundar, V.; Sannasiraj, S.A. Enhancement of Hydrodynamic Performance of an Oscillating Water Column with Harbour Walls. *Renew. Energy* **2019**, *132*, 142–156. [CrossRef]
42. Gaspar, L.A.; Teixeira, P.R.F.; Didier, E. Numerical Analysis of the Performance of Two Onshore Oscillating Water Column Wave Energy Converters at Different Chamber Wall Slopes. *Ocean Eng.* **2020**, *201*, 107119. [CrossRef]
43. Zheng, S.; Zhu, G.; Simmonds, D.; Greaves, D.; Iglesias, G. Wave Power Extraction from a Tubular Structure Integrated Oscillating Water Column. *Renew. Energy* **2020**, *150*, 342–355. [CrossRef]
44. Zhou, Y.; Zhang, C.; Ning, D. Hydrodynamic Investigation of a Concentric Cylindrical OWC Wave Energy Converter. *Energies* **2018**, *11*, 985. [CrossRef]
45. Wan, C.; Yang, C.; Fang, Q.; You, Z.; Geng, J.; Wang, Y. Hydrodynamic Investigation of a Dual-Cylindrical OWC Wave Energy Converter Integrated into a Fixed Caisson Breakwater. *Energies* **2020**, *13*, 896. [CrossRef]
46. Collazo, C.P.; Rodriguez, J.G.I.; Greaves, D.; University of Plymouth. Wave Energy Capture Device. International Patent Application No. PCT/GB2016/051403, 24 November 2016.
47. Perez-Collazo, C.; Greaves, D.; Iglesias, G. A Novel Hybrid Wind-Wave Energy Converter for Jacket-Frame Substructures. *Energies* **2018**, *11*, 637. [CrossRef]
48. Hughes, S.A. *Physical Models and Laboratory Techniques in Coastal Engineering*; World Scientific Publishing Co. Pte. Ltd.: Singapore, 1993; ISBN 981-02-1540-1.
49. Sarmento, A.J.N.A.; Falcão, A.F.d.O. Wave Generation by an Oscillating Surface-Pressure and Its Applications in Wave Energy Extraction. *J. Fluid Mech.* **1985**, *150*, 467–485. [CrossRef]
50. Weber, J.W. Representation of Non-Linear Aero-Thermodynamic Effects during Small Scale Physical Modelling of OWC WECs. In Proceedings of the 7th European Wave and Tidal Energy Conference, Porto, Portugal, 11–13 September 2007; pp. 11–14.
51. Falcão, A.F.d.O.; Henriques, J.C.C. Model-Prototype Similarity of Oscillating-Water-Column Wave Energy Converters. *Int. J. Mar. Energy* **2014**, *6*, 18–34. [CrossRef]
52. Elhanafi, A.; Macfarlane, G.; Fleming, A.; Leong, Z. Scaling and Air Compressibility Effects on a Three-Dimensional Offshore Stationary OWC Wave Energy Converter. *Appl. Energy* **2017**, *189*, 1–20. [CrossRef]
53. Simonetti, I.; Cappietti, L.; Elsafti, H.; Oumeraci, H. Evaluation of Air Compressibility Effects on the Performance of Fixed OWC Wave Energy Converters Using CFD Modelling. *Renew. Energy* **2018**, *119*, 741–753. [CrossRef]
54. Morris-Thomas, M.T.; Irvin, R.J.; Thiagarajan, K.P. An Investigation into the Hydrodynamic Efficiency of an Oscillating Water Column. *J. Offshore Mech. Arct. Eng.* **2007**, *129*, 273–278. [CrossRef]
55. Dizadji, N.; Sajadian, S.E. Modeling and Optimization of the Chamber of OWC System. *Energy* **2011**, *36*, 2360–2366. [CrossRef]
56. Sheng, W.; Lewis, A.; Alcorn, R. On Wave Energy Extraction of Oscillating Water Column Device. In Proceedings of the 4th International Conference on Ocean Energy, Dublin, Ireland, 17–19 October 2012.
57. Hann, M.; Perez-Collazo, C. Chapter 7: Physical Modelling. In *Wave and Tidal Energy*; Greaves, D., Iglesias, G., Eds.; John Wiley & Sons Ltd.: West Sussex, UK, 2018; pp. 233–288. ISBN 978-1-119-01444-7.
58. Nielsen, K. Annex II Report 2003. In *Development of Recommended Practices for Testing and Evaluating Ocean Energy Systems*; IEA—Ocean Energy Systems: Lisbon, Portugal, 2003; pp. 1–62.
59. Mansard, E.P.; Funke, E.R. The Measurement of Incident and Reflected Spectra Using a Least Squares Method. In Proceedings of the International Conference on Coastal Engineering (ICCE), Sydney, Australia, 23–28 March 1980; Volume 1.
60. Baquerizo, A.; Losada, M.A.; Smith, J.M. Wave Reflection from Beaches: A Predictive Model. *J. Coast. Res.* **1998**, *14*, 291–298.
61. Fusco, F.; Nolan, G.; Ringwood, J.V. Variability Reduction through Optimal Combination of Wind/Wave Resources—An Irish Case Study. *Energy* **2010**, *35*, 314–325. [CrossRef]

Journal of
Marine Science and Engineering

MDPI

Review

A Review and Design Principle of Fixed-Bottom Foundation Scour Protection Schemes for Offshore Wind Energy

Dongyue Gao [1], Xinying Pan [1,2,*], Bingchen Liang [1,2], Bo Yang [1], Guoxiang Wu [1,2] and Zhenlu Wang [1,2]

[1] College of Engineering, Ocean University of China, Qingdao 266100, China; gaodongyue4900@stu.ouc.edu.cn (D.G.); bingchen@ouc.edu.cn (B.L.); yangbo1011@ouc.edu.cn (B.Y.); guoxiang@ouc.edu.cn (G.W.); wangzhenlu@ouc.edu.cn (Z.W.)
[2] Shandong Province Key Laboratory of Ocean Engineering, Ocean University of China, Qingdao 266100, China
* Correspondence: xinying@ouc.edu.cn

Abstract: Foundation scour is the erosion of sediments around pile foundations by wave and current in offshore wind energy. This phenomenon destabilizes foundations and poses a threat to pile safety. Therefore, scour protection becomes a crucial challenge in offshore wind projects. This paper reviews and synthesizes recent publications and patented technologies related to scour protection. Considering the primary engineering concerns, the paper proposes design principles for effective scour protection schemes to standardize evaluation criteria. These principles prioritize efficacy, independence, and cost-efficiency, enabling the analysis of scour protection scheme applicability. In addition, this paper summarizes and describes common protection schemes in the literature. The effectiveness of their protection is analyzed and summarized, and their economic and performance independence is evaluated. This paper categorizes flow-altering scour protection schemes found in the literature. Based on a comprehensive understanding of the mechanisms and engineering requirements of scour protection, the paper proposes a focus on determining the erosion reduction rate curve ($Ep - U/U_c$ curve) as a key criterion for evaluating the effectiveness of protection schemes under varying flow velocities and the erosion reduction rate of scour protection schemes under extreme conditions. The study highlights the necessity of establishing a comprehensive design evaluation methodology, which is crucial for addressing the significant challenges related to scour encountered in offshore wind power projects.

Keywords: ocean engineering; offshore wind energy; scour protection; scouring damage

1. Introduction

Recently, renewable energy has become increasingly important in ensuring energy security and reducing greenhouse gas emissions, etc. In various renewable energy sources, wind energy occupies an important position. At present, the scale of offshore wind power development in the world has accelerated significantly. In 2012, the installed capacity of Western countries, China, and India accounted for more than 95% of the global installed capacity, and more than 60% of the global wind power capacity is located in Europe and North America [1,2]. Data released by WindEurope show that, in 2019, a record of 3,623,000 KW (3623 MW) of new offshore wind capacity was installed in Europe, up 19.6% from 2018, with a cumulative installed capacity of 2,272,000 KW (22.07 GW) [3]. By 2030, Europe will have invested nearly EUR 20 billion in the wind power market, 60% of which is targeted at the wind power market [4,5]. In terms of vision, it is estimated that by 2050 wind energy will meet more than 20% of global electricity demand [1,2]. Outside Europe, China is also rapidly growing as a growth engine. According to China's National Energy Administration, in 2019, China installed 1.98 million kilowatts (1980 MW) of new offshore wind power, with a cumulative installed capacity of 5.93 million kilowatts (5930 MW) [3]. Up to July 2023, China's total renewable energy power generation reached

1.322 billion kilowatts (KW), historically surpassing coal power and accounting for about 48.8% of the country's total installed capacity [6,7]. The installed capacity of wind power is 389 million kilowatts. Meanwhile, China's wind power and photovoltaic power generation amounted to 729.1 billion kilowatt-hours, a year-on-year increase of 23.5% [6]. According to BloombergNEF, China's wind power sector achieved a record high with a newly installed capacity of 77.1 GW, representing a year-on-year increase of 58% in 2023. The offshore wind power capacity reached 7.6 GW, showing a 48% increase year-on-year and Chinese companies occupy four out of the top five positions in the global rankings of newly added capacity among wind turbine manufacturers [8].

Currently, the cost issue remains a major constraint to the development of offshore wind power, which is still about 50% more expensive than land-based wind power from the point of view of investment per-megawatt (MW) [9]. Typically, offshore wind turbines are 20% more expensive than similar onshore wind turbines, and the base class is 350% more expensive than onshore wind units [10]. According to the National Renewable Energy Laboratory (NREL) statistics for offshore wind projects, offshore wind energy expenditures are mainly for items, such as wind turbines, assembly and installation of wind structures, substructures, and foundations [9]. The turbine accounts for 33.6% of the total cost, the assembly and installation part accounts for 17.9%, the substructure and foundation accounts for 12.8, as shown in Figure 1. The data from Chinese companies show that the foundation cost accounts for 20% to 30% of the total investment in offshore wind farms, which is much higher than the similar proportion for onshore wind farms [3]. For floating offshore wind platforms, sub-structures and foundations are the highest cost component, accounting for about 36.2%.

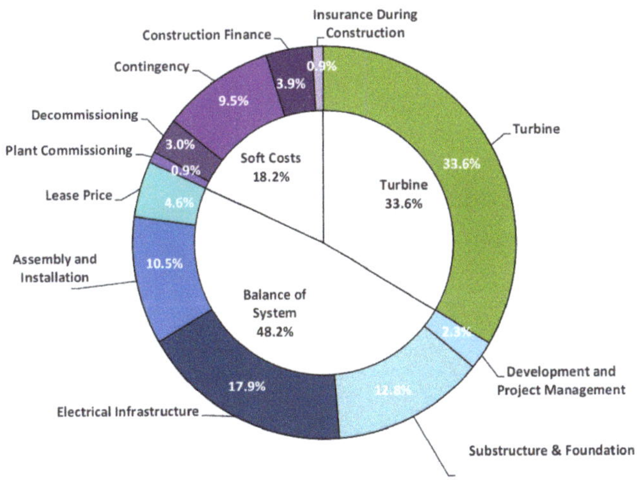

Figure 1. Fixed-bottom offshore wind system cost (with permission from Office of Scientific and Technical Information, U.S. Department of Energy) [9].

Scouring is a major challenge to the safety of pile foundation structures in offshore engineering [11,12]. The schematic diagram of scouring are shown in Figure 2. Chinese offshore wind power companies currently face the problem of pile scour during the operational phase of offshore wind farms. A large amount of scour seriously affects the safety of the structure, becoming one of the main problems of wind farms, requiring a large amount to detect and control local scour of the pile foundation structure, the hazards of which are as follows [12–14] (see Figure 3):

(1) Scouring phenomena induce a reduction in the depth of foundation penetration, consequently increasing the length of the cantilevered section of pile foundation.

(2) The bearing capacity of pile foundation is diminished by scouring, particularly affecting the self-vibration frequency of the entire structure.
(3) Scouring leads to an escalation in the ultimate load and fatigue load on the foundation, thereby impacting the fatigue life of pile foundation.
(4) Scouring results in the submergence of the submarine cable around the foundation, deviating from its intended design of being buried in the soil, affecting the state of its force distribution.
(5) Scouring can lead to environmental issues. During the scouring process, sediment and pollutants carried by the flow can contaminate water bodies, resulting in water pollution.

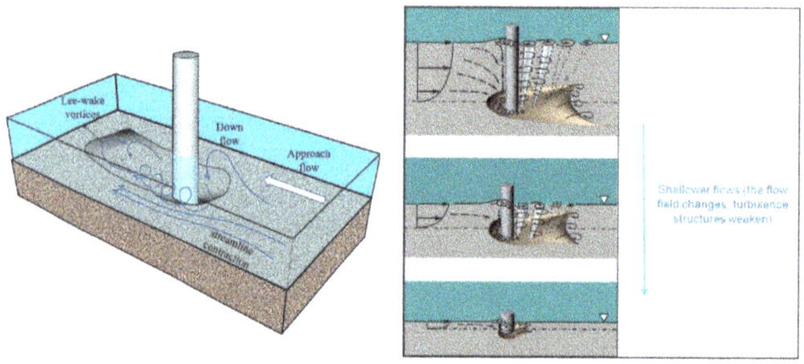

Figure 2. The erosion morphology and mechanism of monopile foundation.

Figure 3. Damage to the foundation of wind power caused by scouring.

Therefore, there is a clear engineering background and practical significance to design a safe and reasonable scour protection scheme for marine engineering structures. It can effectively reduce the consumption of human and material resources for wind farms, significantly improve the safety of wind power foundation, and reduce the chance of collapse of wind farms during the operation.

This paper reviews the scour protection countermeasure schemes for pile foundations in marine engineering. The types of structures mentioned in the paper, such as monopiles and pier and bridge foundations, are similar. Although monopiles may be larger, the differences can be ignored in experimental and numerical studies. Scour mechanisms similar to those of offshore wind pile foundations can be found in offshore areas and inland rivers, although they have different hydrodynamic environments [15]. Scour protection countermeasure schemes for bridge piers and port piers are good references to protect offshore wind pile foundations and are included in this paper.

This paper focuses on the scour protection scheme of monopile foundation that has specific application in practical engineering. There are many types of scour protection schemes for offshore pile structures, with different methods of application, mechanisms of action and scour protection effects. The research reports of wind power companies also mentioned the lack of specific standards and regulations in the offshore wind power industry. The selection and construction of scour protection scheme is mostly dependent on the experience of engineers. Therefore, this paper presents the design principles of scour protection scheme for marine engineering and analyzes the specific schemes in the relevant literature. It is based on the current demand of the marine engineering industry and the actual situation faced by scour protection in the design and construction of offshore wind power.

The rest of this paper is organized as follows. Section 2 briefly introduces the types of fixed wind turbine pile foundation structures and application water depths for the main scenarios of scour protection schemes. Section 3 describes the design principles for scour protection schemes, which are recommended as basic guidelines. Section 4 focuses on the existing flow-altering scour protection schemes in the literature. Section 5 introduces the bed-strengthening protection scheme. Section 6 summarizes the crucial issues of current research into scour protection schemes. Section 7 applies the design principle of scour protection scheme to analyze the engineering applicability of existing scour protection schemes in the literature. A summary and outlook are provided in Section 8.

2. Types of Fixed-Bottom Offshore Wind System Foundations

The types of pile foundations used in offshore wind power can be categorized into the fixed type and floating type, with fixed-type turbines being more commonly utilized. In this section, the main fixed-bottom foundation types are introduced.

2.1. Monopile Foundation

A monopile foundation consists of welded steel tubes made of rolled steel plates, and the tower is supported directly by the foundation pile legs or by connecting the two through a transition section. The structure of a monopile foundation is shown in Figure 4. The pile legs are inserted below the seabed and the depth of insertion depends on the actual environmental loads and the geological conditions of the seabed. The typical single foundation diameter is 3–8 m [5]. Chinese companies typically use 4.5–9 m diameter steel pipes for subsea installations. Monopile foundations are usually applied to shallow water depths, ranging from 0–30 m. In a wind farm of China Three Gorges Group in Dalian City, where the average water depth is 20 m, a large diameter monopile foundation is used as the foundation structure [16].

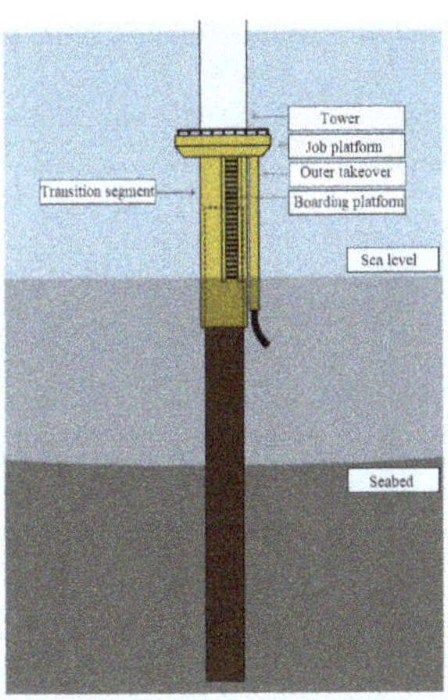

Figure 4. Monopile foundation structure.

Monopile foundation is currently the most widely used type of foundation in offshore wind projects. In European waters, 4258 offshore wind monopile foundations have been installed as of 2019, with a share of 81%. According to statistics, more than 75% of the completed offshore wind power projects are monopile foundations [15]. It has the advantages of mature technology, simple structure, convenient and quick construction, strong adaptability, good economy, and low cost. Monopile foundations are suitable for areas with a sandy soil or soft clay layer, good bearing capacity, and stable seabed. Simultaneously, after the installation of the foundation, it is usually necessary to carry out sea bed scouring protection. Traditional anti-scouring schemes are sand quilt, riprap, bionic grass, curing soil, and other bed-strengthening methods. But they have also shown some drawbacks in terms of effectiveness, maintenance, environment, and cost [3].

2.2. Gravity Foundation

The gravity foundation is one of the main types of offshore wind turbine foundation structures. It mainly rely on the foundation structure and internal ballast weight to resist the overturning moment and sliding force generated by the upper unit and external environment, as shown in Figure 5. This ensures the stability of the foundation and tower structure. It primarily relies on the foundation structure and internal ballast weight to counteract the overturning moment and sliding force generated by the upper unit (wind turbine) and external environmental factors. This ensures the stability of the foundation and tower structure. Gravity foundations are suitable for foundation conditions such as compacted clay and hard rock. However, they are not suitable for soft-foundation seabeds due to the high bearing capacity of the foundation. They are usually applicable to the sea area with water depths of 0–10 m, and some articles think that they can be extended to the sea area with water depths of 0–30 m [16].

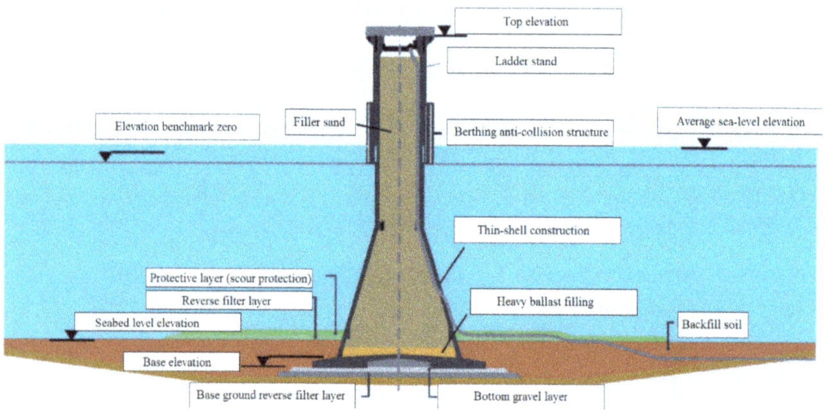

Figure 5. Gravity foundation structure.

The advantage of the gravity foundation is that it has well stability, while the pile structure can be manufactured by prefabrication and other means, reducing the link of offshore piling operations and reducing construction and installation costs [3]. It has a certain effect in reducing local scouring. Compared to other structural types, gravity foundations require higher seabed conditions and are suitable for shallow water depths.

2.3. Multi-Pile Bearing Foundation

Multi-pile bearing foundations consist of a foundation pile and concrete bearing platform, as shown in Figure 6. They have higher rigidity and better performance in resisting horizontal loads, and are suitable for medium water depth and less-demanding geological conditions on the seabed. They require traditional port construction equipment and construction techniques, and are less difficult to construct. Before being used in offshore wind power, they were a common engineering structure for port terminals. They are usually welded and manufactured in advance on land, and can be applied to water depths of 5–50 m [5]. They have the advantages of better applicability to soft ground.

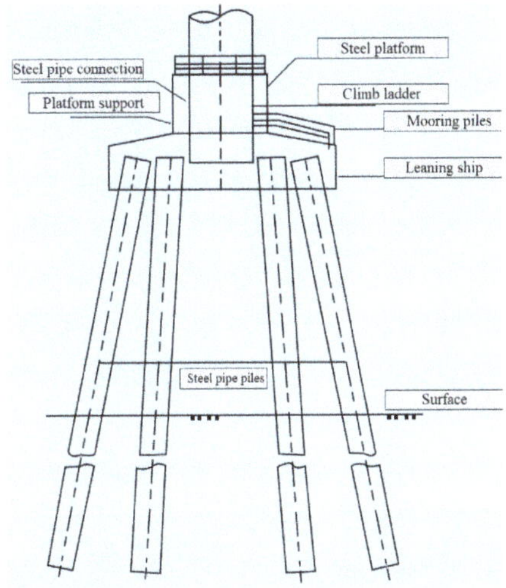

Figure 6. Multi-pile bearing foundation.

2.4. Tripod Foundation

Depending on the number of piles, tripod foundations can be categorized into three-legged and multi-legged foundations. The three-legged tripod foundation, characterized by a standard support structure comprising a main cylinder, three pile casings, and struts, as shown in Figure 7, exhibits notable engineering features. This foundation design involves the precise placement of three steel pipe piles, each with a medium diameter, in an equilateral triangular configuration on the seabed. The upper portion of the foundation is reinforced by a steel casing, providing crucial support to the three-legged truss structure and resulting in the formation of a relatively stable combined foundation. The adaptability of tripod foundations to varying water depths further enhances their versatility and expands their potential deployment in diverse offshore environments.

The utilization of tripod foundations has primarily been observed in European waters, where they have demonstrated applicability within water depth ranges of 10–35 m [5]. This foundation type offers several advantages that contribute to its suitability for offshore installations. Foremost, the inherent stability of the three-legged configuration ensures robust resistance against external forces. The triangular arrangement of the steel pipe piles facilitates the uniform load distribution and effective mitigation of lateral forces, thereby guaranteeing overall structural stability.

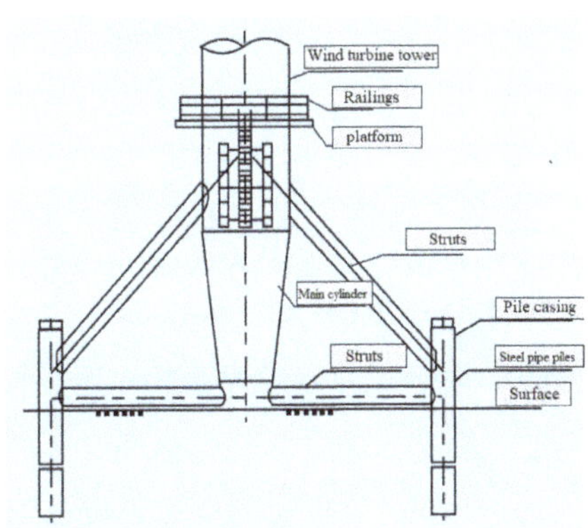

Figure 7. Tripod foundation.

2.5. Jacket Foundation

Jacket foundations are commonly employed in offshore structures and typically consist of three or four pile legs that are interconnected by spars, forming a spatial truss structure with sufficient strength and stability. The interconnections between the pile legs are typically achieved through welding, as illustrated in Figure 8. This welding method effectively addresses the challenge of underwater connections. Jacket foundations can be designed with multiple piles or barrels, providing flexibility in adapting to different site conditions. They are particularly suitable for water depths ranging from 20 to 50 m [16].

One of the key advantages of jacket foundations is their robust load-bearing and overturning resistance. The spatial truss structure imparts significant strength and stability to the foundation, enabling it to withstand the dynamic loads and environmental forces experienced in offshore environments. Additionally, jacket foundations have relatively low requirements for piling equipment, making them more accessible during the installation phase.

However, it is important to consider some challenges associated with jacket foundations. The structure of jacket foundations requires a significant amount of steel, resulting in higher material costs. The welded joints, particularly in the node areas of the steel pipes, are more susceptible to fatigue and corrosion due to the harsh marine environment. Therefore, proper inspection, maintenance, and corrosion protection measures are crucial to ensure the long-term integrity and performance of the jacket foundation.

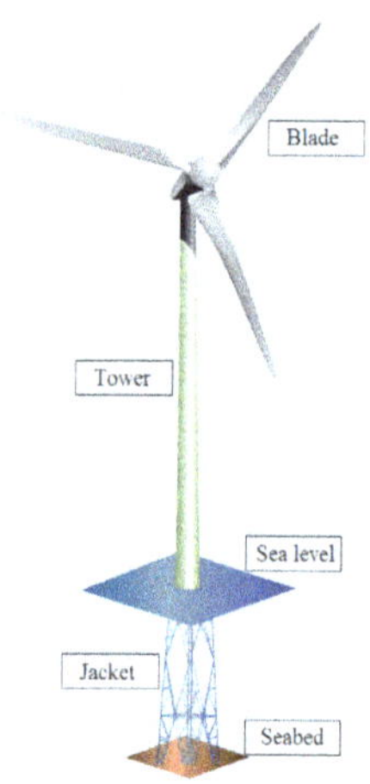

Figure 8. Jacket foundation.

2.6. Suction Cylinder Foundation

Suction cylinder foundations, also known as negative pressure cylinder foundations, are a type of foundation that can be classified into single-cylinder or multiple-cylinder structures. They consist of two main components: the lower cylinder body, which is open at the bottom and sealed at the top; and the outreach section, which can be constructed using reinforced concrete prestressed structures or steel structures, as shown in Figure 9.

This foundation type is specifically designed for deployment in marine areas characterized by sandy soil or soft clay seabeds. The installation process involves creating a negative pressure environment within the cylinder, allowing it to sink and stabilize itself through self-weight and resistance on the side of the cylinder. The suction effect generated by the negative pressure facilitates the penetration and anchoring of the foundation into the seabed.

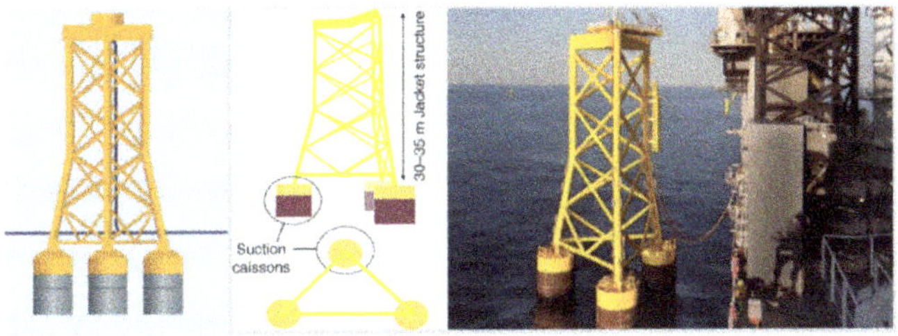

Figure 9. Suction cylinder foundation (with permission from Wiley, 2019) [17].

Suction cylinder foundations offers several advantages in suitable offshore environments. They eliminate the need for traditional piling methods, such as driven piles or drilled shafts, which can be challenging and time-consuming in certain seabed conditions. The self-weight and resistance provided by the foundation's cylinder contribute to its stability, ensuring long-term structural integrity. This foundation type is particularly suitable for marine areas with water depths ranging from 30 to 60 m [17].

The approximate distribution of different pile foundation types along the water depth is shown in Figure 10. In brief, the gravity foundation is the most suitable for a near-shore water depth of 0–20 m, and the monopile foundation can be applied to a water depth of about 30 m. When the water depth increases to 40–50 m, the tripod foundation and multi-pile bearing foundation are more commonly applied. When the water depth continues to increase, the main pile foundation structures are the jacket foundation and suction cylinder foundation [17].

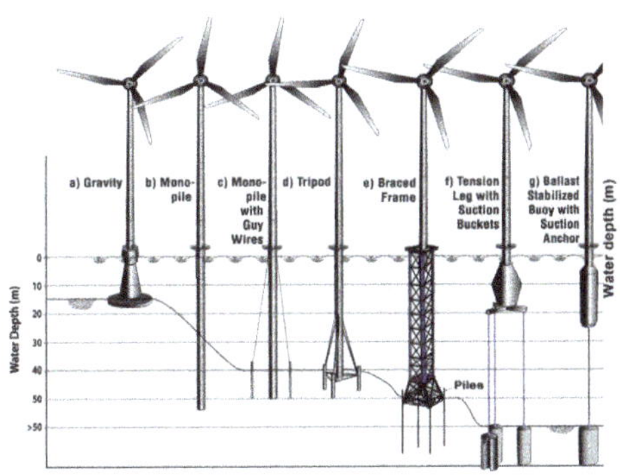

Figure 10. Different pile foundation structure types suitable for different water depth (with permission from Elsevier Books) [18–20].

3. Scour Protection Scheme Design Principle

The study of scour protection schemes for pile foundation structures divides the scour protection countermeasure schemes into the following two main categories, which are flow-altering (or flow-disturbing) schemes and bed protection schemes [21]. The bed protection scheme reduces the erosion of the sub-bed by hydrodynamic elements such as waves and currents and improves the shear resistance of the bed by arranging stones, sand covers, metal frames, and cured soil in the areas around the structure that are susceptible to scouring and erosion. Tafarojnoruz et al. [21] concluded that flow-altering schemes can be divided into four categories according to the type of scheme and the law of flow disturbance, as follows: (1) flow-altering schemes through piles, (2) structure attachment schemes, (3) bed attachment schemes, and (4) other schemes. Some of the scour protection schemes in the literature do not consider their actual application via engineering, which can have a significant impact on the performance of the pile structure itself or the surrounding sea environment.

Currently, the existing research on scour protection programs lacks comprehensive design principles and industry standards. In light of this deficiency, this paper aims to provide design principles for scour protection schemes, taking into account the specific context of wind power project construction carried out by Chinese enterprises. To achieve this objective, a thorough analysis of the relevant journal literature and patents pertaining to scour protection design has been conducted. Figure 11 shows the diagram of scour protection scheme design principle. The elements in the design principles of a scour protection program are well grounded in the literature [22].

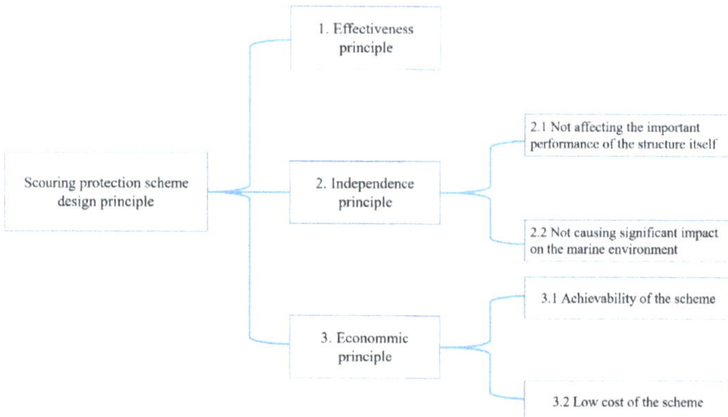

Figure 11. Design principle of scouring protection scheme.

3.1. Effectiveness Principle

The effectiveness principle in scour protection refers to the ability of a protection scheme to meet the safety requirements for scour protection throughout the entire lifecycle of a project, including construction, commissioning, and operation. This principle ensures that the scheme effectively controls the scour volume and maximum scour depth within acceptable limits defined by safety standards. It aims to ensure the safety of pile foundation structures under extreme working conditions where scour poses a significant risk.

To satisfy the effectiveness principle, a scour protection scheme must be designed to control the local scour volume and depth under extreme sea conditions. This requires considering factors such as the length of the cantilever section, pile bearing capacity, self-vibration frequency, fatigue life, and cable overhang length. By controlling the scour volume and depth within a controllable range, the scheme mitigates hazards associated with these factors.

One key parameter used to assess the effectiveness of a scour protection scheme is the scour depth reduction rate, denoted as $E_{p\,\mathrm{min}}$. This parameter represents the scheme's ability to minimize scour depth under the most unfavorable conditions. By focusing on reducing scour depth, the scheme can best demonstrate its effectiveness in protecting the integrity and stability of the pile foundation structures.

Effectiveness principle is of utmost importance in the design and implementation of a scour protection scheme. It ensures that the scheme provides adequate protection against scour hazards throughout the project's lifespan. By meeting the requirements of the effectiveness principle, the scour protection scheme establishes a robust foundation for the overall safety and performance of the project.

3.2. Independence Principle

The independence principle means that the scour protection scheme is independent to other properties of the pile foundation structure. Under the premise of meeting the scour protection, it does not affect other important properties of the structure, including the mechanical properties, such as tensile and shear stress resistance, and the chemical properties, such as corrosion resistance, and will not have a significant impact on the surrounding environment. It can be divided into the following two points.

Not affecting the important performance of the structure itself. The important properties of the structure itself mainly include mechanical properties of the structure and chemical properties of the structure material. Mechanical properties mainly include the load-bearing properties, such as tensile–compressive resistance and shear stress resistance. The stability properties relate to the vibration of the structure itself, and the fatigue load relates to the fatigue life. Chemical properties mainly refer to the corrosion resistance of the structure, the high salinity of the marine environment can accelerate the chemical corrosion of steel and concrete structures [23–25]. As a result, the design and construction of anti-corrosion coating is a major important part in the construction process of marine engineering structures. Relevant studies and specifications have design standards for the safe service life of the corrosion protection process for structures, and also this part of the process is one of the main costs of engineering construction [26]. Therefore, the chemical performance of pile foundation structures against corrosion and other chemical properties is one of the key principles to be considered in designing scour protection schemes.

Not causing a significant impact on the marine environment of the project. Significant impact on the environment means that the erosion of the bed surface will increase, causing an increase in the range of seabed scour and a significant change in the topography, which in turn will affect the ecological environment of the surrounding sea and other possible significant impacts. Marine environmental protection has become a major consensus in the marine engineering industry and in major countries around the world. Scour protection solutions should minimize the impact on the surrounding marine environment during the whole life cycle of the construction and operation of marine projects.

3.3. Economic Principle

The construction cost of pile foundations for offshore wind power and other marine projects accounts for about 20–30% of the total cost [3], much higher than the construction cost of similar wind power pile foundations onshore. Offshore wind power and other renewable energy industry has an important economic indicator: Levelized Cost of Energy (LCOE) [9,27,28], which is an important economic indicator to guide the offshore wind power industry for engineering construction. Many latest metrics are also based on this indicator [29]. It was first proposed by the National Renewable Energy Laboratory (NREL) in 1995. The LCOE model is calculated as follows [28,30,31]:

$$LCOE = \frac{(CapEx \times FCR) + OpEx}{(\frac{AEP_{net}}{1000})} \quad (1)$$

where $LCOE$ is the levelized cost of energy (USD per megawatt-hour [USD/MWh]), FCR is the fixed charge rate (%) , $CapEx$ is the capital expenditures (USD per kilowatt [USD/KW]), $AEPnet$ is the net average annual energy production (megawatt-hours per megawatt per year [MWh/MW/yr]), $OpEx$ is the operational expenditures (USD/KW/yr).

Based on Equation (1), scour protection of pile structures is mainly included in the construction costs. In terms of economy, the following two principles are considered.

(1) Achievability of the scheme. The scour protection solution should meet the existing process conditions and be able to be produced without major modifications to the production process. For some complex pile structures, it is difficult to assemble and produce them through the existing process, which requires major modifications to the production line to meet the production requirements. This will largely increase the construction cost. The authors prefer that scour protection solutions can be mass-produced through prefabricated structures for simple installation, and do not recommend more complex configurations.

(2) Low cost of the scheme. The scour protection scheme should try to meet the requirements of having a lower cost, modular construction, being easy to apply in the project,

and, compared to onshore wind power and other power generation equipment, better competitiveness, in order to meet the market requirements.

In the detailed analysis of the scour protection scheme, it is crucial to prioritize the effectiveness of the designed scheme. Once the effectiveness is ensured, the requirements outlined in principles 2.1 and 3.1 (as shown in Figure 11) should be met. With the above principles satisfied, further consideration should be given to principles 2.2 and 3.2, taking into account the specific conditions of the project and making appropriate trade-offs to achieve optimal results. If the scour protection scheme fails to meet the requirements outlined by the first three principles, it should not be implemented and is considered to be vetoed due to its inability to fulfill the necessary design criteria. This prioritization is illustrated in Figure 12. The order of priority is as follows: principle 1 takes precedence over principles 2.1 and 3.1, which, in turn, take precedence over principles 2.2 and 3.2 (principle (1) > principle (2.1, 3.1) >> principle (2.2, 3.2)).

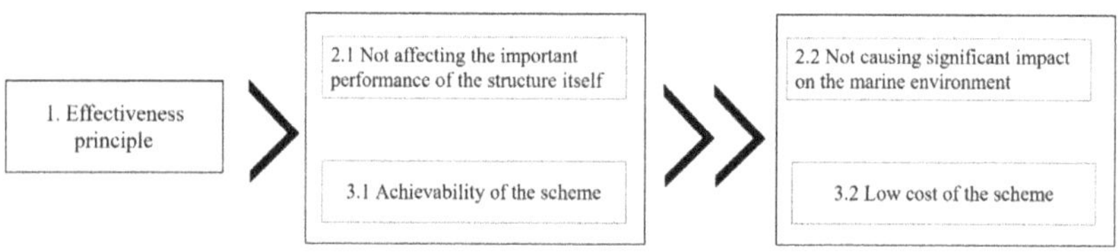

Figure 12. The priority of scour protection scheme design principle.

The following section provides a detailed description of the existing scour protection schemes in the literature by focusing on the scrambled scour protection scheme. It can reduce the effect of scour by changing the characteristics of the flow field around the structure foundation and weakening the pressure difference in front of the pile due to the presence of the pile foundation structure in the flow field. There is a large amount of literature on riprap protection as the main protection measure; this paper will not go into details here. The above mentioned design principles are used to screen the scour protection schemes, and a reasonable scour protection scheme for marine engineering pile foundation structures can be selected to meet the engineering construction requirements.

4. Flow-Altering Protection Scheme

Flow-altering protection schemes achieve the effect of reducing scour by changing the flow field characteristics around the structure. The flow structure around a monoplie foundation is shown in Figure 13. We can learn more about this from Sumer et al. [32] and Roulund [33].

The formation of a horseshoe vortex in front of the pile requires two necessary conditions [32]: the existence of a boundary layer for the traveling water in front of the pile, and a sufficiently large reverse pressure gradient in front of the pile. On this basis, Du et al. [34,35] summarized Baker [36], Dargahi [37], Roulund [33], Zhao [38], etc., for the study of the pressure in front of the pile, and concluded that the pressure is not uniformly distributed along the water depth near the pile surface. The pressure distribution is shown in Figure 14, along the height direction of the pile [34]. This uneven pressure distribution in front of the pile causes the boundary layer separation between the flow and the pile surface, thus creating an initial horseshoe vortex that, once formed, in turn increases the pressure at the bed surface. This is the main hydrodynamic factor for local scour generation. The main function of the flow-altering protection scheme is to reduce the scouring effect by reducing the pressure difference in front of the pile.

Flow-altering protection schemes can be introduced in the following four major categories, namely: (1) openings through piers, as shown in Table 1; (2) structure attachment, as shown in Table 2; (3) bed attachment, as shown in Table 3; (4) pile alteration schemes, as shown in Table 3.

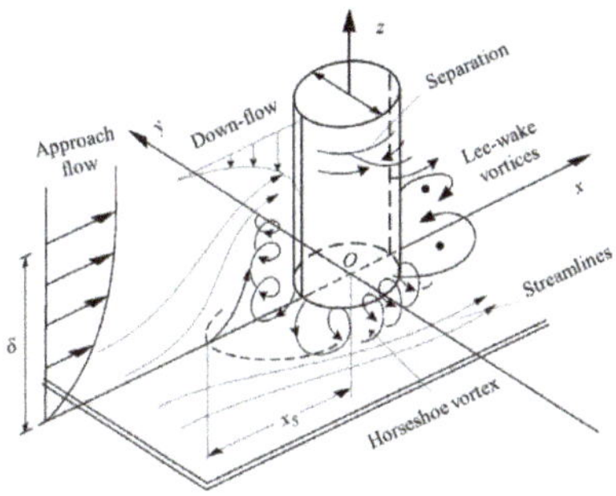

Figure 13. Monopile foundation pile circumferential field structure (with permission from *Journal of Marine Science and Engineering*, 2020, open access) [33,35].

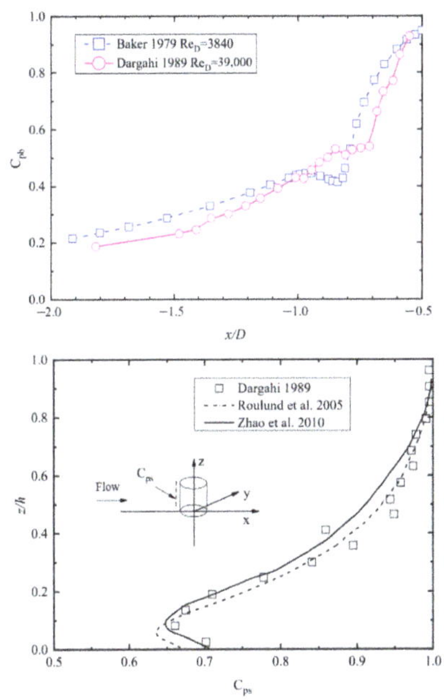

Figure 14. Relative pressure distribution before pile [33,36–38].

Table 1. Openings through piers scheme.

Class	Protection	Paper	Year
Openings through piers scheme	Internal flow-guiding tube scheme	Abd et al. [39]	2003
		Soltani et al. [40]	2013
		Entesar et al. [41]	2013
	Pile slots scheme	Entesaret al. [41]	2013
		Chiew et al. [42]	1992
		Kumar et al. [43]	1999
		Liang et al. [44]	2015
		Ali et al. [45]	2012
		Carmelo et al. [46]	2009
		Gaudio et al. [47]	2012
	Equivalent piles scheme	Vitall et al. [48]	1994
		Yagci et al. [49]	2017

Table 2. Structure attachment scheme.

Class	Protection	Paper	Year
Structure attachment scheme	Collor scheme	Moncada-M et al. [50]	2009
		Tafarojnoruz et al. [45]	2012
		Kumar et al. [43]	1999
		Tang et al. [15]	2022
		Tang et al. [51]	2023
		Liang et al. [44]	2015
		Jahangirzadeh et al. [52]	2014
	Vane scheme	Aly et al. [11]	2021
		Parker et al. [53]	1998
		Gupta [54]	1987
		Alireza et al. [55]	2015
		Khaple et al. [56]	2017
		Gaudio et al. [47]	2012
		Ghorbani et al. [57]	2008
	Pile roughness and threaded piles	Aly et al. [11]	2021
		Ghodsian et al. [58]	2009
		Abdelhaleem et al. [59]	2019
		Dey et al. [60]	2006
		Izadinia et al. [61]	2012
		Muhawenimana et al. [62]	2022
		Vahdati et al. [63]	2019
	Extended foundations	Melville et al. [64]	1996
		Liang et al. [44]	2015
		Yao et al. [65]	2020

Table 3. Bed attachment scheme and pile alteration scheme.

Class	Protection	Paper	Year
Bed attachment scheme	Sacrificial piles scheme	Haque et al. [66]	2007
		Chiew et al. [67]	2003
		Keshavarzi et al. [68]	2018
		Garg et al. [69]	2022
		Mohsen [70]	2021
		Mohsen et al. [71]	2018
		Tafarojnoruz et al. [45]	2012
		Li et al. [72]	2022
	Deflector scheme	Odgaard et al. [73]	1983
		Chauhan et al. [74]	2022
		Ghorbani et al. [57]	2008
		Zarei et al. [75]	2019
		Safaripor et al. [76]	2022
	Sand barrier scheme	Guan et al. [77]	2014
		Hamidifar et al. [78]	2018
		Mahdi et al. [79]	2022
		Grimaldi et al. [80]	2009
		Liang et al. [44]	2015
		Tafarojnoruz et al. [45]	2022
		AI-Awadi et al. [81]	2021
		Pagliara et al. [82]	2010
		Gaudio et al. [47]	2012
Pile alteration scheme		AI-Shukur [83]	2020
		Farooq et al. [84]	2020
		Baranwal et al. [85]	2020
		Aly et al. [11]	2020

The maximum scour depth reduction rate is usually used as an important indicator to determine the effectiveness of scour protection schemes, which is usually expressed by the following equation [21].

$$E_p = \frac{d_{se} - d_{sec}}{d_{se}} \quad (2)$$

where E_p is the maximum scour depth reduction rate, representing the scour protection effect of this scheme; d_{se} is the maximum scour depth without protection scheme; d_{sec} is the maximum scour depth after applying protection scheme.

4.1. Openings through Piers Scheme

There are three main forms of the openings through a piers scheme: internal flow-guiding tube, pile slots, and equivalent piles (group pile replacement) [21]. Table 4 shows the maximum and minimum scour reduction rate for openings through a piers scheme.

Table 4. Scour reduction rate of openings through piers scheme.

	Flow-Guiding Tube Scheme	Pile Slots Scheme	Equivalent Piles Scheme
E_p (Upper limit)	45%	35%	39%
E_p (Lower limit)	37.5%	26.1%	22%

Internal flow-guiding tube scheme reduces the pressure difference generated by the current in front of the pile by cutting several holes in the pile body and guiding the current through the holes to pass through the structure, thus achieving the effect of scour resistance. Figure 15 shows a deflector structure, for which α and d represents the angle and diameter of the inner flow-guiding tube. The scour protection ability of this scheme was found to be related to the hole diameter d and the Froude number Fr [21]. El-Razek et al. [39] found that this protection scheme can reduce the scour depth by a maximum of 39%. Somaye et al. [40] reduced the maximum scour depth of 37.5% by a similar arrangement. Entesar [41] found that the maximum scour depth was reduced by 45% and the scour volume was reduced by 68% by arranging the deflector tube in the pile body.

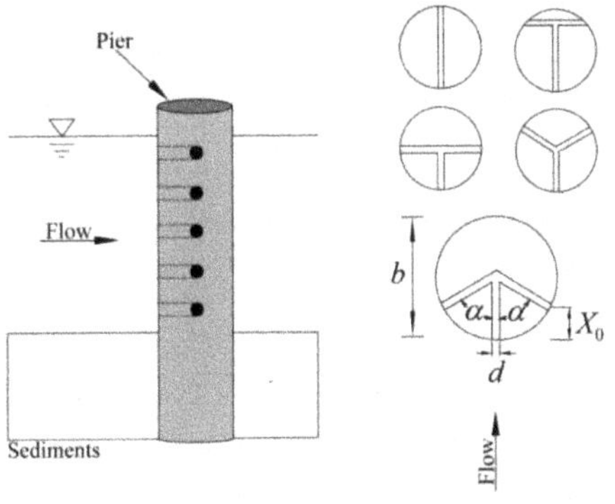

Figure 15. Flow-guiding tube scheme (with permission from *Journal of Hydraulic Research*, 2010) [21].

Pile slots are used to reduce the effect of scouring by opening inflow slots on the structure to guide the flow diversion through the structure and reduce the pressure in front of the structure pile, as shown in Figure 16. It is generally believed that the larger the diameter of the hole, the stronger its scouring protection [15,21,41–43]. Liang et al. [44] adjusted the hole size and arrangement position in the experiment, the scour depth reduction rate was always below 26.1% under the unidirectional flow and wave-current coupling conditions, thus the scour protection effect was considered less than ideal. In other experiments, the single slotting scheme only has a scour depth reduction rate less than 35%, such as the experiments of Tafarojnoruz et al. [45]. It can achieve a scour depth reduction of 35% scour protection effect in the most ideal condition when its opening diameter is maximum. The combination of pile grooving and other protection methods to form a combined protection scheme can achieve a better scour protection effect in some experiments, such as Grimaldi et al. [46], who combined the grooving method with a sand barrier to have a maximum scour depth reduction of 45%. Gaudio et al. [47] combined the grooving scheme with a horizontal plate, which could have a maximum scour depth reduction of 81.8%.

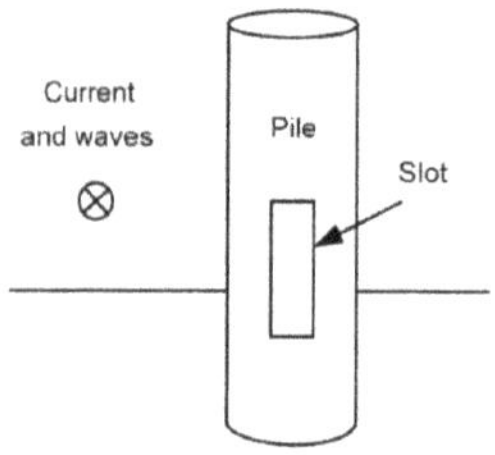

Figure 16. Pile slots scheme (with permission from *Science China Technological Sciences*, 2015) [44].

Equivalent piles are used for local scour reduction by replacing a monopile with a group pile structure of equal support capacity, as shown in Figure 17. The parameter y_L represents the length of equivalent piles. Vittal et al. [48] arranged three structures at 120° instead of a monopile structure and has a scour protection capability of 39% reduction in maximum scour depth.

Oral et al. [49] investigated the use of cylindrical hexagonal arrays as equivalent pile structures, set four array densities of 0.14, 0.2, 0.32, and 0.56, and compared them with a single circular pile having the same area, as shown in Figure 18. The experimental results found that for the combination of equivalent piles with higher array densities, the scour characteristics are similar to those of individual solid cylinders, showing more of their overall scour characteristics. When the array density of the equivalent pile combination is smaller, the local scour characteristics of individual cylinders start to become obvious. In addition, the equivalent piles can reduce the maximum scour depth and scour volume compared with the same square of single cylinder. The whole column arrangement with lower density has better scour protection effect, when the array density is 0.14, as shown in Figure 19. The maximum scour depth can be reduced by 22% and the scour volume can be reduced by 27% [49]. It can be concluded that the load-bearing capacity of the support structure depends largely on its cross-sectional area, and the experimental results show that the equivalent pile structure of hexagonal array can be used as an alternative to monopile support, −1.0.

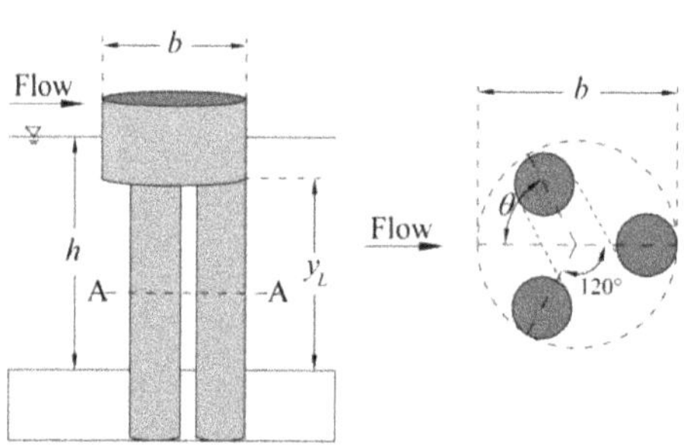

Figure 17. Equivalent piles scheme [21].

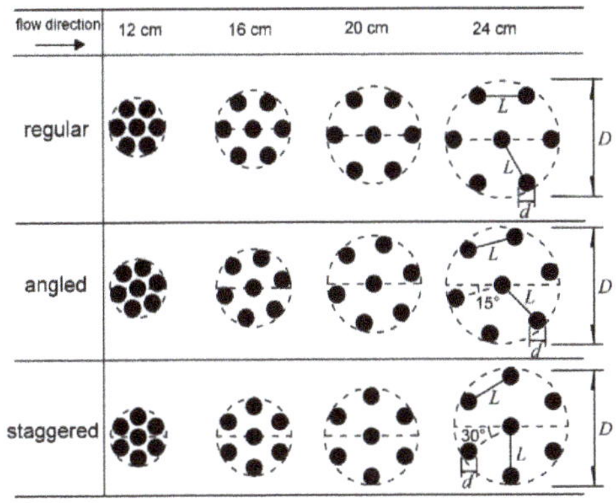

Figure 18. Hexagonal equivalent pile structure (with permission from *Applied Ocean Research*, 2017) [49].

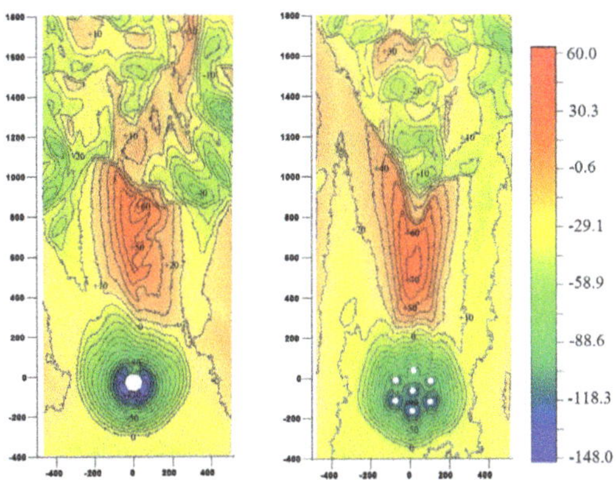

Figure 19. Equivalent pile structure scour protection effect [49].

4.2. Structure Attachment

The structural attachment method achieves the effect of changing the flow field and thus reducing scour by installing accessory structures around the pile foundation and the pile body. Such protection schemes usually have specific options such as horizontal plates (also known as collars), vertical plates, vanes, pile threads, rough pile bodies, and extended foundations. Table 5 shows the maximum and minimum scour reduction rate for structural attachments scheme.

Table 5. Scour reduction rate for structural attachments scheme.

	Vanes Scheme	Vertical Plates Scheme	Threaded Piles Scheme	Extended Foundations Scheme
E_p (Upper limit)	90%	61.6%	52%	89.4%
E_p (Lower limit)	32%	42.4%	12.85%	50%

The collar schemes are divided into two main categories. One is placed above the bed surface to reduce the scour by preventing the water from diving in front of the pile. Another type is usually arranged at the bed surface or at the position where the top plate is flush with the bed surface, which generally acts directly on the bed surface to protect it from scour.

The placement height of the horizontal plate is a major factor affecting its scour protection effect. Moncada-M et al. [50] found that when the horizontal plate was arranged on the bed surface or under the bed surface, its position could effectively reduce scouring, mainly playing the effect of the horizontal plate directly protecting the bed surface. Tafarojnoruz et al. [45] found through experiments that under certain hydrodynamic environmental conditions the protection effectiveness of horizontal plates arranged above the bed surface is weaker than that of protection schemes such as sacrificial piles and pile trenching; however, horizontal plates can be easily combined with other protection schemes and applied as a supplementary scheme. Pandey et al. [86] found that the horizontal plate scheme can effectively reduce the maximum depth compared with the control group without protection scheme, and the development pattern of maximum scour depth over scouring time is consistent with the unprotected group, as shown in Figure 20. Mashahir et al. [87] concluded that, compared with the unprotected control group, the maximum depth of scour under horizontal plate protection is inconsistent with the unprotected group.

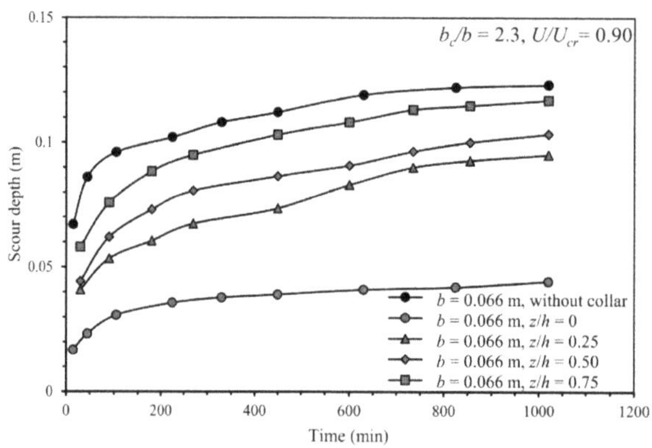

Figure 20. Horizontal plate protection scheme erosion trend over time (with permission from Ocean Engineering, 2020) [86].

Kumar et al. [43] gave the following predictive equation for the scour protection capacity of horizontal plates:

$$E_p = 0.057\left(\frac{W}{D}\right)^{1.612}\left(\frac{y_0 - y_{col}}{y_0}\right)^{0.837}, y_{col} > 0 \quad (3)$$

where W is the diameter of the horizontal plate; D is the diameter of the structure; y_0 is the water depth; and y_{col} is the position of the plate from the bed. Tang et al. [15] compared the experiment results of the physical model with the predicted values of the above equation, and found that the protection effect predicted by the equation had a large deviation from the actual measured values, as shown in Figure 21. The protection ability of the horizontal plate under different hydrodynamic environments is not consistent, as shown in Figure 22. This phenomenon may be related to factors such as flow velocity and sediment particle size.

When the horizontal plate is placed below a certain position on the bed, the volume of scour below the horizontal plate is very small [15,51]. When it is higher than this position, more scour will be generated below the horizontal plate. The scouring protection ability is weakened with the increase in the height of the placement position, as shown in Figure 23. Therefore, when considering the horizontal plate protection scheme, we should first consider the layout position in the horizontal plane or the area below it. For the effect of horizontal plate diameter on scour protection ability, Liang et al. [44] experimentally concluded that diameters of three times the pile diameter have better scour protection ability than those that are two times the pile diameter.

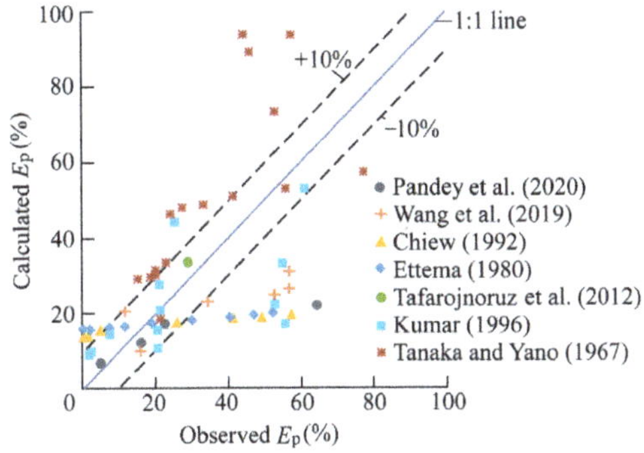

Figure 21. Kumar et al.'s prediction equation versus measured data (with permission from the author, open access) [42,45,86,88–91].

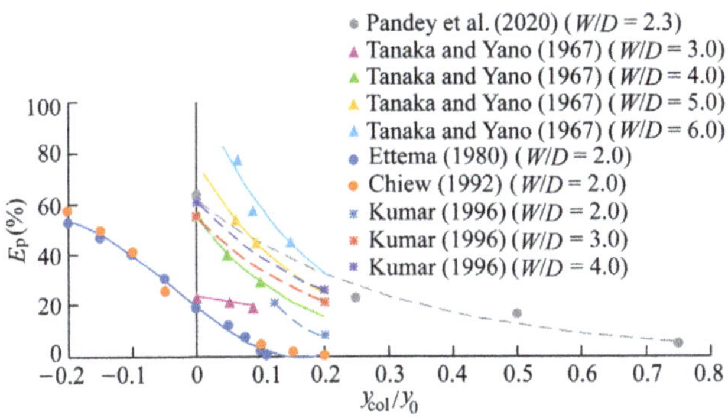

Figure 22. Reduction rate of different experiments in horizontal plate protection schemes [42,86,89–91].

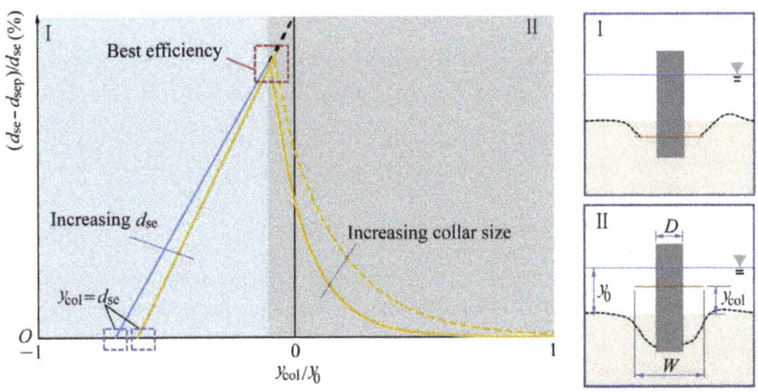

Figure 23. The most effective placement of horizontal plate protection scheme [15].

Vertical plates and vanes are another major category of structural attachments. In 1960s, researchers began to conduct research on such scour protection schemes, using flat plates and vanes to reduce the scour depth [21]. It has been suggested that such protection schemes can separate the flow around the pile structure and thus reduce the strength of the horseshoe vortex [53]. The vane scheme shown in Figure 24 can reduce the scour depth by 90% [21].

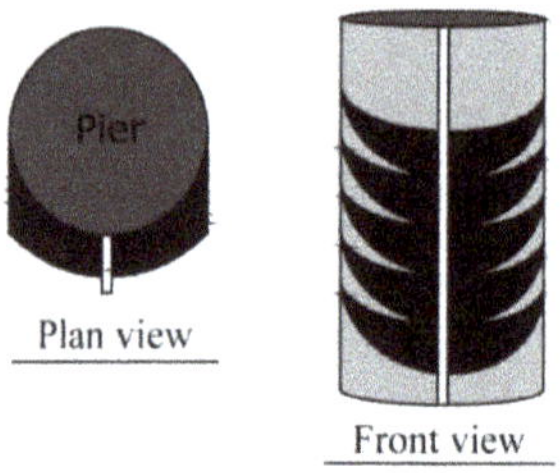

Figure 24. Vanes scheme [21].

Gupta proposed a triangular vane, which placed at the bottom of the structure as shown in Figure 25. It can destroy the flow characteristics at the bottom of the structure and reduce the strength of the horseshoe vortex [54]. The experimental results of this scheme showed that the scour depth was reduced by 32% in unsteady flow and 67% in the experimental clear water velocity condition.

Aly-Mousaad et al. [11] demonstrated by the computational fluid dynamics (CFD) method that the triangular vane protection scheme can reduce the bed shear stress by about 30% under certain water flow conditions, which in turn reduces the scour volume and scour depth. The vertical plate scheme can be reduced 10–15%. The paper reveals the mechanism of the triangular vane scheme and theoretically demonstrates the feasibility of the scheme.

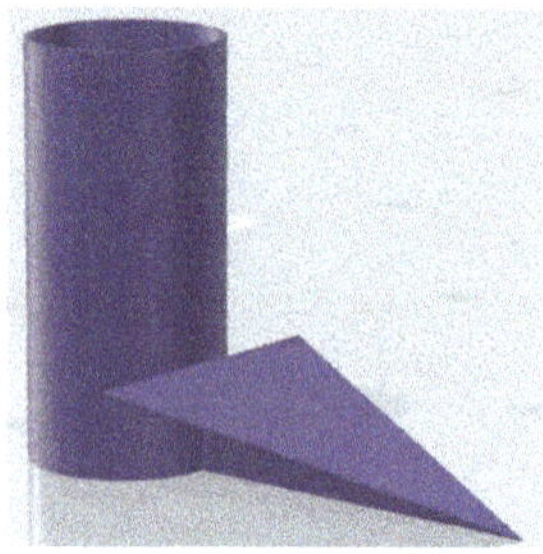

Figure 25. Triangular vane.

The structure of the vertical plate scheme is shown in Figure 26. Dey et al. [60] found that the vertical plate scheme can reduce the maximum scour depth by 61.6% on average. Khaple et al. [55] concluded that the ability of scour protection increases with the increase in vertical plate length, and this ability is independent of the sediment particle size. Khaple et al. [56] found experimentally that the vertical plate length has the best scour protection ability when it is twice the pile diameter, and the maximum scour depth is reduced by 42.4%, and the authors proved that this scheme significantly weakens the pile front vortex structure by observing the flow field. In the experiments of Gaudio et al. [47], the maximum scour depth was reduced by 25.3% when two symmetrical submerged vertical plates were placed on both sides of the pile front and combined with the sand barrier scheme. Ghorbani et al. [57] investigated the effect of the placement angle and position of the submerged vertical plate on scouring, and concluded that the best scouring protection effect was achieved when the vertical plate was set directly in front and the opening angle was 18.5°.

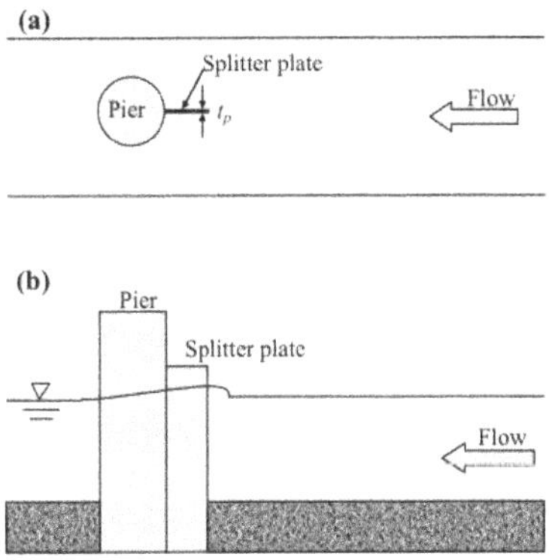

Figure 26. Vertical plate scheme, (**a**) plan view, (**b**) elevation view (with permission from *Acta Geophysica*, 2017) [56].

Increasing the pile roughness and threaded piles can be seen as one class of scour protection schemes. Ghodsian et al. [58] argued that introducing rough structures or attaching rough elements to the surface of existing structures generates minute turbulence on the surface and generates kinetic energy upstream of the jetty, thus delaying the water separation and moving the delay point downstream of the pile. As a result, the intensity of the horseshoe vortex is weakened and moved away from the riverbed. Ghodsian et al. therefore concluded that the method of roughing the surface of structures is effective in reducing the maximum depth of scour and the volume of scour. Fahmy Salah [59] experimentally evaluated the efficiency of different roughness on the surface of circular piers. The effectiveness of increasing the surface roughness of the structure in reducing the maximum scour depth and influencing the upstream slope angle of the regional scour pit was demonstrated. It was observed experimentally that roughed piers could reduce the maximum scour depth, the impact area and the scour volume reduced by 29.6%, 13.7%, and 42.52%, respectively.

Threaded piles are designed to change the flow field and reduce scour by wrapping cables around the perimeter of the pile. Dey et al. [60] first proposed this scheme, which controls the flow field around the pile and the scour around structure by using one, two, or three cables wrapped around the body of the structure. The maximum scour depth reduction under wave conditions was 46.3% when the thread diameter to pile diameter ratio was 0.1 and the thread winding angle was 15°. Izadinia et al. [61] investigated the effect of the scheme of threaded piles and the combination of threaded piles and horizontal plates on the scour depth reduction. The best protection effect was achieved when the ratio of thread diameter to pile diameter was 0.15 and the thread winding angle was 15°. The scour reduction was 12.85%. The maximum scour depth reduction was 52.85% when the combination of threaded pile and horizontal plate scheme was used for protection. In the experiment of Valentin et al. [62], the reduction in scour depth of threaded piles was 32% and 52% for coarse and fine sediments, respectively, and it was found that the scour protection was more effective for the bed of fine sediments as the thread diameter increased. Vahdati et al. [63] investigated the effect of threaded piles on scouring of group piles and found that the maximum scour depths of the front and rear piles were reduced by 46% and 12%, respectively. Threaded piles scheme had no scouring protection effect in the experiments with three downstream side-by-side piles.

Extended foundations usually extend the diameter range of the foundation. In offshore wind power and other marine projects, the foundations of structures in offshore are vulnerable to scouring. Usually gravity foundations can reduce the impact of scouring [5,92]. Chiew [42] and Coleman [93] argue that extended foundations not only increase the load-bearing capacity of structures, but also have the effect of reducing scour. Wu et al. [5] argue that the application of gravity-based foundations is usually in sea area less than 10 m water depth.

Melville et al. [64] demonstrated the effectiveness of the extended foundation scheme for scour protection by experiments and proposed that the foundation installation location Y should be below the bed surface and $0 < Y < 2.4D$, D is the pile diameter of the structure. The maximum scour depth reduction rate of the group with the best effect in their experiments was 50%. Liang et al. [44] found that the extended foundation with three times the pile diameter has better scour protection effect compared with the extended foundation with two times the pile diameter, and the maximum scour depth is reduced by 89.4% and 61%, respectively. Yao et al. [65] found that, unlike the scour development pattern under an unprotected foundation, scour development under an extended foundation starts from behind the pile and extends to the front of the pile. The extended foundation can delay the local scour development process, and no significant scour is generated at the beginning of scour initiation compared to the control group without the scour protection scheme.

4.3. Bed Attachment Scheme

The bed attachment scheme refers to the effect of changing the characteristics of the flow field around the structure and thus reducing the scouring volume by influencing the wave and current through the structures placed on the sea bed, and there are mainly the following types: sacrificial piles, deflectors, sand barriers, etc. Table 6 shows the maximum and minimum scour reduction rate for the bed attachment scheme.

Table 6. Bed attachment scheme erosion reduction rate.

	Sacrificial Pile Scheme	Deflector Scheme	Sand Barrier Scheme
E_p (Upper limit)	65%	46%	42.6%
E_p (Lower limit)	32.2%	34%	17.2%

Sacrificial piles are the most common scour protection scheme installed in the sea bed. See Figure 27. The effect of altering the flow field around the protected structure is achieved by installing one or more flow disturbance piles in front of or around the pile. These sacrificial piles are subject to scour erosion, creating a highly deflected flow around the structure and thus creating a low scour capacity wake behind the sacrificial piles to protect the structure behind from erosion [66,67]. Melville et al. [64] argue that the effectiveness of the sacrificial pile scheme depends on factors such as its number, size relative to the protected piles, geometric arrangement order, and characteristics of the flow field. Keshavarzi et al. [68] experimentally explored the effect of the distance between the front and rear piles on the scour of the pile foundation and found that the scour of the sacrificial piles increased with the spacing when the spacing between the two piles was $1 < L/D < 2.5$, and the maximum scour depth of the front pile was 22% greater than that of the rear pile when $L/D = 2.5$. When $2.5 < L/D < 10$, Garg et al. [69] found that the protection scheme of placing a sacrificial pile in the headwater direction could reduce the maximum scour depth by 39%. The same phenomenon observed by Keshavarzi et al. [68], where violent scouring occurs near the front pile and the upstream sacrificial pile protects the downstream main pile from the direct impact of the impinging water flow. Garg et al. [69] also found in their experiments that the maximum 100% scour protection could be achieved when a horizontal plate of 3 times the pile diameter was combined with the sacrificial pile for protection. Ranjbar-Zahedani et al. [70] designed a triangular block placed in front of the pile, as shown in Figure 28, which can reduce the maximum scour depth of the post-pile by 40–60%. Tafarojnoruz et al. [45] designed a pile-rowing scheme that can reduce the maximum scour depth by 32.2%.

In addition, Li et al. [72], inspired by mangrove protection of shoreline, proposed a wrap-around skirt pile as a protection measure for monopile scour protection scheme, as shown in Figure 29. The maximum scour depth reduction rate of this method is 65%, which can reduce the sediment scour volume by 90%.

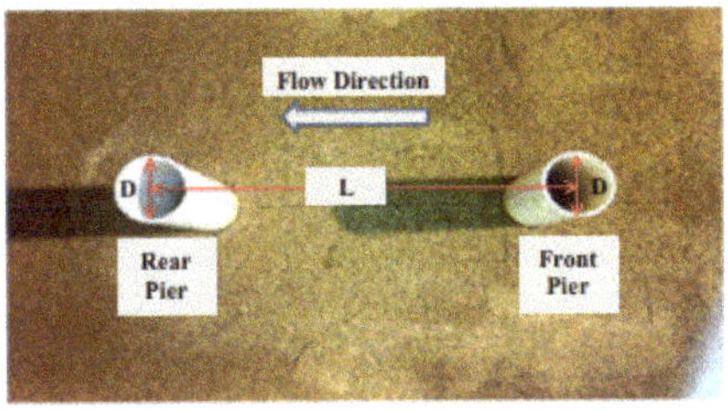

Figure 27. Front-to-rear sacrificial pile scheme (with permission from *Environmental Fluid Mechanics*, 2018) [68].

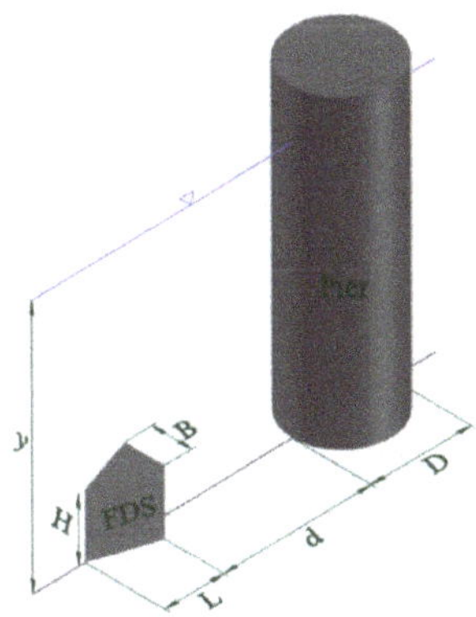

Figure 28. Triangular sacrificial pile (with permission from *Journal of Hydraulic Research*, 2021) [70].

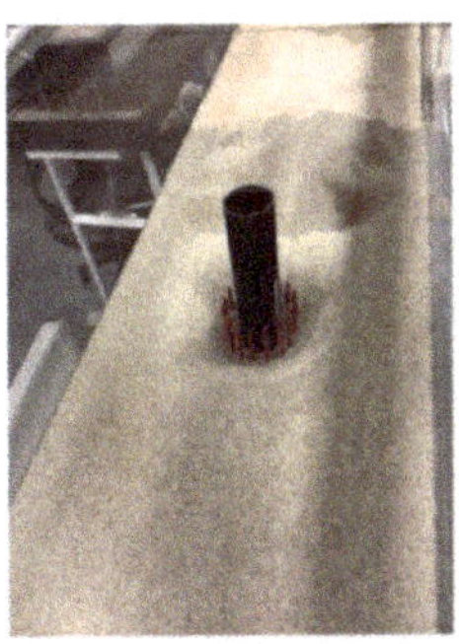

Figure 29. Wrap-around skirt pile scheme (with permission from *Ocean Engineering*, 2022) [72].

The arrangement of the deflector scheme is presented in Figure 30. The scheme operates by inducing secondary circulation in the deflector region, thereby altering the magnitude and direction of bed shear stress in the surrounding area. Consequently, the flow velocity distribution and sediment transport rate are modified. Odgaard and Kennedy [73] introduced the application of deflectors on sand beds to mitigate and control scour. Their investigations revealed that deflectors induced changes in the flow field, leading to alterations in bed shear stress magnitude and direction, subsequently influencing sediment transport patterns. Chauhan et al. [74] comprehensively elucidated the mechanism underlying deflector implementation for scour protection. They emphasized that during flood periods, bridges are susceptible to severe scour-related issues. Placing deflectors upstream of the structure generates a vortex at the rear, while downstream flow establishes a vertical shear layer. These combined effects reduce flow velocity ahead of the pile by mitigating the pressure gradient, thereby modifying sediment transport and diminishing scour.

Tafarojnoruz [21] highlighted key control parameters for the deflector scheme, including blade height (h_v), height-to-length ratio (h_v/l_v, where l_v denotes blade length), and entry angle (α_v). Lauchlan et al. [21,94] contended that when the aspect ratio $h_v/l_v < 1$, the deflector's influence on sediment transport surpasses its impact on the flow field, akin to sacrificial piles. Lauchlan et al. [94] further observed that the most effective scour protection is achieved with $h_v/l_v > 1$, resulting in a 34 % reduction in maximum scour depth and a 50% decrease in scour volume. Tafarojnoruz [21] concluded, based on extensive experiments, that the deflector can reduce maximum scour depth by 50% under both clear water and dynamic bed scour conditions. Ghorbani et al. [57] demonstrated that flow velocity oscillations and dynamic bed scour diminish the deflector scheme's scour protection capabilities and overall effectiveness. In their comparative analysis, Ghorbani et al. found that the double-bladed deflector outperformed the single-bladed deflector in reducing scour. Vaghefi et al. [75,76] substantiated the scour protection effect of deflectors through experimental investigations in river bend sections. For group pile structures comprising three piles, the maximum scour depth was reduced by 35%. In single pile experiments, the maximum scour depth diminished by 46%, thus illustrating the deflector's effectiveness in large river bends.

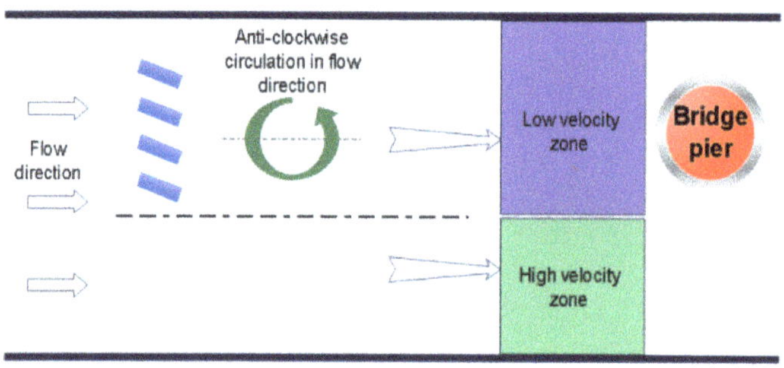

Figure 30. Mechanism of the deflector scheme (with permission from *ISH Journal of Hydraulic Engineering*, 2022) [74].

Sand barriers are commonly employed in river management to prevent the undercutting of river beds. By limiting sediment transport, they effectively influence bed dynamics and reduce scour [77–79]. Grimaldi et al. [80] implemented a sand barrier downstream of a pile structure to control scour under constant flow conditions, as illustrated in Figure 31. The most significant reduction in scour depth, amounting to 26%, was achieved when the sand barrier was placed immediately downstream of the pile structure. However, arranging the sand barrier at a position of $0.5D$ downstream of the pile structure resulted in reductions of over 80% in both scouring range and volume of scoured sediment, demonstrating the most comprehensive effectiveness. Liang et al. [44] conducted experiments involving current and unidirectional wave conditions, yielding scour depth reduction rates (E_p) of 42.6% and 13.6%, respectively, compared to a control group without any protection scheme. Tafarojnoruz et al. [45] observed a maximum scour depth reduction rate (E_p) of 17.2% for a sand barrier scheme under the influence of current. According to the existing literature [45,80–82], it is generally believed that placing the sand barrier in close proximity to the downstream surface of the pile structure effectively reduces scour behind the pile, while the presence of scour behind the sand barrier is not prominent. Aysar [81] experimentally concluded that the relative position of the sand barrier behind the pile structure plays a crucial role in reducing scour depth and is a significant factor affecting scour protection capacity. The best protection effect is achieved when the relative position (L_b/D) is 0 to 0.32 times the pile diameter behind the pile. For relative flow velocities (V/V_c) of 0.48, 0.64, 0.8, and 0.96, the scour reduction rates are 16%, 30%, 23%, and 28% when $L_b/D = 0$, and 12%, 28%, 17%, and 25% when $L_b/D = 0.32$, respectively. The flow rate also influences the scour protection effectiveness of the sand barrier scheme.

The sand barrier can be used in combination with other forms of scour protection schemes [79]. In the experiments of Gaudio et al. [47], the best scour reduction rate is 25.3% for the combined scheme of sand barrier and deflector blade and the reduction is 63.3% for the combined scheme with horizontal plate. The authors concluded that there is an improvement compared with the maximum scour depth reduction rate of 17.2% in the Tafarojnoruz et al. [45] experiment.

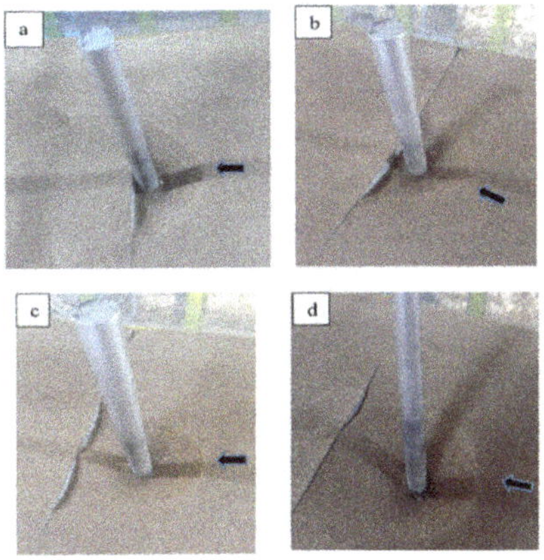

Figure 31. Sand barrier as a structural erosion protection, (**a**) $L_b/D = 0.32$, (**b**) $L_b/D = 1$, (**c**) $L_b/D = 2.5$, (**d**) $L_b/D = 4$ (With permission from *Smart Science*, 2021) [81].

4.4. Pile Alteration Scheme

The pile alteration scheme is mainly used to reduce the obstruction of incoming flow by changing the shape of the structure or the foundation of the structure. It can reduce the flow velocity and pressure in the local area of high flow velocity and high pressure, to reduce the bed shear stress, and thus to achieve the effect of reducing scouring.

Al-Shukur et al. [83] illustrated the effect of pile type change on local scouring, as shown in Figure 32. In the experiment, the structure with rectangular pile type has the largest local scour depth, and the maximum scour depth is larger in comparison with other pile types at three different velocity. The structure with cylindrical pile type also has a larger scour depth, and the structure with streamlined pile type has the smallest maximum scour depth, indicating that pile type change can make the structure with a better scour protection effect. In the experiment of Farooq et al. [84], the maximum scour depths of six pile-type structures were compared, and it was found that the maximum scour depths of round, diamond, pointed-nose, octagonal, and elliptical structures were reduced by 17.7%, 22.4%, 10.4%, and 15.1%, respectively, compared with those of rectangular pile-type structures. Consistent conclusions were also reached in the experiments of Baranwal et al. [85].

Aly et al. [11] designed a streamlined extended foundation as shown in Figure 33. Aly et al. calculated the different hydrodynamic characteristics of the circular and streamlined foundations at the same inlet velocity by means of computational fluid dynamics (CFD). The results show that the near-bottom shear stress around the pile perimeter of the cylindrical structure is about 1 Pa and the flow velocity is 0.5 m/s, while the near-bottom shear stress around the pile perimeter of the streamlined foundation is 0.8 Pa and the flow velocity is 0.45 m/s. Compared with the streamlined foundation, the shear stress of the cylindrical foundation is greater and the flow velocity is smaller. The authors concluded that under the shear stress, the cylindrical structure is more prone to sediment initiation and transport in the 45° angle direction on both sides, while in contrast for the streamlined foundation, only sediment with smaller particle size can be eroded and transported along the streamlined foundation. Aly et al. [11] concluded that this can prove that streamlined foundations have better scour protection effect compared to cylindrical foundations.

For multi-pile bearing structures, it has been found that changing the relative position of the bearing can achieve the effect of scour protection. Yang et al. [95] found that in this type of pile foundation structure, burying the bearing-structure under the bed would have a better scour protection effect. The scour pattern of this form of group pile structure depends strongly on the flow type, with different erosion topography under wave–flow coaction, pure current action and pure wave action, and the scour intensity under wave–flow coaction and current action is greater than that under wave action. Under wave action, the scour of this multi-pile bearing is influenced by the angle of incoming flow, which causes a larger scour range when the incoming flow faces the sharp angle of the bearing.

Pier Shape		V=0.18	V=0.25	V=0.3
		Measured scour depth (cm)	Measured scour depth (cm)	Measured scour depth (cm)
Circular		3.9	6.1	6.9
Rectangular		4.3	6.8	7.6
Octagonal		4.2	5.2	5.9
Joukowsky		4.7	5.5	6.1
Chamfered		4.1	5.9	6.7
Oblong		4.1	4.6	5.8
Elliptical		3.6	4.9	5.6
Sharp nose		3	4.5	4.9
Hexagonal		2.8	3.6	4.1
Streamline		1.9	2.6	3

Figure 32. Al-Shukur [83] measured scouring depth of different pile types (with permission from the author, open access).

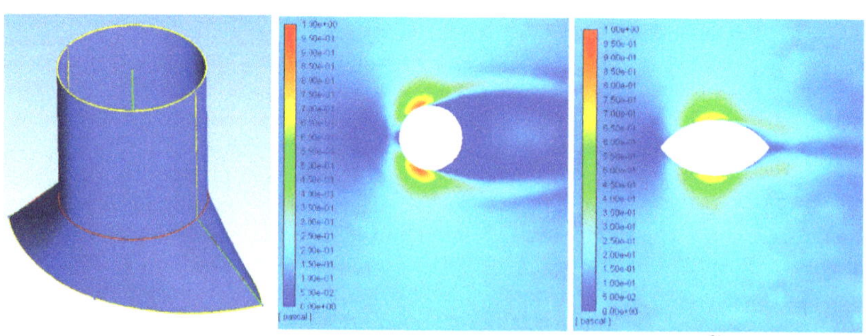

Figure 33. Streamlined extension foundation (with permission from *Ocean Engineering*, 2021) [11].

5. Bed-Reinforced Scour Protection Scheme

The bed-strengthening scheme is the most common method to reduce local scour [96], mainly riprap, cement strengthening [97], bionic grass [98], etc. Riprap protection is most widely used. Tang et al. [15] studied the role of riprap protection from three aspects, such as the failure mechanism of riprap protection scheme, the selection of riprap size and quantitative damage analysis.

It is generally believed that the damage failure of the riprap protection scheme occurs under dynamic bed conditions [99]. When the bed as a whole is scoured by the moving bed, the overall change of the bed topography will destroy the structure of the riprap layer and cause the overall damage of the riprap protection. When the relative flow velocity $V/V_c > 0.35$, smaller rocks can undergo shear damage, causing the local destabilization of the riprap protection layer [99,100]. Compared with rigid materials such as horizontal plates, the deposits in the interstices of riprap protection are more susceptible to erosion by water flow and affect the effect of scour protection, in which the horseshoe vortex plays a major role [15,101,102]. Nielsen et al. [102] considered the flow velocity of water in the pore space and concluded that the vortex formed by the water in the pore space causes erosion of sediment.

The design scheme of riprap protection mainly considers the size range, thickness, and placement depth of the riprap layer [15,103]. Chiew [104] assumes that the rock is coarse sediment and applies the flow rate at which the round pile jetty begins to scour as the threshold velocity and $V/V_c > 0.3$ as the design criterion for the minimum shear damage size. Croad et al. [105] proposed a formula for calculating the throw size based on experimental studies and previous experimental data. De Vos et al. [106] proposed a formula for calculating the throw size required for scour protection of monopile structures under the action of combined waves and currents as follows:

$$\tau_{cr,pred} = 83 + 3.569\tau_c + 0.765\tau_w \tag{4}$$

where $\tau_{cr,pred}$ is the critical initiating shear stress for riprap protection design; τ_c and τ_w are the bed shear stresses due to current and wave breaking action, respectively. All parameters in the equation are in N/m^2. Equation (4) relates the critical shear stress $\tau_{cr,pred}$ required for riprap protection design to the bed shear stresses induced by currents and waves, and the riprap size is designed by the required bed shear stress. The authors conclude that the required stone size can be significantly reduced and the design solution is more cost effective when compared with the equation for the typical case in the European North Sea waters. In the second part of the paper the authors consider the optimization of the design process by allowing finite motion of the top stone [107].

Melville and Coleman [99] proposed a quantitative equation for the design of riprap protection rock sizes:

$$\frac{d_{r50}}{y_0} = \frac{A}{S_s - 1^{\alpha}} Fr^{\beta} \tag{5}$$

where y_0 is the average flow depth; S_s is the gravity of the riprap layer; Fr is the Froude number of flow; and A, α, b are coefficients.

Lauchlan and Melville [100] tested the effect of riprap placement depth on scour and found that when the riprap layer is located below the bed surface, it can effectively reduce the local scour depth and has better scour protection.

In addition, the pore grouting reinforcement of thrown rock layers [108,109], the analysis of differences between large and small experiments [110], with other kinds of filling materials [111–114] is also studied.

6. Main Problems on Scour Protection Countermeasure

The main problems of scour protection scheme research in the literature are the reliability of the scour protection scheme and inconsistency of the experimental environment of various scour protection scheme-related research, the difficulty of horizontal comparison, the large variance of maximum scour depth reduction rate of important indexes, etc. At present, the relevant research on scour protection schemes should start from the following aspects:

1. Reliability of the scour protection scheme. Reliability refers to the lack of field data on scour and scour protection schemes [115], and field data are especially important for the study of scour protection schemes, especially the effect of the flooding period.

Some papers show that during floods, when the pile becomes submerged or when the flow is relatively deep, countermeasures may not properly reduce scour hole [116,117]. Many researchers believe that the actual marine environment has large differences from the laboratory simulation environment, and some factors cannot be considered by model tests.

2. Consistency of comparison of various protection schemes. Due to the inconsistent hydrodynamic environment and bed conditions of various types of studies in the literature, as shown in Figure 34, experiments in different studies were conducted at different experimental sites and environments [15]. The experimental environment lacked consistency. Therefore, it is difficult to make a cross-sectional comparison between different types of scour protection schemes, and the maximum scour depth reduction rate of similar scour protection schemes has a large variance. It is necessary to consider examining the magnitude of scour reduction capacity of each scour protection scheme under consistent environmental conditions.

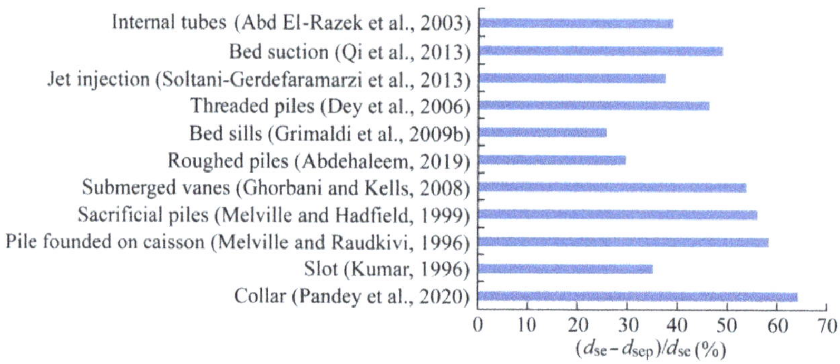

Figure 34. Comparison of erosion reduction rates of various erosion protection schemes in the literature [39,40,57,59,60,64,80,86,89,118,119].

3. Protection (E_p)-flow rate (U/U_c) curve. Through the above part of the study, we found that the main problems of the current research in the category of scour protection schemes for marine engineering structures are that the maximum scour depth reduction rate E_p has a large variance under different hydrodynamic conditions, and the flow velocity is the most important factor affecting E_p. Since similar scour protection schemes have large variance, the authors expect that the maximum scour depth reduction rate is related to the flow velocity as a function of the protection (E_p)-flow velocity (U/U_c) curve, which is more essential feature to reflect the protection ability of scour protection schemes. The maximum scour depth reduction rate may increase and then decrease with the increase in flow velocity. There is a scour reduction rate $E_{p\ min}$ under the most unfavorable conditions in the dynamic bed, or it may fail directly and cannot play the role of scour protection. $E_{p\min}$ is an important parameter to be considered in the design and selection of scour protection scheme.

7. Applicability Analysis of Scour Protection Schemes

The applicability of different types of scour protection schemes summarized in Sections 4 and 5 is analyzed, based on the design principles of scour protection schemes for marine engineering pile foundation structures given in Section 2. The applicability of the protection schemes is shown in Table 7.

The openings through a piers scheme includes equivalent pile, pile slots, and flow-guiding tube scheme. In practical engineering applications, the openings significantly reduce the strength of the pile from the view point of structural capacity against forces. The equivalent pile scheme has good application prospects and needs to focus on the structure capacity of the pile foundation. Its protection design concept is close to the design principle of inherent safety, which can make it less prone to failure under extreme hydrodynamic conditions and satisfy the principles of independence and economy. It has the ability to protect against scour without destroying other safety properties of the pile foundation. The flow-guiding tube scheme is not suitable for steel pile foundations in offshore projects. The flow guiding tube scheme can affect the corrosion resistance of the pile foundation structure, shorten the safety service life. Steel pile foundations have a hollow structure inside and are susceptible to seawater corrosion in a dynamic marine environment. It requires a dense layer of corrosion-resistant material to be applied to the outer layer of the steel structure to ensure the safety service life. The safety service life usually exceeds 20 years. The pile slots significantly affects the mechanical properties of the structure. It has greater impact on the tensile and shear strength of the structure and directly affects the strength of the structure. Partial studies have suggested that during flood events, the implementation of slots does not demonstrate effective mitigation of local scour [117]. In the actual engineering application, the pile slot scheme rarely appears.

Table 7. Applicability analysis of scour protection countermeasure scheme.

Class	Protection	Principle of Independence			Principle of Economy
		Does Not Affect Mechanical Properties	Does Not Affect Chemical Properties	Does Not Affect the Environment	Easy to Produce
Openings through piers scheme	Flow-guiding tube	✓	×	✓	×
	Pile slots	×	×	✓	✓
	Equivalent pile	✓	✓	✓	✓
Structure attachment scheme	Horizontal plate	✓	✓	✓	✓
	Vertical plate	✓	✓	✓	✓
	Vanes	✓	✓	✓	×
	roughed pile	✓	×	✓	×
	Extend foundation	✓	✓	✓	✓
Bed attachment scheme	Sacrificial piles	✓	✓	×	✓
	Deflectors	✓	✓	×	✓
	Sand barriers	✓	✓	×	✓
	Riprap scheme	✓	✓	✓	✓

Structural attachment schemes include horizontal plates, vertical plates, vanes, threaded piles, roughed pile bodies, and extended foundations. The horizontal plate protection scheme has been extensively studied. By manipulating bypass flow and fortifying the bed layer, it achieves scour protection independently from the pile foundation structure itself, preserving structural performance while minimizing environmental impact. This scheme boasts advantages such as simplicity in construction, easy installation, and adherence to economic principles. Notably, several projects have already successfully implemented the horizontal plate scheme. The vertical plate scheme bears resemblance to the horizontal plate structure and is affixed to the structure through attachment methods. It can be manufactured and installed using prefabrication techniques, offering a straightforward design with low economic costs. The primary function of vertical plates is to disrupt the horseshoe vortex structure around the object, thereby reducing hydrodynamic factors that contribute to foundation scouring. As a result, it minimizes the environmental impact, reducing the likelihood of extensive scouring and broader ecological changes.

Vanes are installed on the pile body and attached to the bottom of the pile foundation. The implementation of vanes inside offshore zones may be impossible, since the water body may prevent the correct construction of near-bed structures. The attachment of vanes to the pile body necessitates comprehensive structural construction to ensure their stable installation, preventing damage or detachment. This approach increases construction costs and difficulties, deviating from the principle of economy. Threaded piles and roughed piles significantly diminish the utility of anti-corrosion materials for the pile body, consequently compromising the service life of anti-corrosion coatings. Threaded piles and roughed piles schemes escalate construction costs, conflicting with the principles of independence and economy. The extended foundation solution, exemplified by gravity foundations, has matured and found extensive application in numerous projects. It has evolved into a suitable pile foundation structure for offshore applications, satisfying the design principles of independence and economy.

The bed attachments represented by sacrificial piles, deflectors, sand barriers, etc., achieve the effect of changing the flow field around the pile and thus reducing scour through the structures placed on the bed. The impact of these scour protection schemes is mainly on the marine environment around the pile structure. The sacrificial piles and deflectors scheme expand the scour volume and scour range around the pile structure, which needs to be considered in the project.

The pile alteration schemes need to consider the applicability of the pile shape and should meet the economic principle of easy construction. Some of the pile foundation structure shapes such as long streamlined cylinders have been widely used in practical projects such as cross-sea bridges, while some of the pile shapes in the literature are difficult to build and implement.

Riprap protection, as the most widely used scour protection solution, does not affect the basic performance of the pile foundation structures. It can satisfy the principles of independence and economy. Destabilization of riprap layers by the progression of bed forms past the pier is the dominantfailure mode under live-bed conditions. Edge, shear, and winnowing mechanisms play secondary roles. Relevant design empirical formulas can be applied for the design of riprap protection schemes. Combining turbulence-inducing protective measures with riprap protection can mitigate the occurrence of riprap failure [100,120].

Under the condition of satisfying the above design principles, the scour protection schemes such as equivalent pile, horizontal plate, vertical plate, extended foundation, riprap protection, part of bed attachment, part of pile type, etc., could be selected to focus on the scour protection effectiveness of the scheme. The scour protection scheme that can meet the engineering needs and is applicable to the actual offshore environment shall be selected from the above schemes.

8. Summary and Outlook

This paper introduces the current situation of research and use of scour protection countermeasures for offshore pile foundation structures and puts forward the design principles of scour protection programs for offshore engineering pile foundation structures. Combined with the characteristics of existing scour protection schemes, this paper elaborates on the classification of scour protection schemes for offshore pile foundation structures according to the mechanism of action and analyzes the engineering applicability of scour protection schemes. Through the analysis, it is proposed that under the condition of meeting the design principles of scour protection schemes, the effectiveness of scour protection schemes such as equivalent piles, horizontal plates, vertical plates, extended foundation, slope protection, local bed attachment, and local pile type should be selected for critical research.

It is particularly important to construct an evaluation method for the effectiveness of scour protection schemes for marine engineering structures in future research. At present, there is no method for evaluating the effectiveness of scour protection schemes in the literature. For the scour protection scheme, the evaluation method should be reflected in the following aspects:

(1) Screening by the principles of scour protection scheme design;
(2) Making the reduction rate (E_p)-flow velocity (U/U_c) curve for this protection scheme and finding the maximum scour depth reduction rate (E_p) under the most unfavorable conditions;
(3) Enhancement factor K for the effectiveness of combined protection of flow-altering protection schemes and bed-reinforcement schemes, compared to bed-reinforcement schemes alone;
(4) Generalization study of scour protection schemes. Scour protection schemes can be applied to a wide range of marine engineering structures and hydrodynamic environments.

Author Contributions: Conceptualization, D.G. and X.P.; methodology, D.G.; software, D.G.; validation, B.L., B.Y. and G.W.; investigation, D.G.; resources, X.P. and B.L.; data curation, Z.W.; writing—original draft preparation, D.G.; writing—review and editing, X.P.; funding acquisition, X.P. and B.L. All authors have read and agreed to the published version of the manuscript.

Funding: This research was funded by The National Key Research and Development Program of China (Grant No. 2021YFB2601100).

Institutional Review Board Statement: Not applicable.

Informed Consent Statement: Not applicable.

Data Availability Statement: Data are contained within the paper.

Conflicts of Interest: The authors declare no conflicts of interest.

References

1. Timilsina, G.R.; Cornelis van Kooten, G.; Narbel, P.A. Global wind power development: Economics and policies. *Energy Policy* **2013**, *61*, 642–652. [CrossRef]
2. Tabassum-Abbasi; Premalatha, M.; Abbasi, T.; Abbasi, S. Wind energy: Increasing deployment, rising environmental concerns. *Renew. Sustain. Energy Rev.* **2014**, *31*, 270–288. [CrossRef]
3. Shi, P. Offshore wind power development foundation selection first. *Wind Energy* **2020**, 1–12. Available online: http://www.cwea.org.cn/magazine_down_2020.html (accessed on 9 January 2024). (In Chinese)
4. Blanco, M.I. The economics of wind energy. *Renew. Sustain. Energy Rev.* **2009**, *13*, 1372–1382. [CrossRef]
5. Wu, X.; Hu, Y.; Li, Y.; Yang, J.; Duan, L.; Wang, T.; Adcock, T.; Jiang, Z.; Gao, Z.; Lin, Z.; et al. Foundations of offshore wind turbines: A review. *Renew. Sustain. Energy Rev.* **2019**, *104*, 379–393. [CrossRef]
6. Transcript of China National Energy Administration's Q3 2023 Online Press Conference. 2023. Available online: http://www.nea.gov.cn/2023-07/31/c_1310734825.htm (accessed on 9 January 2024).
7. Xinhua News Agency: Renewable Energy Installed Capacity Exceeded 1.3 Billion Kilowatts in the First Half of the Year, Historically Exceeding Coal Power. 2023. Available online: http://www.news.cn/2023-08/01/c_1212250771.htm (accessed on 9 January 2024).
8. BloombergNEF: China's Goldwind Retains Turbine Supplier Lead, as Global Wind Additions Hit New High. 2024. Available online: https://about.bnef.com/blog/chinas-goldwind-retains-turbine-supplier-lead-as-global-wind-additions-hit-new-high-according-to-bloombergnef/ (accessed on 1 April 2024).
9. Stehly, T.; Duffy, P. 2021 Cost of Wind Energy Review. 2022. Available online: https://www.osti.gov/biblio/1907623/ (accessed on 1 April 2024).
10. Morthorst, P.; Kitzing, L. 2—Economics of building and operating offshore wind farms. In *Offshore Wind Farms*; Woodhead Publishing: Cambridge, UK, 2016; pp. 9–27. [CrossRef]
11. Aly, A.M.; Dougherty, E. Bridge pier geometry effects on local scour potential: A comparative study. *Ocean Eng.* **2021**, *234*, 109326. [CrossRef]
12. Wang, X.; Lin, P.; Wang, H. Dynamic characteristics and online monitoring of offshore wind power foundation erosion. *J. Tsinghua Univ. (Nat. Sci. Ed.)* **2023**. (In Chinese) [CrossRef]
13. Qiu, X. *Research on Swiping Measurement and Reinforcement Technology of Large-Diameter Single Pile Foundation of Offshore Wind Power*; Technical Report; Clean Enengy Research Institute, China Huaneng Group Co. Ltd.: Beijing, China, 2023.
14. He, Y. Preliminary Study on the Interaction between Water-Sediment Processes and River Ecological Environment. Ph.D. Thesis, Wuhan University, Wuhan, China, 2006.
15. Tang, Z.; Melville, B.; Singhal, N.; Shamseldin, A.; hai Zheng, J.; wei Guan, D.; Cheng, L. Countermeasures for local scour at offshore wind turbine monopile foundations: A review. *Water Sci. Eng.* **2022**, *15*, 15–28. [CrossRef]
16. Jun, H. Analysis of the basic characteristics of offshore wind power and its applicability in China's waters. *Wind Energy* **2020**, *10* , 36–40. (In Chinese) [CrossRef]
17. Bhattacharya, S., Overview of a Wind Farm and Wind Turbine Structure. In *Design of Foundations for Offshore Wind Turbines*; John Wiley & Sons Ltd.: Hoboken, NJ, USA, 2019; Chapter 1, pp. 1–50. [CrossRef]
18. O'Kelly, B.; Arshad, M. 20—Offshore wind turbine foundations—Analysis and design. In *Offshore Wind Farms*; Woodhead Publishing: Cambridge, UK, 2016; pp. 589–610. [CrossRef]
19. Malhotra, S. Design and Construction Considerations for Offshore Wind Turbine Foundations in North America. In Proceedings of the ASME 2007 26th International Conference on Offshore Mechanics and Arctic Engineering, San Diego, CA, USA, 10–15 June 2007 ; Volume 24, pp. 1533–1542. [CrossRef]
20. Malhotra, S. Selection, Design and Construction of Offshore Wind Turbine Foundations. In *Wind Turbines*; IntechOpen: Rijeka, Croatia, 2011. [CrossRef]
21. Tafarojnoruz, A.; Gaudio, R.; Dey, S. Flow-altering countermeasures against scour at bridge piers: A review. *J. Hydraul. Res.* **2010**, *48*, 441–452. [CrossRef]

22. Chen, J.; Qu, Y.; Sun, Z. Protection mechanisms, countermeasures, assessments and prospects of local scour for cross-sea bridge foundation: A review. *Ocean Eng.* **2023**, *288*, 116145. [CrossRef]
23. Price, S.J.; Figueira, R.B. Corrosion Protection Systems and Fatigue Corrosion in Offshore Wind Structures: Current Status and Future Perspectives. *Coatings* **2017**, *7*, 25. [CrossRef]
24. Momber, A.; Plagemann, P.; Stenzel, V. Performance and integrity of protective coating systems for offshore wind power structures after three years under offshore site conditions. *Renew. Energy* **2015**, *74*, 606–617. [CrossRef]
25. Momber, A.; Plagemann, P.; Stenzel, V. The adhesion of corrosion protection coating systems for offshore wind power constructions after three years under offshore exposure. *Int. J. Adhes. Adhes.* **2016**, *65*, 96–101. [CrossRef]
26. Momber, A. Quantitative performance assessment of corrosion protection systems for offshore wind power transmission platforms. *Renew. Energy* **2016**, *94*, 314–327. [CrossRef]
27. Loth, E.; Qin, C.; Simpson, J.G.; Dykes, K. Why we must move beyond LCOE for renewable energy design. *Adv. Appl. Energy* **2022**, *8*, 100112. [CrossRef]
28. Bruck, M.; Sandborn, P. Pricing bundled renewable energy credits using a modified LCOE for power purchase agreements. *Renew. Energy* **2021**, *170*, 224–235. [CrossRef]
29. Vanegas-Cantarero, M.M.; Pennock, S.; Bloise-Thomaz, T.; Jeffrey, H.; Dickson, M.J. Beyond LCOE: A multi-criteria evaluation framework for offshore renewable energy projects. *Renew. Sustain. Energy Rev.* **2022**, *161*, 112307. [CrossRef]
30. Aquila, G.; Nakamura, W.T.; Junior, P.R.; Souza Rocha, L.C.; de Oliveira Pamplona, E. Perspectives under uncertainties and risk in wind farms investments based on Omega-LCOE approach: An analysis in São Paulo state, Brazil. *Renew. Sustain. Energy Rev.* **2021**, *141*, 110805. [CrossRef]
31. Filimonova, I.; Kozhevin, V.; Provornaya, I.; Komarova, A.; Nemov, V. Green energy through the LCOE indicator. *Energy Rep.* **2022**, *8*, 887–893. [CrossRef]
32. Sumer, B.; Fredsoe, J. *The Mechanics of Scour in the Marine Environment*; World Scientific: Singapore, 2002; Volume 17. [CrossRef]
33. Roulund, A.; Sumer.; B.Mutluand. Numerical and experimental investigation of flow and scour around a circular pile. *J. Fluid Mech.* **2005**, *534*, 351–401. [CrossRef]
34. Du, S. Study on the Local Scour Pattern of Monopiles under Water under the Action of Wave Flow. Ph.D. Thesis, Ocean University of China, Qingdao, China, 2020. (In Chinese)
35. Liang, B.; Du, S.; Pan, X.; Zhang, L. Local Scour for Vertical Piles in Steady Currents: Review of Mechanisms, Influencing Factors and Empirical Equations. *J. Mar. Sci. Eng.* **2020**, *8*, 4. [CrossRef]
36. Baker, C. The laminar horseshoe vortex. *J. Fluid Mech.* **1979**, *95*, 347 – 367. [CrossRef]
37. Dargahi, B. The turbulent flow field around a circular cylinder. *Exp. Fluids* **1989**, *8*, 1–12. [CrossRef]
38. Zhao, M.; Cheng, L.; Zang, Z. Experimental and numerical investigation of local scour around a submerged vertical circular cylinder in steady currents. *Coast. Eng.* **2010**, *57*, 709–721. [CrossRef]
39. Abd El-Razek, M.; Kassem, M.; Bayoumy, M. Scour reduction around bridge piers using internal openings through the pier. *Alex. Eng. J.* **2003**, *42*, 241–248.
40. Soltani-Gerdefaramarzi, S.; Afzalimehr, H.; Chiew, Y.M.; Lai, J. Jets to control scour around circular bridge piers. *Can. J. Civ. Eng.* **2013**, *40*, 204–212. [CrossRef]
41. EL-Ghorab, E.A. Reduction of scour around bridge piers using a modified method for vortex reduction. *Alex. Eng. J.* **2013**, *52*, 467–478. [CrossRef]
42. Chiew, Y. Scour Protection at Bridge Piers. *J. Hydraul. Eng.* **1992**, *118*, 1260–1269. [CrossRef]
43. Kumar, V.; Raju, K.G.R.; Vittal, N. Reduction of Local Scour around Bridge Piers Using Slots and Collars. *J. Hydraul. Eng.* **1999**, *125*, 1302–1305. [CrossRef]
44. Liang, S.; Zhang, Y.; Yang, J. An experimental study on pile scour mitigating measures under waves and currents. *Sci. China Technol. Sci.* **2015**, *58*, 1031–1045. [CrossRef]
45. Tafarojnoruz, A.; Gaudio, R.; Calomino, F. Evaluation of Flow-Altering Countermeasures against Bridge Pier Scour. *J. Hydraul. Eng.* **2012**, *138*, 297–305. [CrossRef]
46. Grimaldi, C.; Gaudio, R.; Calomino, F.; Cardoso, A.H. Countermeasures against Local Scouring at Bridge Piers: Slot and Combined System of Slot and Bed Sill. *J. Hydraul. Eng.* **2009**, *135*, 425–431. [CrossRef]
47. Gaudio, R.; Tafarojnoruz, A.; Calomino, F. Combined flow-altering countermeasures against bridge pier scour. *J. Hydraul. Res.* **2012**, *50*, 35–43. [CrossRef]
48. Vittal, N.; Kothyari, U.C.; Haghighat, M. Clear-Water Scour around Bridge Pier Group. *J. Hydraul. Eng.* **1994**, *120*, 1309–1318. [CrossRef]
49. Yagci, O.; Yildirim, I.; Celik, M.F.; Kitsikoudis, V.; Duran, Z.; Kirca, V.O. Clear water scour around a finite array of cylinders. *Appl. Ocean Res.* **2017**, *68*, 114–129. [CrossRef]
50. Moncada-M, A.T.; Aguirre-Pe, J.; Bolívar, J.; Flores, E. Scour protection of circular bridge piers with collars and slots. *J. Hydraul. Res.* **2009**, *47*, 119–126. [CrossRef]
51. Tang, Z.; Melville, B.; Shamseldin, A.; Guan, D.; Singhal, N.; Yao, Z. Experimental study of collar protection for local scour reduction around offshore wind turbine monopile foundations. *Coast. Eng.* **2023**, *183*, 104324. [CrossRef]
52. Jahangirzadeh, A.; Basser, H.; Akib, S.; Karami, H.; Naji, S.; Shamshirband, S. Experimental and Numerical Investigation of the Effect of Different Shapes of Collars on the Reduction of Scour around a Single Bridge Pier. *PLoS ONE* **2014**, *9*, e98592. [CrossRef]

53. Parker, G.; Toro-Escobar, C.; Voigt, R.L.J. *Countermeasures to Protect Bridge Piers from Scour*; Technical Report; St. Anthony Falls Laboratory: Minneapolis, MN, USA, 1998.
54. Gupta, A. Hydrodynamic modification of the horseshoe vortex at a vertical pier junction with ground. *Phys. Fluids* **1987**, *30*, 1213–1215. [CrossRef]
55. Pourzaker Arabani, A.; Hajikandi, H. Reduction of Local Scour Around A Bridge Pier Using Triple Rectangular Plates. *Curr. World Environ.* **2015**, *10*, 47–55. [CrossRef]
56. Khaple, S.; Hanmaiahgari, P.; Gaudio, R.; Dey, S. Splitter Plate as a Flow-Altering Pier Scour Countermeasure. *Acta Geophys.* **2017**, *65*. [CrossRef]
57. Ghorbani, B.; Kells, J. Effect of submerged vanes on the scour occurring at a cylindrical pier. *J. Hydraul. Res.* **2008**, *46*, 610–619. [CrossRef]
58. Ghodsian, M.; Vaghefi, M. Experimental study on scour and flow field in a scour hole around a T-shape spur dike in a 90 bend. *Int. J. Sediment Res.* **2009**, *24*, 145–158. [CrossRef]
59. Abdelhaleem, F.S.F. Roughened bridge piers as a scour countermeasure under clear water conditions. *ISH J. Hydraul. Eng.* **2019**, *25*, 94–103. [CrossRef]
60. Dey, S.; Sumer, B.M.; Fredsøe, J. Control of Scour at Vertical Circular Piles under Waves and Current. *J. Hydraul. Eng.* **2006**, *132*, 270–279. [CrossRef]
61. Izadinia, E.; Heidarpour, M. Simultaneous use of cable and collar to prevent local scouring around bridge pier. *Int. J. Sediment Res.* **2012**, *27*, 394–401. [CrossRef]
62. Muhawenimana, V.; Foad, N.; Ouro, P.; Wilson, C. Local Scour Patterns around a Bridge Pier with Cable-Wrapping. *Fluids* **2022**, *8*, 3. [CrossRef]
63. Vahdati, V.; Torabipour, A.; Correia, J.; Fazeres Ferradosa, T.; Taveira-Pinto, F. Combined solutions to reduce scour around complex foundations: An experimental study. *Mar. Syst. Ocean Technol.* **2019**, *15*, 81–93. [CrossRef]
64. Melville, B.W.; Raudkivi, A.J. Effects of Foundation Geometry on Bridge Pier Scour. *J. Hydraul. Eng.* **1996**, *122*, 203–209. [CrossRef]
65. Yao, W.; Draper, S.; An, H.; Cheng, L.; Harris, J.M.; Whitehouse, R.J. Effect of a skirted mudmat foundation on local scour around a submerged structure. *Ocean Eng.* **2020**, *218*, 108127. [CrossRef]
66. Haque, A.; Rahman, M.; Islam, G.M.T.; Hussain, M. Scour mitigation at bridge piers using sacrificial piles. *Int. J. Sediment Res.* **2007**, *22*, 49–59.
67. Chiew, Y.; Lim, S. Protection of bridge piers using a sacrificial sill. *Proc. Inst. Civ. Eng. Water Marit. Eng.* **2003**, *156*, 53–62. [CrossRef]
68. Keshavarzi, A.; Shrestha, C.; Melville, B.; Khabbaz, H.; Ranjbar Zahedani, M.; Ball, J. Estimation of maximum scour depths at upstream of front and rear piers for two in-line circular columns. *Environ. Fluid Mech.* **2018**, *18*, 537–550. [CrossRef]
69. Garg, V.; Setia, B.; Singh, V.; Kumar, A. Scour protection around bridge pier and two-piers-in-tandem arrangement. *ISH J. Hydraul. Eng.* **2022**, *28*, 251–263. [CrossRef]
70. Ranjbar-Zahedani, M.; Keshavarzi, A.; Khabbaz, H.; Ball, J.E. Optimizing flow diversion structure as an effective pier-scour countermeasure. *J. Hydraul. Res.* **2021**, *59*, 963–976. [CrossRef]
71. Ranjbar Zahedani, M.; Keshavarzi, A.; Khabbaz, H.; Ball, J. Protecting bridge pier against local scour using flow diversion structure. *Proc. Inst. Civ. Eng. Water Manag.* **2018**, *171*, 1–26. [CrossRef]
72. Li, X.; van Paassen, L.; Tao, J. Investigation of using mangrove-inspired skirt pile group as a scour countermeasure. *Ocean Eng.* **2022**, *266*, 113133. [CrossRef]
73. Odgaard, A.J.; Kennedy, J.F. River-Bend Bank Protection by Submerged Vanes. *J. Hydraul. Eng.* **1983**, *109*, 1161–1173. [CrossRef]
74. Chauhan, V.; Singhal, G.D.; Chavan, R. A review of sediment deflection in rivers using submerged vanes. *ISH J. Hydraul. Eng.* **2022**, *29* , 1–17. [CrossRef]
75. Zarei, E.; Vaghefi, M.; Hashemi, S.S. Bed topography variations in bend by simultaneous installation of submerged vanes and single bridge pier. *Arab. J. Geosci.* **2019**, *12*, 178. [CrossRef]
76. Safaripour, N.; Vaghefi, M.; Mahmoudi, A. Experimental study of the effect of submergence ratio of double submerged vanes on topography alterations and temporal evaluation of the maximum scour in a 180-degree bend with a bridge pier group. *Int. J. River Basin Manag.* **2022**, *20*, 427–441. [CrossRef]
77. Guan, D.; Melville, B.W.; Friedrich, H. Flow Patterns and Turbulence Structures in a Scour Hole Downstream of a Submerged Weir. *J. Hydraul. Eng.* **2014**, *140*, 68–76. [CrossRef]
78. Hamidifar, H.; Nasrabadi, M.; Omid, M. Using a bed sill as a scour countermeasure downstream of an apron. *Ain Shams Eng. J.* **2018**, *9*, 1663–1669. [CrossRef]
79. Esmaeili Varaki, M.; Tavazo, N.; Radice, A. Using a Bed Sill as a Countermeasure for Clear-Water Scour at a Complex Pier with Inclined Columns Footed on Capped Piles. *Hydrology* **2022**, *9*, 65. [CrossRef]
80. Grimaldi, C.; Gaudio, R.; Calomino, F.; Cardoso, A.H. Control of Scour at Bridge Piers by a Downstream Bed Sill. *J. Hydraul. Eng.* **2009**, *135*, 13–21. [CrossRef]
81. Al-Awadi, A.T. Aspects of Downstream Bed Sill Location for Investigating the Countermeasure with Local Scour around Cylindrical Bridge Piers. *Smart Sci.* **2021**, *9*, 113–120. [CrossRef]
82. Pagliara, S.; Carnacina, I.; Cigni, F. Sills and gabions as countermeasures at bridge pier in presence of debris accumulations. *J. Hydraul. Res.* **2010**, *48*, 764–774. [CrossRef]

83. Al-Shukur, A.H.; Hadi Obeid, Z. Experimental study of bridge pier shape to minimize local scour. *Int. J. Civ. Eng. Technol.* **2016**, *7*, 162–171.
84. Farooq, R.; Ghumman, A.R. Impact Assessment of Pier Shape and Modifications on Scouring around Bridge Pier. *Water* **2019**, *11*, 1761. [CrossRef]
85. Baranwal, A.; Das, B.S.; Setia, B. A comparative study of scour around various shaped bridge pier. *Eng. Res. Express* **2023**, *5*, 015052. [CrossRef]
86. Pandey, M.; Azamathulla, H.M.; Chaudhuri, S.; Pu, J.H.; Pourshahbaz, H. Reduction of time-dependent scour around piers using collars. *Ocean Eng.* **2020**, *213*, 107692. [CrossRef]
87. Mashahir, M.B.; Zarrati, A.R.; Mokallaf, E. Effect of bed shear stress on development of scouring around bridge piers protected by a collar. In Proceedings of the 32nd IAHR World Congress, Venice, Italy, 1–6 July 2007; pp. 267–280.
88. Wang, S.; Wei, K.; Shen, Z. ; Xiang, Q. Experimental Investigation of Local Scour Protection for Cylindrical Bridge Piers Using Anti-Scour Collars. *Water* **2019**, *11*, 2073–4441. [CrossRef]
89. Kumar, V. Reduction of Scour around Bridge Pier Using Protective Devices. Ph.D. Thesis University of Roorkee, Roorkee, India, 1996.
90. Robert E. Scour at Bridge Piers. Ph.D. Thesis, The University of Auckland, Auckland, New Zealand, 1980.
91. Tanaka, S.; Yano, M. Local scour around a circular cylinder. In Proceedings of the 12th IAHR Congress, Fort Collins, CO, USA, 11–14 September 1967; pp. 125–134.
92. Tavouktsoglou, N. Scour and Scour Protection around Offshore Gravity Based Foundations. Ph.D. Thesis, University College London, London, UK, 2018.
93. Coleman, S.E. Clearwater Local Scour at Complex Piers. *J. Hydraul. Eng.* **2005**, *131* . [CrossRef]
94. Lauchlan, C. Pier Scour Countermeasures. Ph.D. Thesis, University of Auckland, Auckland, New Zealand, 1999.
95. Yang, Y.; Melville, B.W.; Macky, G.H.; Shamseldin, A.Y. Experimental study on local scour at complex bridge pier under combined waves and current. *Coast. Eng.* **2020**, *160*, 103730. [CrossRef]
96. Wang, C.; Yu, X.; Liang, F. A review of bridge scour: Mechanism, estimation, monitoring and countermeasures. *Nat. Hazards* **2017**, *87*, 1881–1906. [CrossRef]
97. OuYang, H.; Dai, G.; Gao, L.; Zhu, W.; Du, S.; Gong, W. Local scour characteristics of monopile foundation and scour protection of cement-improved soil in marine environment - Laboratory and site investigation. *Ocean Eng.* **2022**, *255*, 111443. [CrossRef]
98. Wang, G.; Xu, S.; Zhang, Q.; Zhang, J. An experimental study of the local scour protection methods around the monopile foundation of offshore wind turbines. *Ocean Eng.* **2023**, *273*, 113957. [CrossRef]
99. Melville, B.; Coleman, S. *Bridge Scour*; Water Resources Publication: Littleton, CO, USA, 2000; p. 572.
100. Lauchlan, C.S.; Melville, B.W. Riprap Protection at Bridge Piers. *J. Hydraul. Eng.* **2001**, *127*, 412–418. [CrossRef]
101. Nielsen, A.W.; Mutlu Sumer, B.; Fredsøe, J.; Christensen, E.D. Sinking of armour layer around a cylinder exposed to a current. *Proc. Inst. Civ. Eng. Marit. Eng.* **2011**, *164*, 159–172. [CrossRef]
102. Nielsen, A.W.; Probst, T.; Petersen, T.U.; Sumer, B.M. Sinking of armour layer around a vertical cylinder exposed to waves and current. *Coast. Eng.* **2015**, *100*, 58–66. [CrossRef]
103. Fazeres-Ferradosa, T.; Chambel, J.; Taveira-Pinto, F.; Rosa-Santos, P.; Taveira-Pinto, F.V.C.; Giannini, G.; Haerens, P. Scour Protections for Offshore Foundations of Marine Energy Harvesting Technologies: A Review. *J. Mar. Sci. Eng.* **2021**, *9*, 297. [CrossRef]
104. Chiew, Y.M. Mechanics of Riprap Failure at Bridge Piers. *J. Hydraul. Eng.* **1995**, *121*, 635–643. [CrossRef]
105. Croad, R.N. Protection from Scour of Bridge Piers Using Riprap. Transfund New Zealand Research Report. 1997. Available online: https://www.nzta.govt.nz/assets/resources/research/reports/082/082-Protection-from-scour-of-bridge-piers-using-riprap.pdf (accessed on 1 April 2024).
106. De Vos, L.; De Rouck, J.; Troch, P.; Frigaard, P. Empirical design of scour protections around monopile foundations: Part 1: Static approach. *Coast. Eng.* **2011**, *58*, 540–553. [CrossRef]
107. De Vos, L.; De Rouck, J.; Troch, P.; Frigaard, P. Empirical design of scour protections around monopile foundations. Part 2: Dynamic approach. *Coast. Eng.* **2012**, *60*, 286–298. [CrossRef]
108. Zhang, F.; Chen, X.; Feng, T.; Wang, Y.; Liu, X.; Liu, X. Experimental study of grouting protection against local scouring of monopile foundations for offshore wind turbines. *Ocean Eng.* **2022**, *258*, 111798. [CrossRef]
109. Wang, W.; Yan, J.; Chen, S.; Liu, J.; Jin, F.; Wang, B. Gridded cemented riprap for scour protection around monopile in the marine environment. *Ocean Eng.* **2023**, *272*, 113876. [CrossRef]
110. Wu, M.; De Vos, L.; Arboleda Chavez, C.E.; Stratigaki, V.; Whitehouse, R.; Baelus, L.; Troch, P. A study of scale effects in experiments of monopile scour protection stability. *Coast. Eng.* **2022**, *178*, 104217. [CrossRef]
111. Craswell, T.; Akib, S. Reducing Bridge Pier Scour Using Gabion Mattresses Filled with Recycled and Alternative Materials. *Eng* **2020**, *1*, 188–210. [CrossRef]
112. Esteban, M.; López-Gutiérrez, J.S.; Negro, V.; Sanz, L. Riprap Scour Protection for Monopiles in Offshore Wind Farms. *J. Mar. Sci. Eng.* **2019**, *7*, 440. [CrossRef]
113. Zolghadr, M.; Bejestan, M.S. Six legged concrete (SLC) elements as scour countermeasures at wing wall bridge abutments. *Int. J. River Basin Manag.* **2021**, *19*, 319–325. [CrossRef]
114. Yoon, T.H. Wire Gabion for Protecting Bridge Piers. *J. Hydraul. Eng.* **2005**, *131*, 942–949. [CrossRef]

115. Harasti, A.; Gilja, G.; Potočki, K.; Lacko, M. Scour at Bridge Piers Protected by the Riprap Sloping Structure: A Review. *Water* **2021**, *13*, 3606. [CrossRef]
116. Tafarojnoruz, A.; Lauria, A. Large eddy simulation of the turbulent flow field around a submerged pile within a scour hole under current condition. *Coast. Eng. J.* **2020**, *62*, 489–503. [CrossRef]
117. Tafarojnoruz, A.; Gaudio, R.; Calomino, F. Effects of a slotted bridge pier on the approach flow. In Proceedings of the XXXIII Convegno Nazionale di Idraulica e Costruzioni Idrauliche IDRA 2012, Brescia, Italia, 10–14 September 2012; pp. 1–10.
118. Melville, B.; Anna, H.; Use of sacrificial piles as pier scour countermeasures. *J. Hydraul. Eng.* **1999**, *125*, 1221–1224. [CrossRef]
119. Qi M.; Chiew Y.; Hong J. Suction Effects on Bridge Pier Scour under Clear-Water Conditions. *J. Hydraul. Eng.* **2013**, *139*, 621–629. https://api.semanticscholar.org/CorpusID:129807525. [CrossRef]
120. Tang, Z.; Melville, B.; Shamseldin, A.; Singhal, N.; Guan, D.; Stolte, A. Performance of riprap armour at vibrating offshore wind turbine monopile foundations. *Coast. Eng.* **2023**, *186*, 104392. [CrossRef]

Journal of
*Marine Science
and Engineering*

MDPI

Article

Advancing Offshore Renewable Energy: Integrative Approaches in Floating Offshore Wind Turbine-Oscillating Water Column Systems Using Artificial Intelligence-Driven Regressive Modeling and Proportional-Integral-Derivative Control

Irfan Ahmad *, Fares M'zoughi, Payam Aboutalebi, Aitor J. Garrido and Izaskun Garrido

Automatic Control Group—ACG, Institute of Research and Development of Processes—IIDP, Department of Automatic Control and Systems Engineering, Faculty of Engineering of Bilbao, University of the Basque Country—UPV/EHU, Po Rafael Moreno no3, 48013 Bilbao, Spain; fares.mzoughi@ehu.eus (F.M.); payam.aboutalebi@ehu.eus (P.A.); izaskun.garrido@ehu.eus (I.G.)

* Correspondence: irfanahmad.irfan@ehu.eus

Abstract: This research investigates the integration of Floating Offshore Wind Turbines (FOWTs) with Oscillating Water Columns (OWCs) to enhance sustainable energy generation, focusing on addressing dynamic complexities and uncertainties inherent in such systems. The novelty of this study lies in its dual approach, which integrates regressive modeling with an aero-hydro-elasto-servo-mooring coupled system with a deep data-driven network and implements a proportional-integral-derivative (PID) control mechanism to improve system stability. By employing Artificial Neural Networks (ANNs), the study circumvents the challenges of real-time closed-loop control on FOWT structures using the OpenFAST simulation tool. Data-driven models, trained on OpenFAST datasets, facilitate real-time predictive behavior analysis and decision-making. Advanced computational learning techniques, particularly ANNs, accurately replicate the dynamics of FOWT-OWC numerical models. An intelligent PID control mechanism is subsequently applied to mitigate structural vibrations, ensuring effective control. A comparative analysis with traditional barge-based FOWT systems underscores the enhanced modeling and control methodologies' effectiveness. In this sense, the experimental results demonstrate substantial reductions in the mean oscillation amplitude, with reductions from 5% to 35% observed across various scenarios. Specifically, at a wave period from 20 s and a wind speed of 5 m/s, the fore-aft displacement was reduced by 35%, exemplifying the PID control system's robustness and efficacy under diverse conditions. This study highlights the potential of ANN-driven modeling as an alternative to managing the complex non-linear dynamics of NREL 5 MW FOWT models and underscores the significant improvements in system stability through tailored PID gain scheduling across various operational scenarios.

Keywords: neural computation techniques; marine aerogenerators; wave energy converters; smart regulation; proportional-integral-derivative (PID) strategy; vibration reduction; dynamic structural management

1. Introduction

Offshore wind energy represents a progressive and eco-friendly approach to electricity production, capitalizing on the consistent winds found offshore. Its adoption is on the rise, as it outperforms conventional onshore wind farms in terms of power generation efficiency [1]. Initially confined to shallow waters with fixed bottoms, the advent of advanced technology has paved the way for floating wind turbines. These turbines are moored to the ocean floor with adaptable links, making it feasible to venture into deeper waters [2]. Switching to FOWTs offers several benefits, including access to steadier winds, minimized visual intrusion, and greater compliance flexibility with noise regulations [3]. The proliferation of offshore wind farms can be attributed to technological progress, supportive policies, and significant financial backing, all contributing to increased power output and a decrease in carbon emissions [4].

Renewable energy plays a crucial role in global initiatives to address climate change and secure energy supplies. Offshore wind energy, particularly in Europe, has emerged as a front-runner among renewable energy options [5]. As depicted in Figure 1, there has been a notable trend in the growth of the average capacity of offshore wind turbines per project from 2000 to 2025. Initially averaging 1.5 MW at the start of the millennium, the capacity of these turbines is expected to reach between 10 and 12 MW by 2025, underscoring the rapid advancements in turbine technology and the expansion of offshore wind projects. This expected growth trend anticipates a focus on larger capacity units in the industry, particularly in markets outside China where the average size is anticipated to be between 7 and 8 MW [6].

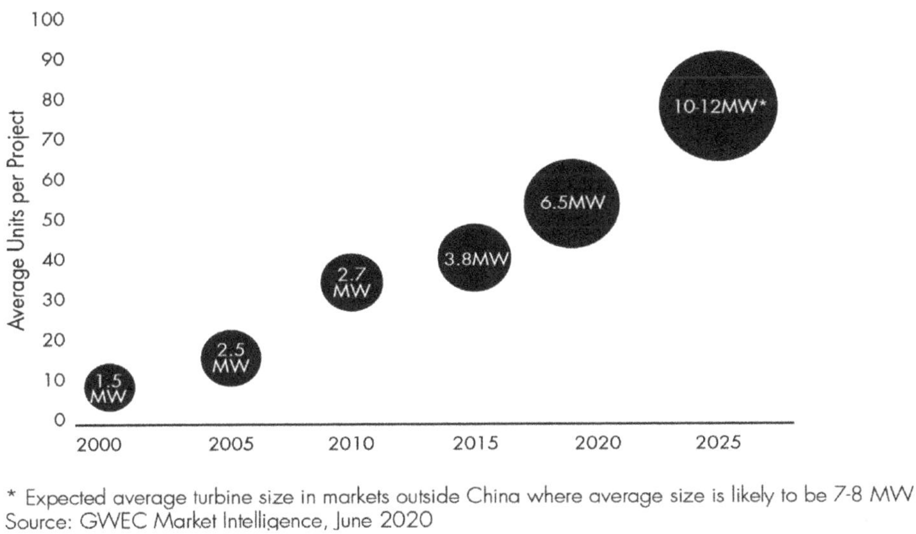

Figure 1. Evolution of FOWTs and project size in units per project.

Recent trends in the field include the integration of Wave Energy Converters (WECs) with FOWTs. This hybrid approach, specifically the incorporation of OWCs with FOWTs, has been recognized as a promising strategy for improving renewable energy generation. The combination of FOWTs and OWCs aims to stabilize platforms and improve energy harvest, as shown in Figure 2. The functioning of an OWC is based on a capture chamber with an opening at the bottom, allowing water to flow in response to incoming waves. The motion of water leads to the compression and expansion of air within the chamber, later driving self-rectifying air turbines at the apex of the chamber. Different models of WECs have been implemented across Europe, exemplified by the NEREIDA Wave Power Plant in Spain and the Limpet facility in Scotland, signifying notable advancements in the field of renewable energy [7].

The creation of these hybrid offshore structures encompasses complex dynamics [8]. Noteworthy advancements in modeling and control strategies for FOWTs combined with OWCs have been achieved, with machine learning playing a pivotal role [9]. These developments have significantly enhanced the efficiency and dependability of such systems [10]. The design of hybrid offshore structures presents complexities due to their coupled aero-hydro-servo-elastic dynamics [11]. While bottom-fixed turbines are ideal for shallow waters, floating turbines excel in deeper marine environments. The design of floating wind turbines is categorized into three main types according to their stabilization methods: buoyancy-stabilized (barge platform), mooring-stabilized (tension leg platform), and ballast-stabilized (spar buoy) [12].

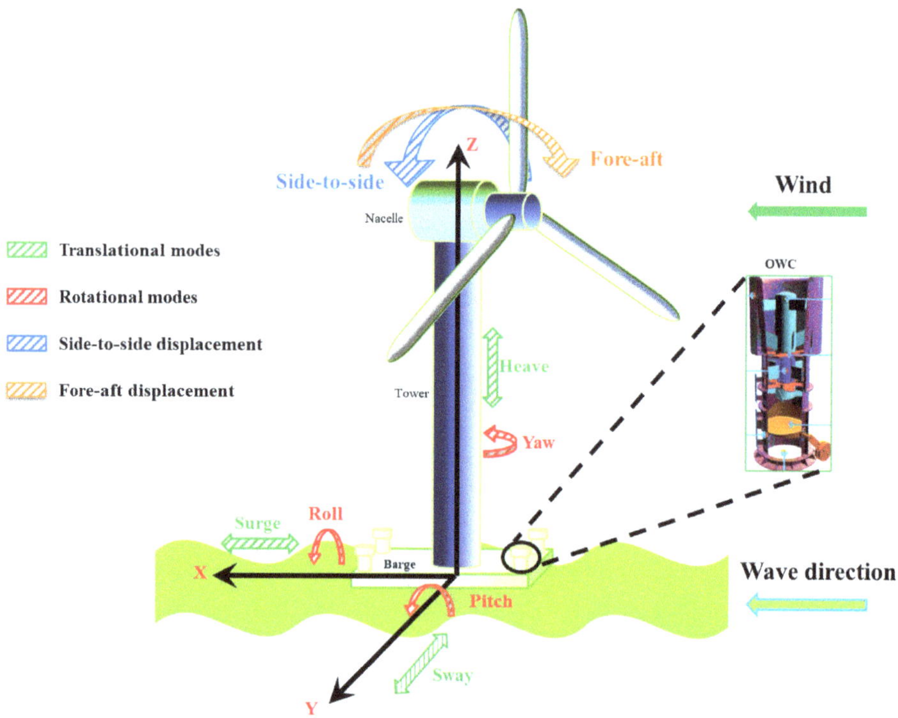

Figure 2. A novel hybrid system for FOWT-OWCs.

Considerable progress has been realized in the development of modeling and control methodologies for FOWTs coupled with OWCs [13]. Research efforts are intensively focused on discovering new strategies to enhance both the efficiency and dependability of these sophisticated systems. The application of machine learning, recognized for its prowess in identifying patterns and forecasting based on extensive data collections, has proven to be an instrumental asset in this area [14]. Utilizing artificial intelligence, machine-learning approaches facilitate the crafting of precise and streamlined models for FOWTs integrated with OWCs.

2. Technical Literature Review

Machine learning is revolutionizing the domain of wind turbine regulation, marking a pivotal shift in research related to wind turbine control and surveillance through the integration of advanced machine learning and deep learning algorithms [15]. A key focus area is the stabilization of FOWTs for marine energy uses, in which deep reinforcement learning (DRL) techniques, including actor-critic networks in conjunction with a globally asymptotically stable observer, are employed to dynamically manage FOWTs across diverse environmental settings [16]. This simulation-driven analysis illustrates the advantage of such methodologies over conventional linear quadratic regulator (LQR) techniques in stabilizing FOWTs. Innovative, model-independent controllers utilizing reinforcement learning (RL) and Bayesian optimization (BO) offer adjustments without dependency on traditional mathematical models, aiming to boost energy production and minimize turbine stress [17]. Additionally, data-oriented predictive control tactics employing deep learning alongside multi-objective optimization tackle the model complexity and the dilemma of conflicting control aims in FOWTs [18]. These approaches enable accurate individual blade adjustment, optimizing the energy yield and ensuring platform steadiness in variable wind scenarios [19]. In the field of FOWT monitoring and safety, deep learning significantly contributes to the analysis of mooring line tension. Through simulations under assorted environmental conditions, it has been discerned that surge movements primarily affect mooring line tension, regardless of the mooring configuration, whereas the elasticity of blades and towers plays a minor role in tension predictions [20].

Gaussian process metamodels have recently been utilized as an innovative approach for encapsulating the hydrodynamic and structural dynamics of FOWTs [21]. These metamodels process inputs such as wave height, forces, and moments at the tower-platform junction to forecast platform movements and rotations. The investigation assesses three varieties of Gaussian process metamodels, showcasing their capability in accurately simulating platform behaviors. Additionally, a multi-criteria decision-making (MCDM) framework for the development of offshore wind farms in Ireland has been introduced, incorporating technical, financial, environmental, and societal factors to evaluate the sustainability of offshore wind locations [22]. Utilizing interval type-2 fuzzy sets and energy economic metrics such as the levelized cost of electricity (LCoC), this framework offers a refined decision-support system [23]. Table 1 summarizes various soft computing techniques employed in FOWT applications, detailing their specific areas of application and the resulting benefits or outcomes. These methods enhance the performance, stability, and efficiency of FOWTs by addressing complex dynamic and control challenges.

Table 1. Overview of soft computing methods applied to FOWTs.

Soft Computing Method	Application Area	Outcome/Benefits	Source
Genetic Algorithms (GA)	Structural optimization of FOWT platforms	Enhanced design for load mitigation and cost-effectiveness	Lemmer et al., 2018 (ASME Digital Collection) [24]
Artificial Neural Networks (ANN)	Prediction of aerodynamic forces	Improved real-time performance prediction	Raissi et al., 2018 (Journal of Computational Physics) [25]
Fuzzy Logic Systems	Control systems for platform stability	Increased system stability and response to environmental changes	M'zoughi et al., 2023 (International Journal of Energy Research) [26]
Support Vector Machines (SVM)	Fault detection in turbine systems	Early detection of potential faults, reducing downtime	Perdomo et al., 2017 (Applied Mathematics and Modeling) [27]
Particle Swarm Optimization (PSO)	Parameter tuning in turbine control systems	Optimized control parameters leading to better energy capture	Wu et al., 2022 (Applied Sciences) [28]
Deep Learning (Convolutional Neural Networks)	Aerodynamic data modeling	Enhanced accuracy in predicting aerodynamic properties	Prantl et al., 2017 (Advances in Aerodynamics) [29]
Recurrent Neural Networks (RNN)	Prediction of dynamic aerodynamic forces	Accurate modeling of unsteady aerodynamics for airfoils	Moin et al., 2022 (Engineering Proceedings) [30]
Physics-informed Neural Networks	Solving forward and inverse problems in fluid dynamics	Integration of physical laws into neural networks for improved predictions	Raissi et al., 2019 (Journal of Computational Physics) [31]

For the modeling of FOWTs, several innovative methodologies and technologies have been developed to advance their performance. J. Jonkman and collaborators [32] have been at the forefront with the introduction of OpenFAST for wind turbine behavior, a comprehensive tool that integrates fatigue, aerodynamics, structures, and turbulence aspects with a gain-scheduled proportional-integral approach. This simulator is instrumental in deciphering FOWT dynamics and facilitates the creation of robust control algorithms, including a standard collective blade pitch control mechanism [33]. Addressing the critical issue of vibrations in FOWTs, the TORA concept has been developed [34]. TORA is designed to enhance the structural stability of FOWTs, contributing to their smoother and more dependable functioning. Furthermore, M.A. Lackner and his team have introduced FAST-SC, a customized structural control system tailored for FOWTs [35]. This system allows for the meticulous management of the turbine's structural elements, optimizing its performance comprehensively.

OpenFAST [36] is a pivotal tool in the development of diverse control strategies for FOWTs. It facilitates the exploration of active and passive control methods, including strategies focused on blade, torque, and rotational speed adjustments, and the application of the Tuned Mass Damper (TMD) for enhanced stability. In the pursuit of augmenting platform stability, a novel PID complementary airflow control method has been integrated into Offshore Wind Converters [37]. This technique guarantees consistent performance amidst variable weather conditions. Furthermore, collective torque control is identified as a key factor in the operational efficiency of FOWTs, with PID control systems widely implemented to reduce discrepancies between target and actual values, thus ensuring adequate control over FOWT operations [38].

There are various modeling techniques for FOWT-OWCs with semi-submersible configurations, which examine their dynamics within both time and frequency analytical domains. However, there is a need for intelligent machine learning models and control mechanisms for hybrid system stability. Therefore, this article has two primary novel objectives. The first is to develop novel control-oriented regressive intelligent modeling specifically for the hybrid design of FOWTs and OWCs. The second objective involves utilizing estimated models to implement gain scheduling PID feedback control. This control, aided by numerical tools and air valve control strategies, aims to ensure overall system control and stability. OWCs are utilized in this study primarily for platform stabilization. Consequently, their power output is generally lower compared to that of wind turbines. For instance, the OWC plant at the Mutriku Wave Power Plant in Spain has an installed capacity of 296 kW, while the wind turbines have a capacity of 5 MW [39].

The paper's structure has been outlined as follows: Section 3 gives a detailed explanation of the subsystems within the FOWT-OWC system, along with their mathematical modeling. Section 4 delves into the proposed designs for the hybrid platform's geometry and the associated hydrodynamic calculations. Section 5 discusses the proposed PID control for managing platform pitch and mitigating unwanted vibrations. Experimental findings, corroborated through cross-validation, are detailed in Section 6. The paper ends with the final section, offering conclusions and suggestions for future research directions.

3. Theoretical Foundations

3.1. Model of Wave Elevation

A straightforward model of wave elevation is presented as a unidirectional, regular sine wave, with surface dynamics described according to the Airy wave theory [40].

$$z_\omega(t) = Asin(\omega t) = Asin(2\pi f t) = Asin(\frac{2\pi}{\lambda}ct) \tag{1}$$

where $c = f\lambda$ is defined as the propagation velocity, A is the wave amplitude from the Still Water Level (SWL), and λ is calculated by measuring the distance between two consecutive waves. From Equation (1), the temporal fluctuation of a wave is represented as a macroscopic illustration of the oscillatory motion of water molecules at a designated location. To facilitate the application of this oscillatory behavior to any position on the wave's surface, a new variable that accounts for the spatial dimension along the wave front is introduced. Therefore, Equation (1) is reformulated as follows:

$$z_\omega(x,t) = Asin(\frac{2\pi}{\lambda}(ct - x\theta)) = \frac{H}{2}sin(\omega t - kx\theta) \tag{2}$$

where $k = \frac{2\pi}{\lambda}$ is the wave number, H is the wave height, x is the axis in the direction of wave propagation, and θ represents the wave angle in the direction of the x-axis. As explained below, this can be generalized by superposing an n-fold number of waves [38].

$$z_\omega(x,t) = \sum_{i=1}^{N} K_i sin(\omega_i t - k_i + \theta_i) \tag{3}$$

$$K_i = \sqrt{2S_i \Delta\omega_i} \tag{4}$$

where N is the number of waves, S_i is the spectral density, k_i is the number of each wave component, and ω_i is the angular frequency. The two most widely recognized theoretical wave spectra are the Bretschneider spectrum [41] for fully developed waves and the JONSWAP spectrum for partially developed waves. The generalized representation of the spectrum can be expressed as

$$S_i(\omega_i) = (1 - 0.287ln(\gamma))\frac{5\omega_p^4}{16\omega^5}K_s^2\gamma^\beta e^{\frac{5\omega_p^4}{16\omega^5}} \tag{5}$$

where β is $exp(-\frac{(\omega-\omega_p)^2}{2\omega_p^2\alpha^2})$ and $\alpha = \begin{Bmatrix} 0.07, if\omega \leq \omega_p \\ 0.09, if\omega > \omega_p \end{Bmatrix}$, K_s is the wave height, and ω_p is the peak angular frequency. Depending on the wave condition, a value between 1 and 5 is chosen for the heat ratio parameter γ. The value of the standard JONSWAP spectrum γ is 3.3 [42].

3.2. Wind Turbine

The turbine set up a mechanical system that transforms wind energy into mechanical energy; subsequently, a generator converts this mechanical energy into electrical energy. The output power and torque can be characterized as follows:

$$P_w = \frac{1}{2}C_p(\vartheta,\lambda)\rho\pi r^2 v_{wind}^3 \tag{6}$$

$$Q_w = \frac{1}{2}C_Q(\vartheta,\lambda)\rho\pi r^2 v_{wind}^3 \tag{7}$$

where C_p and C_Q represent the power and torque coefficients, respectively. ρ denotes the air density $\frac{\text{kg}}{\text{m}^3}$ and r the the wind rotor radius (m). ϑ is the blade pitch angle (dgrees). The tip-speed ratio (TSR), λ, is defined as follows:

$$\lambda = \Omega_t \frac{R}{V} \tag{8}$$

where R denotes the radius of the turbine's rotor and Ω_t specifies the turbine's rotational speed in radians per second ($\frac{rad}{s}$). The power coefficient, a nonlinear function, is dependent on ϑ and λ can be expressed as

$$\begin{cases} C_p(\vartheta,\lambda) = 0.22(\frac{116}{\lambda_i} - 0.4\vartheta - 5)e^{-\frac{12.5}{\lambda_i}} \\ \frac{1}{\lambda_i} = \frac{1}{\lambda+0.087\vartheta} - \frac{0.035}{\vartheta^3+1} \end{cases} \tag{9}$$

The parametric values of the floating offshore wind turbine considered in this manuscript are presented in [43] Table 2.

Table 2. NREL 5 MW floating offshore wind turbine (FOWT) specifications.

Parameter	Value
Hub Height	90 m
Rotor Diameter	126 m
Center of mass location	38.23 m
Blade Count	3
Initial rotational speed	12.1 rpm
Blade Mass	53,220 kg
Hub Mass	240,000 kg
Nacelle Mass	347,660 kg
Tower mass	56,780 kg
Output Generated Power	5 MW
Wind Speed Thresholds (Cut-in, Rated, Saturated)	773.8 m

3.3. Equation of Motion of the Hybrid FOWT-OWCs

This section delineates the theoretical framework for a hybrid model designed to integrate OWC-WECs into a 5 MW floating barge-mounted wind turbine. Frequency-domain numerical tools, based on linear theory, were employed to analyze this design. Incorporating a WEC into the system potentially reduces overall costs by utilizing shared mooring structures and energy generation infrastructure. The model was constructed using MultiSurf for geometry design and WAMIT for computational diffraction-radiation analysis, assuming standard specifications for well and Power-Take-Off (PTO) equipment [43]. The complete nonlinear time-domain motion equations for the 5 MW FOWT with an OWC-equipped platform are presented as follows [44]:

$$M_{ij}(\xi, u, t)\ddot{\xi} = F_l\left(\xi, \dot{\xi}, u, t\right) \tag{10}$$

In the equation, ξ and $\ddot{\xi}$ represent the first and second time derivatives of the jth DOF, respectively. M_{ij} is a component of the inertia mass matrix, which exhibits nonlinear dependence on the system's DOFs, ξ, time (t), and control inputs (u). The term on the right side of the equation denotes the generalized external forces impacting the integrated system. These forces include aerodynamic loads on the blades and nacelle, as well as hydrodynamic forces on the platform, encompassing elastic and servo forces associated with the ith DOF. ξ from Equation (10) is defined as follows:

$$\xi = \begin{bmatrix} roll\ (\text{deg}) \\ pitch\ (\text{deg}) \\ yaw\ (\text{deg}) \\ surge\ (m) \\ heave\ (m) \\ sway\ (m) \\ fore-aft\ (m) \\ side-to-side\ (m) \end{bmatrix} \tag{11}$$

The generalized linear system of equations of motion within the frequency domain is formulated as follows [44]:

$$I_F(\omega)\ddot{\xi} + D_F(\omega)\dot{\xi} + C_F\xi = \hat{F}(\omega) + \hat{F}_{PTO}(\omega) \tag{12}$$

In the frequency domain, $I_F(\omega)$, $D_F(\omega)$, and $C_F(\omega)$ represent the inertia, damping, and stiffness matrices of the FOWT, respectively. The term $\hat{F}(\omega)$ denotes the aggregate forces attributable to hydrodynamic effects and viscous drag induced by wave interactions, whereas $\hat{F}_{PTO}(\omega)$ encapsulates the force contributions from the OWCs.

$$I_F(\omega) = A_{Hyd}(\omega) + M_{pltfrm}(\omega) + M_{Twr} \tag{13}$$

$I_F(\omega)$ includes the frequency-dependent 8x8 matrix. $A_{Hyd}(\omega)$, $M_{pltfrm}(\omega)$ and M_{Twr} represent the platform added mass, actual platform mass, and tower mass, respectively. The damping matrix is delineated by Equation (14), incorporating $D_{Hyd}(\omega)$ and D_{Twr}, which pertain to the damping properties of the floating barge platform and the flexible tower, respectively. D_{Vscs} signifies the nonlinear viscosity effects on the platform, while D_{chmbr} represents the comprehensive external damping resulting from the power take-off (PTO) system's operation.

$$D_F(\omega) = D_{Hyd}(\omega) + D_{Twr} + D_{Vscs} + D_{chmbr} \tag{14}$$

$$C_F(\omega) = C_{Hyd}(\omega) + C_{Morng} + C_{Twr} \tag{15}$$

where the stiffness matrix $C_F(\omega)$ consists of the hydrostatic restoration matrix of the platform obtained by WAMIT $C_{Hyd}(\omega)$, the mooring lines spring stiffness coefficients that give matrix C_{Morng}, and the stiffness matrix of the tower C_{Twr}.

The internal pressure within the enclosure encompassing the four interconnected OWCs can be postulated to exhibit uniformity, as the internal free surface functions analogously to a piston. In this context, the influence of the OWCs on the overarching dynamic system is characterized, as delineated in reference [23], by an externally applied force:

$$\hat{F}_{PTO}(\omega) = -p(\omega)S \tag{16}$$

where p represents the pressure differential across the turbine and S denotes the area of the internal free surface; the observed variations in air density and pressure due to processes of compression and decompression correspond to an isentropic transformation. Assuming the air behaves as an ideal gas, the temporal variation in air density provides an analytical description of the chamber's state when at rest, which is defined as

$$\rho = \rho_a \left(\frac{p}{p_o}\right)^{\frac{1}{\alpha}} \tag{17}$$

where α defines the heat capacity ratio of air. Upon linearizing the time derivative of the air density,

$$\dot{\rho} = \rho_a \left(\frac{1}{\alpha p_o}\right)\dot{p} \tag{18}$$

Then, within the chamber, the linearized mass flow can be quantitatively determined using the following formulation:

$$\dot{m} = \frac{d(\rho V)}{dt} = \frac{\rho_a}{\alpha p_o}\dot{p}V_o + \rho_o\dot{V} \tag{19}$$

where V is the air volume inside the chamber.

A Wells turbine, characterized by a diameter D and rotational velocity N, exhibits a linear correlation between the pressure and flow coefficients. This relationship is expressed using the non-dimensional parameters typical of turbomachinery analysis, as outlined in reference [45]:

$$\psi = K\zeta \tag{20}$$

The pressure and flow coefficients are defined as

$$\psi = \frac{p}{\rho_a N^2 D^2} \tag{21}$$

$$\zeta = \frac{\dot{m}}{\rho_a N D^3} \tag{22}$$

The linear relationship can be described by considering the non-dimensional flow rate, under the assumption that the pressure drop is proportional to this flow rate, as follows:

$$\psi_C = K_C \zeta_C = \frac{p}{\rho_a g H} \tag{23}$$

$$\zeta_C = \frac{2\pi \dot{m}}{\rho_a \omega S H} \tag{24}$$

where g represents the acceleration due to gravity. Hence, following these formulations, the mass flow through the turbine can be expressed as

$$\dot{m}(\omega) = \frac{S\omega p}{2\pi g K_c} \tag{25}$$

Upon integrating Equations (19) and (25), the pressure characterized by a complex amplitude is expressible within the frequency domain as follows:

$$\hat{p}(\omega) = i\omega \frac{\gamma}{S\omega[1 + (\varepsilon\gamma)^2]}\hat{V} - \omega^2 \frac{\varepsilon\gamma^2}{S\omega[1 + (\varepsilon\gamma)^2]}\hat{V} \tag{26}$$

where $\hat{V}$ denotes the complex amplitude of the oscillatory volume displacement in air, and γ and ε represent constants defined by the following relationships:

$$\gamma = 2\pi \rho_a g K_C \tag{27}$$

$$\varepsilon = \frac{V_a}{\gamma\, p_a S} \tag{28}$$

The total PTO force can be rewritten by combining Equations (16) and (26):

$$\hat{F}_{PTO}(\omega) = i\omega B_{PTO}\hat{x}_r + \omega^2 K_{PTO}\hat{x}_r \tag{29}$$

where $\hat{x}_r$ is the complex relative displacement amplitude. According to Equation (29), the dissipative term becomes proportional to the volume variation. In this context, $\hat{x}_r$ represents the complex amplitude of the relative displacement. As delineated in Equation (29), the linear load exerted by the PTO includes a dissipative component that is directly proportional to the relative velocity, as well as a reactive component that is induced by the compressed air within the chamber and corresponds to the relative acceleration. Additionally, the dissipative component is proportional to the variation in volume. The reactive term is proportional to the rate of volume change when the damping coefficient B_{PTO} and the spring coefficient K_{PTO} are normalized by the area of the internal free surface. These PTO damping and spring coefficients are determined as per Equation (26):

$$B_{PTO}(\omega) = \frac{\gamma}{\omega[1 + (\varepsilon\gamma)^2]} \tag{30}$$

$$K_{PTO}(\omega) = \frac{\varepsilon\gamma^2}{\omega^2[1 + (\varepsilon\gamma)^2]} \tag{31}$$

Finally, the following results have been derived for the system's frequency-dominant equations of motion for the 8-DOFs FOWT:

$$I_F(\omega)\hat{\ddot{\xi}} + (D_F(\omega) + B_{PTO}(\omega))\hat{\dot{\xi}} + (C_F + K_{PTO}(\omega))\hat{\xi} = \hat{F}(\omega) \tag{32}$$

4. Proposed Hybrid FOWT-OWC Model

4.1. Platform Geometry Design

To implement active structural control, four Oscillating Water Columns (OWCs) were integrated into a 5 MW Floating Offshore Wind Turbine (FOWT). The initial phase involves designing the geometry of the hybrid system. This process begins with the architectural design of the hybrid platform. The platform's geometry has been developed using MultiSurf, a computational tool designed for marine platform design. MultiSurf facilitates the creation of structural elements such as hulls, decks, keels, interiors, and superstructures, as well as the generation of free-form curves and surfaces, as referenced in sources [23,24].

To utilize the geometric buoyant model, the WAMIT tool was interfaced with MultiSurf to compute the hydrodynamic loads exerted by water pressure on wet surfaces. The geometries are illustrated in Figures 3 and 4 using the panel method. This study evaluates two representative platforms to highlight their unique characteristics. Figure 3 shows the first platform, a conventional barge type, which has been meshed with 8960 rectangular panels. The second platform, illustrated in Figure 4, is a barge platform with four corner OWCs. Each OWC measures 5 m × 5 m × 10 m and is meshed with 9840 rectangular panels for configurations with open moonpools and 10,240 rectangular panels for configurations with closed moonpools. The OWCs are positioned 1 m from the sidewalls. Detailed specifications of the barge platform and the four identical OWCs are provided in Table 3.

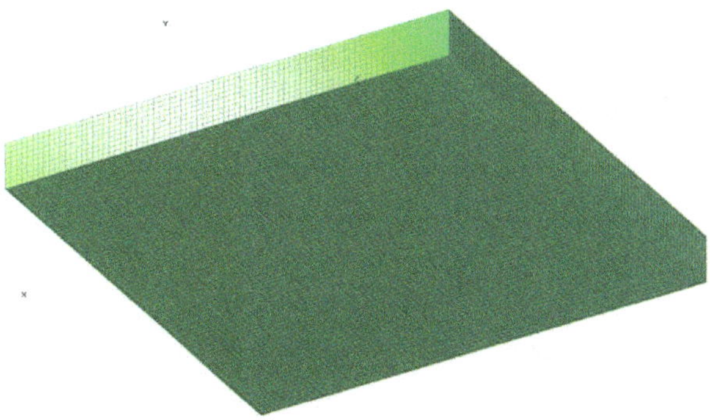

Figure 3. Standard barge platform WAMIT panels.

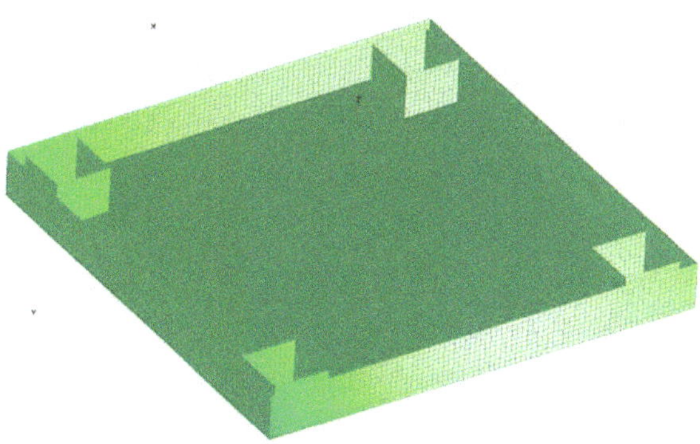

Figure 4. Standard barge platform equipped with four open moonpools, modeled using WAMIT panels.

Table 3. Features of the standard barge and the four OWC-based barge platforms [45].

Parameters	Specifications
Platform Dimensions (width × length × height)	40 m × 40 m × 10 m
OWC Dimensions (width × length × height)	5 m × 5 m × 10 m
Freeboard Levels of Both Platforms' Drafts	4 m, 6 m
Water Displacement (Simple Barge)	6400 m^3
Water Displacement (with Integrated OWCs)	6000 m^3
Total Mass including Ballast	7,466,330 kg
Center of Mass Position below SWL	0.28768 m
Roll Inertia Relative to Center of Mass	726,900,000 kg·m^2
Pitch Inertia Relative to Center of Mass	726,900,000 kg·m^2
Yaw Inertia Relative to Center of Mass	1,453,800,000 kg·m^2
Anchor Depth	150 m
Distance between Opposing Anchors	773.8 m
Length of Unstretched Mooring Line	473.3 m
Length of Mooring Line Resting on Seabed	250 m
Mooring Line Diameter	0.0809 m
Mooring Line Density	130.4 kg/m
Mooring Line Extensional Stiffness	589,000,000 N

4.2. Advanced Hydrostatic and Hydrodynamic Computations

Evaluating the hydrodynamic and hydrostatic parameters during the geometric design of the proposed quartet of OWC-based barge platforms is crucial. Therefore, detailed assessments of these characteristics were performed using the WAMIT numerical tool. Initially developed for the linear analysis of surface wave interactions with various floating and submerged structures, the WAMIT diffraction panel program facilitates these evaluations. Hydrostatic and hydrodynamic coefficients were calculated by integrating the MultiSurf file directly into WAMIT's diffraction-radiation module, resulting in the generation of the matrices A_{Hyd}, B_{Hyd}, and C_{Hyd}. All hydrostatic data can be represented as surface integrals over the mean body wetted surface S_b using the Gauss divergence theorem. WAMIT allows us to evaluate all three forms of volume under the assumption that the coordinates of the center of buoyancy are set to zero:

$$\forall = -\iint xn_1dS = -\iint yn_2dS = -\iint zn_3dS \tag{33}$$

with the center of buoyancy parameters

$$x_b = \frac{-1}{2\forall}\iint S_b n_1 x^2 dS \tag{34}$$

$$y_b = \frac{-1}{2\forall}\iint S_b n_2 y^2 dS \tag{35}$$

$$z_b = \frac{-1}{2\forall}\iint S_b n_3 z^2 dS \tag{36}$$

The hydrostatic and gravitational restoring coefficients can be ascertained through a matrix that is configured with respect to their respective coordinates.

$$\begin{bmatrix} 0 & 0 & 0 & 0 & 0 & 0 \\ 0 & 0 & 0 & 0 & 0 & 0 \\ 0 & 0 & a_{33} & a_{34} & a_{35} & 0 \\ 0 & 0 & 0 & a_{44} & a_{45} & a_{46} \\ 0 & 0 & 0 & 0 & a_{55} & a_{56} \\ 0 & 0 & 0 & 0 & 0 & 0 \end{bmatrix} \tag{37}$$

The matrix elements are given by

$$a_{33} = \rho g \iint S_b n_3 dS, \qquad a_{34} = \rho g \iint S_b y n_3 dS \qquad a_{35} = -\rho g \iint S_b x n_3 dS$$
$$a_{44} = \rho g \iint S_b y^2 n_3 dS + \rho g \forall z_b - m g z_g, \qquad a_{45} = -\rho g \iint S_b x y n_3 dS$$
$$a_{46} = -\rho g \forall x_b + m g x_g \qquad a_{55} = \rho g \iint S_b x^2 n_3 dS + \rho g \ \forall z_b - m g z_g$$
$$a_{56} = -\rho g \forall y_b + m g y_g$$

where m is the body mass, and x_g, y_g, and z_g are the center of gravity coordinates. Finally, the following equation describes the added mass and damping coefficients,

$$A_{ij} - \frac{iB_{ij}}{\omega} = \rho \iint S_b n_i \phi_j dS \tag{38}$$

where i is the imaginary unit, ω is the frequency, ρ is the density, S_b is the surface of integration, n_i is the ith component of the normal vector, and ϕ_j is a function of a field component.

To incorporate the hydrodynamic data and additional mass attributes into OpenFAST, the WAMIT v9 software was utilized. Figure 5 elucidates the methodology for the integration of modules to facilitate the creation of aero-hydro-servo-elastic simulations.

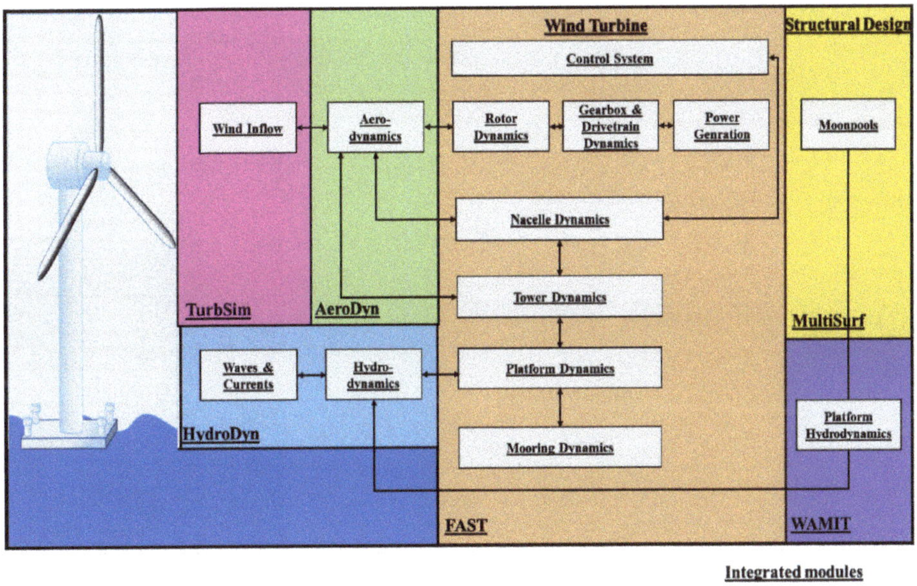

Figure 5. Integration of essential modules for the simulation of aero-hydro-servo-elastic dynamics.

The generator torque is defined as a tabular function of the filtered generator speed, covering five control regions: 1, 2a, 2b, and 3. This methodology conforms to the specifications established for the National Renewable Energy Laboratory (NREL) standard 5 MW wind turbine, as illustrated in Figure 6.

The framework for data collection, simulation, and network development is illustrated in the flow diagram in Figure 7. As depicted in the flowchart, five steps are utilized to establish the modeling and control of the hybrid framework.

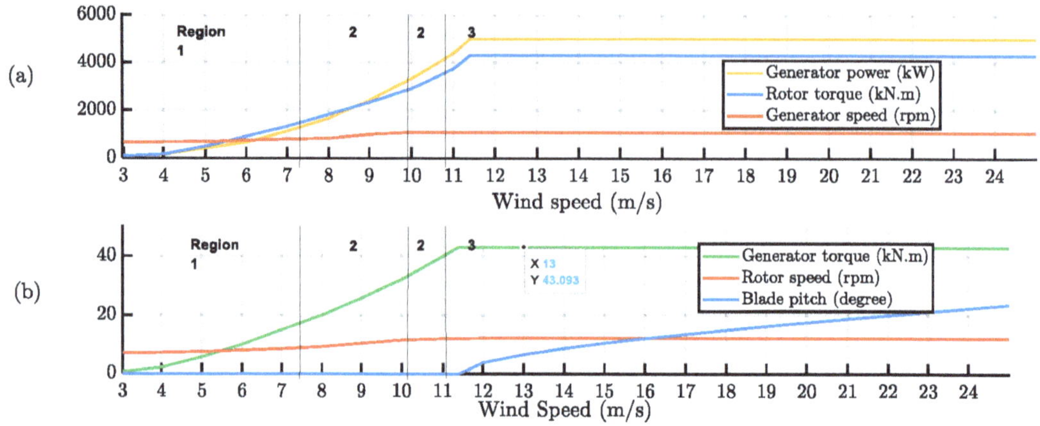

Figure 6. (**a**) Power-versus-speed and (**b**) torque-versus-speed response of the variable-speed controller.

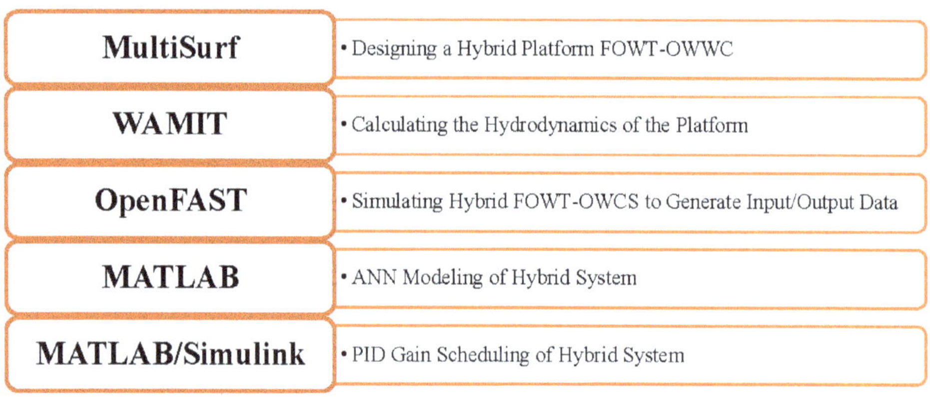

Figure 7. Overview of computational tools and their applications for the design and analysis of a hybrid FOWT-OWC system.

4.3. Advanced Deep Learning-Based Hybrid Modeling for the Hybrid System

OpenFAST was used multiple times to generate datasets for developing models based on Response Amplitude Operators (RAOs), as depicted in Figure 8. There are four recurrent ANN models that were developed. Each network comprises an input layer, ten hidden layers with ten fully connected neurons each, and an output layer with two neurons for estimating tower fore-aft displacement and platform pitch.

A visual representation of the dataset is shown in Figure 9. The process to determine the optimal number of hidden layers and neurons involved starting with minimal numbers and incrementally increasing them during the training of new network architectures.

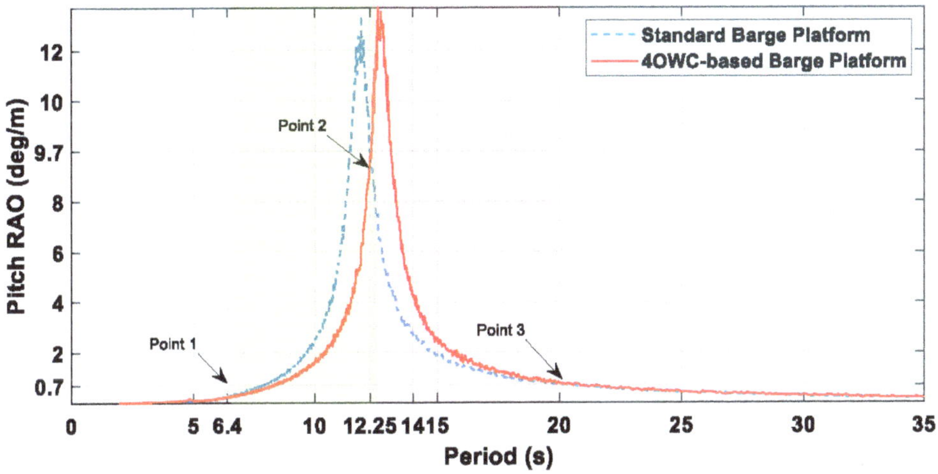

Figure 8. RAOs of a standard barge platform and 4 OWC-based barge platform pitch.

	Valve position				Valve position			
	Amplitudes	Periods	Winds	Voltages	Amplitudes	Periods	Winds	Voltages
Closed Valves	1m	5 s	5 m/s	0 V	1 m	14 s	5 m/s	0V
	1 m	5 s	8 m/s	0 V	1 m	14 s	8 m/s	0 V
	1 m	5 s	11 m/s	0 V	1 m	14 s	11 m/s	0 V
	1 m	5 s	14 m/s	0 V	1 m	14 s	14 m/s	0 V
	1 m	5 s	17 m/s	0 V	1 m	14 s	17 m/s	0 V
Half-Open Valves	1 m	5 s	5 m/s	24 V	1 m	14 s	5 m/s	24 V
	1 m	5 s	8 m/s	24 V	1 m	14 s	8 m/s	24 V
	1 m	5 s	11 m/s	24 V	1 m	14 s	11 m/s	24V
	1 m	5 s	14 m/s	24V	1 m	14 s	14 m/s	24 V
	1 m	5 s	17 m/s	24 V	1 m	14 s	17 m/s	24 V
Open-Valves	1 m	5 s	5 m/s	48 V	1 m	14 s	5 m/s	48V
	1 m	5 s	8 m/s	48 V	1 m	14 s	8 m/s	48V
	1 m	5 s	11 m/s	48 V	1 m	14 s	11 m/s	48V
	1 m	5 s	14 m/s	48 V	1 m	14 s	14 m/s	48V
	1 m	5 s	17 m/s	48 V	1 m	14 s	17 m/s	48 V
Closed Valves	1 m	10 s	5 m/s	0 V	1 m	20 s	5 m/s	0 V
	1 m	10 s	8 m/s	0 V	1 m	20 s	8 m/s	0 V
	1 m	10 s	11 m/s	0 V	1 m	20 s	11 m/s	0 V
	1 m	10 s	14 m/s	0 V	1 m	20 s	14 m/s	0 V
	1m	10 s	17 m/s	0 V	1 m	20 s	17 m/s	0 V
Half-Open Valves	1 m	10 s	5 m/s	24 V	1 m	20 s	5 m/s	24 V
	1 m	10 s	8 m/s	24 V	1 m	20 s	8 m/s	24 V
	1 m	10 s	11 m/s	24 V	1 m	20 s	11 m/s	24 V
	1 m	10 s	14 m/s	24V	1 m	20 s	14 m/s	24 V
	1 m	10 s	17 m/s	24 V	1 m	20 s	17 m/s	24 V
Open-Valves	1 m	10 s	5 m/s	48 V	1 m	20 s	5 m/s	48 V
	1 m	10 s	8 m/s	48 V	1 m	20 s	8 m/s	48 V
	1 m	10 s	11m/s	48 V	1 m	20 s	11 m/s	48 V
	1 m	10 s	14 m/s	48V	1 m	20 s	14 m/s	48 V
	1 m	10 s	17 m/s	48 V	1 m	20 s	17 m/s	48 V

Figure 9. Comprehensive dataset collected from FAST-NERL software for the training.

The outputs can be defined as follows:

$$y_k(t) = \phi_o\left(\sum_{i=1}^{10} w_{ik} y_i(t) + b_k\right), k = \{1;2\} \quad (39)$$

where the output of each node can be defined as

$$y_i(t) = \phi_h\left(\sum_{j=1}^{3} w_{ji}Z_j(t) + b_i\right), i = \{1, \ldots, 10\} j = \{1; 2; 3\} \tag{40}$$

where $Z(t) = [Z_1 Z_2 Z_3]^T = [z(t) v(t) u(t)]^T$ is the input vector, $z(t)$ is the wave elevation, $v(t)$ denotes wind speed, and $u(t)$ is the control input.

$$y_k(t) = \phi_o\left(\sum_{i=1}^{10} w_{ik}\phi_h\left(\sum_{j=1}^{3} w_{ji}Z_j(t) + b_i\right) + b_k\right) \tag{41}$$

$$\theta_p = y_1(t) = \phi_o\left(\sum_{i=1}^{10} w_{i1}\phi_h\left(\sum_{j=1}^{3} w_{ji}Z_j(t) + b_i\right) + b_1\right) \tag{42}$$

$$TTD_{FA} = y_2(t) = \phi_o\left(\sum_{i=1}^{10} w_{i2}\phi_h\left(\sum_{j=1}^{3} w_{ji}Z_j(t) + b_i\right) + b_2\right) \tag{43}$$

where ϕ_o and ϕ_h are the activation functions of the output and hidden layers, respectively. TTD_{FA} and θ_p are the top-tower displacement and platform pitch. For the training of datasets, the inputs considered are shown in Figure 10. The estimated outputs are shown in Figures 11 and 12.

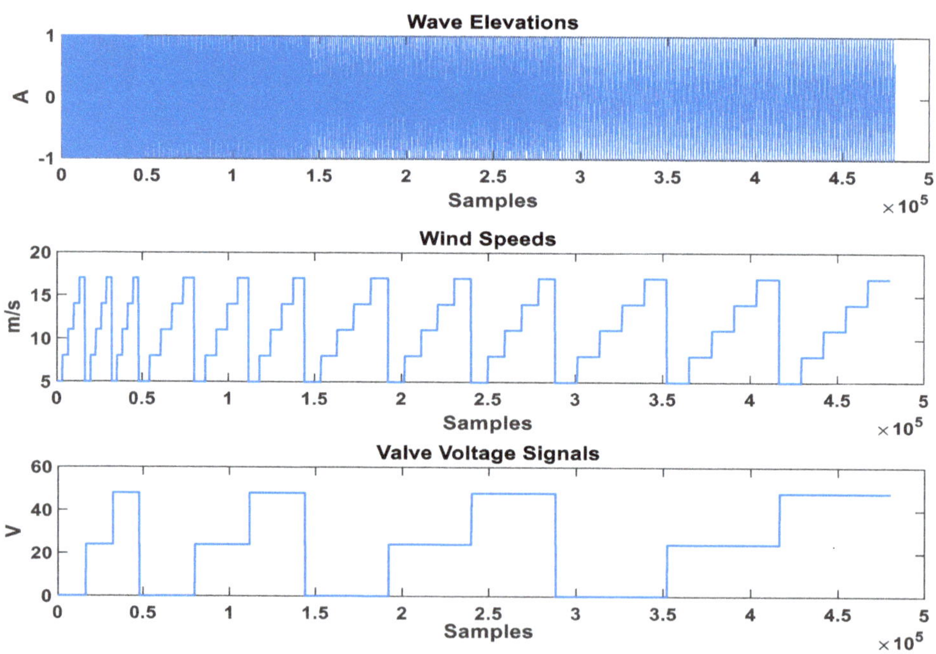

Figure 10. Network inputs: wave elevations, wind speeds, and valve voltage signals.

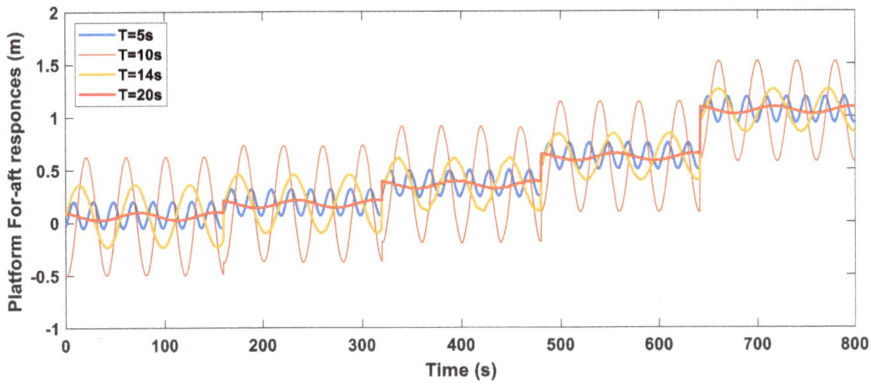

Figure 11. OpenFAST output of the fore-aft displacement across various wave periods, each with varying wind speeds (5, 8, 11, 14, and 17 m/s) and wave height of 1 m.

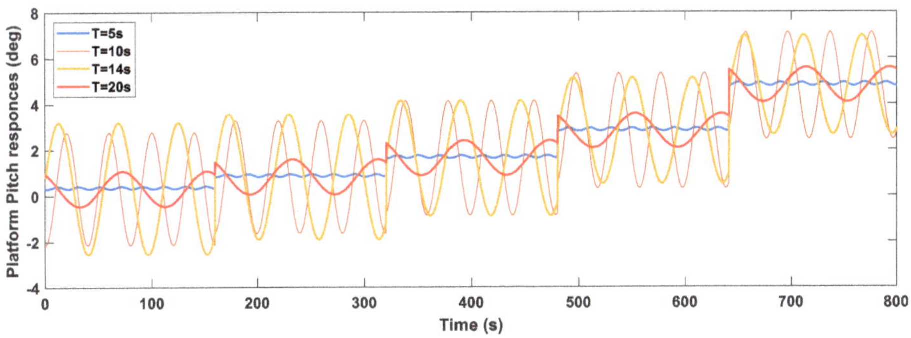

Figure 12. Pitch responses across various wave periods, each with varying wind speeds (5, 8, 11, 14, and 17 m/s) and wave height of 1 m.

Figure 10 illustrates the input variables used in the training of the computational ANN models, including wave elevations, wind speeds, and valve voltage signals. Figure 11 shows the top tower fore-aft displacement responses of the FOWT-OWC system across various wave periods and wind speeds. It demonstrates how the ANN model can predict displacement under different environmental conditions. Figure 12 depicts the platform pitch responses of the FOWT-OWC system across various wave periods and wind speeds. The diagram shown in Figure 13 outlines the workflow for developing a machine-learning model using a Multilayer Perceptron (MLP) architecture. The process begins with a dataset that undergoes preprocessing, including normalization, to prepare for input into the MLP model. The database contains parameters for top-tower displacement and platform pitch. The model-training phase involves an optimization process using the Levenberg–Marquardt algorithm. This was performed until the lowest Mean Squared Error (MSE) was achieved. Various hyper-parameters were tested, including learning rates (0.01, 0.001, 0.0001) and batch sizes (32, 64, 128), along with different configurations of hidden layers. A configuration with a learning rate of 0.001, a batch size of 32, and an optimal 10 hidden layers of neurons demonstrated effective results. The use of 10 hidden layers was chosen based on extensive empirical testing and optimization, demonstrating that this configuration provides the best trade-off between model complexity and performance, ensuring accurate predictions without overfitting.

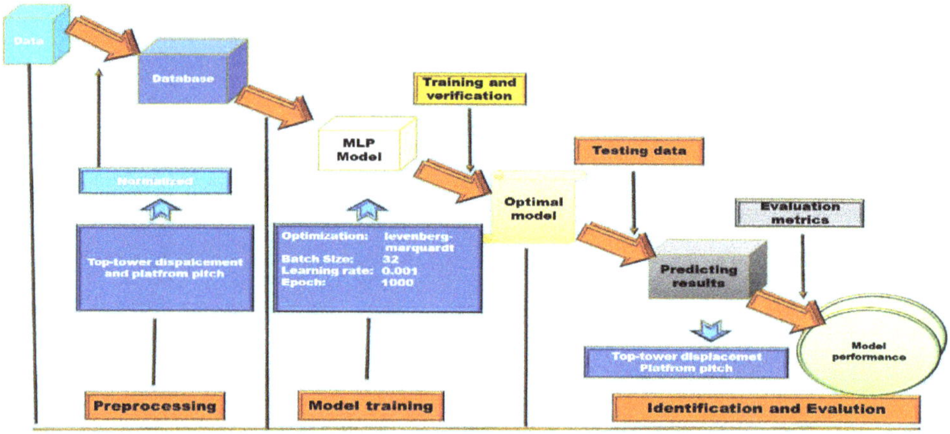

Figure 13. Model processing, training, identification, and evaluation.

This configuration balances computational efficiency and model performance, yielding the best outcomes in terms of prediction accuracy and system stability.

The architecture of an NN model is illustrated in Figure 14. Once training and verification were completed, the model was tested against a separate set of data to determine its accuracy and efficacy. The optimal model was then used to predict results, specifically the top-tower displacement and platform pitch. Evaluation metrics, such as accuracy, precision, and MSE, were applied to assess the model's performance. The results were fed back into the model for further refinement, ensuring that the predictions aligned as closely as possible with actual measured values. This iterative process was designed to enhance the accuracy of the MLP model for reliable predictive analysis in practical applications.

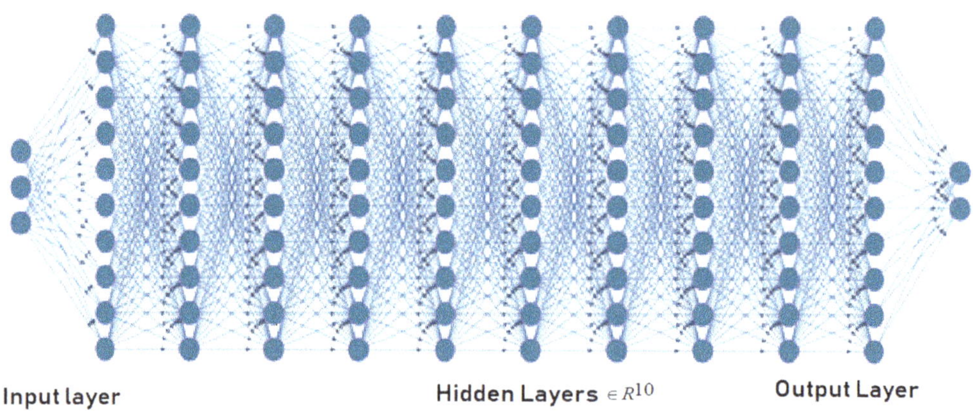

Figure 14. Architecture of a NN model with three inputs, ten hidden layers, and two outputs.

Several training functions were examined to train the network. The trainlm function, while requiring more memory, is often the fastest backpropagation method and is recommended as a primary supervised technique. The trainrp function employs resilient backpropagation (Rprop) to update weight and bias variables, mitigating the negative impacts of partial derivative magnitudes. Conjugate gradient algorithms, such as traincgb, initially follow the steepest descent direction and periodically reset the search direction. The traincgb function uses conjugate gradient backpropagation with Powell–Beale restarts to update weight and bias values.

The trainbr function applies Bayesian regularization with Levenberg–Marquardt optimization to update weight and bias variables, balancing squared errors and regularization terms for a generalizable network. The most effective results were achieved using Levenberg–Marquardt optimization techniques, as shown in Table 4.

Table 4. Error graphs for validation.

Training Function	Performance	MSE	R	Epochs	Training Function	Performance	MSE	R	Epochs
trainrp	Validation	542	0.9994	479	trainscg	Validation	341	0.9998	914
	Training		0.9994			Training		0.9999	
	Test		0.9995			Test		0.9998	
traincgb	Training	428	0.9995	675	trainbr	Training	319	0.9997	942
	Validation		0.9996			Validation		0.9998	
	Test		0.9996			Test		0.9998	
traincgf	Training	351	0.9998	343	trainblm	Training	316	0.9999	953
	Validation		0.9996			Validation		0.9999	
	Test		0.9998			Test		0.9999	
traincgp	Training	344	0.9996	513					
	Validation		0.9997						
	Test		0.9996						

4.4. Proposed Control Integration: PID Gain Scheduling Approach

Both platform pitch and tower top displacement rise significantly when exposed to high wind speeds. The control strategy following the development of the four estimated models for FOWT-OWCs incorporated PID gain scheduling across four networks, enhancing system responsiveness and adaptability. This method focuses on precise measurement and scaling of control variables, ensuring accurate input for the PID controllers and optimal system performance under various conditions. PID gain scheduling is a method that adaptively modifies controller gains according to the system's current operational conditions. Its main objective is to reduce the discrepancy between a predefined setpoint (zero reference) and the actual output of the system, with a special emphasis on managing the platform pitch. This reduction is accomplished by perpetually fine-tuning the control valve signal, which is determined by the measured error. Consequently, PID controllers serve as a crucial stabilizing element, refining the system's reaction to maintain compliance with specified performance criteria.

Figure 15 outlines the processes and interactions in a structured and understandable manner by clearly separating the offline and online stages. During the offline stage, the ANN models undergo training to produce the platform pitch θ_p and fore-aft top-tower displacement TTD_{FA}. Subsequently, the ANN_Predict function processes these variables. Following this, the decision logic applies manual decision-making principles to generate control gains K_P, K_I, K_D, which are then stored in a Look-Up Table (LUT) within the Gain Scheduler.

In the online stage, real-time wind and wave conditions $V(t)$ and $Z(t)$ are input into the LUT, which provides the appropriate control gains K_P, K_I, K_D to the PID controller. The PID controller utilizes these gains to adjust the reference pitch angle $\theta_p ref$, generating a control signal for the FOWT. The FOWT system outputs the actual pitch angle θ_p and TTD_{FA}, which are then fed back into the PID controller to maintain the desired pitch angle.

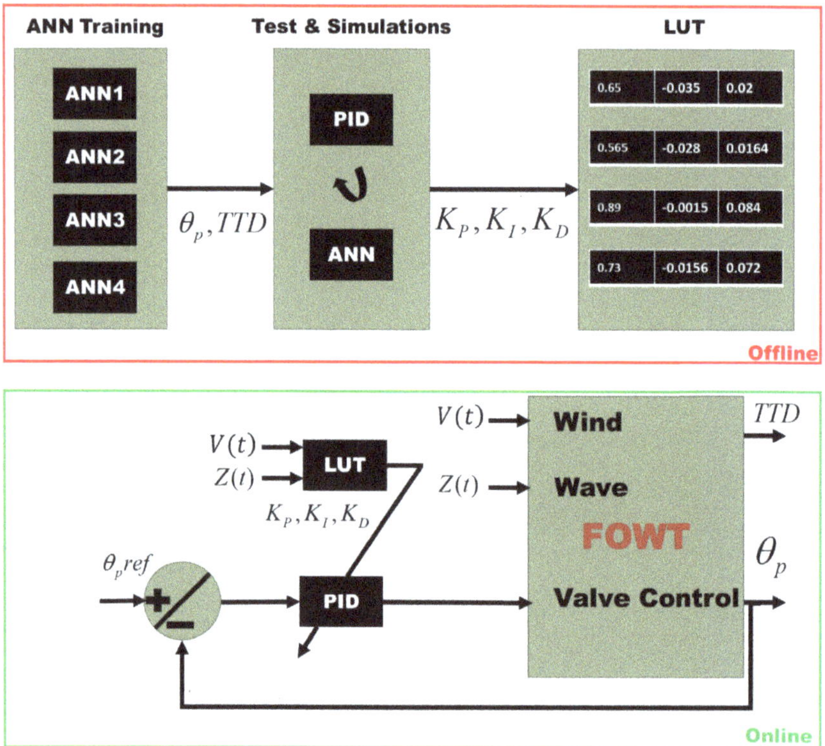

Figure 15. Schematic diagram of an adaptive control system utilizing ANNs and PID controller with a gain scheduling mechanism.

5. Model Validation and Control Results

This section details the simulations conducted to assess the effectiveness of the proposed modeling and control method for the hybrid FOWT-OWC system.

The comprehensive validation process is outlined in Figure 16, and reveals a robust predictive model with exceptional performance metrics. The first figure sets a remarkable precedent, with near-perfect correlation coefficients exceeding 0.9997 across all datasets, showcasing the model's high correlation with the datasets and the effectiveness of the underlying algorithm. Subsequent figures illustrate a commendable level of generalizability, with correlations consistently around or above 0.90. Such results are indicative of a well-tuned model that has been meticulously trained to translate the complexities of the data while maintaining commendable performance consistency when exposed to new, unseen datasets.

Moreover, the moderate performance depicted in the third figure, with correlations stabilizing between 0.76 to 0.78, underscores the model's reliability in providing stable predictions despite varying data conditions. The fourth figure reinforces these findings, demonstrating the model's resilience with high training and overall data correlation coefficients of 0.97, while a slight reduction in the test set correlation suggests a balanced approach to model fitting, avoiding overfitting while still capturing essential data patterns. These results collectively signal a promising direction for future deployment, offering a strong foundation for confident, data-driven decision-making and further affirming the model's potential for practical application across diverse scenarios.

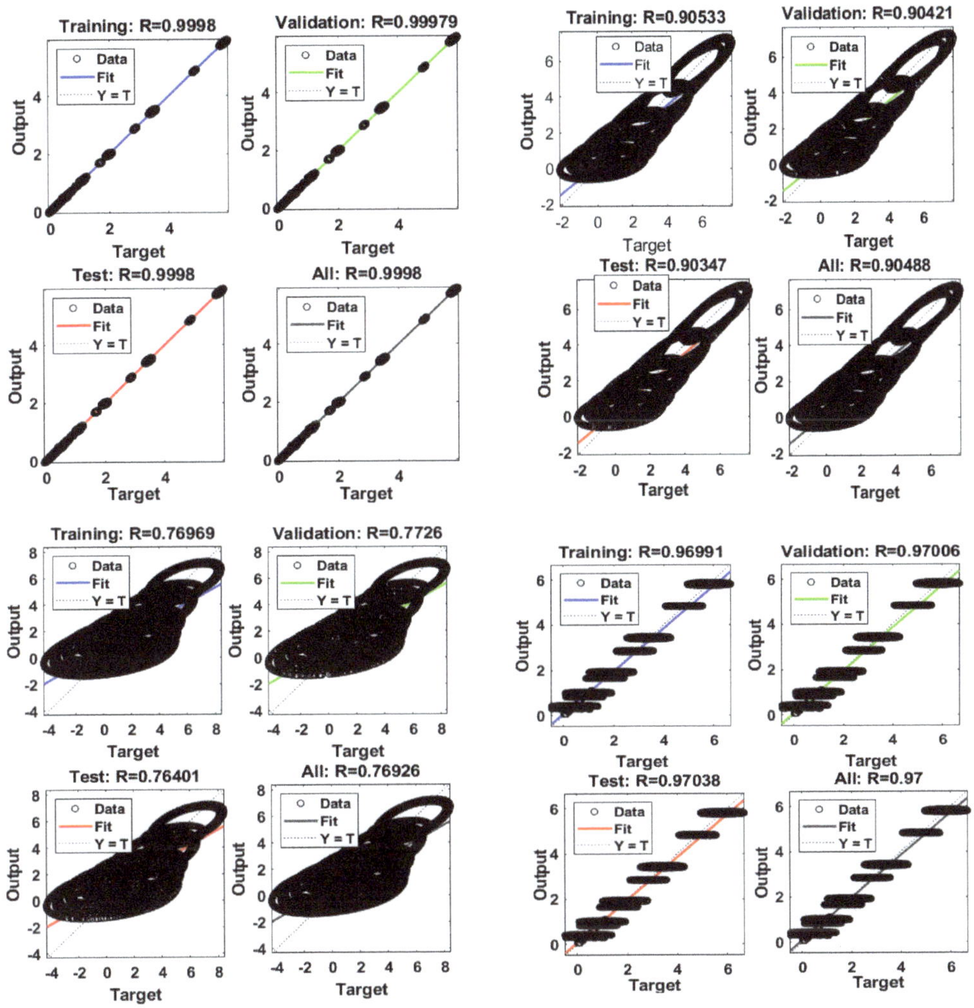

Figure 16. Performance evaluation of predictive models with regression. Plots for training, validation, and testing of all data sets.

The series of validation graphs shown in Figure 17 demonstrates the robust training model efficiency and predictive accuracy. The blue, green, and red lines represent training, validation, and testing, respectively. The model achieved optimal validation performance, with the best validation MSE remarkably low at 0.001169 by epoch 96, 0.68048 by epoch 34, 2.1952 by epoch 7, and 0.16825 by epoch 23, indicating rapid convergence and a strong learning capability. The MSE on a logarithmic scale swiftly declined from the initial epochs, underscoring the model's ability to generalize without overfitting, as the test errors closely followed the validation errors. This consistency in low error rates across all phases highlights the model's well-tuned balance between bias and variance, emphasizing its readiness for real-world application with a high degree of confidence in its predictive stability.

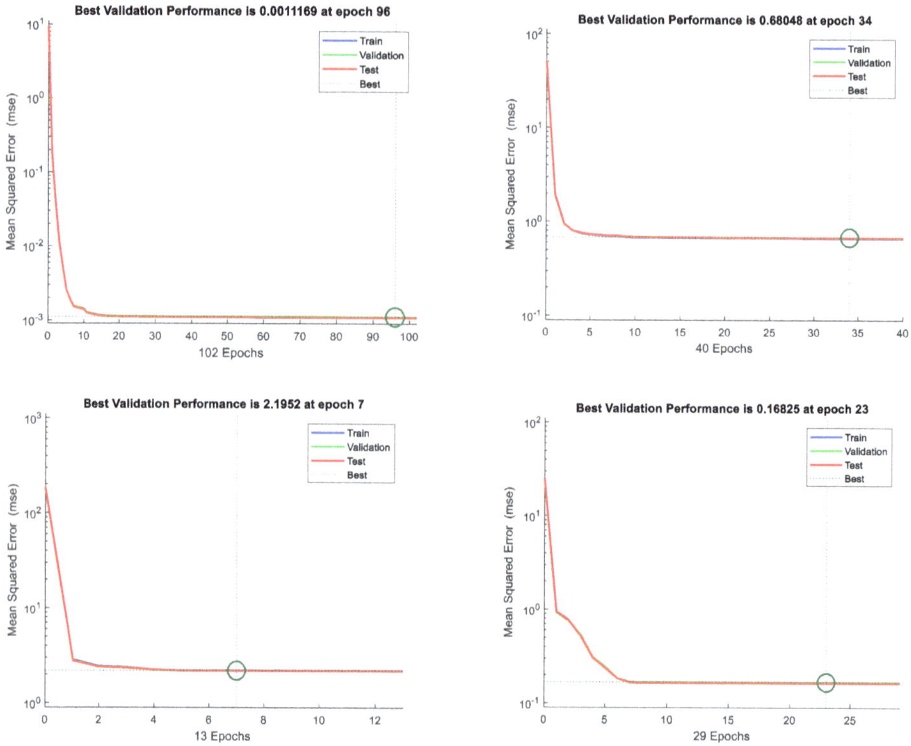

Figure 17. Performances analysis of four NN models with three inputs, ten hidden layers, and two outputs.

The set of error histograms from the predictive model evaluation provides insightful data on the distribution of prediction errors across training, validation, and test datasets. The histograms are plotted (see Figure 18) with errors calculated as the difference between targets and model outputs, and they are segmented into 20 discrete bins, offering a clear visual representation of the error magnitude and frequency. In each histogram, most errors cluster around the zero-error bin, which is a positive indication of the model's accuracy. Notably, the concentration of errors in bins close to zero across all datasets suggests that the model predictions are well-aligned with the actual values. The similar error distributions in the training, validation, and test sets imply that the model is not overfitted to the training data and has a consistent error profile when applied to unseen data. The distribution tails are thin, indicating fewer instances of large errors, which enhances the model's credibility for practical applications.

The graphs illustrated in Figure 19 are the errors of four distinct models across a 600-s horizon, with a particular focus on fore-aft and platform pitch errors. Models N1, N2, N3, and N4 exhibit an impressive level of accuracy, as evidenced by their error metrics closely reaching the zero line, indicating predictions that consistently align with the actual values. These models demonstrate exceptional reliability, maintaining a steady course even when faced with the complexities of dynamic forecasting. In general, the collective performance of these models paints a promising picture of predictive accuracy and offers a robust foundation for complex forecasting in dynamic environments.

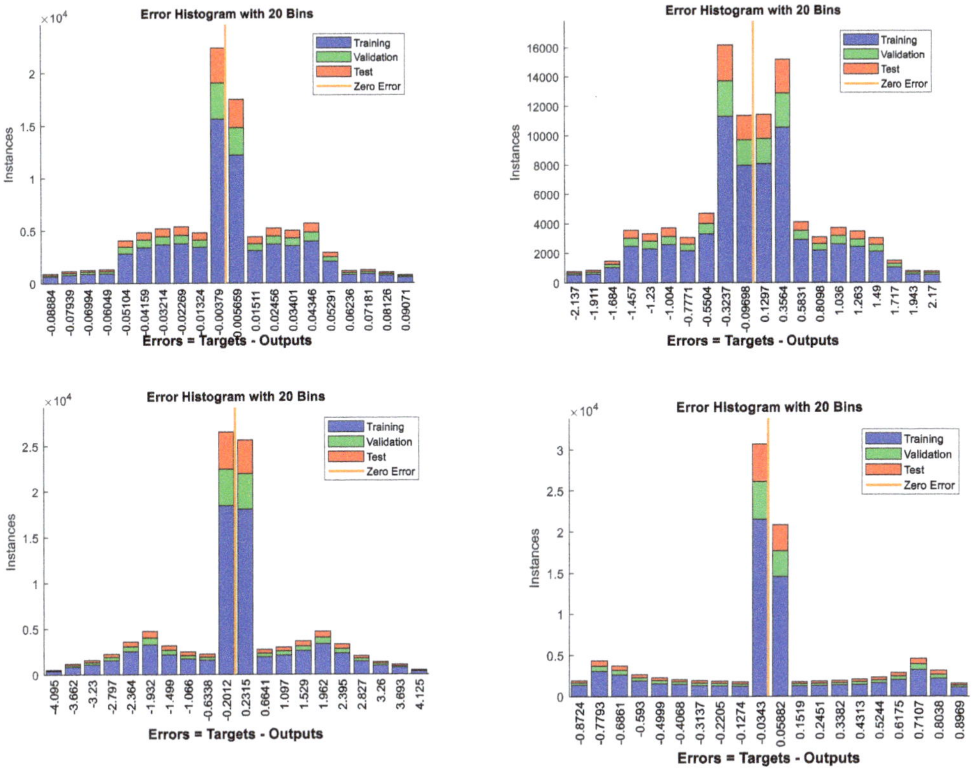

Figure 18. Error histograms analyzing the distribution of four NN models with three inputs, ten hidden layers, and two outputs.

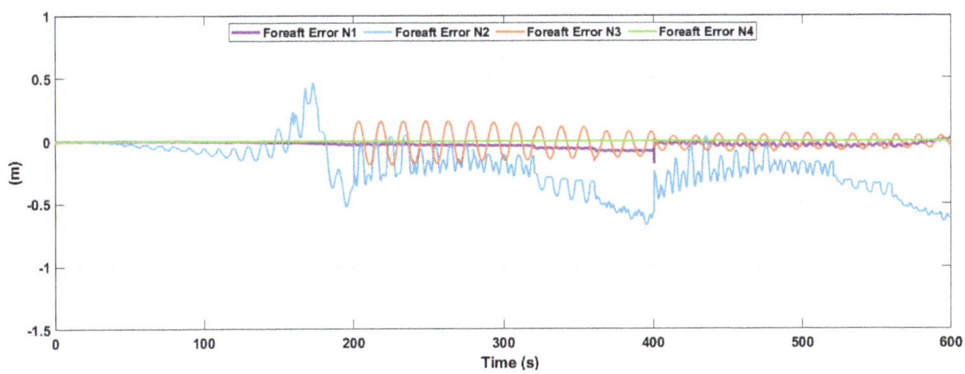

Figure 19. *Cont.*

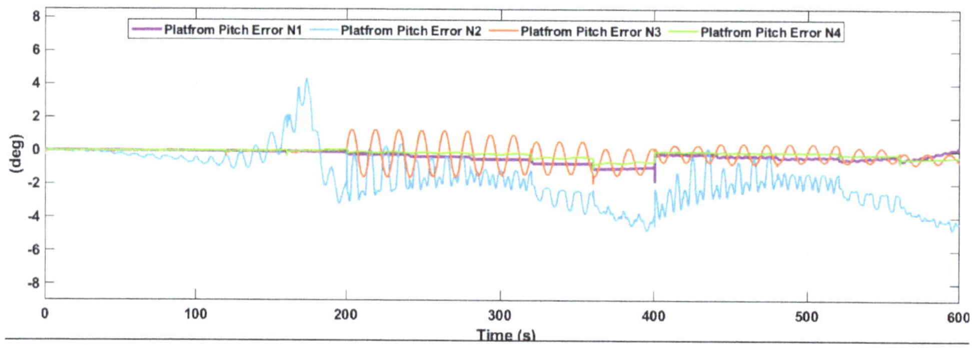

Figure 19. Comprehensive training errors across four NN models of fore-aft displacement and platform pitch.

For the top-tower fore-aft displacement (TTD_{FA}), a set of graphical analyses is presented in Figure 20. A detailed overview of the neural network's training performance is rigorously compared against FAST simulations across a spectrum of wave periods. For the shortest wave period of 5 s, the trained network demonstrates excellent synchronization with the simulation data, capturing the rapid oscillatory patterns with minimal deviation. As the wave period increases to 10 and 14 s, the network maintains this high level of reliability, despite the longer periods introducing more complex dynamics to the training task. The graphs show that the network adeptly adjusts to these changes, with the error between the simulation and the trained network remaining consistently low. The longest wave period of 20 s tests the limits of the network's predictive capacity. The corresponding graph indicates that while the overall trend and periodicity are captured, there is a slight increase in the deviation from the FAST simulation data. This is due to the inherent challenges in modeling such extended patterns, or could reflect a need for further training or refinement of the network for these conditions. Across all periods, however, the consistent performance of the trained network, especially in lower frequency waves, is indicative of a robust training regime that has prepared the network to handle a diverse range of scenarios with varying wind speeds. These results are encouraging for the application of the trained network in real-world situations in which adaptability to different environmental conditions has been considered carefully.

(a)

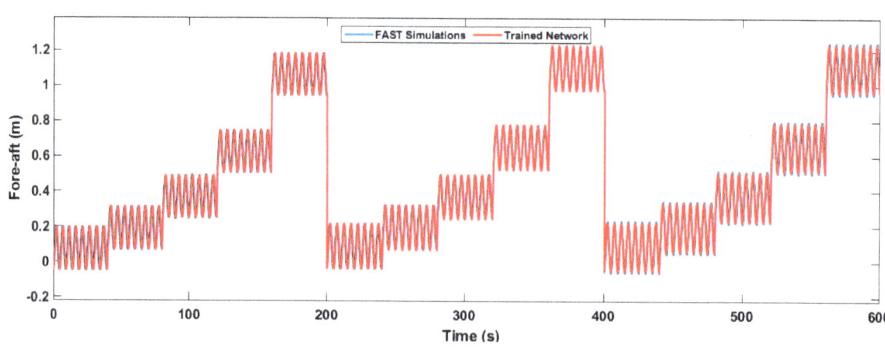

Figure 20. *Cont.*

(b)

(c)

(d)

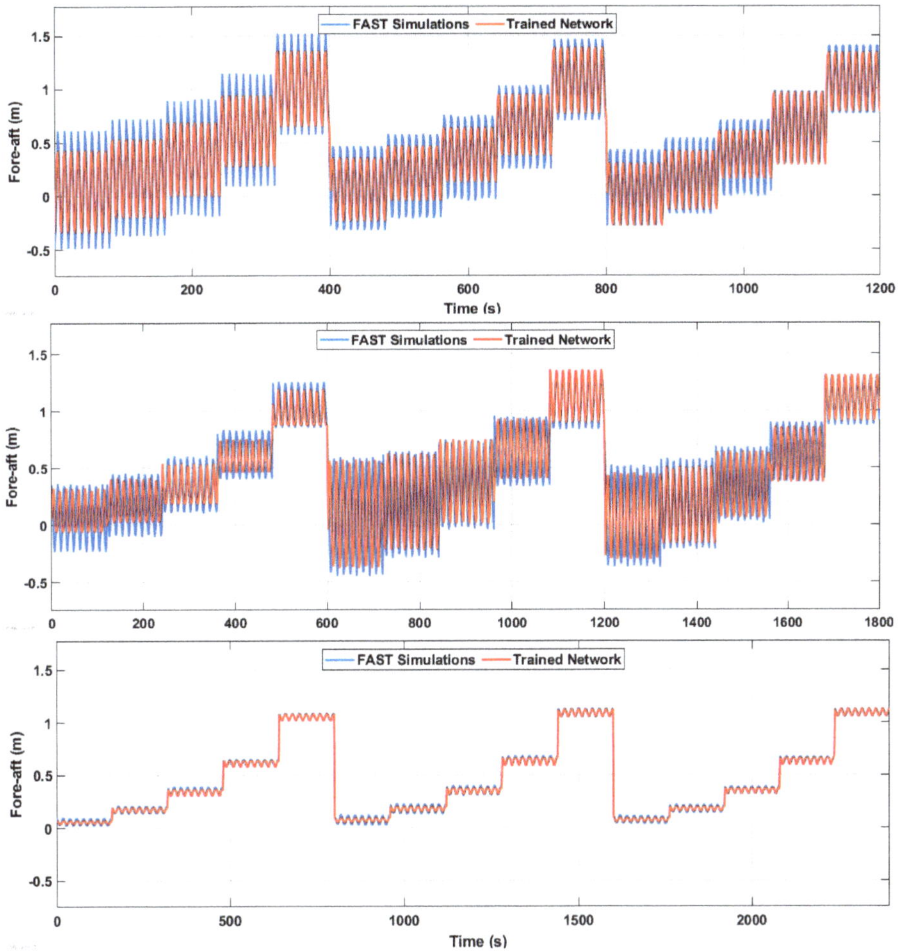

Figure 20. Comprehensive training results of fore-aft displacement across different wave periods of (**a**) 5 s, (**b**) 10 s, (**c**) 14 s, and (**d**) 20 s, each with varying wind speeds (5, 8, 11, 14, and 17 m/s) and wave height of 1 m.

Figure 21 presents the training results of the Trained Model, set against FAST Data Network outputs, and using varying wave periods for the platform pitch. Each graph reveals the model's performance over extended time frames, capturing the dynamics of platform pitch in response to simulated maritime conditions. The first graph, depicting the scenario with a 5-s wave period, shows an exceptional alignment between the Trained Model and the FAST Data Network, suggesting that the model has effectively internalized the system dynamics within this range. As the wave period increases to 10, 14, and 20 s in subsequent graphs, the Trained Model consistently mirrors the FAST Data Network's pitch response, albeit with minor variations that become more pronounced with longer wave periods. These discrepancies are due to the increased complexity and potential non-linearities introduced at extended intervals. However, even at a 20-s wave period, the Trained Model demonstrates an impressive ability to replicate the complex patterns of the FAST simulations, exhibiting its robustness and adaptability.

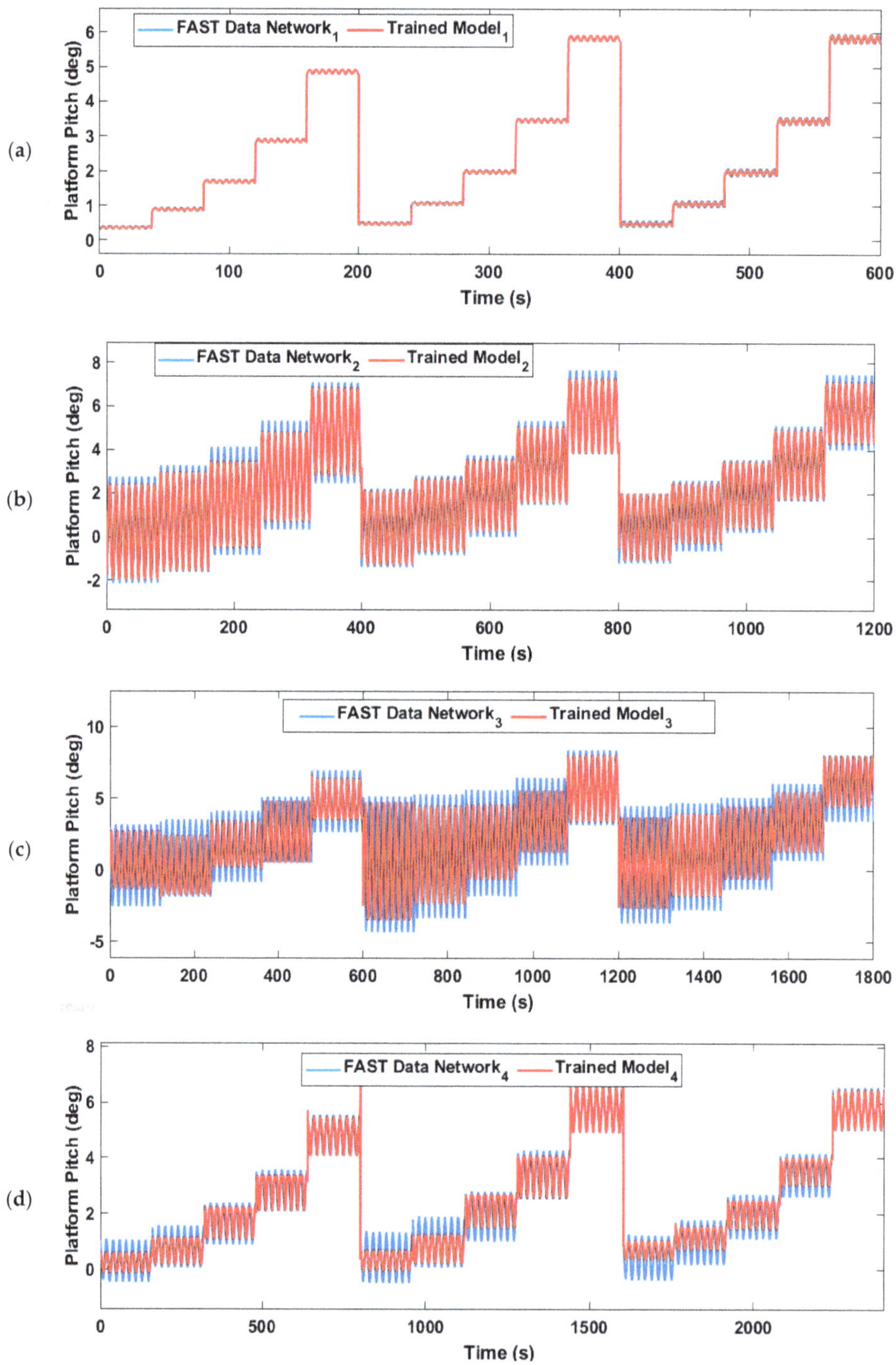

Figure 21. Comprehensive training results for platform pitch across different wave periods of (**a**) 5 s, (**b**) 10 s, (**c**) 14 s, and (**d**) 20 s, each with varying wind speeds (5, 8, 11, 14, and 17 m/s) and wave height of 1m.

Overall, the Trained Model's performance across these varying conditions highlights its refined learning capabilities and potential for real-world application. Despite the challenges posed by longer wave periods and the intricate behaviors they induce, the model shows it can predict with high accuracy, making it a valuable tool for navigating the complexities of maritime environments.

The series of control implementation graphs in Figure 22, demonstrates the performance of a PID-controlled system, in which the green lines represent the control actions and their resulting system stability, indicated by the reduced oscillations. The first graph reveals that the control actions closely follow the predicted model values with minimal oscillations, suggesting that the PID controller is well-tuned for the system's dynamics within this specific scenario. The small oscillation amplitude indicates a finely adjusted control response that quickly stabilizes the platform pitch. Moving to the second graph, as the system is subjected to what may be a different set of conditions or a longer wave period, there is a slight increase in the oscillation magnitude. Despite this, the control action remains effective, keeping the platform pitch oscillations within a narrow band, indicative of a robust control system that compensates for the increased complexity of the input signal.

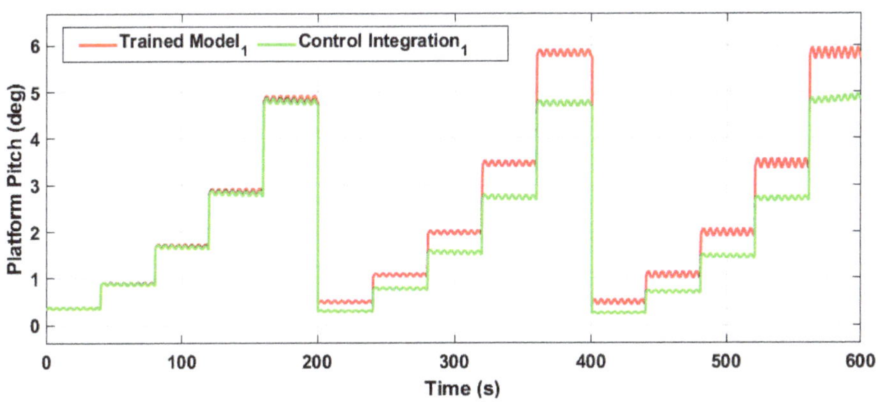

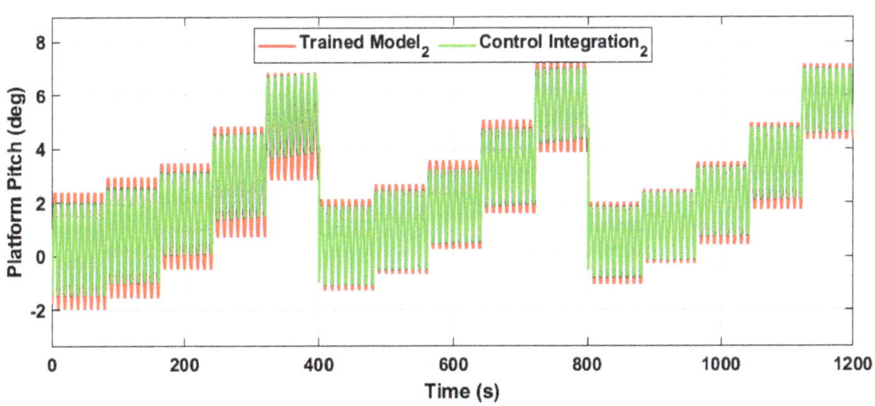

Figure 22. *Cont.*

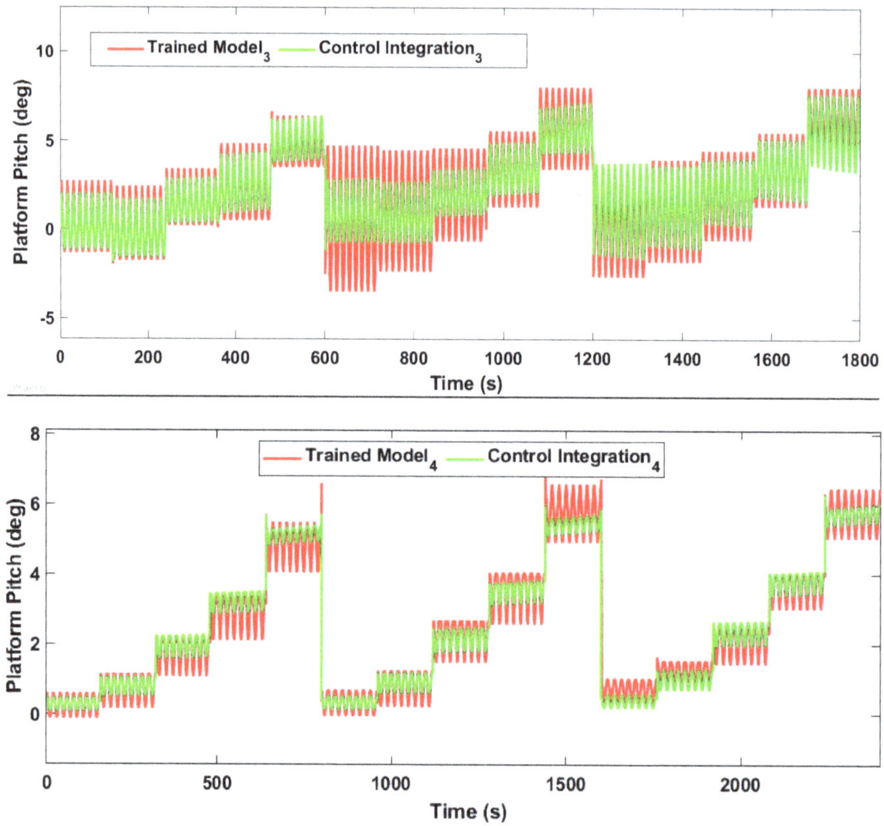

Figure 22. PID control design for platform pitch across several wave periods (5 s, 10 s, 14 s, and 20 s), each with varying wind speeds (5, 8, 11, 14, and 17 m/s) and wave height of 1 m.

The third graph shows the response of the system to yet another set of conditions, potentially with even longer wave periods. Here, the control action successfully dampens oscillations, although there is a noticeable transient deviation after each significant change in the platform pitch. The transient peaks suggest the system may be approaching the limits of its design parameters, yet it still manages to return to a stable state quickly without prolonged or escalating oscillations. In the fourth graph, despite further complexity due to extended intervals or increased environmental challenges, the PID controller, improved by gain scheduling, demonstrates a commendable job of maintaining stability. The control actions result in bounded oscillations, indicating that the system has a good transient response and can settle within an acceptable range after being subjected to disturbances.

The effectiveness of the PID control system in reducing oscillations across different wave periods is presented in Table 5. The data reveal that the mean oscillation amplitude is significantly reduced when the control system is applied, demonstrating significant reductions in oscillation amplitudes across different conditions. For instance, at a wave period of 20 s and a wind speed of 5 m/s, the fore-aft displacement is reduced by 35%, indicating the control system's robustness. The consistent reduction in oscillation percentage, ranging from 5% to 35%, underscores the PID system's capability to enhance stability and control in FOWT-OWC integrated systems under diverse operational scenarios. These findings highlight the potential of the PID control system in practical applications requiring precise oscillation control.

Table 5. Impact of wave periods, wind speeds, and wave elevations on fore-aft displacement, pitch response, and oscillation reduction with PID control.

Scenario	Wave Period (s)	Wind Speed (m/s)	Wave Elevation (m)	Valve Voltage (V)	Fore-Aft Displacement (m)	Pitch Response (deg)	% Reduction in Oscillation	Mean Std Deviation
1	5	5	1.2	25	0.3	1.5	20%	0.05
2	5	8	1.4	28	0.35	2.0	15%	0.08
3	5	11	1.5	30	0.4	2.5	10%	0.1
4	5	14	1.6	32	0.45	3.0	5%	0.12
5	10	5	1.3	26	0.32	1.6	25%	0.04
6	10	8	1.5	29	0.37	2.1	18%	0.07
7	10	11	1.7	31	0.43	2.6	12%	0.09
8	10	14	1.8	33	0.49	3.1	8%	0.11
9	14	5	1.4	27	0.34	1.7	30%	0.03
10	14	8	1.6	30	0.39	2.2	20%	0.05
11	14	11	1.8	32	0.46	2.7	15%	0.07
12	14	14	2.0	34	0.52	3.2	10%	0.1
13	20	5	1.5	28	0.36	1.8	35%	0.02
14	20	8	1.7	31	0.41	2.3	25%	0.04
15	20	11	1.9	33	0.48	2.8	18%	0.06
16	20	14	2.1	35	0.55	3.3	12%	0.08

Statistically, the lower oscillation amplitudes across all four scenarios suggest that the PID gain scheduling is effectively calibrated. The control system appears to possess both a high degree of precision and an ability to quickly adapt to varying conditions, maintaining the platform pitch within tightly controlled limits. This is consistent with a well-designed control system that can mitigate the risk of instability even when dealing with complex, dynamic environmental inputs.

Figure 23 shows the PID controller's voltage output over time for various wave periods and wind speeds. Specifically, it includes wave periods of 5 s, 10 s, 14 s, and 20 s, each plotted with their respective time scales: 600 s, 1200 s, 1800 s, and 2400 s. These time scales correspond to the selected wave periods, ensuring a comprehensive representation of the controller's performance. The stepwise increase in voltage across all graphs indicates a controlled and adaptive approach to system regulation, with the gain scheduling effectively modulating the PID gains to manage the dynamic environment.

(a)

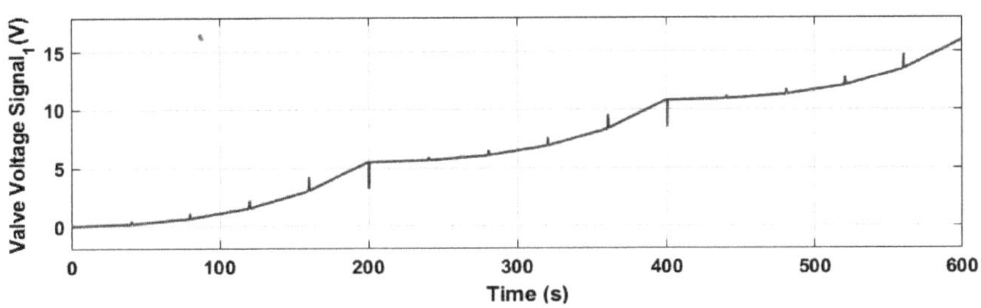

Figure 23. *Cont.*

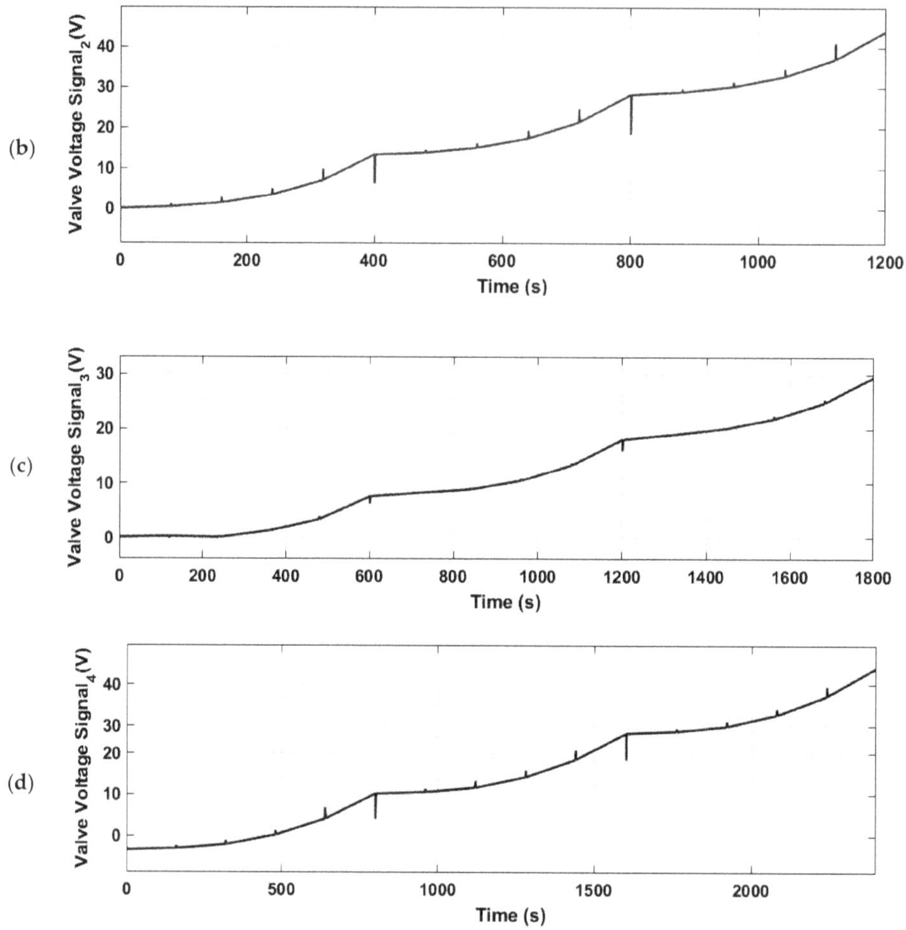

Figure 23. Control signals for the fore-aft displacement across different wave periods of (**a**) 5 s, (**b**) 10 s, (**c**) 14 s, and (**d**) 20 s, each with varying wind speeds (5, 8, 11, 14, and 17 m/s) and wave height of 1 m.

In the first graph, the voltage response is moderate, reflecting proportional and deliberate action to minor disturbances. The second graph shows a stronger response, suggesting the controller's compensation for more significant disturbances. The third and fourth graphs extend this pattern, with the controller addressing sustained or evolving disturbances, maintaining system stability throughout. The consistent valve voltage increase without abrupt fluctuations highlights the PID controller's effectiveness in ensuring smooth and stable system control over time.

The PID control tuning process was conducted using Simulink MATLAB to ensure precise optimization of the PID parameters. The control design of the FOWT-OWC system was modeled in Simulink, and initial PID parameters were estimated through theoretical and empirical methods. Simulations were run to observe system responses, with iterative adjustments made using Simulink PID Tuner for optimal performance. The tuning process ensured the control system could handle various environmental conditions, maintain stability, and minimize overshoot and settling time. The final PID parameters were validated through extensive testing, demonstrating the control strategy's effectiveness and reliability in practical applications, as shown in Table 6. These configurations are reflective of strategic adjustments made to ensure optimal system performance across varying maritime conditions. For N1, which operates within a 5-m wave environment, the proportional gain is set at 0.65, indicating a strong responsive action is favored in this scenario. This is complemented by a derivative gain of 0.02, which moderates the rate of change in the system's response, providing a dampening effect to potential oscillations. N2, adapting to a 10-m wave period, utilizes a slightly lower proportional gain of 0.565, demonstrating a controlled and less aggressive approach to system error correction. The derivative gain here is adjusted to 0.0164, fine-tuning the system's responsiveness to changes over time. In the case of N3, contending with a 14-m wave period, the proportional gain is increased to 0.89, reflecting a robust control strategy to swiftly address system deviations. The corresponding derivative gain of 0.084 is indicative of a strategy designed to provide stability and counteract the inertia that comes with larger wave impacts. Finally, parameters for N4, a 20-m wave period, show a proportional gain of 0.73, balancing prompt corrective action with the need for stability in more substantial wave conditions. The derivative gain is set at 0.072, suggesting a tailored approach to maintain control without over-dampening the response of system. The integral gains for all networks are notably negative; instead of accumulating positive corrections, they accumulate negative corrections.

Table 6. Control parameters for four distinct networks.

	Control parameters		
	P	I	D
N1 (5 m)	0.65	−0.035	0.02
N2 (10 m)	0.565	−0.28	0.0164
N3 (14 m)	0.89	−0.015	0.084
N4 (20 m)	0.73	−0.0156	0.072

This unique adjustment offers advantages in these specialized applications, as it implies a reduction of the integral response, which could potentially be beneficial in systems where over-integration of the error could lead to instability or performance issues. Overall, the selection of PID parameters demonstrates a thoughtful approach to achieving a balance between responsiveness and stability, ensuring that each network can effectively cope with the dynamic challenges presented by its specific operational wave period.

The reliance on simulation data poses a challenge, as it may not capture all real-world variabilities. Additionally, assumptions regarding environmental conditions and system parameters can affect the generalizability of the findings. Consequently, there is a necessity for field tests to validate the effectiveness of the proposed ANN models and PID control strategies in practical applications. The authors plan to incorporate Convolutional Neural Networks (CNNs) and Recurrent Neural Networks (RNNs) in future comparative analyses to leverage their advanced spatial and temporal processing capabilities. This strategic expansion is intended to enhance the modeling accuracy and increase the predictive precision of their simulations, thereby broadening the scope and depth of their methodology.

6. Conclusions

This study significantly contributes to offshore renewable energy by integrating FOWTs with OWCs. The dynamic complexities and uncertainties inherent in these systems have been effectively addressed through the innovative application of ANNs for regressive modeling and an advanced proportional-integral-derivative control mechanism. This approach leverages data-driven models trained on OpenFAST datasets to facilitate real-time predictive behavior analysis and decision-making. The results demonstrated a substantial reduction in platform pitch motion across diverse operational conditions, which is vital for improving system reliability and longevity. The deployment of the intelligent control system, tailored for this application, was pivotal in achieving these outcomes. A comparative analysis with ITI-barge-based systems highlighted that the proposed modeling and control approaches significantly enhanced system stability and efficiency, as evidenced by the successful mitigation of platform pitch motion, directly correlating with increased platform stability and overall system performance.

The findings underscore the efficacy of ANN-driven modeling and advanced control strategies as viable alternatives to traditional methods, offering superior performance in managing the intricate dynamics of these systems. This research not only advances the current understanding and methodologies in the field but also sets a robust framework for future innovations in feedback control for renewable energy systems. The introduction of a feedback control mechanism was critical in achieving the observed improvements in system stability, providing a closed-loop system that continuously adjusts based on real-time data to maintain optimal performance. The methodologies and results presented in this study pave the way for significant advancements in offshore renewable energy, marking a critical step towards more sustainable energy solutions. By establishing a model for feedback control and system stability, this research provides a foundation for future work aimed at enhancing the efficiency and resilience of renewable energy technologies.

Author Contributions: Conceptualization, I.A., F.M., P.A., I.G. and A.J.G.; methodology, I.A., F.M., P.A., I.G. and A.J.G.; software, I.A., F.M., P.A., I.G. and A.J.G.; validation, A.J.G.; data curation, I.A., F.M. and P.A.; writing—original draft preparation, I.A., F.M. and P.A.; writing—review and editing, F.M., P.A., I.G. and A.J.G.; supervision, I.G. and A.J.G. All authors have read and agreed to the published version of the manuscript.

Funding: This research work was partially funded by the Basque Government through Grant IT1555-22, MICIU/AEI/10.13039/501100011033 and ERDF/EU through Grants PID2021-123543OB-C21 and PID2021-123543OB-C22, the University of the Basque Country (UPV-EHU) through grant PIF20/299, the UPV-EHU/MIU/Next Generation, EU through Margarita Salas grant MARSA22/09 and the María Zambrano grant MAZAM22/15.

Data Availability Statement: All data generated or analyzed during this study are included in this published article.

Conflicts of Interest: The authors declare that they have no conflicts of interest. This research was conducted in the absence of any commercial or financial relationships that could be construed as a potential conflict of interest.

References

1. Jung, C.; Schindler, D. Efficiency and effectiveness of global onshore wind energy utilization. *Energy Convers. Manag.* **2023**, *280*, 116788. [CrossRef]
2. Chen, M.; Li, C.B.; Han, Z.; Lee, J.-B. A simulation technique for monitoring the real-time stress responses of various mooring configurations for offshore floating wind turbines. *Ocean Eng.* **2023**, *278*, 114366. [CrossRef]
3. Zhou, B.; Zhang, Z.; Li, G.; Yang, D.; Santos, M. Review of key technologies for offshore floating wind power generation. *Energies* **2023**, *16*, 710. [CrossRef]
4. Goyal, R. Advancements in Offshore Wind Energy Technology: Challenges and Opportunities for Sustainable Power Generation. *J. Sustain. Solut.* **2024**, *1*, 1–4.
5. Jolly, S.; Steen, M.; Hansen, T.; Afewerki, S. Renewable energy and industrial development in pioneering and lagging regions: The offshore wind industry in southern Denmark and Normandy. *Oxf. Open Energy* **2023**, 2, oiad010. [CrossRef]
6. Guo, X.; Chen, X.; Chen, X.; Sherman, P.; Wen, J.; McElroy, M. Grid integration feasibility and investment planning of offshore wind power under carbon-neutral transition in China. *Nat. Commun.* **2023**, *14*, 2447. [CrossRef]
7. Garrido, I.; Garrido, A.J.; Lekube, J.; Otaola, E.; Carrascal, E. Oscillating water column control and monitoring. In Proceedings of the OCEANS 2016 MTS/IEEE Monterey, Monterey, CA, USA, 19–23 September 2016; pp. 1–6.
8. Karimirad, M. *Offshore Energy Structures: For Wind Power, Wave Energy and Hybrid Marine Platforms*; Springer: Cham, Switzerland, 2014.
9. Ahmad, I.; M'zoughi, F.; Aboutalebi, P.; Garrido, I.; Garrido, A.J. A regressive machine-learning approach to the non-linear complex FAST model for hybrid floating offshore wind turbines with integrated oscillating water columns. *Sci. Rep.* **2023**, *13*, 1499. [CrossRef] [PubMed]
10. Stetco, A.; Dinmohammadi, F.; Zhao, X.; Robu, V.; Flynn, D.; Barnes, M.; Keane, J.; Nenadic, G. Machine learning methods for wind turbine condition monitoring: A review. *Renew. Energy* **2019**, *133*, 620–635. [CrossRef]

11. Jessen, K.; Laugesen, K.; Mortensen, S.M.; Jensen, J.K.; Soltani, M.N. Experimental validation of aero-hydro-servo-elastic models of a scaled floating offshore wind turbine. *Appl. Sci.* **2019**, *9*, 1244. [CrossRef]
12. Uzunoglu, E.; Karmakar, D.; Guedes Soares, C. Floating offshore wind platforms. In *Floating Offshore Wind Farms*; Springer: Cham, Switzerland, 2016; pp. 53–76.
13. Ahmad, I.; M'zoughi, F.; Aboutalebi, P.; Garrido, I.; Garrido, A.J. Fuzzy logic control of an artificial neural net-work-based floating offshore wind turbine model integrated with four oscillating water columns. *Ocean. Eng.* **2023**, *269*, 113578. [CrossRef]
14. Gajendran, M.K.; Kabir, I.F.S.A.; Vadivelu, S.; Ng, E.Y.K. Machine Learning-Based Approach to Wind Turbine Wake Prediction under Yawed Conditions. *J. Mar. Sci. Eng.* **2023**, *11*, 2111. [CrossRef]
15. Memari, M.; Shakya, P.; Shekaramiz, M.; Seibi, A.C.; Masoum, M.A.S. Review on the Advancements in Wind Turbine Blade Inspection: Integrating Drone and Deep Learning Technologies for Enhanced Defect Detection. *IEEE Access* **2024**, *12*, 33236–33282. [CrossRef]
16. Kim, T.; Kim, C.; Song, J.; You, D. Optimal control of a wind farm in time-varying wind using deep reinforcement learning. *Energy* **2024**, *303*, 131950. [CrossRef]
17. Soler, D.; Mariño, O.; Huergo, D.; de Frutos, M.; Ferrer, E. Reinforcement learning to maximize wind turbine energy generation. *Expert Syst. Appl.* **2024**, *249*, 131950. [CrossRef]
18. Lamnabhi-Lagarrigue, F.; Annaswamy, A.; Engell, S.; Isaksson, A.; Khargonekar, P.; Murray, R.M.; Nijmeijer, H.; Samad, T.; Tilbury, D.; Hof, P.V.D. Systems & Control for the future of humanity, research agenda: Current and future roles, impact and grand challenges. *Annu. Rev. Control* **2017**, *43*, 1–64. [CrossRef]
19. Tsai, F.-M.; Kao, S.-L.; Sujanto, R.Y.; Tseng, M.-L.; Hsu, T.-W.; Chou, C.-C. Causality of Risk Assessment Attributes under Uncertainty in Taiwan's Offshore Wind Farms Development. *J. Mar. Sci. Eng.* **2023**, *11*, 225. [CrossRef]
20. Martinez, A.; Iglesias, G. Global wind energy resources decline under climate change. *Energy* **2024**, *288*, 129765. [CrossRef]
21. Cheng, A.; Low, Y.M. A new metamodel for predicting the nonlinear time-domain response of offshore structures subjected to stochastic wave current and wind loads. *Comput. Struct.* **2024**, *297*, 107340. [CrossRef]
22. Jiang, H.; Wang, H.; Vaz, M.A.; Bai, X. Research on dynamic response prediction of semi-submersible wind turbine platform in real sea test model based on machine learning. *Appl. Ocean Res.* **2024**, *142*, 103808. [CrossRef]
23. Milles, A.; Merabet, E.; Benbouhenni, H.; Debdouche, N.; Colak, I. Robust control technique for wind turbine system with interval type-2 fuzzy strategy on a dual star induction generator. *Energy Rep.* **2024**, *11*, 2715–2736. [CrossRef]
24. Lemmer, F.; Schlipf, D.; Cheng, P.W. Structural optimization of FOWT platforms using genetic algorithms. *J. Offshore Mech. Arct. Eng.* **2018**, *140*, 011402. [CrossRef]
25. Raissi, M.; Perdikaris, P.; Karniadakis, G.E. Hidden physics models: Machine learning of nonlinear partial differential equations. *J. Comput. Phys.* **2018**, *357*, 125–141. [CrossRef]
26. M'zoughi, F.; Garrido, I.; Garrido, A.J.; De La Sen, M. Fuzzy Airflow-Based Active Structural Control of Integrated Oscillating Water Columns for the Enhancement of Floating Offshore Wind Turbine Stabilization. *Int. J. Energy Res.* **2023**, *2023*, 4938451. [CrossRef]
27. Perdomo, O.; Wei, F.S. On the flapping motion of a helicopter blade: Applied Mathematics and Modeling. *Appl. Math. Model.* **2017**, *46*, 299–311. [CrossRef]
28. Wu, M.-Y.; Wu, Y.; Yuan, X.-Y.; Chen, Z.-H.; Wu, W.-T.; Aubry, N. Fast Prediction of Flow Field around Airfoils Based on Deep Convolutional Neural Network. *Appl. Sci.* **2022**, *12*, 12075. [CrossRef]
29. Prantl, L.; Bonev, B.; Thuerey, N. High-dimensional aerodynamic data modeling using a machine learning method based on a convolutional neural network. *Adv. Aerodyn.* **2017**, *1*, 15.
30. Moin, H.; Khan, H.Z.I.; Mobeen, S.; Riaz, J. Airfoil's Aerodynamic Coefficients Prediction using Artificial Neural Network. In Proceedings of the 2022 19th International Bhurban Conference on Applied Sciences and Technology (IBCAST), Islamabad, Pakistan, 16–20 August 2022; pp. 175–182.
31. Raissi, M.; Perdikaris, P.; Karniadakis, G.E. Physics-informed neural networks: A deep learning framework for solving forward and inverse problems involving nonlinear partial differential equations. *J. Comput. Phys.* **2019**, *378*, 686–707. [CrossRef]
32. Cordle, A.; Jonkman, J. State of the art in floating wind turbine design tools. In Proceedings of the ISOPE International Ocean and Polar Engineering Conference (ISOPE), Maui, HI, USA, 19–24 June 2011.
33. Santoni, C.; Khosronejad, A.; Seiler, P.; Sotiropoulos, F. Toward control co-design of utility-scale wind turbines: Collective vs. individual blade pitch control. *Energy Rep.* **2023**, *9*, 793–806. [CrossRef]
34. Shah, S.A.A.; Gao, B.; Ahmed, N.; Liu, C. Advanced robust control techniques for the stabilization of translational oscillator with rotational actuator based barge-type OFWT. *Proc. Inst. Mech. Eng. Part M J. Eng. Marit. Environ.* **2021**, *235*, 327–343. [CrossRef]
35. Stewart, G.M.; Lackner, M.A. The effect of actuator dynamics on active structural control of offshore wind turbines. *Eng. Struct.* **2011**, *33*, 1807–1816. [CrossRef]
36. Aslmostafa, E.; Hamida, M.A.; Plestan, F. Nonlinear control strategies for a floating wind turbine with PMSG in Region 2: A comparative study based on the OpenFAST platform. *Ocean Eng.* **2024**, *300*, 117507. [CrossRef]
37. Danayiyen, Y.; Dinçer, K.; Nuhoğlu, Y. A Novel Fractional Order Proportional Integral-Fractional Order Proportional Derivative Controller Design Based on Symbiotic Organisms Search Algorithm for Speed Control of a Direct Current Motor. *Electrica* **2024**, *24*, 327–335. [CrossRef]

38. Didier, F.; Liu, Y.-C.; Laghrouche, S.; Depernet, D. A Comprehensive Review on Advanced Control Methods for Floating Offshore Wind Turbine Systems above the Rated Wind Speed. *Energies* **2024**, *17*, 2257. [CrossRef]
39. Ibarra-Berastegi, G.; Sáenz, J.; Ulazia, A.; Serras, P.; Esnaola, G.; Garcia-Soto, C. Electricity production, capacity factor, and plant efficiency index at the Mutriku wave farm (2014–2016). *Ocean. Eng.* **2018**, *147*, 20–29. [CrossRef]
40. Komar, P.D.; Gaughan, M.K. Airy Wave Theory and Breaker Height Prediction. In Proceedings of the 13th International Conference on Coastal Engineering, Vancouver, BC, Canada, 10–14 July 1972; pp. 405–418.
41. Bretschneider, C.L. Wave Variability and Wave Spectra for Wind-Generated Gravity Waves (No. 118). Ph.D. Thesis, Texas A&M University, College Station, TX, USA, 1959.
42. Mazzaretto, O.M.; Menéndez, M.; Lobeto, H. A global evaluation of the JONSWAP spectra suitability on coastal areas. *Ocean Eng.* **2022**, *266*, 112756. [CrossRef]
43. Chaudhuri, A.; Datta, R.; Kumar, M.P.; Davim, J.P.; Pramanik, S. Energy Conversion Strategies for Wind Energy System: Electrical, Mechanical and Material Aspects. *Materials* **2022**, *15*, 1232. [CrossRef] [PubMed]
44. Aboutalebi, P.; Garrido, A.J.; Garrido, I.; Nguyen, D.T.; Gao, Z. Hydrostatic stability and hydrodynamics of a floating wind turbine platform integrated with oscillating water columns: A design study. *Renew. Energy* **2024**, *221*, 119824. [CrossRef]
45. Kim, D.; Bae, Y.H. Multibody Analysis of Wave Energy Converters and a Floating Platform in the Time Domain. *J. Mar. Sci. Eng.* **2024**, *12*, 265. [CrossRef]

Journal of
Marine Science and Engineering

MDPI

Article

Research on Decoupling Duty Cycle Optimization Control Method of a Multiport Converter for Dual-Port Direct Drive Wave Power Generation System

Lei Huang *, Shixiang Wang, Baoyi Pan, Haitao Liu, Jiyu Zhang and Shiquan Wu

School of Electrical Engineering, Southeast University, Nanjing 210096, China; wangshixiang@seu.edu.cn (S.W.); 220232860@seu.edu.cn (B.P.); 220213149@seu.edu.cn (H.L.); 230229410@seu.edu.cn (J.Z.); 220222725@seu.edu.cn (S.W.)

* Correspondence: huanglei@seu.edu.cn

Abstract: Dual-port direct drive wave energy power generation systems (DP-DDWEPGS) have received widespread attention due to their smooth and zero-free output power, compared to single-port direct drive wave energy power generation systems (SP-DDWEPGS) which have the disadvantage of large out-put power fluctuations. To further enhance the performance of the DP-DDWEPGS, optimal power capture control is proposed to achieve maximum power point tracking. Meanwhile, a multiport converter is applied to the DP-DDWEPGS to solve the problem caused by an excessive number of switching devices in the overall system converter. The multiport converter fulfills all the functional requirements of the DP-DDWEPGS while reducing the number of switching devices. However, switch multiplexing of the multiport converter also introduces coupling relationships between each port and the wave force exhibits time-varying characteristics, necessitating advanced control methods with superior fast-tracking capability. Therefore, in this paper, a decoupling duty cycle optimization model predictive control for DP-DDWEPGS is proposed. Based on the characteristics of switching multiplexing, NSC finite control set model predictive control (FCS-MPC) decouples the current prediction and the cost function, reduces the number of candidate voltage vectors in each operation, and shortens the operation time by 70%. To address the issues of high ripple value and increased error due to decoupling in FCS-MPC, duty cycle optimization control is added, greatly reducing the fluctuations in electromagnetic force and power of the permanent magnet linear generator (PMLG). Based on the established simulation model, the feasibility and superiority of the multiport converter and decoupling duty cycle optimization model predictive current control method are verified.

Keywords: dual-port direct drive wave energy power generation systems (DP-DDWEPGS); optimal power capture control; decoupling duty cycle optimization model predictive current control (MPCC-DD); nine-switch converter (NSC); hybrid energy storage system (HESS); permanent magnet linear generator (PMLG)

1. Introduction

Direct drive wave energy power generation systems (DDWEPGS) exhibit high energy conversion efficiency due to the elimination of gearboxes, hydraulic equipment and air compressor, compared with non-direct wave energy converters [1,2]. The DDWEPGS mainly consists of two configurations: the single-port direct drive wave energy power generation system (SP-DDWEPGS) and the dual-port direct drive wave energy power generation system (DP-DDWEPGS). The SP-DDWEPGS has only one power output port, whereas the DP-DDWEPGS is equipped with dual power output ports as shown in Figure 1 [3]. Under the driving of a wave, the velocity of the floats exhibits a periodic variation. As the float of the DP-DDWEPGS directly drives the translator of the linear permanent magnet generator (PMLG), the output power of the PMLG also varies in periodic fluctuation [4]. By adjusting the translators' electromagnetic force, the DP-DDWEPGS can achieve two complementary output powers, resulting in a total output power that is smooth and free of zero-crossings [5]. This feature makes the performance of the DP-DDWEPGS superior to that of the SP-DDWEPGS. But it is worth noting that DP-DDWEPGS employs a dual-electrical-ports dual-mechanical-ports machine system. This results in differences in the system dynamics and equivalent circuit compared to SP-DDWEPGS. Consequently, DP-DDWEPGS has a unique optimal power capture strategy that has not been extensively studied in previous literature.

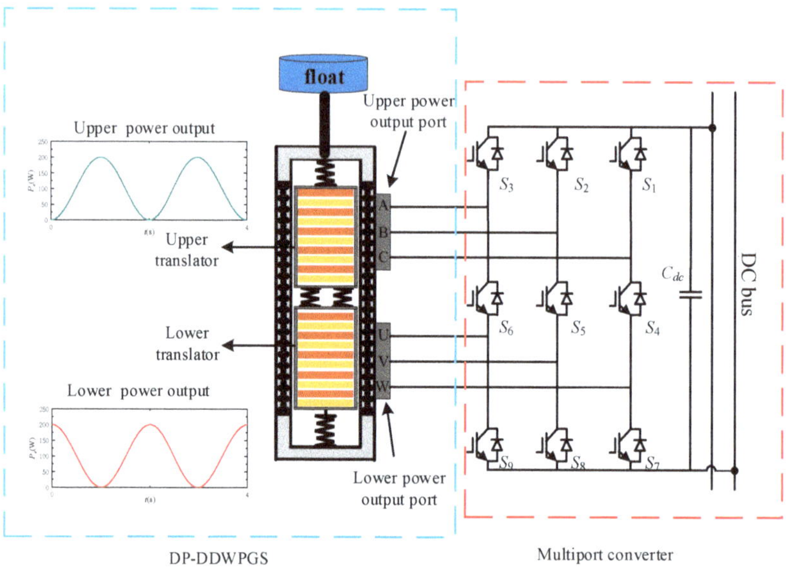

Figure 1. DP-DDWEPGS with multiport converter.

Meanwhile, the dual power outputs of the DP-DDWEPGS require two discrete three-phase voltage source rectifiers (VSRs). Due to the fluctuating nature of wave energy conversion, DP-DDWEPGS must be coupled with a hybrid energy storage system (HESS) through two sets of DC-DC converters. These converters result in an excessive number of switching devices in the overall system. This configuration leads to a higher failure rate, poor stability, and increased costs. To address these issues, the multiport converter was proposed to reduce the number of switching devices in the converter by sharing the switching legs, which provides excellent application prospects [6].

As a typical multiport converter, the nine-switch converter (NSC) features two AC ports and one DC port, as shown in Figure 1. The three ports of the NSC are derived by switch multiplexing two three-phase voltage source rectifiers (VSRs). While maintaining the full functions of VSRs, the NSC reduces the number of switching devices by 25% [7,8]. However, the control method of the NSC differs from that of the VSRs. Switch multiplexing introduces coupling relationships between the ports of the NSC, preventing the independent and free control of each port as is possible with VSRs [9–11]. Additionally, conventional linear controllers require different modulation strategies for the NSC under common-frequency and difference-frequency modes. This makes the conventional control methods for the NSC particularly complex, and it is difficult to achieve fast tracking with the linear controller in a nonlinear environment [12]. To address the issue, finite control set model predictive control (FCS-MPC) is applied to the NSC. FCS-MPC considers the voltage vectors corresponding to the switching states of the switching devices as a finite control set. In each calculation, it uses all the voltage vectors in the control set to predict the system behavior for the next state, then selects the switching state that can minimize the desired cost function. Compared to linear controllers, FCS-MPC is advantageous due to its fast response in dynamic processes, elimination of the need for a pulse width modulator, and its ability to easily incorporate nonlinearities and NSC system constraints [13]. The determination of the switching states in the finite control set of FCS-MPC has a significant impact on the overall control performance [14]. The NSC has a total of 27 switching states, as shown in Table A1 in Appendix A. Gao et al. [15] calculate the 27 switching states of NSC and sum the cost functions of the dual ports into a single overall cost function. However, calculating 27 switching states per operation imposes a significant burden on the microcontroller. Although there are 27 possible switching states for the NSC, some of these states are redundant. It is found that only 15 switching states are sufficient to control the dual AC loads independently. These 15 switching states are considered a finite solution set of predictive control schemes to minimize computation [16]. Furthermore, a dual predictive current control for NSC was proposed to separate the control of the induction generator from the grid control [17]. The two controllers operate alternately and independently to decouple the cost function. The finite control set contains only eight candidate voltage vectors, significantly reducing the computational burden, with extremely fast computational speed.

However, it is worth noting that the standard FCS-MPC applies only one voltage vector in each control cycle, resulting in a high ripple in the steady state [18]. To address this issue, an improved model predictive direct power control is proposed for a pulse width modulation rectifier by using a duty cycle control [19]. This approach introduces the concept of duty cycle control by allocating the operating time between non-zero voltage vectors and zero vectors within the control cycle. The non-zero vectors and their operating time are selected based on the principle of minimizing the effect of the non-zero vectors and the power error. In direct torque control, to reduce torque and flux ripples, a finite control set of new candidate voltage vectors with different duty cycles is synthesized by inserting zero vectors along the optimal voltage vectors [20].

Additionally, due to the volatility of the wave, the HESS is commonly used with DDWEPGS [21,22]. However, HESS connected to the DC bus through bidirectional DC-DC converters, which results in the redundancy of switching devices, high failure rate, and power multilevel flow [23]. An integrated dual-input DC-DC converter is proposed to address this problem, but it lacks research on power bidirectional flow [24].

In this paper, an equivalent circuit diagram of DP-DDWEPGS is established by hydrodynamic analysis. Based on the equivalent circuit diagram, optimal power capture control is proposed to achieve maximum power point tracking for DP-DDWEPGS. Meanwhile, a multiport converter is proposed to address the issues of high fault rates, high costs, and low stability caused by the excessive number of switching devices in DP-DDWEPGS. This multiport converter is derived by switch multiplexing two three-phase VSRs and two DC-DC converters and can perform all the functions of these converters while reducing the number of switching devices by 25%. However, the coupling relationships and constraints between the ports of the multiport converter make the design of linear controllers complex. The time-varying wave speed and displacement lead to time-varying electromagnetic forces in the generator, necessitating rapid control response. FCS-MPC is employed to meet these requirements. Furthermore, decoupling model predictive current control (MPCC-D) is proposed to decouple NSC dual ports and the cost function. As a result, the computational load is reduced by 80%, significantly speeding up the calculations. However, since MPCC-D applies a single voltage vector only once per control cycle and each control cycle activates only one port, it results in high ripple and increased fluctuations in steady state. Duty cycle optimization control is proposed to address this issue, allocating the operating time between optimal voltage vectors and zero voltage vectors in each control cycle, which greatly reduces ripple and fluctuations.

This paper is organized as follows: Section 2 details the optimal power capture analysis of the DP-DDWEPGS. Section 3 describes in detail the mathematical model analysis of DP-DDWEPGS. Section 4 provides an in-depth study of the improved FCS-MPC combining decoupling and duty cycle control. Section 5 verifies the feasibility of the proposed control strategy multi-port converter through simulation. Finally, the paper is summarized in Section 6.

2. Optimal Power Capture Analysis of the DP-DDWEPGS

The proposed DP-DDWEPGS consists of dual translators connected by the spring and a float rigidly connected to the upper translator. By analyzing the forces between them, the maximum power point can be obtained.

2.1. Hydrodynamic Model of Float

The decomposition of the forces acting on the float is shown in Figure 2. The hydrodynamic equations are as follows [1]:

$$m_b\ddot{x}(t) = F_{ex}(t) + F_{rad}(t) + F_h(t) - F_{line}(t) \tag{1}$$

where $x(t)$ is the float swing displacement with respect to the horizontal plane, m_b is the float mass, $F_{ex}(t)$ is the wave excitation force, $F_{rad}(t)$ is the radiation force, $F_h(t)$ is hydrostatic resilience, $F_{line}(t)$ is the rope force connecting the float to the power take off (PTO) device.

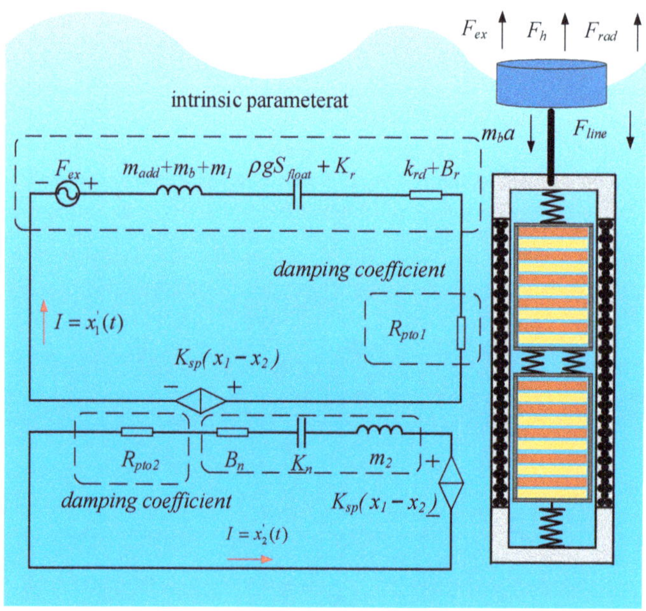

Figure 2. Equivalent circuit diagram of DP-DDWEPGS.

$F_{rad}(t)$ consists of two components, acceleration and velocity, and can be expressed in regular wave changes as

$$F_{rad}(t) = -k_{rd}\dot{x}(t) - m_{add}\ddot{x}(t) \tag{2}$$

where k_{rd} is the radiative damping and m_{add} is the added mass.

$F_h(t)$ can be obtained from the buoyancy equation

$$F_h(t) = -\rho g S_{float}x(t) \tag{3}$$

where ρ is the density of seawater, g is the acceleration of gravity, and S_{float} is the buoyant area of the float.

The hydrodynamic equilibrium equation can be obtained by bringing Equations (2) and (3) into Equation (1)

$$(m_{add} + m_b)\ddot{x}(t) + k_{rd}\dot{x}(t) + \rho g S_{float}x(t) = F_{ex}(t) - F_{line}(t) \tag{4}$$

2.2. Optimal Power Capture of DP-DDWEPGS

Decoupling the force on the float from the force on the PTO device leads to the force equation of the dual-translator

$$\begin{cases} m_1\ddot{x}_1(t) = F_{line}(t) - k_{sp}(x_1(t) - x_2(t)) - F_{em1}(t) - B_r\dot{x}_1(t) - K_r x_1(t) \\ m_2\ddot{x}_2(t) = k_{sp}(x_1(t) - x_2(t)) - F_{em2}(t) - B_n\dot{x}_2(t) - K_n x_2(t) \end{cases} \tag{5}$$

where m_1 and m_2 are the masses of the upper and lower translator, k_{sp} is the spring coefficient, $x_1(t)$and $x_2(t)$ are the dual translator displacements, $F_{em1}(t)$ and $F_{em2}(t)$ are the dual translator electromagnetic forces, K_r and B_r are the spring coefficient and elastic damping of the up end-stop spring, K_n and B_n are the spring coefficient and elastic damping of the restoring-spring.

When the PMLG moves coaxially with the PTO device, without considering the motion offset of the translator with respect to the device, in order to maximize the active power emitted by the PMLG, the electromagnetic force and velocity need to be kept in-phase in order to reduce the generation of reactive power [1], and hence the following can be obtained:

$$\begin{cases} F_{em1}(t) = R_{pto1}\dot{x}_1(t) \\ F_{em2}(t) = R_{pto2}\dot{x}_2(t) \end{cases} \tag{6}$$

where R_{pto1} and R_{pto1} are the damping coefficients of the upper translator and the lower translator.

From Equations (4) and (5), considering the upper translator is rigidly connected to the float, $x(\omega) = x_1(\omega)$, $x'(\omega) = x'_1(\omega)$, an equivalent circuit diagram can be obtained as shown in Figure 2, considering $m_{add} + m_b + m_1$ and m_2 as inductance values, $k_{rd} + B_r$ and B_n as resistance values, and $\rho g S_{float} + K_r$ and K_n as capacitance values. These parameters are referred to as the intrinsic parameters of the wave power generator. $k_{sp}(x_1 - x_2)$ is considered as a controlled voltage source. The velocity of the float is then equivalent to the current in the first circuit of Figure 2, and the velocity of the lower translator is equivalent to the current in the second circuit with a controlled voltage source of Figure 2.

Bringing (6) into Equation (5) and performing the Laplace transform, then converting to the frequency domain yields:

$$\frac{x_1(\omega)}{x_2(\omega)} = \frac{k_{sp} - \omega^2 m_2 + j\omega(R_{pto2} + B_n) + K_n}{k_{sp}} \tag{7}$$

In DP-DDWEPGS, the velocity phase difference between the dual translators is $\pi/2$, which leads to the following equation:

$$k_{sp} + K_n = \omega^2 m_2 \tag{8}$$

The total output power of DP-DDWEPGS is the sum of the output power of the dual translators, in order to ensure the stability of the total instantaneous power and reduce the power superposition fluctuations, the ideal output power of the dual translators should have the same amplitude, which can be obtained from the following conditions:

$$F_{em1}(\omega)x'_1(\omega) = F_{em2}(\omega)x'_2(\omega) = \frac{1}{2}P_{pto} \tag{9}$$

Let $x_1'(\omega) = \lambda x_2'(\omega)$, at a single frequency, λ is a constant.

Performing the Laplace transform transforms Equations (4) and (5) into the frequency domain, combining with $x(\omega) = x_1(\omega)$, $x'(\omega) = x'_1(\omega)$ and $\lambda = x_1'(\omega)/x_2'(\omega)$ gives

$$\begin{cases} F_{ex}(\omega) = j\omega(m_{add} + m_b + m_1)x'(\omega) + (k_{rd} + B_r)x'(\omega) \\ \quad +(\rho g S_{float} + K_r)\frac{x'(\omega)}{j\omega} + F_{em1} + k_{sp}(x_1(\omega) - x_2(\omega)) \\ k_{sp}(x_1(\omega) - x_2(\omega)) = j\omega m_2 x_2'(\omega) + F_{em2} + B_n x_2'(\omega) + K_n\frac{x_2'(\omega)}{j\omega} \end{cases} \tag{10}$$

Combining the two formulas in Equation (10) and bringing in $\lambda = x_1'(\omega)/x_2'(\omega)$ yields

$$\begin{aligned} F_{ex}(\omega) &= j\omega(m_{add} + m_b + m_1 + \tfrac{m_2}{\lambda})x'(\omega) + (k_{rd} + B_r + \tfrac{B_n}{\lambda})x'(\omega) \\ &\quad +(\rho g S_{float} + K_r + \tfrac{K_n}{\lambda})\frac{x'(\omega)}{j\omega} + (1+\lambda)R_{pto1}x'(\omega) \end{aligned} \tag{11}$$

The principle of analog circuits can be employed to determine the optimal R_{pto}. In Equation (11), the upper translator velocity $x'(\omega)$ is used as the current and the excitation force $F_{ex}(\omega)$ is used as the voltage, and the damping coefficient $(1 + \lambda)R_{pto1}$ is used as the resistance value. To achieve the maximum power from waves for the DP-DDWEPGS, the damping coefficient of the generator is equal to the modulus of the intrinsic parameter of the wave power generator, and the damping coefficient is

$$\begin{cases} (1+\lambda)R_{pto1} = \sqrt{[\omega(m_{add} + m_b + m_1 + \frac{m_2}{\lambda}) - \frac{1}{\omega}(\rho g S_{float} + K_r + \frac{K_n}{\lambda})]^2 + (k_{rd} + B_r + \frac{B_n}{\lambda})^2} \\ R_{pto2} = \lambda^2 R_{pto1} \end{cases} \tag{12}$$

3. Mathematical Model Analysis of DP-DDWEPGS

The proposed multiport converter applied to DP-DDWEPGS consists of a nine-switch converter (NSC) and an integrated DC-DC converter, and its topology and control block diagram are shown in Figure 3. NSC is interfaced with a dual-port permanent magnet linear generator (DP-PMLG), functioning as a rectifier. Concurrently, an integrated bidirectional DC-DC converter facilitates the connection between the DC bus and the HESS to maintain power stability on the load side.

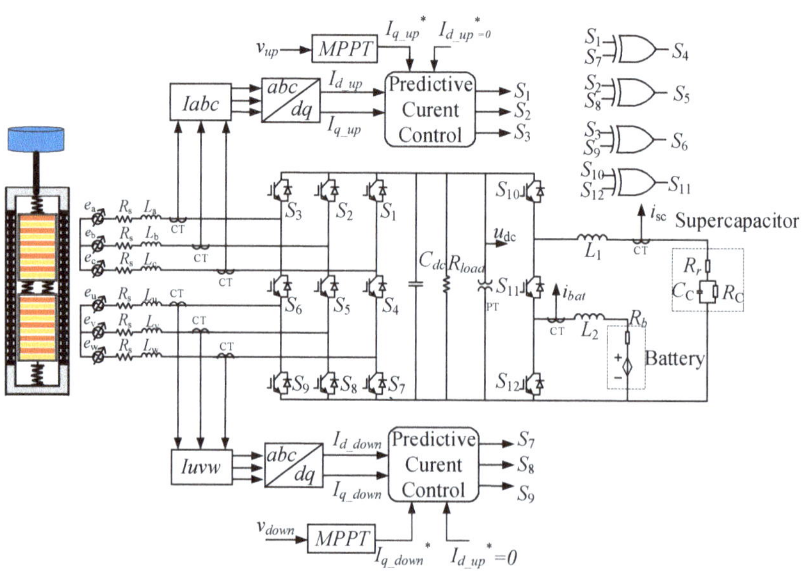

Figure 3. Topology and control block diagram of proposed multiport converter.

3.1. Mathematical Modeling of DP-DDWEPGS' Generator Side

The nine-switch converter configuration is derived from the back-to-back converter through switch multiplexing. In this arrangement, each of the AC terminals is linked to either $+V_{dc}$ or ground, necessitating two switches to be active and one switch to be inactive in each leg of the converter. This constraint yields three distinct switching states per leg, amounting to a total of 27 switching states, as elaborated in Table A1.

Dual translators of the PMLG in DPDDWEPGS have identical parameters; therefore, only one port needs to be analyzed. According to the generator convention, the voltage equation of PMLG in the d/q coordinate system, which is based on mover magnetic field orientation, can be obtained as follows [25]

$$\begin{cases} u_d = -R_s i_d - L_d \frac{di_d}{dt} + \frac{\pi v}{\tau} L_q i_q \\ u_q = \frac{\pi v}{\tau} \psi_f - R_s i_q - L_q \frac{di_q}{dt} - \frac{\pi v}{\tau} L_d i_d \end{cases} \tag{13}$$

where u_d, i_d is the voltage and current of the d-axis equivalent winding, u_q, i_q is the voltage and current of the q-axis equivalent winding, L_d, L_q is the inductance of the d-axis and q-axis equivalent windings, τ is pole pitch of PMLG, and ψ_f is the flux-linkage of the permanent magnet.

The active power can be expressed as

$$P_{em} = \frac{3\pi v}{2\tau}(\psi_f i_q + (L_d - L_q) i_d i_q) \tag{14}$$

If $i_d = 0$ control strategy is used, the electromagnetic force of PMLG can be expressed as

$$F_{em} = R_{PTO} v = \frac{P_{em}}{v} = \frac{3\pi}{2\tau} \psi_f i_q \tag{15}$$

Conventional model predictive current control (MPCC) for the derivative phase of electron current, discretized using the Eulerian approximation

$$\frac{di}{dt} \approx \frac{i(k+1) - i(k)}{T_s} \tag{16}$$

According to Equations (13) and (16), d/q axis predictive current can be expressed as

$$\begin{cases} i_d(k+1) = (1 - T_s \frac{R_s}{L_d}) i_d(k) + T_s \frac{\pi v(k)}{\tau} \frac{L_q}{L_d} i_q(k) - T_s \frac{u_d(k)}{L_d} \\ i_q(k+1) = (1 - T_s \frac{R_s}{L_d}) i_q(k) + T_s \frac{\pi v(k)}{\tau L_q} \psi_f - T_s \frac{\pi v}{\tau} \frac{L_d}{L_q} i_d(k) - T_s \frac{u_q(k)}{L_q} \end{cases} \tag{17}$$

The MPCC for dual translators is consistent in both Equation (17), and the cost function. The $i_d = 0$ control strategy is implemented in this system, and the q axis current is controlled to achieve target damping. The cost function is used to realize the fast following of the actual current to the reference value of d/q axis current. Therefore, the cost function of the upper translator and lower translator are expressed as

$$\begin{cases} g_{up\_j} = (i^*_{d\_up}(k+1) - i_{d\_up}(k+1))^2 + (i^*_{q\_up}(k+1) - i_{q\_up}(k+1))^2 \\ g_{down\_j} = (i^*_{d\_down}(k+1) - i_{d\_down}(k+1))^2 + (i^*_{q\_down}(k+1) - i_{q\_down}(k+1))^2 \end{cases} \tag{18}$$

where g_{up_j} is the cost function of the upper translator, and g_{down_j} is the cost function of the lower translator. The reference value of i_q at MPPT (maximum power point tracking) can be obtained from Equations (6), (12), and (15)

$$\begin{cases} i^*_{q\_up}(k+1) = \frac{2\tau}{3\pi\psi_f} R_{pto1} v_1(k) \\ i^*_{q\_down}(k+1) = \frac{2\tau}{3\pi\psi_f} R_{pto2} v_2(k) \end{cases} \tag{19}$$

Considering the upper translator and lower translator have an equal effect [15], the total cost function is written as

$$J = g_{up\_j} + g_{down\_j} \tag{20}$$

3.2. Mathematical Modeling of DP-DDWEPGS' Hybrid Energy Storage System Side

The integrated bidirectional DC-DC converter is achieved through switch multiplexing, like the nine-switch converter. However, it differs in that all three of its ports are DC-powered. In this study, a HESS comprising supercapacitors and batteries is employed to mitigate system power fluctuations. The supercapacitor handles high-frequency power fluctuations, while the battery addresses low-frequency variations. This configuration offers benefits such as rapid response, prolonged service life, and cost-effectiveness.

In addressing wave power fluctuations, the equilibrium of power required to stabilize the total power within the DC link is delineated into two distinct components [26]: (1) average power component P_{avg} and (2) transient power component P_{tran}. The power balance equation can be articulated as follows:

$$P_{load} - P_g = P_{sc} + P_{bat} = P_{tran} + P_{avg} \tag{21}$$

where P_{load} is the load power and P_g is the generator power, the requisite net power to stabilize the DC bus voltage within a designated range can be expressed as follows:

$$P_{tran} + P_{avg} = i_{tot} u_{dc} \tag{22}$$

where i_{tot} denotes the total current, u_{dc} is the busbar voltage, it is acknowledged that i_{tot} comprises a transient current component i_{tran}, and an average current component i_{avg}, with i_{tran} being the reference current for the supercapacitor and i_{avg} being the reference amount for the battery current. Their reference values can be obtained as

$$\begin{cases} i_{bat}^*(s) = i_{avg}(s) = \frac{\omega_c}{s+\omega_c} i_{tot}(s) \\ i_{sc}^*(s) = i_{tran}(s) = i_{tot}(s) - i_{avg}(s) \end{cases} \tag{23}$$

where ω_c is the cutoff frequency of the LPF.

4. Decoupling Duty Cycle Optimization Model Predictive Control

4.1. Model Predictive Control of NSC

The voltage vector model of the NSC forms the basis for the current model prediction and cost function evaluation steps. In this context, NSC for DP-DDWEPGS, with its 27 voltage vectors, is utilized, as shown in Table A1. The cost function, which encompasses all variables of the dual-port system, is predicted using a conventional current model. We refer to this type of control as MPCC, and its control algorithm is shown in Figure 4.

The algorithm to derive the optimal voltage vector requires 27 calculations, shown in Table A1, which poses a computationally intensive task for an embedded system. Additionally, the algorithm centralizes the variables of the upper and lower ports into a single cost function. This approach results in a cost function that is dominated by the port with the higher current difference, consequently ignoring the port with the lower current difference.

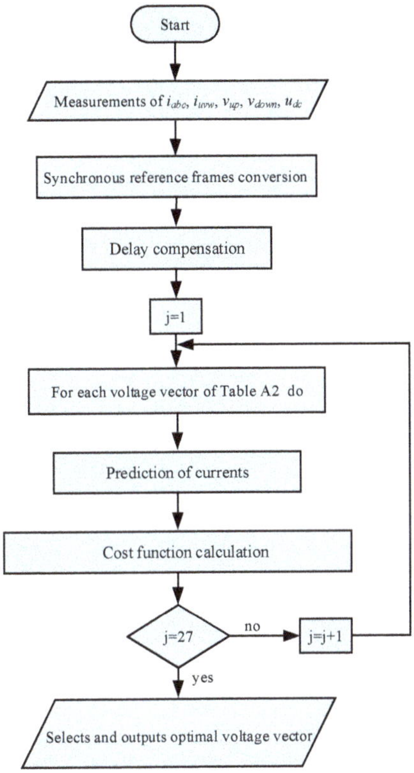

Figure 4. Flowchart of overall control algorithm of MPCC.

4.2. Decoupling MPCC

NSC is derived from the back-to-back converter through switch-multiplexing, which allows the NSC to function as a dual-port converter while maintaining the same control strategy as the back-to-back converter. This is achieved through the decoupling strategy proposed in this paper (MPCC-D). The decoupling strategy is outlined as follows: when the lower three switches are all on, the upper port operates as a three-phase VSR, referred to as state A, as shown in Figure 5a. Conversely, when the upper three switches are all on, the lower port operates as a three-phase VSR, referred to as state B, as shown in Figure 5b.

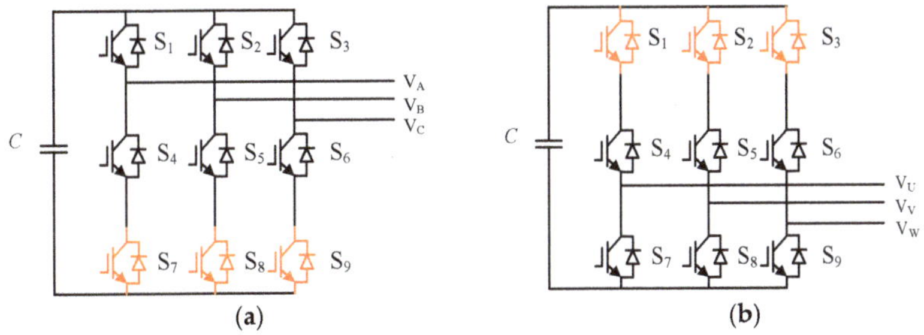

Figure 5. Decoupling strategy. (**a**) State A ([S_7, S_8, S_9] = [1, 1, 1]); (**b**) State B ([S_1, S_2, S_3] = [1, 1, 1]).

In state A, the upper port three-phase VSR has only eight voltage vectors (V_0~V_7 shown in Table A1), and in state B, the lower port three-phase VSR also has only eight voltage vectors (V_0~V_7). Decoupling of the upper and lower port MPCC is achieved when the upper and lower port MPCC are operated alternately, with each MPCC operating at half the discretization time, as shown in Figure 6. At this time, the cost function also realizes decoupling and is divided into two parts corresponding to each port (24).

$$\begin{cases} J_{stateA} = g_{up\_j} \\ J_{stateB} = g_{down\_j} \end{cases} \tag{24}$$

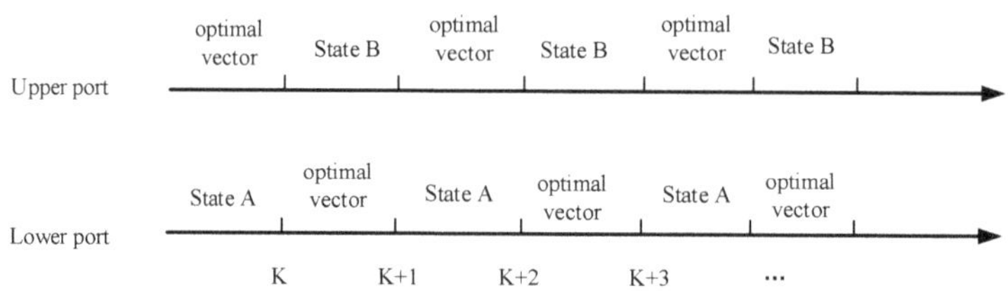

Figure 6. Port operation timing in discrete time.

After the decoupling of the dual ports of the NSC and cost function, the optimal voltage vector can be obtained with only eight calculations, greatly reducing the computation time. At the same time, since states A and B are composed of zero vectors [1, 1, 1], each port inserts zero vectors between the optimal voltage vectors, creating a time gap. This process eliminates the delay from the prediction stage, making the delay compensation link unnecessary.

4.3. Duty Cycle Optimization of Decoupling MPCC

To reduce ripple and fluctuations in maximum power point tracking and electromotive force, decoupling duty cycle optimization model predictive current control (MPCC-DD) is proposed in this paper. This method targets the given value of i_q from Equation (20) and, by adjusting the action time of the optimal voltage vector and the zero vector, ensures that the actual value of i_q is exactly equal to its given value before the end of the next control cycle. Figure 7 shows the schematic diagram of the dead beat.

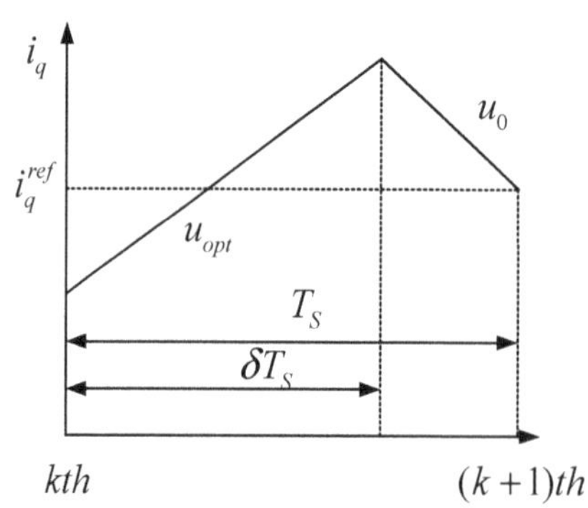

Figure 7. Schematic diagram of dead beat.

From Figure 7, it can be seen that the optimal voltage vector u_{opt} combined with the zero vector u_0 acts in the same control cycle. The predicted value of i_q at the moment of $(k + 1)$ is equal to the given value of i_q from MPPT. δ is the duty cycle of u_{opt}.

Derivation of Equation (13) with respect to time yields

$$\frac{di_q}{dt} = \frac{-u_q + \omega_r \psi_f - R_s i_q}{L_q} - \omega_r i_d \tag{25}$$

According to Equation (25), the slope of i_q after the action of different voltage vectors can be obtained as follows:

$$\begin{cases} S_0 = \frac{di_q}{dt}\Big|_{u_q=0} = \frac{\omega_r\psi_f - R_s i_q}{L_q} - \omega_r i_d \\ S_{opt} = \frac{di_q}{dt}\Big|_{u_q=u_{opt}} = \frac{\omega_r\psi_f - R_s i_q}{L_q} - \omega_r i_d - \frac{u_q}{L_q} \end{cases} \tag{26}$$

where S_0 denotes the i_q slope corresponding to the zero vector, and S_{opt} denotes the i_q slope corresponding to the optimal voltage vector.

Making the value of i_q at the next moment equal to the given value of i_q^{ref}, the equation for i_q is given by

$$i_q(k+1) = i_q^{ref} = i_q(k) + S_{opt}\delta T_s + S_0(1-\delta)T_s \tag{27}$$

The optimal vector duty cycle can be obtained

$$\delta = \frac{i_q^{ref} - i_q(k) - S_0 T_s}{(S_{opt} - S_0)T_s} = \frac{i_q^{ref} - i_q(k) - T_s\left(\frac{\omega_r\psi_f - R_s i_q(k)}{L_q} - \omega_r i_q(k)\right)}{\left(-\frac{u_q(k)}{L_q}\right)T_s} \tag{28}$$

Since the parameters of the dual translator are the same, except for the different i_q^{ref}, the other control modes are exactly the same, and the specific control diagram is shown in Figure 8.

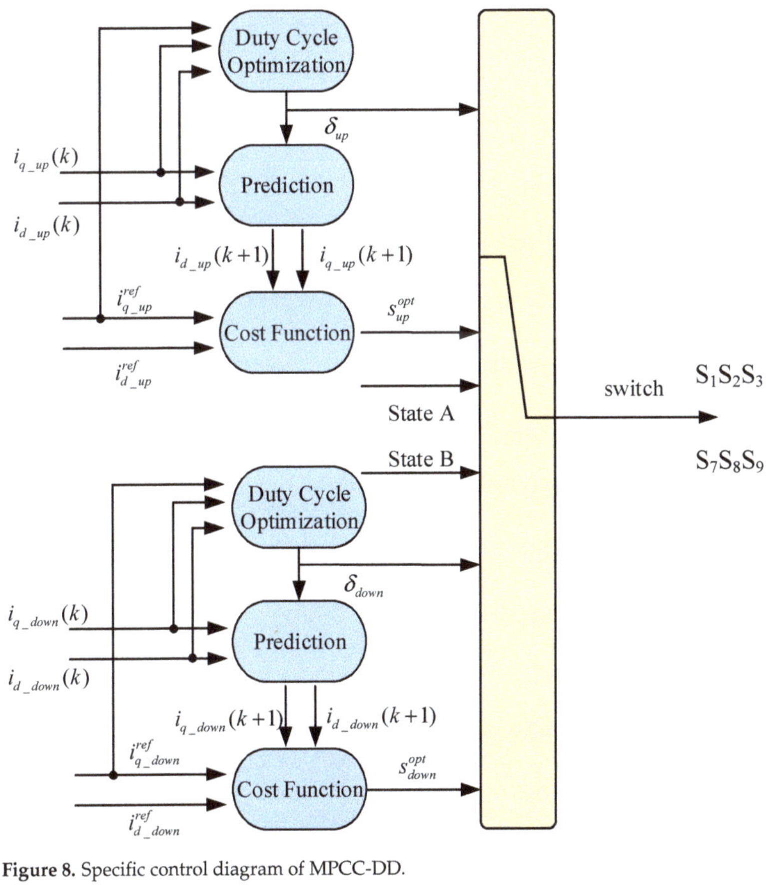

Figure 8. Specific control diagram of MPCC-DD.

The MPCC of the NSC dual ports is alternated and the duty cycle optimization calculation is added so that the acting voltage vector and zero vector work together to reduce the maximum power point fluctuation. We refer to this type of control as MPCC-DD, and its overall control algorithm is shown in Figure 9.

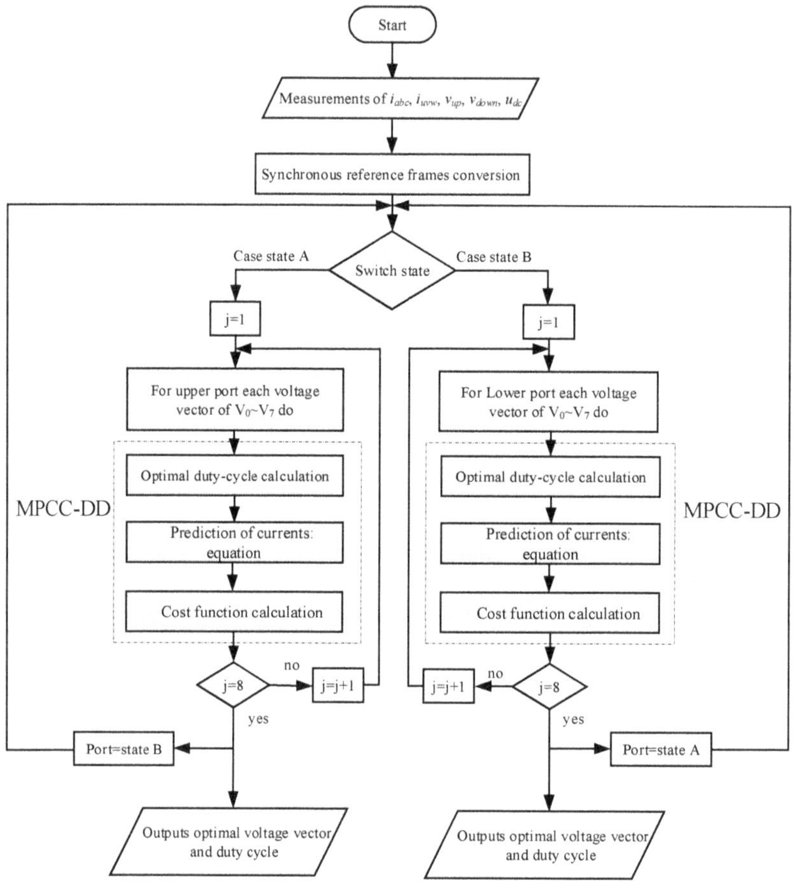

Figure 9. Flowchart of overall control algorithm of MPCC-DD.

5. Simulation Results and Analysis of DP-DDWEPGS

This section introduces the implementation of MPCC-DD under local optimal energy capture. The parameters of the PMLG are as follows (dual translators have the same parameters): L_d = 0.045 H, L_q = 0.045 H, Ψ_f = 5 Wb, τ = 0.1 m. DC load is 120 Ω and DC bus voltage is 200 V.

5.1. Local Optimal Power Capture

According to the sea conditions along the coast of China, the JONSWAP spectrum with a period T of 6.5 s and a significant wave height H_s of 1.75 m is selected [27]. The excitation force on the float from the irregular waves can be obtained. By performing a fast Fourier transform, five main frequencies of the wave excitation force can be identified, with the decomposed parameters listed in Table 1. It is shown in Figure 10 that the fitting excitation force at the selected five main frequencies basically matches the original excitation force and can be a good substitute for it.

Table 1. Main frequency of excitation force.

Frequency (Hz)	Amplitude (N)	Phase (rad)
$f_1 = 0.0333$	876	1.6057
$f_2 = 0.1$	3023	−0.40143
$f_3 = 0.1333$	3541	0.05236
$f_4 = 0.1667$	4009	2.1468
$f_5 = 0.2667$	1098	−0.8203

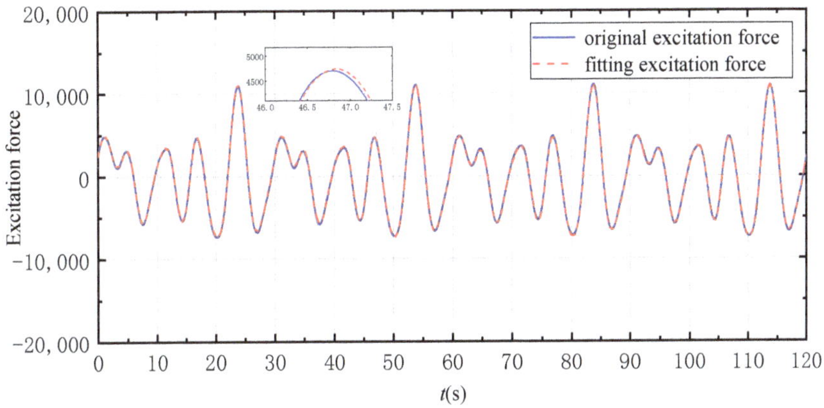

Figure 10. Fitting excitation force and original excitation force.

In practice, it is challenging for the PMLG to accurately track different frequency points simultaneously, and the spring in the DP-DDWEPGS exhibits a delay in adjustment between different frequencies. Therefore, the local optimal power is selected in the paper for further analysis. According to Equations (10) and (12), the power captured by DP-DDWEPGS at a single frequency can be obtained, as shown in formula (29).

$$P_i = \frac{{F_{exi}}^2 R_{pto}}{\left[\omega_i m_\Sigma - \frac{1}{\omega_i}(\rho g S_{float} + k_r + \frac{k_{l1}}{\lambda})\right]^2 + \left[k_{rd} + B_r + \frac{B_{l1}}{\lambda} + R_{pto}\right]^2} \tag{29}$$

where ω_i (i = 1, 2, 3, 4, 5) is the frequency selected from Table 1, F_{exi} is the amplitude of the excitation force corresponding to ω_i, P_i is the power captured by the DP-DDWEPGS with frequency ω_i, $R_{pto} = R_{pto1} + R_{pto2}/\lambda$, $m_\Sigma = m_{add} + m_b + m_1 + m_2/\lambda$.

The power corresponding to each of the five frequencies is calculated through Equation (29), as shown in Figure 11. Each of the five frequencies has its respective optimal damping coefficient, where P_i (i = 1, 2, 3, 4, 5) reaches its maximum value. It can be observed that ω_4 is the frequency with the maximum power in the excitation force.

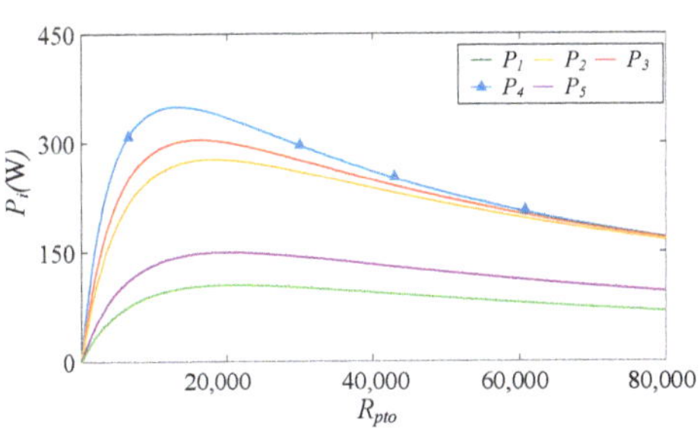

Figure 11. Output power for each frequency.

Meanwhile, the optimal damping coefficient derived from ω_4 allows the system to capture the maximum power, as detailed in Table 2. Therefore, the associated R_{pto} of ω_4 is chosen as the local optimal damping coefficient of the generator for this paper.

Table 2. Total power at five optimal damping coefficients of main frequency of excitation force.

R_{pto}	ΣP_i (i = 1, 2, 3, 4, 5) (W)
21,110 (f_1 = 0.0333)	1162.43
18,003 (f_2 = 0.1)	1168.67
15,911 (f_3 = 0.1333)	1177.58
13,190 (f_4 = 0.1667)	1180.03
20,110 (f_5 = 0.2667)	1166.77

5.2. Comparison of MPCC, MPCC-D, MPCC-DD

Based on the analysis in Section 5.1, the local optimal damping coefficient can be determined. And in Equation (6), the local optimal damping coefficient is used to establish the reference value for the electromagnetic forces of the dual translators under optimal power capture. The electromagnetic force of the PMLG is controlled by the armature current. In this paper, zero d-axis current control is employed, and the electromagnetic force is related to the q-axis current, as described in Equation (15). To match the electromagnetic force with the local optimal damping coefficient, the i_q reference value is calculated through Equation (15). Meanwhile, three control methods are implemented in this paper to control the q-axis current of the PMLG to achieve maximum power capture. Based on the previous analysis, frequency ω_4 of the excitation force has the maximum power. To compare and verify the effectiveness of the controllers, a simulation model based on the excitation force at the frequency ω_4 is established, and comparative simulations are conducted to evaluate the performance of the three controllers. The simulation results are presented in Figure 12.

The q-axis current tracking under MPCC, MPCC-D, and MPCC-DD is shown in Figure 12, where $\Delta i_{q\_up} = i_{q\_upref} - i_{q\_up}$, $\Delta i_{q\_down} = i_{q\_downref} - i_{q\_down}$.

Figure 12a–f show the dual translators' reference and actual currents of the q-axis. Due to the decoupling control of the dual ports, where only one port operates per control cycle, the current ripple in MPCC-D is larger compared to MPCC. Therefore, this paper introduces duty cycle optimization control. As seen in Figure 12c,f, the current ripple in MPCC-DD is significantly reduced. This demonstrates that decomposing a control cycle into the operation of optimal and zero voltage vectors can effectively address the issue of large current ripple in model predictive current control. This improvement is achieved without adding other voltage vectors, meaning that the computational load does not increase significantly.

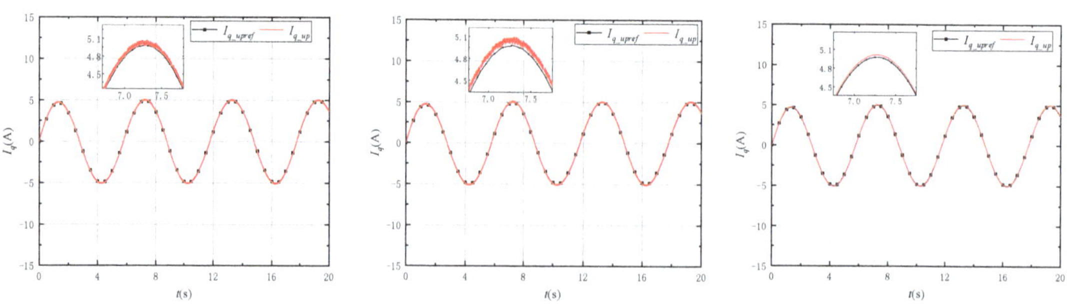

(a) (b) (c)

Figure 12. *Cont.*

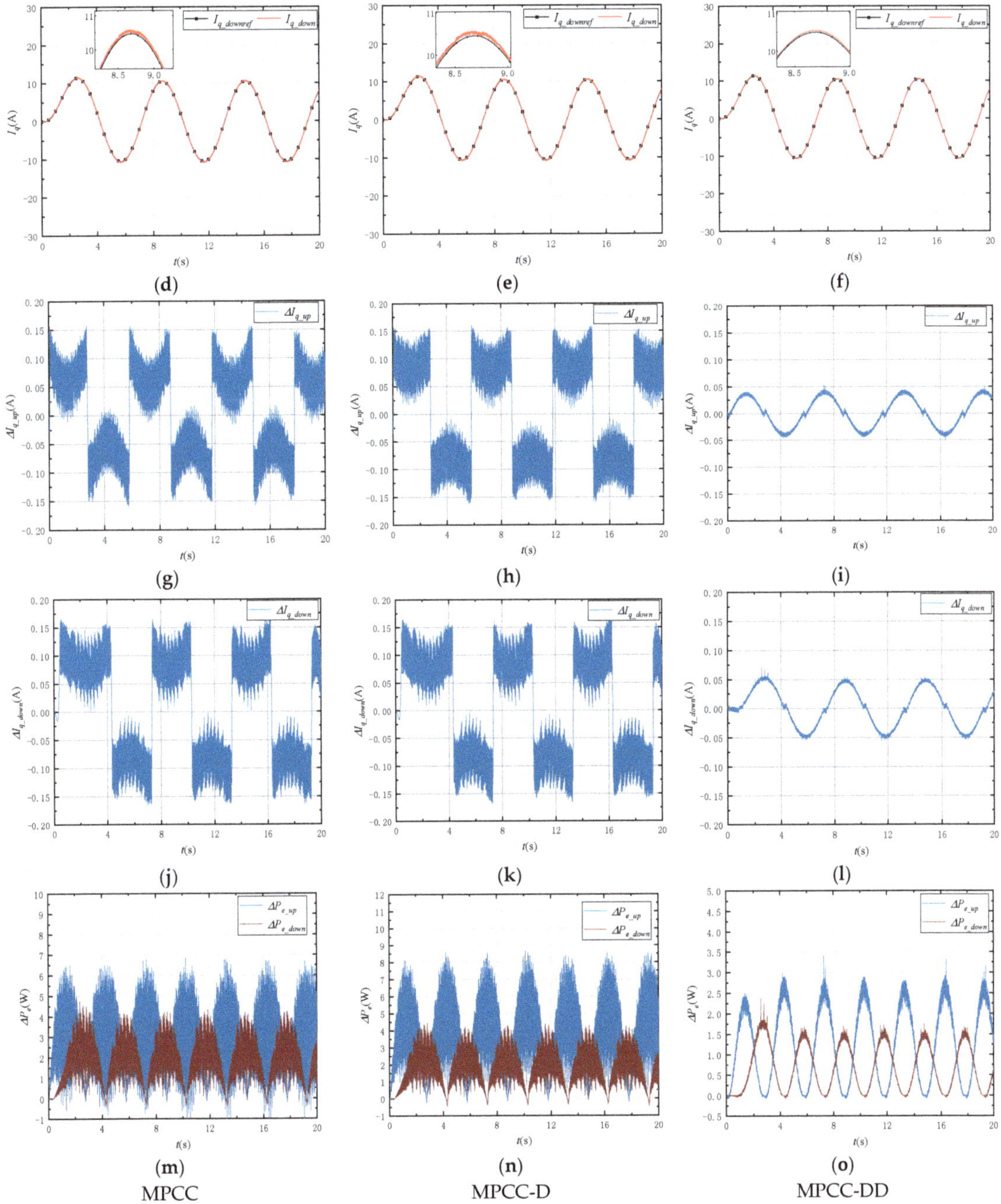

Figure 12. Simulation results under MPCC, MPCC-D, and MPCC-DD. (**a**) i_q of upper translator; (**b**) i_q of dual translator; (**c**) i_q of dual translator; (**d**) i_q of lower translator; (**e**) i_q of lower translator; (**f**) i_q of lower translator; (**g**) Δi_{q_up} of upper translator; (**h**) Δi_{q_up} of upper translator; (**i**) Δi_{q_up} of upper translator; (**j**) Δi_{q_down} of lower translator; (**k**) Δi_{q_down} of lower translator; (**l**) Δi_{q_down} of lower translator; (**m**) Δp_e of dual translator; (**n**) Δp_e of dual translator; (**o**) Δp_e of dual translator.

The differences between the reference and actual currents of the q-axis are shown in Figure 12g–l. These results more intuitively illustrate the advantage of duty cycle optimization in reducing the current ripple. In conventional MPCC, the cost function is the sum of the dual ports' cost functions, as shown in Equations (18) and (19). Consequently, due to the different current magnitudes between the dual ports, the port with the larger current error will dominate the cost function. It is revealed in Figure 12g,j that the current error values for the dual ports are not the same. However, in MPCC-D, the ports are decoupled, and the cost function only reflects the error for the present port under the optimal voltage vector, as shown in Equation (24). Therefore, in MPCC-D, each port selects the optimal voltage vector that minimizes its own error without being influenced by the other port. Consequently, it is shown in Figure 12h,k that the current error values for the dual ports in MPCC-D are nearly identical. And the mutations in Figure 12g,h,j,k result from the velocity commutation of the PMLG translators. Since i_q is proportional to the velocity, at the moment of translator velocity commutation, the value of Δi_q is near its maximum, abruptly changing from positive to negative, thereby causing a mutation. In Figure 12i,l, the commutation mutation is small because the Δi_q value is close to zero at the moment of the translator's velocity commutation.

The error between the theoretical and actual values of power under MPCC, MPCC-D, and MPCC-DD is shown in Figure 12m–o, where $\Delta P_e = P_{e\_ref} - P_e$. In the PMLG used in this paper, $L_d = L_q$, so Equation (14) describes the relationship between i_q and active power. The ripples in active power are primarily caused by that in i_q in the PMLG. In Equation (15), the electromagnetic force of the PMLG is also related to i_q. Under the influence of MPCC-DD, the ripples in i_q are significantly reduced, as shown in Figure 12c,f,i,l. Consequently, the ripples in active power are also greatly reduced, as depicted in Figure 12m–o. This indicates that in MPCC-DD, the active power is much closer to the theoretical value calculated by MPPT, thereby reducing active power loss.

The time required for each main control part of the MPCC, MPCC-D, and MPCC-DD during one execution is shown in Table 3. In the MPCC-D, the control mode is divided into state A and state B, achieving decoupling operation. Decoupling operation only requires the calculation of 8 switching vectors each time, and States A and B alternate during the process, resulting in the computational load of MPCC-D being approximately 20% of that of MPCC. Because of adding the duty cycle optimization, MPCC-DD has a slightly longer operation time than MPCC-D. The switching states of the NSC under MPCC-DD are shown in Figure 13, with state A and state B alternating to achieve decoupling control, accompanied by optimal duty cycle regulation.

Table 3. Time Required for Each Main Control Part Each Cycle.

Control Method	MPCC	MPCC-D	MPCC-DD
Voltage vectors calculations and conversion (10^{-6} s)	18.821	2.836	2.915
Predictions (10^{-6} s)	3.498	0.5	0.563
Cost functions (10^{-6} s)	1.054	0.269	0.274
Duty cycle optimization (10^{-6} s)	—	—	3.078
Else (10^{-6} s)	2.127	1.518	1.775
Total tome(10^{-6} s)	25.5	5.123	8.605

Under the zero d-axis current control strategy, the d-axis current affects the reactive power. The d-axis currents of MPCC and MPCC-DD are shown in Figure 14, and it can be observed that the fluctuation of d-axis currents in MPCC-DD is slightly larger compared with MPCC but remains within the acceptable range. This is because duty cycle control is used in this paper for the q-axis current, which is prioritized in the cost function of Equation (18). However, the simulation results show that MPCC-DD significantly reduces the q-axis current error and ripple, far outweighing the slight increase in the d-axis current error. Moreover, the d-axis current error remains within the acceptable range.

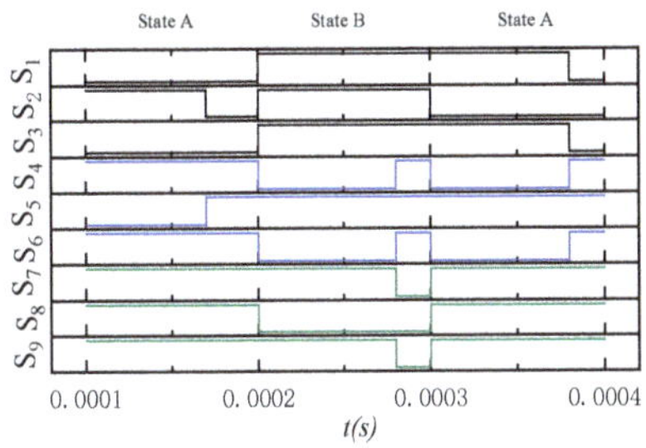

Figure 13. Switching state of the NSC.

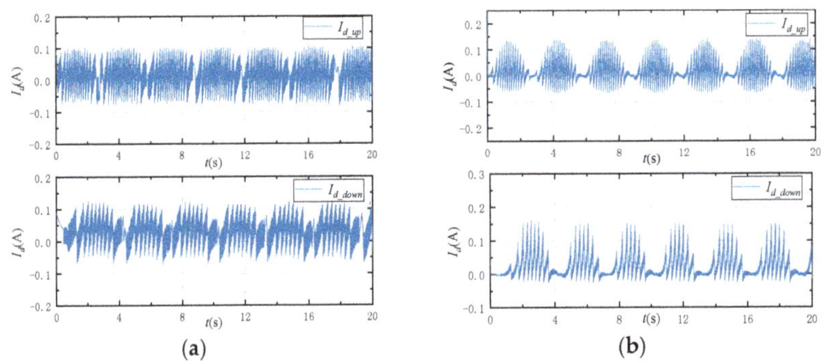

Figure 14. d-axis current. (**a**) i_d of dual translator (MPCC); (**b**) i_d of dual translator (MPCC-DD).

5.3. Simulation Analysis of the Control Effect Whole System

To verify the effectiveness of the proposed control method and optimal power capture strategy, a simulation model of the whole system with generators, NSC, and MPC controllers is built. In addition, different control results with regular wave excitation force under optimal frequency and irregular wave excitation force as JONSWAP spectrum are obtained and analyzed.

5.3.1. Simulation of Optimal Frequency Point of Overall System Operation

With regular wave excitation force, the output power of DP-DDWEPGS, the current of HESS, and the DC voltage of NSC are obtained and shown in Figures 15 and 16.

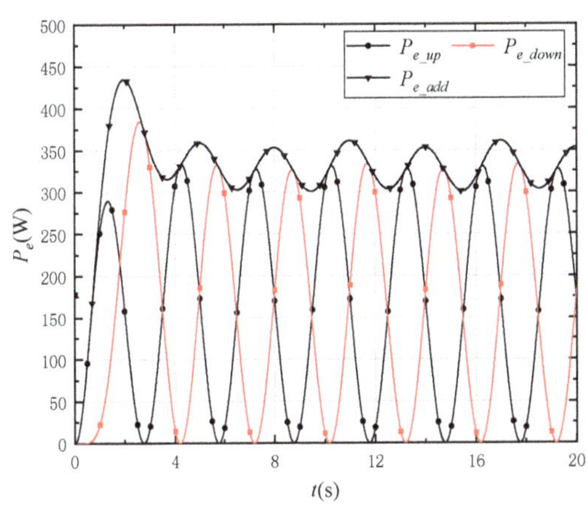

Figure 15. Instantaneous power relationship diagram of dual-translators in DP-DDWEPGS.

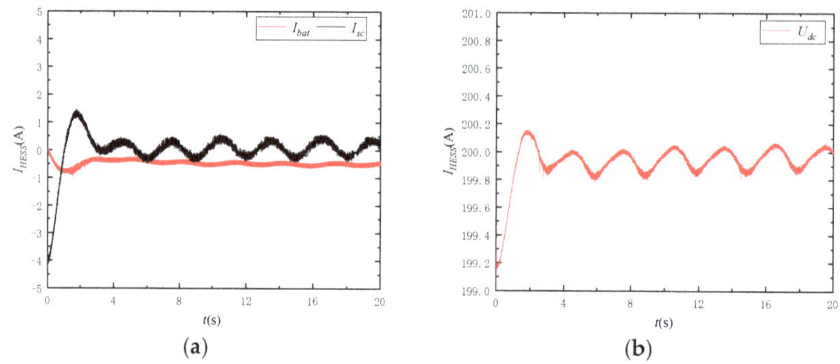

Figure 16. The current and voltage of DC side. (**a**) Current of HESS; (**b**) DC-bus voltage.

As shown in Figure 15. The instantaneous power of the dual translators is complementary, resulting in a smooth, zero-free, and consistent total output instantaneous power, which reduces the impact on the load-side power. Consequently, HESS responds to the high-frequency and low-frequency power with a small amplitude of the response current, as shown in Figure 16a. The supercapacitor suppresses the high-frequency power fluctuation, while the battery suppresses the low-frequency power fluctuation, ensuring that the DC bus voltage is stabilized at a given value. As shown in Figure 16b, the steady-state fluctuation of the DC voltage is 0.2 V, indicating that the system performs well.

5.3.2. Operation Results of DP-DDWEPGS in Irregular Waves

Under the irregular wave excitation force of the JONSWAP spectrum, the generator damping factor of the upper and lower translator is controlled to achieve full complementarity and the optimal damping coefficient under optimal frequency ω_4, as shown in Figure 11. And the simulation results are obtained and shown in Figures 17–19. Firstly, as the current i_q is used to control the electromagnetic force of generators and implement damping control, the different currents $i_{q,}$ under different frequency wave excitation force obtained by Fourier decomposition from the JONSWAP spectrum are implemented in the system and are controlled by using the MPCC-DD controller using the duty cycle control method. The simulation results are obtained and shown in Figure 17.

It can be seen that by using the MPCC-DD controller with the duty cycle control method, the q-axis current under different frequencies can be controlled to follow the reference value well and achieve target damping.

Moreover, an irregular wave excitation with JONSWAP spectrum performance is implemented during system operation. The d-axis current, q-axis current of the upper port, speed of the translator, and output power of the upper and lower power port, respectively, are obtained by using the proposed MPCC-DD controller using the duty cycle control method. The simulation results are shown in Figures 18 and 19.

As we can see, due to the action of irregular waves, the magnitude and frequency of the translator velocity are constantly changing, and the frequency and magnitude of i_q can be found through Equation (15), which also varies with the velocity. The d/q current of the upper and lower power ports can be controlled with a small bias between input and feedback values. This indicates that the proposed controller has the advantages of quick following and good broadband frequency response performance and is suitable for wave power generation systems with variable frequency input power. However, it can be seen that at maximum transient power (about 24 s), the lower d current increases because it is the highest speed and force point, and the angular error also increases. Therefore, to obtain a more perfect performance, instantaneous high speed and force should be considered.

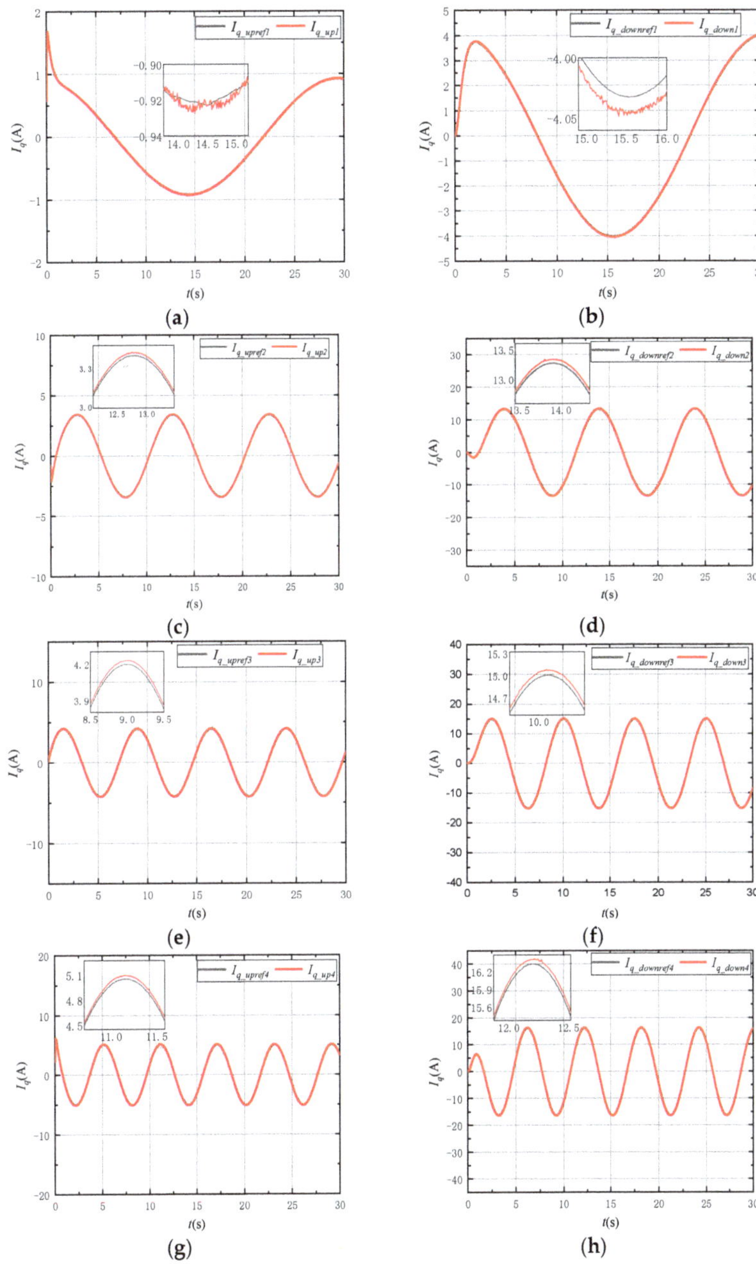

Figure 17. *Cont.*

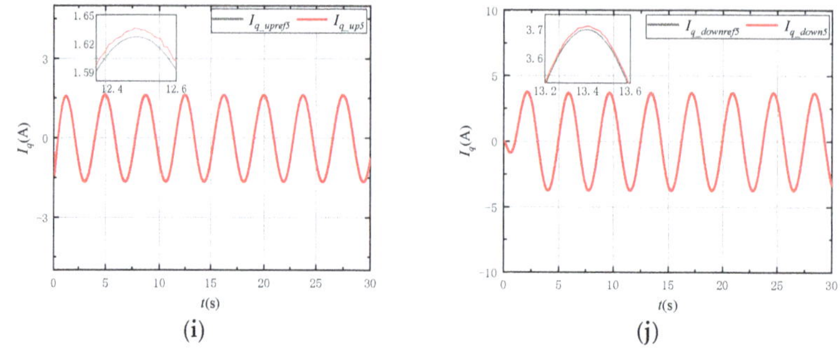

Figure 17. The simulation effect of control of q-axis current under different frequencies. (**a**) i_q of upper power port under frequency f_1; (**b**) i_q of lower power port under frequency f_1; (**c**) i_q of upper power port under frequency f_2; (**d**) i_q of lower power port under frequency f_2; (**e**) i_q of upper power port under frequency f_3; (**f**) i_q of lower power port under frequency f_3; (**g**) i_q of upper power port under frequency f_4; (**h**) i_q of lower power port under frequency f_4; (**i**) i_q of upper power port under frequency f_5; (**j**) i_q of lower power port under frequency f_5.

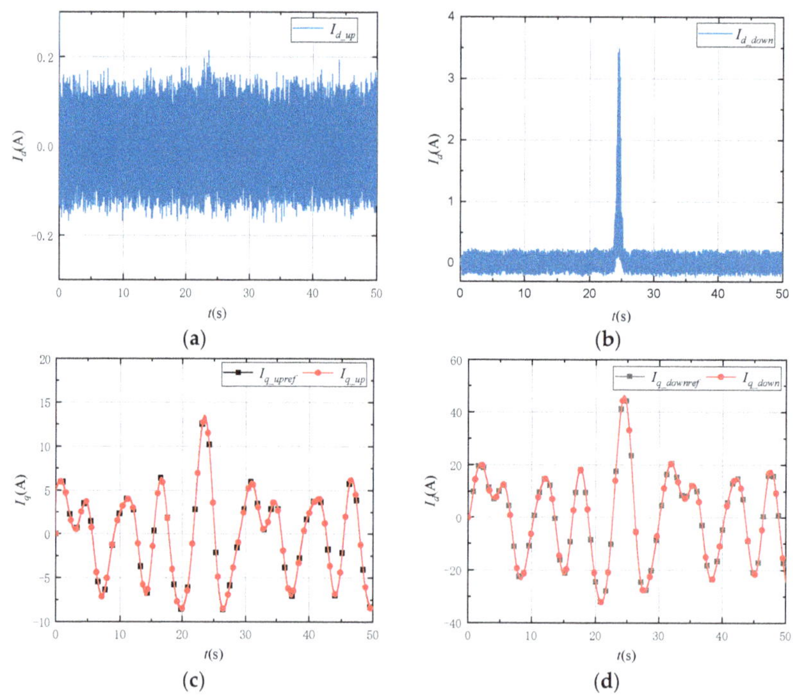

Figure 18. The d/q current of generators under irregular wave excitation. (**a**) i_d of upper under irregular wave excitation; (**b**) i_d of lower under irregular wave excitation; (**c**) i_q of upper under irregular wave excitation; (**d**) i_q of lower under irregular wave excitation.

Figure 19 shows the speed, output power, and actual damping of the upper and lower power ports.

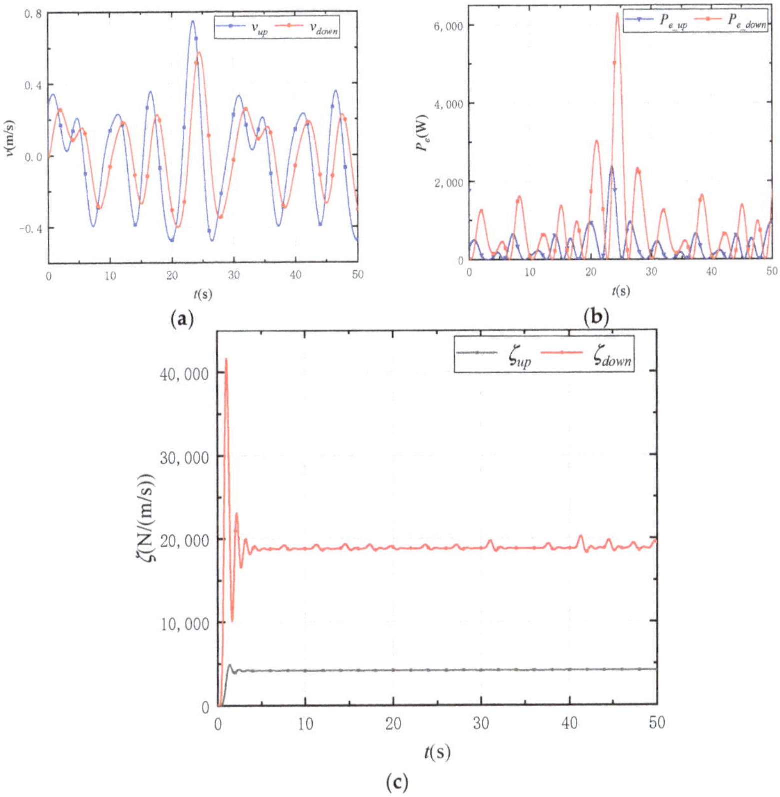

Figure 19. Performance of system under irregular waves. (**a**) Speed of upper and lower power port; (**b**) Dynamic power of upper and lower power port; (**c**) Damping of upper and lower power port.

From the controlled damping, it can be seen that the damping has very small fluctuations, a well-controlled effect. In addition, the spring coefficient is fixed, due to the use of a mechanical spring between the dual translators. The spring coefficient is determined based on the excitation force corresponding to ω_4, which contains the maximum power. The irregular waves consist of multiple frequency components, as shown in Table 1, the output powers of the dual translators are no longer completely complementary under irregular wave conditions. Nevertheless, compared with conventional SP-DDWEPGS, it is observed in Figure 19 that the overall power fluctuations of the DP-DDWEPGS are reduced, and the power complementarity effect still works.

6. Conclusions

In this paper, the equivalent circuit diagram of DP-DDWEPGS is first constructed to implement the optimal power capture control. Then, a multiport converter for DP-DDWEPGS is proposed by employing switch multiplexing, which reduces the number of switching devices and lowers the failure rate and cost compared to conventional three-phase VSR and bidirectional DC-DC converters. By dividing the NSC into two operating states, the NSC decouples the control of its dual ports. Compared to conventional MPCC, the computation time of MPCC-D is reduced by 80%. However, because the MPCC-D applies a voltage vector only once per control cycle and operates with only one port at a time, it results in high current ripples and errors. Therefore, duty cycle optimization is performed using the deadbeat control principle, significantly reducing current ripples and errors. This reduction leads to decreased electromagnetic force ripples in the PMLG, bringing the output power closer to the theoretical value produced by MPPT. Simulation results prove the feasibility of optimal power capture control and reveal that the ripples are effectively reduced in PMLG current and active power. This is achieved with a computational burden still smaller than that of conventional MPCC.

Author Contributions: Methodology, L.H.; Software, J.Z.; Validation, S.W. (Shiquan Wu); Investigation, B.P.; Data curation, H.L.; Writing—original draft, S.W. (Shixiang Wang). All authors have read and agreed to the published version of the manuscript.

Funding: This research was funded by National Natural Science Foundation of China, grant number 41876096.

Institutional Review Board Statement: Not applicable.

Informed Consent Statement: Not applicable.

Data Availability Statement: The original contributions presented in the study are included in the article, further inquiries can be directed to the corresponding author.

Conflicts of Interest: The authors declare no conflict of interest.

Appendix A

Table A1. NSC possible switching states and dual ports voltage vectors.

Switching States [S_1–S_9]	Upper Port Voltage Vector	Lower Port Voltage Vector
[111111000]	V_7 (0)	V_7 (0)
[110111001]	V_2 ($2/3U_{dc}e^{j\pi/3}$)	V_2 ($2/3U_{dc}e^{j\pi/3}$)
[111110001]	V_7 (0)	V_2 ($2/3U_{dc}e^{j\pi/3}$)
[101111010]	V_6 ($2/3U_{dc}e^{j5\pi/3}$)	V_6 ($2/3U_{dc}e^{j5\pi/3}$)
[100111011]	V_1 ($2/3U_{dc}e^{j0}$)	V_1 ($2/3U_{dc}e^{j0}$)
[101110011]	V_6 ($2/3U_{dc}e^{j5\pi/3}$)	V_1 ($2/3U_{dc}e^{j0}$)
[111101010]	V_7 (0)	V_6 ($2/3U_{dc}e^{j5\pi/3}$)
[110101011]	V_2 ($2/3U_{dc}e^{j\pi/3}$)	V_1 ($2/3U_{dc}e^{j0}$)
[111100011]	V_7 (0)	V_1 ($2/3U_{dc}e^{j0}$)
[011111100]	V_4 ($2/3U_{dc}e^{j\pi}$)	V_4 ($2/3U_{dc}e^{j\pi}$)
[010111101]	V_3 ($2/3U_{dc}e^{j2\pi/3}$)	V_3 ($2/3U_{dc}e^{j2\pi/3}$)
[011110101]	V_4 ($2/3U_{dc}e^{j\pi}$)	V_3 ($2/3U_{dc}e^{j2\pi/3}$)
[001111110]	V_5 ($2/3U_{dc}e^{j4\pi/3}$)	V_5 ($2/3U_{dc}e^{j4\pi/3}$)
[000111111]	V_0 (0)	V_0 (0)
[001110111]	V_5 ($2/3U_{dc}e^{j4\pi/3}$)	V_0 (0)
[011101110]	V_4 ($2/3U_{dc}e^{j\pi}$)	V_5 ($2/3U_{dc}e^{j4\pi/3}$)
[010101111]	V_3 ($2/3U_{dc}e^{j2\pi/3}$)	V_0 (0)
[011100111]	V_4 ($2/3U_{dc}e^{j\pi}$)	V_0 (0)
[111011100]	V_7 (0)	V_4 ($2/3U_{dc}e^{j\pi}$)
[110011101]	V_2 ($2/3U_{dc}e^{j\pi/3}$)	V_3 ($2/3U_{dc}e^{j2\pi/3}$)
[111010101]	V_7 (0)	V_3 ($2/3U_{dc}e^{j2\pi/3}$)
[101011110]	V_6 ($2/3U_{dc}e^{j5\pi/3}$)	V_5 ($2/3U_{dc}e^{j4\pi/3}$)
[100011111]	V_1 ($2/3U_{dc}e^{j0}$)	V_0 (0)
[101010111]	V_6 ($2/3U_{dc}e^{j5\pi/3}$)	V_0 (0)
[111001110]	V_7 (0)	V_5 ($2/3U_{dc}e^{j4\pi/3}$)
[110001111]	V_2 ($2/3U_{dc}e^{j\pi/3}$)	V_0 (0)
[111000111]	V_7 (0)	V_0 (0)

Table A2. Acronyms.

Acronyms	Full Form
DP-DDWEPGS	dual-port direct drive wave energy power generation system
SP-DDWEPGS	single-port direct drive wave energy power generation system
FCS-MPC	finite control set model predictive control
DDWEPGS	direct drive wave energy power generation system
PMLG	permanent magnet linear generator
VSR	voltage source rectifier
HESS	hybrid energy storage system
NSC	nine-switch converter
MPCC	model predictive current control
MPCC-D	decoupling model predictive current control
MPCC-DD	decoupling duty cycle optimization model predictive current control

References

1. Xiao, X.; Huang, X.; Kang, Q. A Hill-Climbing-Method-Based Maximum-Power-Point-Tracking Strategy for Direct-Drive Wave Energy Converters. *IEEE Trans. Ind. Electron.* **2016**, *63*, 257–267. [CrossRef]
2. Sun, Z.G.; Cheung, N.C.; Zhao, S.W.; Lu, Y.; Shi, Z.H. Design and simulation of a linear switched reluctance generator for wave energy conversion. In Proceedings of the 2011 4th International Conference on Power Electronics Systems and Applications, Hong Kong, China, 11 August 2011; pp. 1–5.
3. Farrok, O.; Islam, M.R.; Muttaqi, K.M.; Sutanto, D.; Zhu, J. Design and Optimization of a Novel Dual-Port Linear Generator for Oceanic Wave Energy Conversion. *IEEE Trans. Ind. Electron.* **2020**, *67*, 3409–3418. [CrossRef]
4. Rasool, S.; Islam, M.R.; Muttaqi, K.M.; Sutanto, D. Coupled Modeling and Advanced Control for Smooth Operation of a Grid-Connected Linear Electric Generator Based Wave-to-Wire System. *IEEE Trans. Ind. Appl.* **2020**, *56*, 5575–5584. [CrossRef]
5. Liu, H.; Huang, L.; Li, Y.; Yang, J.; Zhang, J. Resonance control to eliminate reactive power of an improved dual-port direct-drive wave energy converter. *Ocean Eng.* **2023**, *288*, 116007. [CrossRef]
6. Wu, H.; Xu, P.; Hu, H.; Zhou, Z.; Xing, Y. Multiport Converters Based on Integration of Full-Bridge and Bidirectional DC-DC Topologies for Renewable Generation Systems. *IEEE Trans. Ind. Electron.* **2014**, *61*, 856–869. [CrossRef]
7. Jarutus, N.; Kumsuwan, Y. A Carrier-Based Phase-Shift Space Vector Modulation Strategy for a Nine-Switch Inverter. *IEEE Trans. Power Electron.* **2017**, *32*, 3425–3441. [CrossRef]
8. Liu, X.; Loh, P.C.; Wang, P.; Blaabjerg, F. A Direct Power Conversion Topology for Grid Integration of Hybrid AC/DC Energy Resources. *IEEE Trans. Ind. Electron.* **2013**, *60*, 5696–5707. [CrossRef]
9. Gao, F.; Zhang, L.; Li, D.; Loh, P.C.; Tang, Y.; Gao, H. Optimal Pulsewidth Modulation of Nine-Switch Converter. *IEEE Trans. Power Electron.* **2010**, *25*, 2331–2343. [CrossRef]
10. Pan, L.; Zhang, J.; Zhang, J.; Pang, Y.; Wang, B.; Wang, K.; Xu, D. A Novel Space-Vector Modulation Method for Nine-Switch Converter. *IEEE Trans. Power Electron.* **2020**, *35*, 1789–1804. [CrossRef]
11. de Andrade, F.C.; Bradaschia, F.; Limongi, L.R.; Cavalcanti, M.C. A Reduced Switching Loss Technique Based on Generalized Scalar PWM for Nine-Switch Inverters. *IEEE Trans. Ind. Electron.* **2018**, *65*, 38–48. [CrossRef]
12. Abdel-Moneim, M.G.; Abdel-Azim, W.E.; Abdel-Khalik, A.S.; Hamed, M.S.; Ahmed, S. Model Predictive Current Control of Nine-Switch Inverter-Fed Six-Phase Induction Motor Drives Under Healthy and Fault Scenarios. *IEEE Trans. Transp. Electrif.* **2024**. [CrossRef]
13. Lee, S.S.; Heng, Y.E.; Roslan, M.A. Finite control set model predictive control of nine-switch AC/DC/AC converter. In Proceedings of the 2016 IEEE International Conference on Power and Energy (PECon), Melaka, Malaysia, 28–29 November 2016; pp. 746–751.
14. Kouro, S.; Cortes, P.; Vargas, R.; Ammann, U.; Rodriguez, J. Model Predictive Control—A Simple and Powerful Method to Control Power Converters. *IEEE Trans. Ind. Electron.* **2009**, *56*, 1826–1838. [CrossRef]
15. Gao, H.; Wu, B.; Xu, D. Nine-switch ac/ac current source converter for microgrid application with model predictive control. *IET Power Electron.* **2017**, *10*, 1759–1766. [CrossRef]
16. Gulbudak, O.; Santi, E. Model predictive control of dual-output nine-switch inverter with output filter. In Proceedings of the 2015 IEEE Energy Conversion Congress and Exposition (ECCE), Montreal, QC, Canada, 20–24 September 2015; pp. 1582–1589. [CrossRef]
17. Guazzelli, P.R.U.; Castro, A.G.D.; Dos Santos, S.T.C.A.; de Oliveira, C.M.R.; Pereira, W.C.A.; Monteiro, J.R.B.A.; Aguiar, M.L.D. Dual Predictive Current Control of Grid Connected Nine-Switch Converter Applied to Induction Generator. In Proceedings of the 2018 13th IEEE International Conference on Industry Applications (INDUSCON), Sao Paulo, Brazil, 12–14 November 2018; pp. 1038–1044.
18. Aciego, J.J.; Gonzalez Prieto, I.; Duran, M.J.; Bermudez, M.; Salas-Biedma, P. Model Predictive Control Based on Dynamic Voltage Vectors for Six-Phase Induction Machines. *IEEE J. Emerg. Sel. Top. Power Electron.* **2021**, *9*, 2710–2722. [CrossRef]
19. Zhang, Y.; Xie, W.; Li, Z.; Zhang, Y. Model Predictive Direct Power Control of a PWM Rectifier With Duty Cycle Optimization. *IEEE Trans. Power Electron.* **2013**, *28*, 5343–5351. [CrossRef]

20. Nikzad, M.R.; Asaei, B.; Ahmadi, S.O. Discrete Duty-Cycle-Control Method for Direct Torque Control of Induction Motor Drives With Model Predictive Solution. *IEEE Trans. Power Electron.* **2018**, *33*, 2317–2329. [CrossRef]
21. Nie, Z.; Xiao, X.; Yi, H.; Kang, Q. Direct drive wave energy converters integrated with a composite energy storage system. In Proceedings of the 2011 International Conference on Electrical Machines and Systems, Beijing, China, 20–23 August 2011; pp. 1–5.
22. Manandhar, U.; Ukil, A.; Gooi, H.B.; Tummuru, N.R.; Kollimalla, S.K.; Wang, B.; Chaudhari, K. Energy Management and Control for Grid Connected Hybrid Energy Storage System Under Different Operating Modes. *IEEE Trans. Smart Grid* **2019**, *10*, 1626–1636. [CrossRef]
23. Copping, A.; Battey, H.; Brown-Saracino, J.; Massaua, M.; Smith, C. An international assessment of the environmental effects of marine energy development. *Ocean. Coast. Manag.* **2014**, *99*, 3–13. [CrossRef]
24. Dong, J.; Chen, G.; Deng, Y.; Wang, K.; He, X. A family of integrated dual-output DC-DC converters: Synthesis methodology and performance analysis. In Proceedings of the 2016 IEEE 8th International Power Electronics and Motion Control Conference (IPEMC-ECCE Asia), Hefei, China, 22–26 May 2016; pp. 342–347.
25. O'Sullivan, A.C.M.; Lightbody, G. Co-design of a wave energy converter using constrained predictive control. *Renew. Energy* **2017**, *102*, 142–156. [CrossRef]
26. Manandhar, U.; Tummuru, N.R.; Kollimalla, S.K.; Ukil, A.; Beng, G.H.; Chaudhari, K. Validation of Faster Joint Control Strategy for Battery- and Supercapacitor-Based Energy Storage System. *IEEE Trans. Ind. Electron.* **2018**, *65*, 3286–3295. [CrossRef]
27. Wu, S.; Liu, C.; Chen, X. Offshore wave energy resource assessment in the East China Sea. *Renew. Energy* **2015**, *76*, 628–636. [CrossRef]

Journal of
Marine Science and Engineering

MDPI

Article

Quantum-Inspired MoE-Based Optimal Operation of a Wave Hydrogen Microgrid for Integrated Water, Hydrogen, and Electricity Supply and Trade

Hady H. Fayek [1], Fady H. Fayek [2] and Eugen Rusu [3,*]

[1] Department of Energy and Renewable Energy Engineering, Faculty of Engineering and Technology, Egyptian Chinese University, Cairo 11786, Egypt; hadyhabib@hotmail.com
[2] Faculty of Pharmacy, Egyptian Chinese University, Cairo 11786, Egypt; habib.fady@yahoo.com
[3] Department of Mechanical Engineering, Faculty of Engineering, "Dunarea de Jos" University of Galati, 800008 Galati, Romania
* Correspondence: eugen.rusu@ugal.ro

Abstract: This research explores the optimal operation of an offshore wave-powered hydrogen system, specifically designed to supply electricity and water to a bay in Humboldt, California, USA, and also sell it with hydrogen. The system incorporates a desalination unit to provide the island with fresh water and feed the electrolyzer to produce hydrogen. The optimization process utilizes a mixture of experts in conjunction with the Quantitative Structure-Activity Relationship (QSAR) algorithm traditionally used in drug design, to achieve two main objectives: minimizing operational costs and maximizing revenue from the sale of water, hydrogen, and electricity. Many case studies are examined, representing typical electricity demand and wave conditions during typical summer, winter, spring, and fall days. The simulation, optimization, and results are carried out using MATLAB 2018 and SAM 2024 software applications. The findings demonstrate that the combination of the QSAR algorithm and quantum-inspired MoE results in higher revenue and lower costs compared to other current techniques, with hydrogen sales being the primary contributor to increased income.

Keywords: wave energy converters; hydrogen energy; mixture of experts; Humboldt Bay; Pacific Ocean; QSAR optimization

1. Introduction

The global focus is shifting toward achieving fully sustainable energy and water management by 2050 [1]. The concept of the water-energy nexus refers to the interdependent relationship between water usage in energy production and energy used for water production [2]. Examples of this nexus include using sustainable energy for water desalination and harnessing seawater to generate electricity through tidal, wave, and wind converters [3].

Wave energy technology, a promising source of renewable energy, is used to generate clean electricity from the movement of ocean waves. Several successful wave energy projects have been implemented, particularly in Europe, with increasing interest in exploring its potential in other regions [4]. Wave energy presents a significant opportunity to contribute to the global transition to renewable energy and helps meet future energy demands sustainably [5]. Hydrogen is emerging as a key player in the future of sustainable energy generation and storage, with the potential to reshape global energy dynamics [6]. The green hydrogen is produced from green energy technology such as PV, wind, or wave applications. It is then stored in the form of gas or liquid to be converted during energy need to electricity or thermal energy. The United States has developed detailed plans to promote hydrogen energy as a crucial element of its clean energy transition. At the core of these efforts is the U.S. National Clean Hydrogen Strategy and Roadmap, which identifies pathways for integrating clean hydrogen into national decarbonization efforts across various economic sectors. This roadmap provides a comprehensive framework for scaling up the production and utilization of clean hydrogen, with detailed projections for 2030, 2040, and 2050 [7]. Green hydrogen, produced from wave energy and seawater desalination, is seen as a promising solution [8]. The hydrogen system typically consists of three components mainly an electrolyzer that converts water into hydrogen, a hydrogen storage tank to store the produced hydrogen, and a fuel cell that converts stored hydrogen back into electricity [9,10].

In recent years, researchers have been exploring the use of hydrogen in sustainable energy generation and storage. One study focused on optimizing the operation of a system involving photovoltaic (PV) cells, hydrogen, batteries, and the electrical grid [11]. Another examined the operation of a combined wind, photovoltaic, battery, and hydrogen system [12]. Many recent studies have aimed to reduce the operational costs of microgrids and power systems. For example, a study presented a method to optimize the operation of a region in Egypt while considering operation costs maximizing the share of renewable energy to reach 100% [13,14].

The application of Mixture of Experts (MoE) models in microgrids offers a promising approach for optimizing energy distribution and management in decentralized energy systems. Microgrids, which consist of interconnected local energy sources such as solar panels, wind turbines, and storage units, require sophisticated decision-making systems to efficiently manage energy flow and ensure reliability. MoE models, with their ability to combine the expertise of multiple specialized models, can be used to model complex and dynamic behavior in microgrid systems [15]. In this context, different experts can be assigned to various tasks, such as forecasting energy demand, predicting renewable energy generation, managing storage units, and controlling energy exchange between grid and microgrid. A gating network determines which expert's output to prioritize, based on current operating conditions, such as weather, load demand, or energy availability. This adaptability allows MoE models to handle uncertainties and variations in renewable energy generation, improving the overall efficiency and reliability of the microgrid [16]. Furthermore, MoE-based systems can potentially offer better scalability and robustness, as they can adapt to new experts or update existing ones as the microgrid evolves. Research into MoE in microgrids could lead to more intelligent and resilient energy management systems, paving the way for the integration of renewable energy sources and the development of smart grid technologies [17,18].

Quantitative Structure-Activity Relationship (QSAR) modeling is a valuable tool used to analyze the relationships between the chemical structure of compounds and experimental observations. The method relies on numerical descriptors, quality of observed data, and statistical techniques to establish correlations [19]. Despite its effectiveness, QSAR has limitations, such as overfitting, limited applicability to new chemical structures, and challenges in providing accurate error estimates [20]. QSAR models are frequently used to optimize chemical compounds for potential clinical trials [21]. In this research, QSAR is employed to optimally operate a wave hydrogen energy microgrid.

From the above studies, it was noticed that no previous research was implemented on how to employ wave and hydrogen energy technologies in the United States, especially in California. In this research, the main contributions covered the following topics:

i. Integration of hydrogen and wave energies to form a microgrid to produce electricity, water, and hydrogen for supplying a bay in the USA and trade.

ii. Employ the QSAR optimization technique to operate the microgrid optimally to achieve minimum cost and maximum revenue in daily operation.
iii. Employ MoE as an artificial intelligence tool for solving the multi-objective goals in the operation of the microgrid.
iv. Compare the performance of the daily wave energy generation, the microgrid cost of operation, and revenue in different seasons namely summer, winter, fall, and spring.

The paper is organized as follows; Section 2 illustrates the modeling of the microgrid while in Section 3, an illustration of the project location is presented. Section 4 illustrates how optimization and artificial intelligence are employed towards optimal operation of the microgrid. Sections 5–7 present results, discussions, and conclusions, respectively.

2. Microgrid Modeling

The microgrid shown in Figure 1 is operated by a wave energy converter namely a point absorber to operate electrolyzer, electrical loads, and water desalination unit. The energy is stored in the form of hydrogen in compressed gas tanks; the hydrogen is converted to electricity by fuel cells. The aim of the microgrid is the production of electricity, hydrogen, and water for use and selling.

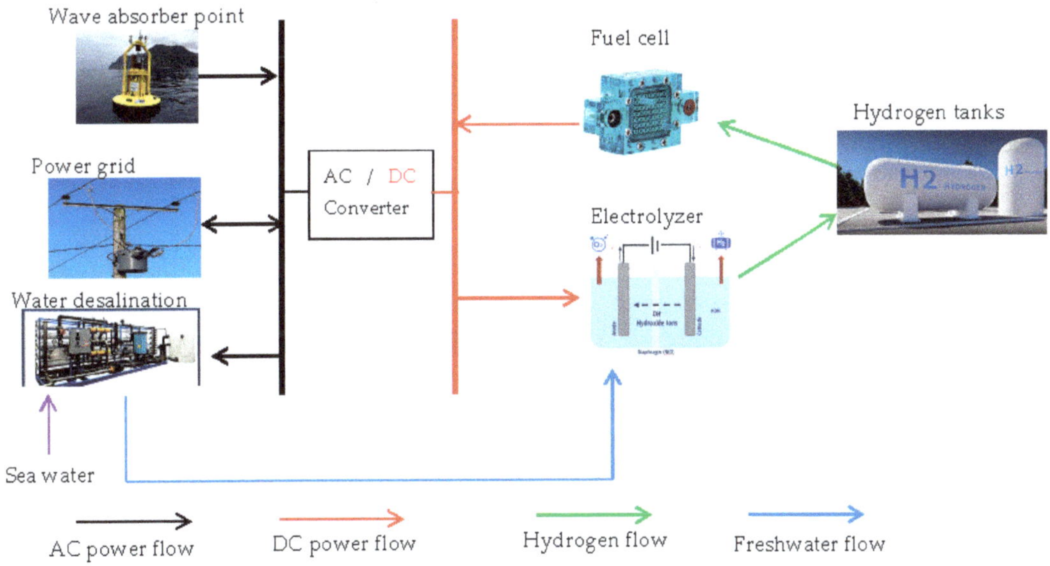

Figure 1. Wave hydrogen energy technologies microgrid.

2.1. Wave Energy Conversion System

A wave energy system works by capturing the kinetic and potential energy from ocean waves and converting it into electrical power. A point absorber wave energy converter is used in this research which is a floating device that harnesses the vertical motion of ocean waves to generate electricity, typically using a hydraulic or mechanical power take-off system to drive a generator. The energy available from the waves is determined by the wave height (H) and the wave period (T), along with other environmental parameters. The total power in the waves (P_{wave}) can be estimated using (1) [22].

$$P_{wave} = \frac{\rho \cdot g^2 \cdot H^2 \cdot T}{64\pi} \quad (1)$$

ρ is the density of seawater which is set to be 1000 kg/m^3, g is the gravitational acceleration (9.81 m/s^2). This power is then captured by a wave energy converter, selected in this research to be a point absorber. The vertical motion of the waves is converted into mechanical energy, which is then transformed into electrical power using a generator. The mechanical power output ($P_{mechanical}$) can be approximated as illustrated in (2) [23].

$$P_{mechanical} = \frac{C_m \cdot H^2}{T} \tag{2}$$

C_m is a constant representing the efficiency of the point absorber. The mechanical power is then converted into electrical power ($P_{electrical}$) by the generator and turbine, considering their respective efficiencies ($\eta_{generator}$ and $\eta_{turbine}$) as illustrated in (3) [24].

$$P_{electrical} = P_{mechanical} \cdot \eta_{turbine} \cdot \eta_{generator} \tag{3}$$

2.2. Water Desalination Unit

The operation of the water desalination unit is outlined in [25] and the equations governing the system are (4) and (5).

$$W_{water}(t) = G_R\left(\frac{P_t(t)}{P_R}\right) \tag{4}$$

$$W_s(t) = W_s(t-1) + G_w(t) - W_{use}(t) \tag{5}$$

W_{water} signifies the quantity of pure water produced, G_R is the nominal capability for pure water production, P_t is the utilized power, and P_R is the nominal power of the unit of desalination. W_s indicates the water stored in the reservoir, G_w refers to the freshwater generated, and W_{use} is the amount of freshwater utilized.

2.3. Hydrogen Energy System

The hydrogen system is composed of three key components: the electrolyzer, the hydrogen storage tank, and the fuel cell. The primary function of the electrolyzer is to produce hydrogen, as described in Equations (6) and (7). The amount of power required to perform the electrolysis process is denoted as P_{el} , while the mass of hydrogen generated during the process is represented by m_{el}

$$P_{el}(t) = \sum_{i=1}^{N_{el}} A_i^{el} N_{el} I_{el} V_{el} \Delta t \tag{6}$$

$$m_{el}(t) = \frac{N_{el}\ I_{el}\ \eta_f \Delta t}{2F} M \tag{7}$$

The fuel cell's primary function is to transform hydrogen into electrical energy, as shown in Equations (8) and (9). The proton exchange membrane fuel cell is used in this research to convert hydrogen to electricity. The power utilized in the redox reaction is denoted as P_{FC}, while the amount of hydrogen consumed during this process is represented by m_{FC}.

$$P_{FC}(t) = \sum_{i=1}^{N_{FC}} A_i^{FC} N_{FC} I_{FC} V_{FC} \Delta t \tag{8}$$

$$m_{FC}(t) = \frac{N_{FC}\ I_{FC}\ \Delta t}{2F} M \tag{9}$$

In this context, A represents the operational status of the cell during electrolysis (where 0 indicates off and 1 indicates on). N refers to the total number of electrolyzers or fuel cells. The variables V and I denote the voltage and current of the cell, respectively. F is the Faraday constant, and η_f represents Faraday's efficiency. The quantity M refers to the mass of hydrogen in kilograms.

After hydrogen exits the electrolyzer, it undergoes compression before being stored in a tank. Taking into account the adiabatic expansion and the variation in hydrogen volume, the storage process can be described by Equation (10).

$$\frac{V_{storage}(t)}{RT}\frac{dY_H}{dt} = n_{stored\ hydrogen} \tag{10}$$

In this equation, Y_H represents the hydrogen performance parameter, $V_{storage}$ is the volume of the stored hydrogen, T is the temperature during the adiabatic process, and R is the ideal gas constant [9].

3. Microgrid Location

Humboldt Bay is located along the northern coast of California, nestled between the Pacific Ocean and the rugged coastal ranges as shown in Figure 2. The bay stretches roughly 15 miles inland, with its waters framed by the Humboldt Bay Heads, which offer natural protection from the open ocean. Situated in Humboldt County, the bay is surrounded by a mix of lush forests, tidal marshes, and hills that create a dramatic and scenic backdrop. The bay itself is one of the largest natural harbors on the West Coast, offering a sheltered environment that has historically supported maritime activities [26]. The surrounding landscape includes diverse ecosystems, from salt marshes to dense redwood forests, which contribute to the bay's ecological importance [27].

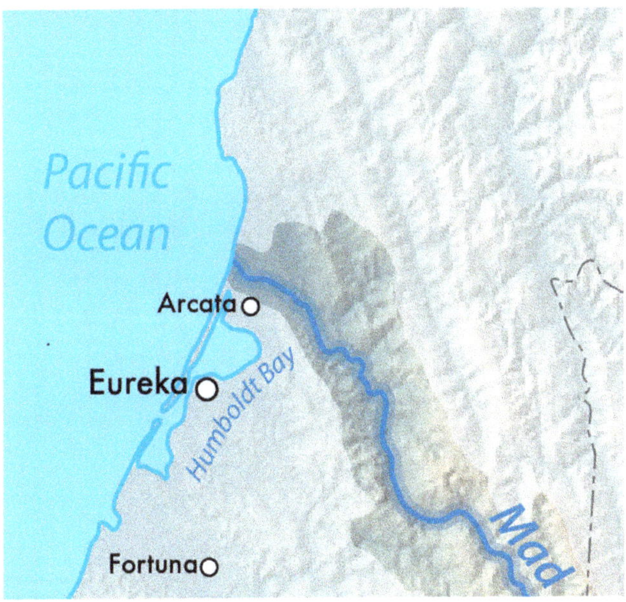

Figure 2. Humboldt Bay, USA location in Pacific Ocean [27].

The bay is positioned near the city of Eureka, which sits along its southern shore, providing easy access to the bay's waters. To the north and south, the bay is bordered by smaller communities, each contributing to the regional economy and culture. The area's geography also makes it a popular destination for outdoor enthusiasts, who come to enjoy the natural beauty, wildlife, and recreational opportunities the bay and its surroundings offer [28]. Humboldt Bay's location in this remote and picturesque corner of California makes it a unique and important natural resource for both the local community and the broader region [29]. The Humboldt Bay area relies on a mix of surface water and groundwater for its water supply, with conservation efforts in place to address periodic droughts. Energy needs are shifting toward sustainability, with decommissioned fossil fuel plants replaced by renewable sources like offshore wind and solar power. The region benefits from renewable energy programs, although challenges remain in infrastructure and grid capacity. Local authorities prioritize water quality and energy efficiency to ensure a sustainable future. The wave energy system will be implemented in Humboldt Bay 5344.78 m distance from the shore, with a water depth of 48 m, latitude of 40.84, and longitude of −124.25. The wave height is illustrated in Figure 3 which is exported from SAM 2024 software application and shows that there is a big wave energy potential especially in winter [30].

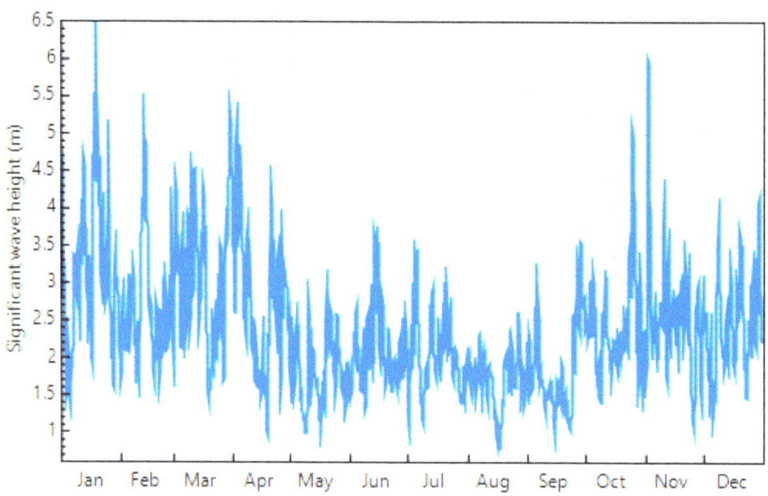

Figure 3. Yearly wave heights in Humboldt Bay, USA.

4. Optimization in Microgrid Operation

4.1. Optimization Problem Definition

The optimization is done to minimize the cost of operation and maintenance while also increasing the revenue from the sale of energy and water. Increasing revenue from the sale of electricity, hydrogen, and freshwater (F_1) and lowering operating costs for fuel cells, electrolyzers, and water desalination units (F_2) are the two main goals of the objective function (F). The weighting factor and normalization procedures are two ways that combine the two objective functions.

Objective functions:

(A) Maximizing income

$$F_1 = \max\sum_{t=1}^{24}(C_E P_E(t) + C_H m_H(t) + C_W W_s(t))/24 \quad (11)$$

where C_E is the price per unit of electricity sold, the electricity that was sold in KWhr is $P_E(t)$, C_H is the cost per unit of hydrogen sold, m_H is how many liters of hydrogen are sold, C_W is the cost per unit of freshwater sold and W_s is the volume of water sold in cubic meters.

(B) Minimization of operation cost

The objective is to minimize the operation cost of water desalination unit, electrolyzer unit, and fuel cell.

$$F_2 = \min \sum_{t=1}^{24} (U_{el}P_{el}(t) + U_{FC}P_{FC}(t) + U_W P_W(t))/24 \tag{12}$$

where the unit costs for running the fuel cell, water desalination, and electrolyzer units are U_{el}, $U_{FC,}$ and U_W, respectively.

There are two ways to handle this multi-objective problem: the normalization approach, which uses the single best solution for each objective, as shown in (13) and the weighting factors, as shown in (14) assuming equal priority for the two objectives.

$$F = \frac{1}{\text{Optimal } F_1}F_1 + \frac{1}{\text{Optimal } F_2}F_2 \tag{13}$$

$$F = \frac{1}{2}F_1 + \frac{1}{2}F_2 \tag{14}$$

Constraints:

i. Normal power flow equations

The system's power generation (from wave and fuel cells) is equal to the power sold to the grid and the power required for system consumption (water desalination power, electrolyzer, and load). The fuel cell and electrolyzer cannot operate simultaneously.

$$P_{Wind}(t) + P_{FC}(t) = P_t(t) + P_{el}(t) + P_{load}(t) + P_E(t) \tag{15}$$

$$P_{FC}(t) \cdot P_{el}(t) = 0 \tag{16}$$

ii. Inequality constraints (limits)

Wave energy conversion limits: Wave energy converter cannot exceed maximum power.

$$0 \leq P_{Wave}(t) \leq P_{Wavemax} \tag{17}$$

$$\Delta P_{Wavemin}(t) \leq \Delta P_{Wave}(t) \leq \Delta P_{Wavemax}(t) \tag{18}$$

The output of a water desalination plant varies from minimum to maximum.

$$W_{watermin}(t) \leq W_{water}(t) \leq W_{watermax}(t) \tag{19}$$

Fuel cell and electrolyzer units operating power limitations

$$P_{elmin} \leq P_{el}(t) \leq P_{elmax} \tag{20}$$

$$P_{FCmin} \leq P_{FC}(t) \leq P_{FCmax} \tag{21}$$

To prevent any damage to the grid component, the power sold to the grid must be less than the maximum amount that the grid could receive from the system.

$$P_E(t) \leq P_{Emax} \tag{22}$$

Hydrogen storage energy should follow (23), (24), and (25)

$$E_H(t) = E_H(t-1)(1-\delta) + \Delta t(P_{el}(t-1)\eta_{el} - \frac{P_{FC}(t-1)}{\eta_{FC}}) \tag{23}$$

$$E_{Hmin} \leq E_H(t) \leq E_{Hmax} \tag{24}$$

$$0.2 \leq SOC \leq 0.8 \tag{25}$$

where the capacity of the storage is E_H, δ is the coefficient of discharge and SOC is the state of charge.

4.2. QSAR Optimization

In quantitative structure-activity relationship (QSAR) studies in drug design, the process typically involves the use of two distinct datasets: the training set and the test set. These datasets are instrumental in the development and validation of predictive models. The training set consists of a diverse array of chemical compounds along with their corresponding biological activities or properties. The goal of the training set is to develop a QSAR model that can accurately predict the biological activity of novel compounds based on their molecular descriptors, which represent the structural features of the compounds [19].

The test set, on the other hand, is utilized to evaluate the model's predictive capability. Unlike the training set, the compounds in the test set are not used during the model training phase, allowing researchers to assess how well the model generalizes to previously unseen data. The performance of the model is typically evaluated by comparing its predictions against the actual observed values in the test set [20,21].

A widely used metric for assessing model performance in QSAR studies is the Q-squared (Q^2) statistic. Q^2 quantifies the proportion of variance in the observed data that the model is able to explain. It ranges from 0 to 1, with values closer to 1 indicating a better fit between the model and the data. In the context of QSAR, a model is considered reproducible if its Q^2 value exceeds 0.8 in the training set. A model is deemed predictive if its Q^2 value is greater than 0.6, while both reproducibility and predictive capability must be satisfied for the model to be regarded as valid [31–33].

The Q^2 statistic is computed in (26):

$$Q^2 = 1 - \frac{SS_{res}}{SS_{tot}} \tag{26}$$

where SS_{res} represents the sum of squared residuals (the differences between predicted and observed values), and SS_{tot} is the total sum of squares (the overall variability in the observed data). The individual components SS_{res} and SS_{tot} can be calculated as illustrated in (27) and (28)

$$SS_{res} = \sum \left(y_{obs} - y_{pred}\right)^2 \tag{27}$$

$$SS_{tot} = \sum (y_{obs} - y_{mean})^2 \tag{28}$$

where y_{obs} is the observed activity value, y_{pred} is the predicted activity value, and y_{mean} is the mean of the observed activity values.

In QSAR studies, outliers and z-scores play crucial roles in data analysis and model development as shown in Figure 4 which illustrates the flowchart of QSAR optimization. Outliers are data points that significantly deviate from the expected trend and can introduce noise or bias, thus negatively affecting model accuracy. Identifying and appropriately handling outliers is vital for ensuring the reliability of QSAR models. Outliers may arise due to factors such as measurement errors, experimental artifacts, or the presence of compounds with rare or unique characteristics.

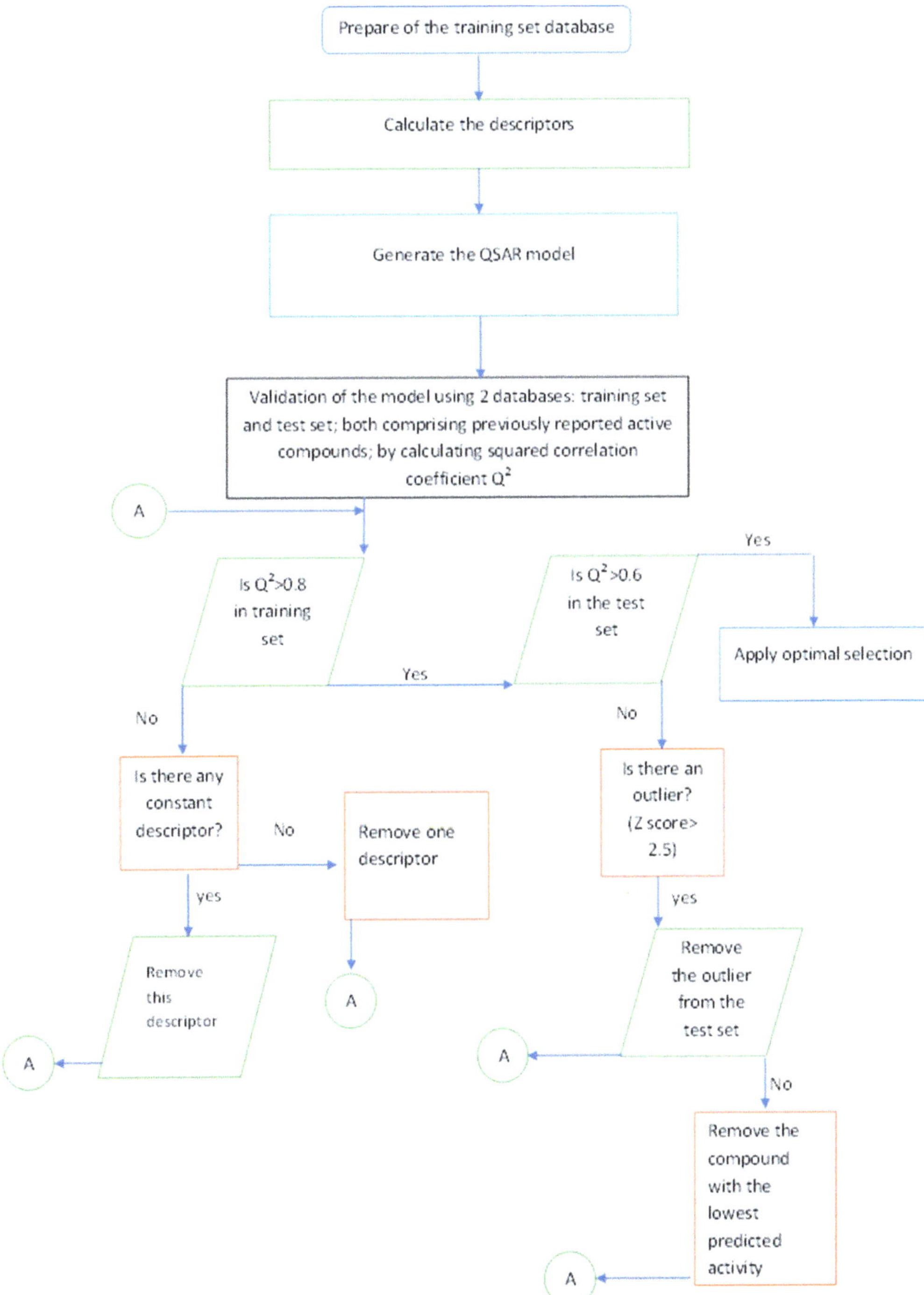

Figure 4. QSAR optimization flowchart.

The z-score is a statistical tool used to quantify how far a data point deviates from the mean of a distribution, measured in standard deviations. In QSAR analysis, z-scores are often employed for both outlier detection and data normalization. A commonly accepted threshold for identifying outliers based on z-scores is 2.5, where values beyond this threshold indicate potential outliers [33].

The z-score for a data point x_i is calculated using the formula in (29):

$$z = \frac{x_i - \mu}{\sigma} \tag{29}$$

where x_i is the observed value, μ is the mean, and σ is the standard deviation of the data distribution.

4.3. *Quantum-Inspired Mixture of Experts Strategy*

The Mixture of Experts (MoE) strategy represents a cutting-edge approach to addressing multi-objective optimization challenges across various domains. This framework combines the strengths of modularization, selective activation, and parallel processing to achieve superior performance in solving complex, multifaceted problems. By design, the MoE strategy decomposes a problem into smaller, specialized tasks, each handled by an "expert" model. These experts are dynamically activated based on contextual information, making the MoE approach a promising solution for balancing trade-offs between conflicting objectives [34].

The MoE framework consists of two primary components: the expert models and a gating network. Each expert model is trained to specialize in a particular objective or subset of the problem space. For instance, in the context of microgrid energy optimization, individual experts might focus on distinct objectives, such as maximizing renewable energy utilization, minimizing operational costs, or enhancing system reliability. The gating network functions as a decision-making mechanism, dynamically assigning tasks to the most relevant expert(s) based on the input features or environmental context. This selective activation ensures computational efficiency by engaging only the required subset of experts, thereby reducing unnecessary processing overhead.

The MoE strategy is particularly well-suited for multi-objective optimization due to its ability to address trade-offs among competing objectives. Traditional optimization techniques often require combining objectives into a single composite function, which can obscure individual priorities and lead to suboptimal solutions. In contrast, MoE retains the granularity of each objective by assigning them to specialized experts, thereby enabling more effective optimization. Moreover, the modular nature of MoE facilitates scalability, as additional experts can be introduced to address emerging objectives or accommodate evolving problem requirements.

From a computational perspective, the MoE strategy offers significant advantages. The independent nature of expert models allows for parallel processing, which enhances scalability and reduces computation time in large-scale optimization problems. Furthermore, the specialization of experts ensures that each model achieves high performance within its designated domain, leading to improved overall optimization outcomes. This is particularly beneficial in applications where objectives are highly diverse and interdependent, such as energy systems, supply chain management, autonomous systems, and healthcare.

In energy systems, for example, the MoE approach can be utilized to optimize the distribution of energy resources, balance operational costs, and enhance sustainability. Each objective is managed by a specialized expert, while the gating network coordinates its interactions to provide an integrated solution. Similarly, in supply chain management, the MoE framework can address the trade-offs between cost efficiency, delivery speed, and inventory levels. The modularity and adaptability of the MoE strategy make it a versatile tool for addressing complex multi-objective challenges across industries.

The implementation of the MoE framework has demonstrated significant potential in various research studies. For instance, recent advancements in machine learning and artificial intelligence have highlighted the efficacy of MoE in optimizing resource allocation, reducing energy consumption, and improving decision-making processes in dynamic environments [18,35]. These findings underscore the transformative role of the MoE strategy in solving real-world optimization problems.

Figure 5 shows how MoE is employed to solve the multi-objective optimization process to optimally operate the wave hydrogen microgrid in this research. The optimal value of each single objective is calculated using QSAR optimization.

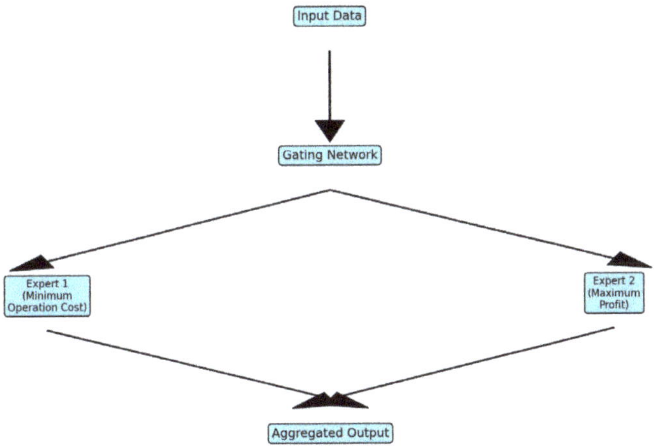

Figure 5. MoE implementation in wave hydrogen microgrid.

The gating network in the MoE framework is a crucial component responsible for dynamically selecting the appropriate experts for a given input. It operates as a mediator that decides which expert model should process the input data based on certain criteria, such as input features or environmental context. Here is a detailed breakdown of how the gating network is typically designed in this research:

a. Input layer: The gating network starts by receiving the same input as the entire MoE system. The inputs included in this research are wave height, water demand, and electricity demand. It is designed in this research to have one neuron.
b. Quantum-Inspired Processing [36]: The inputs are processed to mix between the two objectives based on the normalization of probability amplitudes, to ensure that the sum of the weights is 1. The absolute square of each amplitude to get the selection weights is shown in (30). This ensures that the gating network still produces a valid probability distribution of weights, but the way these weights are formed introduces a quantum-like interference.

$$w_i = \frac{|Optimal\ F_i|^2}{|Optimal\ F_i|^2 + |Optimal\ F_j|^2} \tag{30}$$

c. Output layer: consists of one neuron and the outputs are on/off decision of the water desalination unit, the electrolyzer, and the fuel cell.

5. Results

This study aims to evaluate the performance of a newly proposed quantum-inspired MoE, optimization technique, QSAR, alongside other advanced methods in terms of revenue generation and total cost for a hypothetical microgrid. The analysis is conducted for typical summer, spring, fall, and winter days, considering realistic daily electricity demand and wave height variations. Five optimization scenarios were examined: Normalized QSAR Optimization (NQSAR), Weighting Factor QSAR Optimization (WQSAR), Particle Swarm Optimization (PSO), Genetic Algorithm Optimization (GA), and Quantum-Inspired Mixture of Experts (MoE). The microgrid is assumed to include a 1 GW wave converter located in the Pacific Ocean of Humboldt Bay, with a maximum water load capacity of 3.91 million tons. To ensure consistency and accuracy, all optimization algorithms were implemented and tested using MATLAB 2018 while data of generation was imported from SAM 2024 to MATLAB.

In this study, the power rating of both the electrolyzer and the fuel cell is 10 MW with a capacity of 20 MWhrs. The cost of 1 Kg of hydrogen is assumed to be USD10 while 1 Kwh of electricity is assumed to be USD0.46 similar to 1 m^3 of water. The wave power and energy produced over one year are shown in Figures 6 and 7, respectively using the SAM 2024 version. The yearly accumulative energy produced from the microgrid is 2,292,968,704 kWhr with a capacity factor of 26.2%.

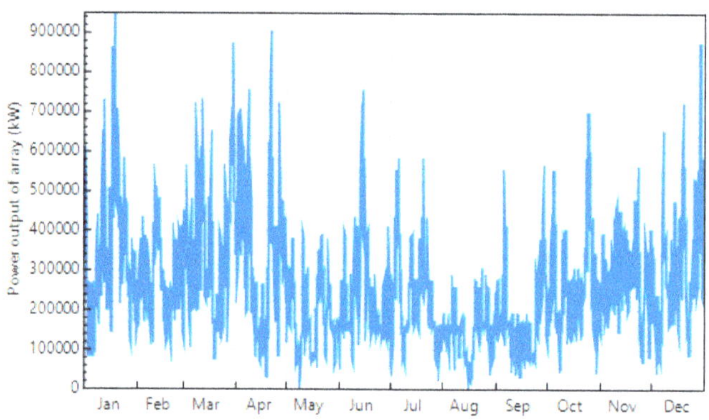

Figure 6. Wave converter output power in a year.

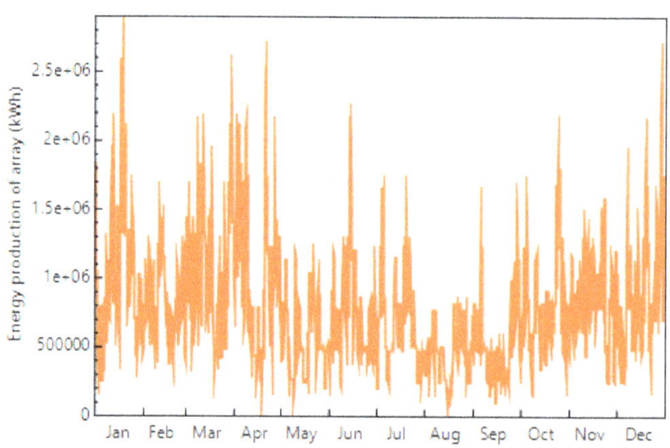

Figure 7. Wave energy production yearly.

5.1. Summer Day

Figures 8 and 9 illustrate the electricity demand and the wave energy production on a typical summer day in Humboldt Bay, Pacific Ocean. Optimization is conducted using five different scenarios to enhance revenue generation while reducing the microgrid's operational expenses. As depicted in Figures 10 and 11, the MoE followed by the NQSAR approach, then the WQSAR, achieves higher revenue and lower operational costs compared to the other two methods. Additionally, the data in Figure 12 indicate that hydrogen sales account for approximately two-thirds of the total income.

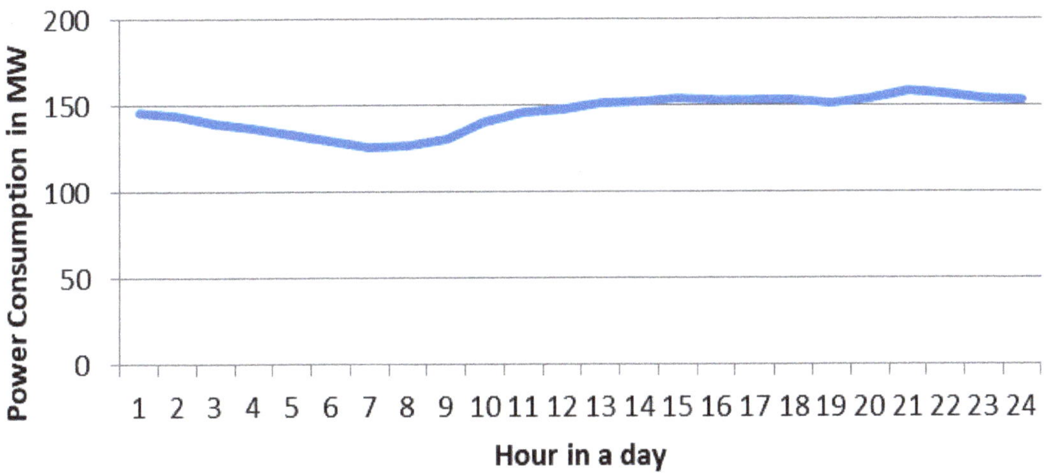

Figure 8. Electrical power consumption on a typical summer day.

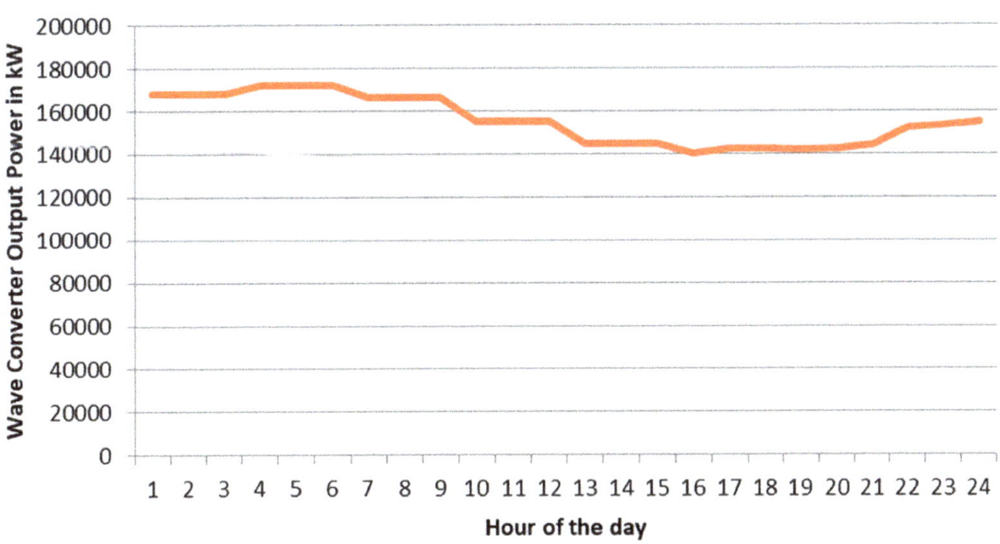

Figure 9. Hourly power produced from a wave converter on a typical summer day.

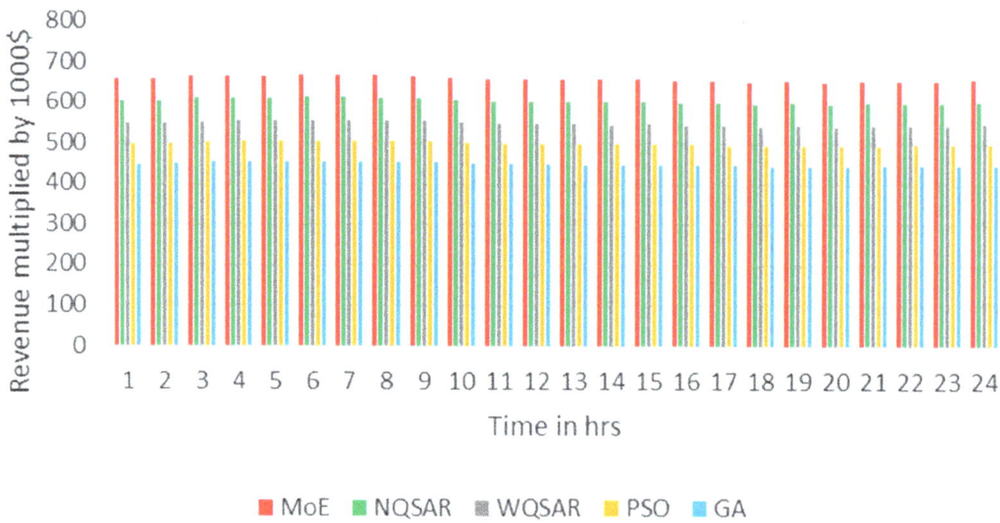

Figure 10. Revenue of the project on summer days using different optimization techniques.

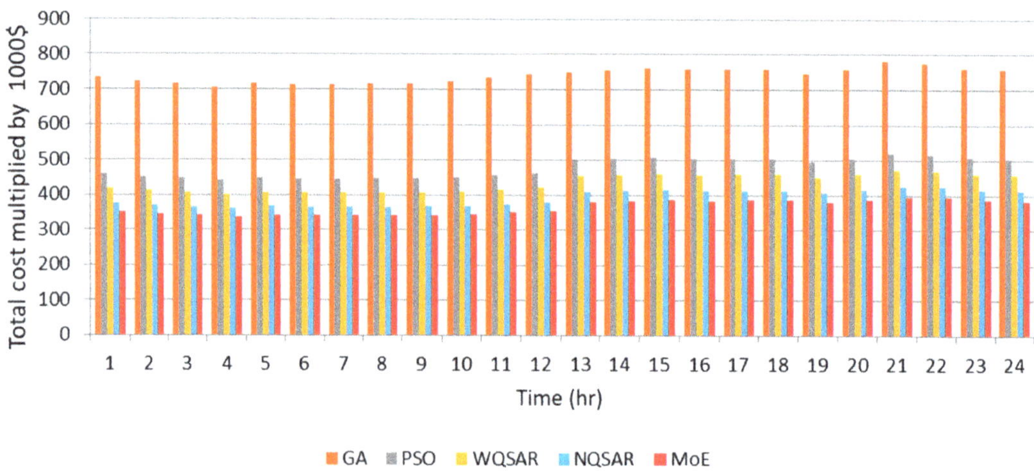

Figure 11. The total operation cost of the microgrid on a summer day using different optimization techniques.

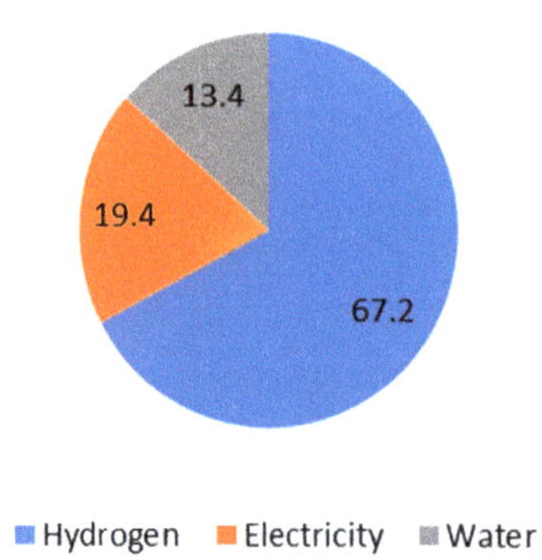

Figure 12. Income share from hydrogen, water, and electricity on a summer day.

5.2. Winter Day

Figure 13 presents the electricity demand on a winter day for Humboldt Bay, Pacific Ocean which is 29% lower than the summer demand, while Figure 14 represents the wave energy production from the converter on a typical winter day which is almost double that of the summer day. Optimization is performed using five scenarios to maximize revenue and minimize the microgrid's operational costs. As shown in Figures 15 and 16, the MoE followed by the NQSAR, then the WQSAR, achieves higher revenue and lower costs compared to GA and PSO. Furthermore, the data in Figure 17 reveal that hydrogen sales contribute approximately 70% of the total income.

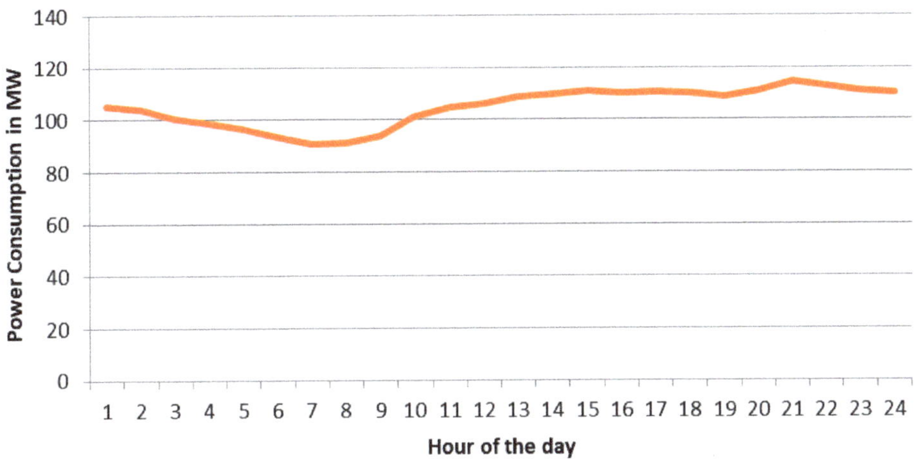

Figure 13. Electrical power consumption on a winter day.

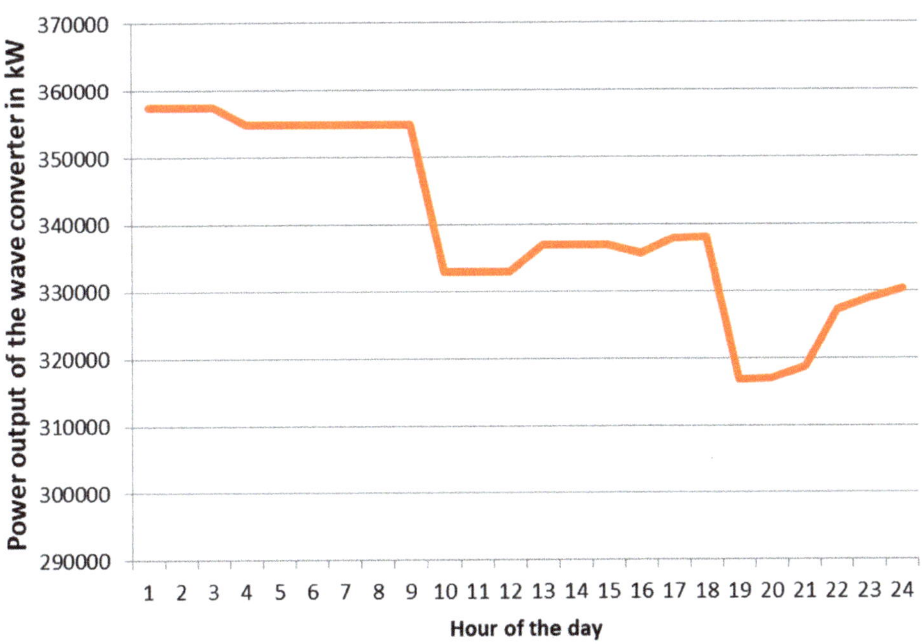

Figure 14. Power produced by a wave converter on a winter day.

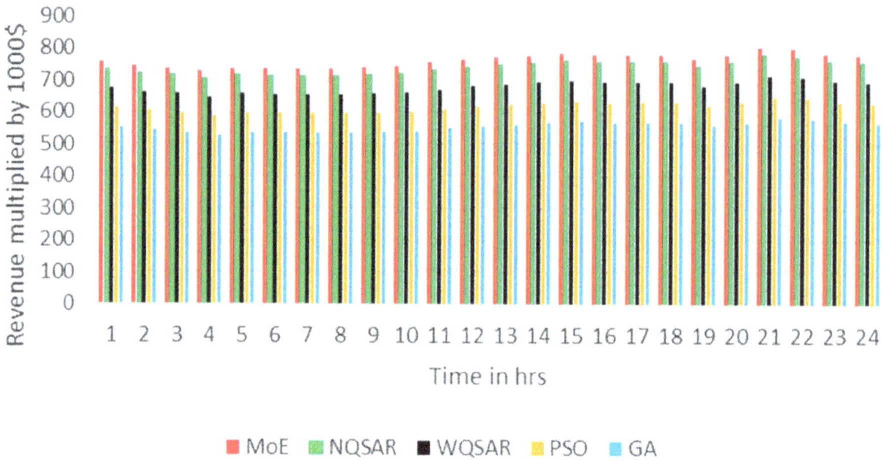

Figure 15. Revenue on a winter day using different optimization techniques.

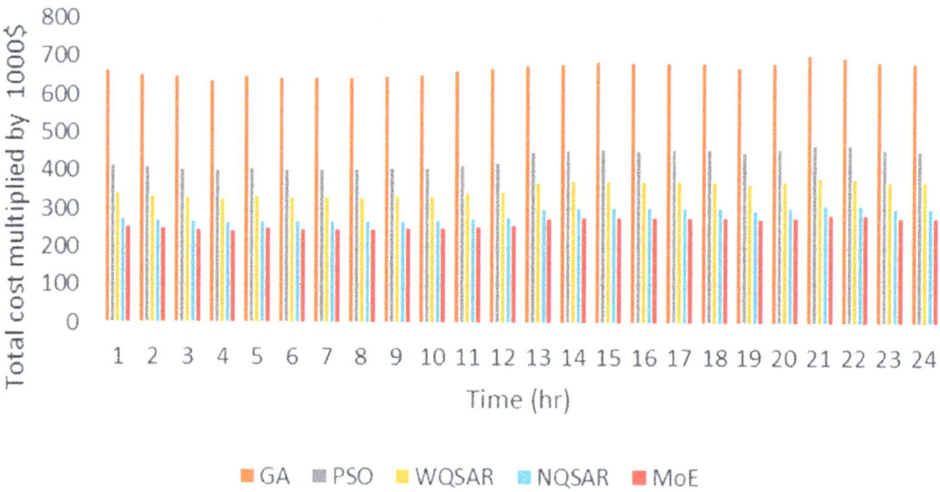

Figure 16. Operation cost of microgrid on a winter day using different optimization techniques.

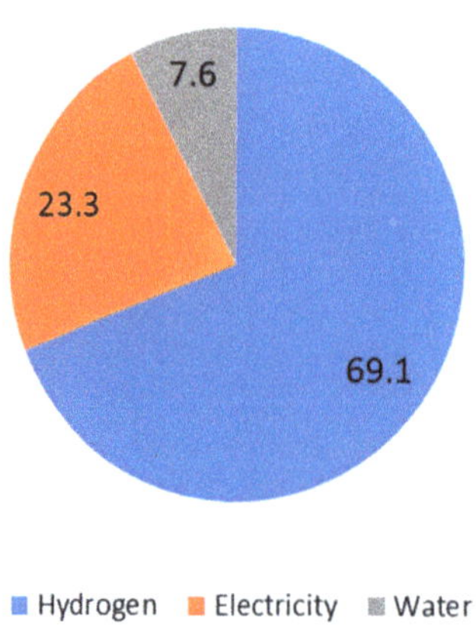

Figure 17. Share out of total income on a winter day.

5.3. Spring Day

Figure 18 presents the electricity demand on a spring day for Humboldt Bay, Pacific Ocean which is 12% lower than the summer demand, while Figure 19 represents the wave energy production from the converter on a typical spring day which is almost 10% lower than that of the winter day. Optimization is performed using five scenarios to maximize revenue and minimize the microgrid's operational costs. As shown in Figures 20 and 21, the MoE, followed by NQSAR, then WQSAR, achieves higher revenue and lower costs compared to GA and PSO. Furthermore, the data in Figure 22 reveal that hydrogen sales contribute approximately 65% of the total income followed by almost 22% from selling electricity.

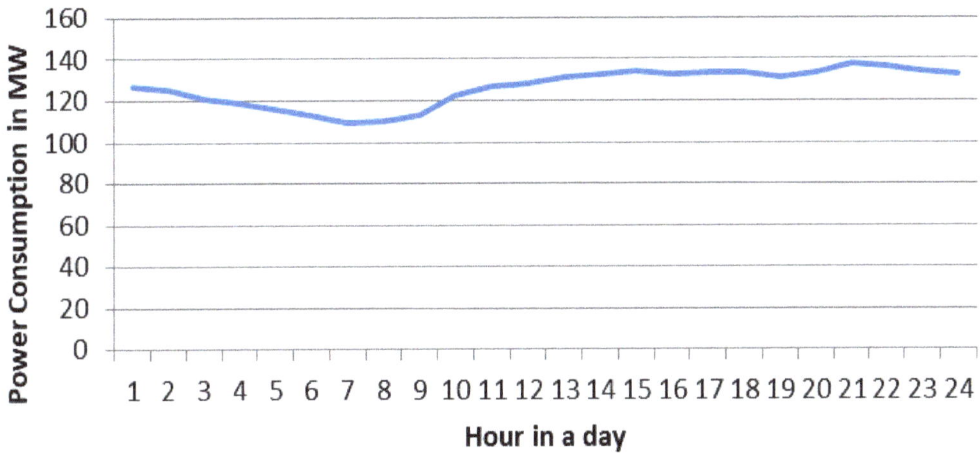

Figure 18. Electrical power consumption on a spring day.

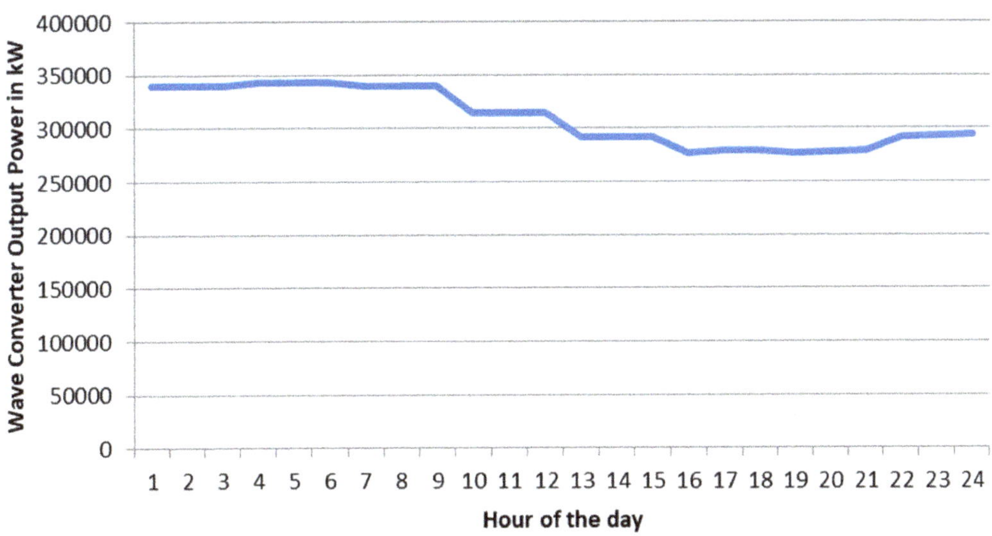

Figure 19. Output power from the wave converter on a spring day.

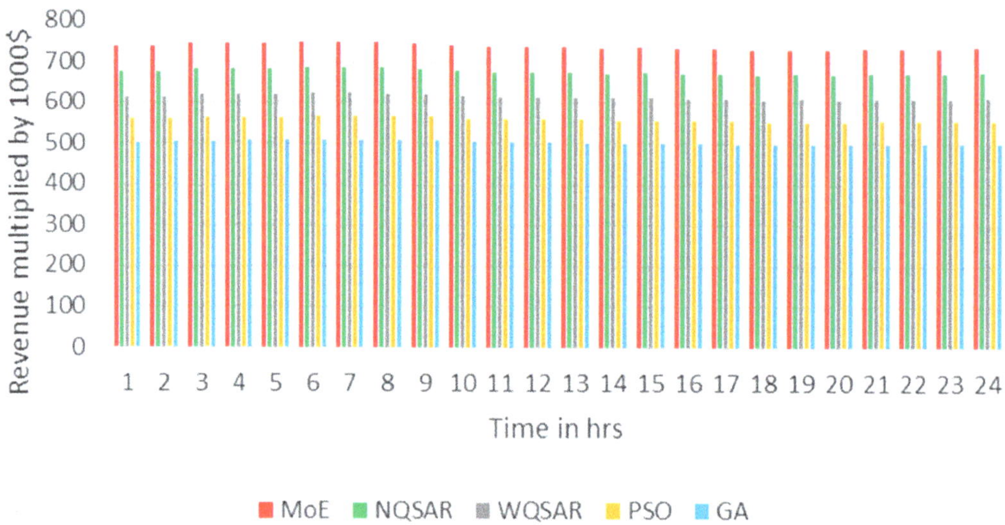

Figure 20. Revenue on a spring day.

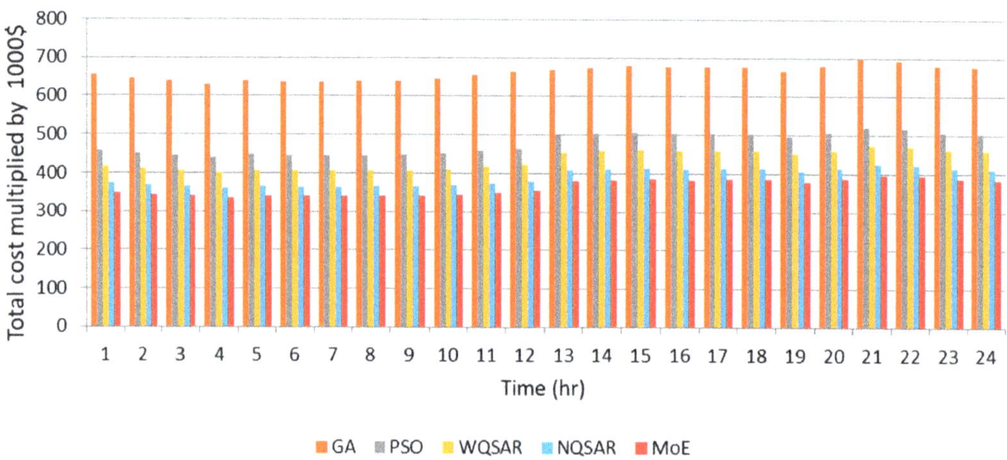

Figure 21. Operation cost of microgrid on a spring day.

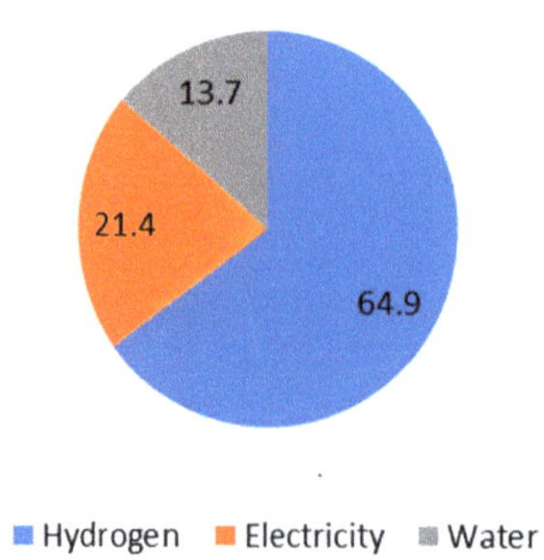

Figure 22. Share of income on a spring day.

5.4. Fall Day

Figure 23 presents the electricity demand on a fall day for Humboldt Bay, Pacific Ocean which is 11% lower than the summer demand, while Figure 24 represents the wave energy production from the converter on a typical fall day which is almost 14% lower than that of the winter day. Optimization is performed using five scenarios to maximize revenue and minimize the microgrid's operational costs. As shown in Figures 25 and 26, the MoE, followed by NQSAR, then WQSAR, achieves higher revenue and lower costs compared to GA and PSO. Furthermore, the data in Figure 27 reveal that hydrogen sales contribute approximately 60% of the total income followed by almost 24% from selling electricity.

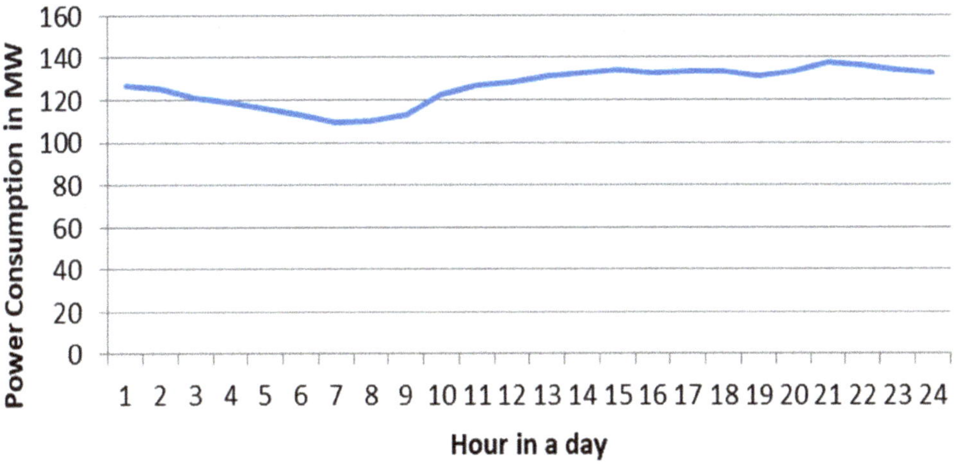

Figure 23. Power consumption on a fall day.

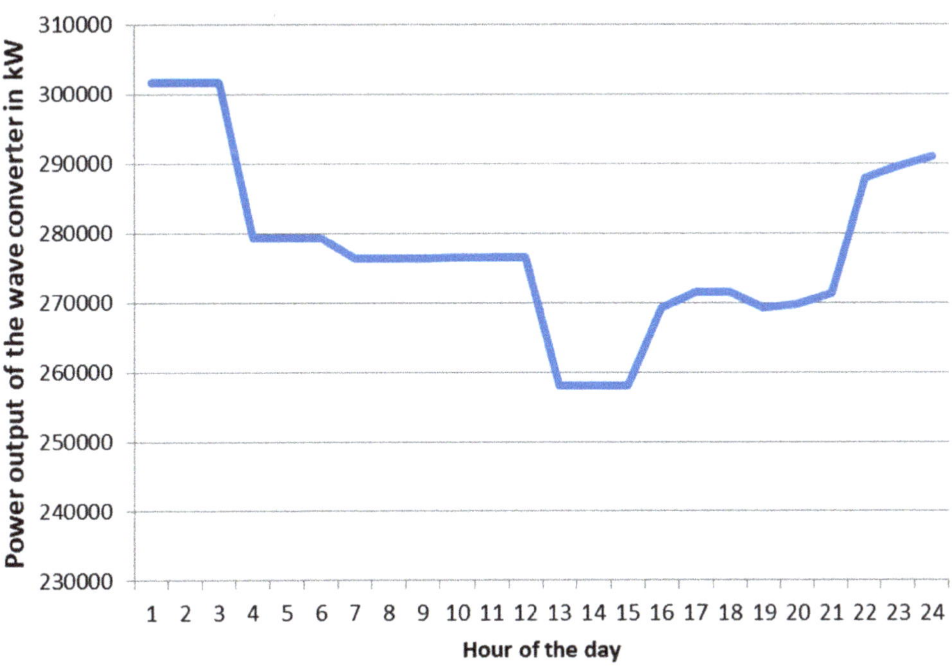

Figure 24. Output power from wave converter on a fall day.

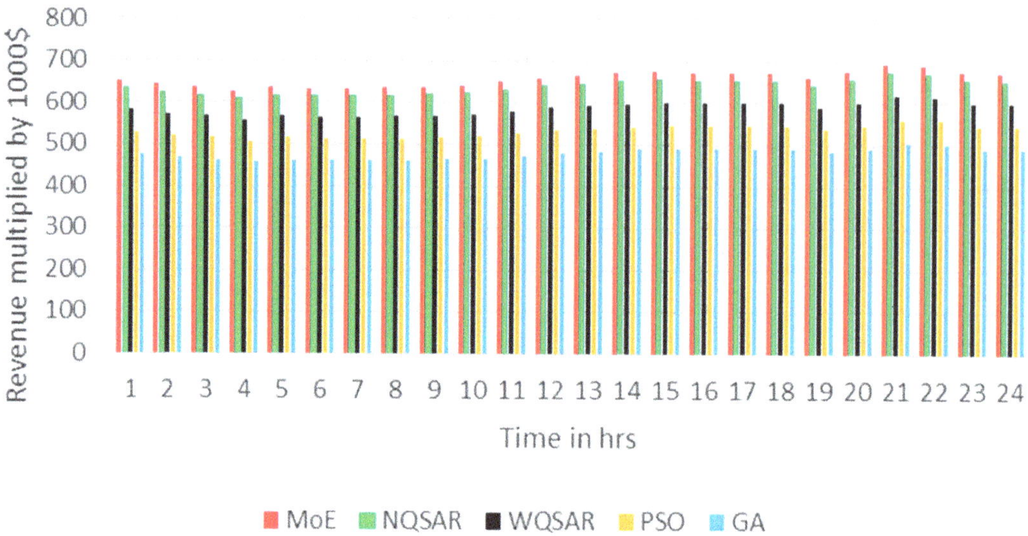

Figure 25. Revenue on a fall day.

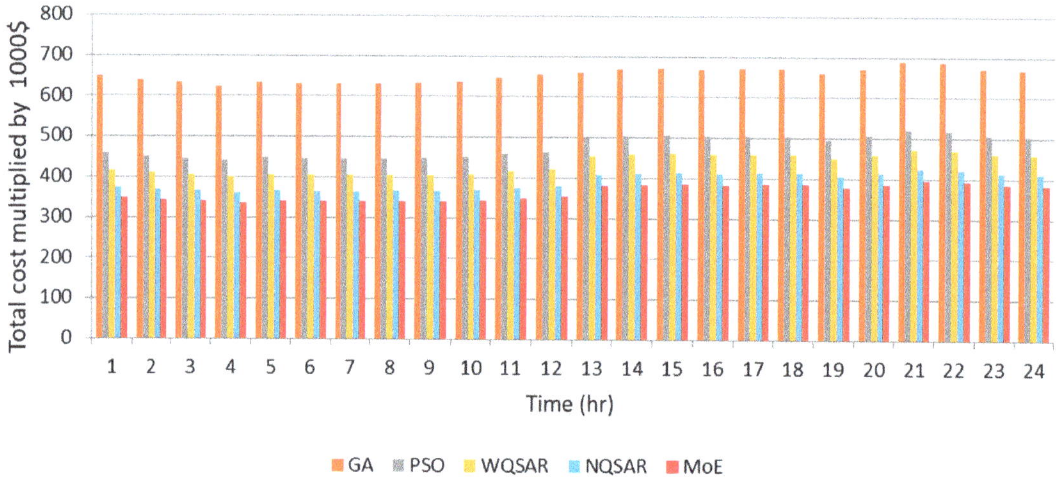

Figure 26. Cost of microgrid operation on a fall day.

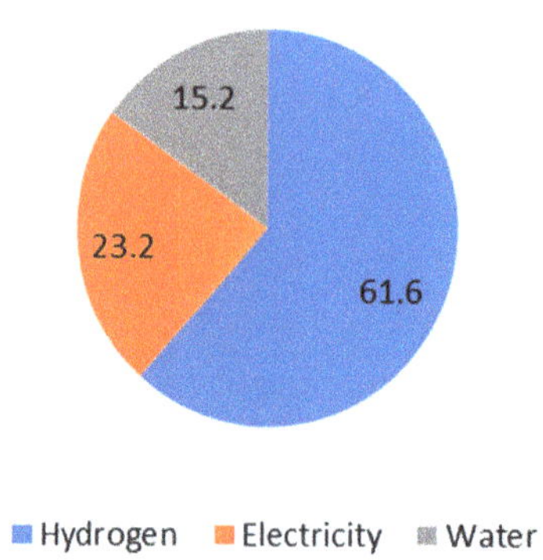

Figure 27. Share of income on a fall day.

6. Discussions

Wave-powered hydrogen, electricity, and water production offer significant environmental advantages, primarily by generating hydrogen with zero direct greenhouse gas emissions, unlike fossil fuel-based hydrogen methods. Additionally, wave energy has a minimal land footprint, reducing habitat disruption compared to large-scale solar or wind farms. The process also supports decarbonization efforts in hard-to-abate sectors, such as shipping and heavy industry, by providing a clean fuel alternative. However, regulatory barriers remain a challenge. The deployment of wave energy, water desalination, and hydrogen infrastructure requires complex permitting processes, environmental impact assessments, and compliance with evolving hydrogen safety standards. Furthermore, the lack of clear policies and incentives for marine renewable hydrogen production can delay project implementation and investment decisions. Addressing these challenges through streamlined regulations, government incentives, and international standardization will be crucial for accelerating the adoption of wave-powered hydrogen solutions.

The seasonal analysis of the microgrid system, optimized using the quantum-inspired Mixture of Experts (MoE) and other advanced algorithms, offers a comprehensive perspective on the performance and revenue potential of integrating wave energy with hydrogen production. The results for typical summer, winter, spring, and fall days highlight distinct variations in electricity demand, wave energy production, and revenue contributions from hydrogen sales and electricity generation.

On a typical summer day, the electricity demand peaks, while wave energy production is relatively lower compared to winter. The optimization results indicate that the MoE, followed by the normalized QSAR (NQSAR) and weighting factor QSAR (WQSAR), outperforms Particle Swarm Optimization (PSO) and Genetic Algorithm (GA) in enhancing revenue and reducing operational costs. Notably, hydrogen sales accounted for approximately two-thirds of the total income, underscoring the economic importance of hydrogen production in the microgrid's operational model.

During a winter day, the electricity demand is approximately 29% lower than in summer, but wave energy production nearly doubles. This seasonal shift enhances the capacity for hydrogen production and storage. The optimization results reaffirm the superiority of the MoE approach, followed by NQSAR and WQSAR, in achieving higher revenue and lower costs. Hydrogen sales contributed an even higher share of the income at approximately 70%, highlighting the critical role of hydrogen as a revenue driver during periods of high wave energy production.

Spring and fall days exhibit intermediate characteristics between summer and winter. In spring, electricity demand is 12% lower than in summer, and wave energy production is about 10% lower than in winter. Similarly, in fall, electricity demand is 11% lower than in summer, and wave energy production is 14% lower than in winter. In both cases, the MoE optimization technique consistently delivered the best results in terms of revenue generation and cost reduction, followed by NQSAR and WQSAR. Hydrogen sales accounted for approximately 65% and 60% of the total income in spring and fall, respectively, with electricity sales contributing a smaller but significant portion (22% in spring and 24% in fall).

These findings emphasize the effectiveness of advanced optimization techniques like MoE in adapting to seasonal variations in demand and resource availability. The consistent superiority of the MoE approach across all seasons demonstrates its robustness and adaptability in optimizing microgrid operations under diverse conditions. Compared to prior studies that primarily focused on singular optimization techniques, this study highlights the advantages of integrating quantum-inspired algorithms in managing complex energy systems. For instance, while traditional methods like PSO and GA are widely used, their performance in this study was outpaced by the MoE and QSAR approaches, particularly in balancing cost efficiency and revenue generation.

The economic viability of the system is further supported by the high contribution of hydrogen sales to total income, which aligns with the growing global interest in hydrogen as a clean energy carrier. The integration of hydrogen production systems into the microgrid provides not only a means for addressing seasonal energy storage needs but also a pathway for monetizing excess wave energy during periods of low electricity demand. These results are consistent with findings in recent renewable energy studies, reinforcing the critical role of hydrogen in future energy systems.

Despite these strengths, some limitations should be noted. The study assumes fixed costs for hydrogen and electricity, which may not reflect real-time market fluctuations. Additionally, while the system's capacity factor (26.2%) is promising, further research is needed to explore the long-term impacts of wave energy variability on operational stability. Future work should also investigate the potential of combining wave energy with other renewable resources, such as marine geothermal energy, to further enhance system resilience and scalability. Furthermore, policy support and economic incentives will play a pivotal role in scaling up such systems for broader adoption.

In this study, the MoE approach was selected over other optimization techniques, such as QSAR, GA, and PSO, due to its superior adaptability, performance, and interpretability in handling the specific challenges of our application. Unlike QSAR, which is primarily effective for linear relationships, MoE excels in capturing non-linear patterns by partitioning the problem space and assigning specialized models (experts) to distinct regions. While GA and PSO are powerful optimization tools, they often suffer from computational inefficiency and suboptimal convergence in high-dimensional spaces. In contrast, MoE leverages a gating network to dynamically allocate resources to the most relevant experts, resulting in faster and more accurate optimization. Additionally, MoE offers enhanced interpretability, as the contributions of individual experts and the gating network can be analyzed to understand their roles in the final solution—a critical advantage in our application. Furthermore, MoE demonstrates greater robustness to noisy data compared to QSAR, GA, and PSO, as the gating network can effectively filter out irrelevant or noisy inputs by assigning low weights to less reliable experts. These attributes collectively justify the selection of MoE as the preferred approach for this study.

To assess the impact of market fluctuations on the feasibility of wave-to-hydrogen production in Humboldt Bay, a sensitivity analysis was conducted on hydrogen, electricity, and water prices. Hydrogen prices varied within a range of USD2.5/kg (optimistic), USD5.0/kg (baseline), and USD10.0/kg (pessimistic), reflecting current market conditions and future projections. Similarly, electricity prices were analyzed at USD0.03/kWh (renewable-rich scenario), USD0.07/kWh (current average), and USD0.15/kWh (high-cost grid dependence). Additionally, variations in water prices were considered, given the importance of water supply in electrolysis. Water costs were assessed within USD0.5/m^3 (low-cost access), USD1.5/m^3 (moderate cost), and USD3.0/m^3 (high-cost regions) to reflect different sourcing conditions, including desalination and municipal supply. The results indicate that lower hydrogen, electricity, and water costs significantly improve project feasibility, reducing the Levelized Cost of Hydrogen (LCOH) and enhancing economic viability. Conversely, high electricity and water prices increase operational costs, posing challenges to competitiveness, particularly in regions with limited freshwater availability. These findings highlight the importance of cost-efficient energy and water sourcing, as well as potential policy incentives, to enhance the feasibility of wave-powered hydrogen production.

Overall, the integration of advanced optimization techniques and hybrid renewable systems positions this study as a significant contribution to the ongoing transition toward sustainable energy solutions, particularly in coastal and resource-rich regions like Humboldt Bay. In future studies, research will be applied to power quality, stability, and control of the proposed microgrid.

7. Conclusions

This study demonstrates the transformative potential of integrating wave energy with hydrogen production using advanced optimization techniques to supply a bay with water and electricity then selling both and the hydrogen. The quantum-inspired Mixture of Experts (MoE) consistently outperformed other methods, achieving superior revenue and cost efficiency across all seasons. Hydrogen production emerged as the primary revenue driver, contributing up to 70% of total income, while the system's capacity factor of 26.2% underscores the viability of wave energy for coastal regions in the United States and worldwide. By addressing seasonal variations and leveraging cutting-edge optimization, this research sets a benchmark for hybrid renewable systems. Future exploration of real-time implementation and the integration of additional resources like marine geothermal energy can further enhance scalability and resilience. These findings provide a solid foundation for advancing sustainable energy solutions, aligning with global clean energy goals.

Author Contributions: Conceptualization, H.H.F.; methodology, H.H.F.; software, H.H.F. and F.H.F.; validation, E.R.; formal analysis, F.H.F.; investigation, E.R.; resources, E.R.; data curation, F.H.F.; writing—original draft preparation, H.H.F.; writing—review and editing, E.R.; visualization, F.H.F.; supervision, E.R.; project administration, H.H.F.; funding acquisition, E.R. All authors have read and agreed to the published version of the manuscript.

Funding: No external fund was received for this research.

Institutional Review Board Statement: Not applicable.

Informed Consent Statement: Not applicable.

Data Availability Statement: Data are contained within the article.

Conflicts of Interest: The authors declare no conflicts of interest.

References

1. IEA. Introduction to the Water-Energy Nexus Report. International Energy Agency. 23 March 2020. Available online: https://www.iea.org/articles/introduction-to-the-water-energy-nexus (accessed on 22 January 2025).
2. Shenouda, A.; Hagras, M.A.; Rusu, E.; Ismael, S.; Fayek, H.H.; Balah, A. Selecting Appropriate Water–Energy Solutions for Desalination Projects in Coastal Areas. *J. Mar. Sci. Eng.* **2024**, *12*, 1901. [CrossRef]
3. Fayek, H.H.; Mohammadi-Ivatloo, B. Tidal Supplementary Control Schemes-Based Load Frequency Regulation of a Fully Sustainable Marine Microgrid. *Inventions* **2020**, *5*, 53. [CrossRef]
4. Li, H.; Wu, J. CFD Simulation of the Wave Pattern Above a Submerged Wave Energy Converter. *J. Mar. Sci. Eng.* **2025**, *13*, 23. [CrossRef]
5. Gomes, R.P.F.; Gato, L.M.C.; Henriques, J.C.C.; Portillo, J.C.C.; Howey, B.; Collins, K.M.; Hann, M.R.; Greaves, D.M. Compact floating wave energy converters arrays: Mooring loads and survivability through scale physical modelling. *Appl. Energy* **2020**, *280*, 115982. [CrossRef]
6. Le, T.T.; Sharma, P.; Bora, B.J.; Tran, V.D.; Truong, T.H.; Le, H.C.; Nguyen, P.Q.P. Fueling the Future: A Comprehensive Review of Hydrogen Energy Systems and Their Challenges. *Int. J. Hydrogen Energy* **2024**, *54*, 791–816. [CrossRef]
7. U.S. Department of Energy. U.S. National Clean Hydrogen Strategy and Roadmap. 2020. Available online: https://www.hydrogen.energy.gov (accessed on 22 January 2025).
8. Taroual, K.; Nachtane, M.; Rouway, M.; Tarfaoui, M.; Faik, A.; Mînzu, V.; Hilmi, K.; Saifaoui, D. Marine Renewable-Driven Green Hydrogen Production toward a Sustainable Solution and a Low-Carbon Future in Morocco. *J. Mar. Sci. Eng.* **2024**, *12*, 774. [CrossRef]

9. Fayek, H.H.; Fayek, F.H.; Rusu, E. Operation of a 100% Off-Shore Renewable Energy Micro-Grid for Water, Hydrogen, and Electricity. In Proceedings of the 2024 International Conference on Machine Intelligence and Smart Innovation (ICMISI), Alexandria, Egypt, 12–14 May 2024.
10. Billah, S.B.; Kabir, K.M.; Islam, M.O.; Barua, S.; Mahmud, M.S.; Hossain, M.S. Hydrogen Energy Storage Based Green Power Plant in Seashore of Bangladesh: Design and Optimal Cost Analysis. In Proceedings of the 2017 International Conference on Innovations in Green Energy and Healthcare Technologies (IGEHT), Coimbatore, India, 16–18 March 2017.
11. Liu, Z.; Wang, H.; Zhou, B.; Yang, D.; Li, G.; Yang, B.; Xi, C.; Hu, B. Optimal Operation Strategy for Wind–Hydrogen–Water Power Grids Facing Offshore Wind Power Accommodation. *Sustainability* **2022**, *14*, 6871. [CrossRef]
12. Gutiérrez-Martín, F.; Amodio, L.; Pagano, M. Hydrogen Production by Water Electrolysis and Off-Grid Solar PV. *Int. J. Hydrogen Energy* **2021**, *46*, 29038–29048. [CrossRef]
13. Fayek, H.H.; Abdalla, O.H. Maximization of Renewable Power Generation for Optimal Operation of the Egyptian Grid. In Proceedings of the 2020 IEEE 29th International Symposium on Industrial Electronics (ISIE), Delft, The Netherlands, 17–19 June 2020; pp. 1033–1038.
14. Fayek, H.H.; Abdalla, O.H. Operation of the Egyptian Power Grid with Maximum Penetration Level of Renewable Energies Using Corona Virus Optimization Algorithm. *Smart Cities* **2022**, *5*, 34–53. [CrossRef]
15. Mohammadzadeh, M.; Akbari, E.; Salameh, A.A.; Ghadamyari, M.; Pirouzi, S.; Senjyu, T. Application of Mixture of Experts in Machine Learning-Based Controlling of DC-DC Power Electronics Converter. *IEEE Access* **2022**, *10*, 117157–117169. [CrossRef]
16. Chen, D.; Zhou, X. AttMoE: Attention with Mixture of Experts for Remaining Useful Life Prediction of Lithium-Ion Batteries. *J. Energy Storage* **2024**, *84 Pt A*, 110780. [CrossRef]
17. Tong, J.; Liu, Z.; Zhang, Y.; Zheng, X.; Jin, J. Improved Multi-Gate Mixture-of-Experts Framework for Multi-Step Prediction of Gas Load. *Energy* **2023**, *282*, 128344. [CrossRef]
18. Hsu, C.-C.; Jiang, B.-H.; Lin, C.-C. A Survey on Recent Applications of Artificial Intelligence and Optimization for Smart Grids in Smart Manufacturing. *Energies* **2023**, *16*, 7660. [CrossRef]
19. Veerasamy. QSAR—An Important In-Silico Tool in Drug Design and Discovery. In *Advances in Computational Modeling and Simulation*; Springer Nature: Singapore, 2022; pp. 191–208.
20. Lewis, R.A.; Wood, D.J. Modern 2D QSAR for Drug Discovery. Wiley Interdiscip. *Rev. Comput. Mol. Sci.* **2014**, *4*, 505–522. [CrossRef]
21. Tropsha, A. Best Practices for QSAR Model Development, Validation, and Exploitation. *Mol. Inform.* **2010**, *29*, 476–488. [CrossRef] [PubMed]
22. Bouhrim, H.; El Marjani, A.; Nechad, R.; Hajjout, I. Ocean Wave Energy Conversion: A Review. *J. Mar. Sci. Eng.* **2024**, *12*, 1922. [CrossRef]
23. Sheng, W. Wave energy conversion and hydrodynamics modelling technologies: A review. *Renew. Sustain. Energy Rev.* **2019**, *109*, 482–498. [CrossRef]
24. Ahn, S.; Haas, K.A.; Neary, V.S. Wave energy resource characterization and assessment for coastal waters of the United States. *Appl. Energy* **2020**, *267*, 114922. [CrossRef]
25. Katakam, V.S.S.; Bahadur, V. Reverse Osmosis-Based Water Treatment for Green Hydrogen Production. *Desalination* **2024**, *581*, 117588. [CrossRef]
26. Humboldt Bay Harbor District. About Humboldt Bay. Available online: https://www.humboldtbay.org (accessed on 15 January 2025).
27. Humboldt Bay Harbor, Recreation, and Conservation District. Humboldt Bay Management Plan. 2007. Available online: https://humboldtbay.org/sites/humboldtbay2.org/files/documents/hbmp2007/HumBayMgmtPLAN_print.pdf (accessed on 10 August 2024).
28. California State Parks. Humboldt Bay and Surrounding Areas. Available online: https://www.parks.ca.gov (accessed on 15 January 2025).
29. California Coastal Commission. Humboldt Bay: A Coastal Resource. Available online: https://www.coastal.ca.gov (accessed on 15 January 2025).
30. National Renewable Energy Laboratory (NREL). *System Advisor Model (SAM)*; Version 2024.12.12; National Renewable Energy Laboratory (NREL): Golden, CO, USA, 2024. Available online: https://sam.nrel.gov (accessed on 22 January 2025).
31. Roy, K.; Kar, S.; Das, R.N. *Understanding the Basics of QSAR for Applications in Pharmaceutical Sciences and Risk Assessment*; Academic Press: San Diego, CA, USA, 2015.
32. Ayoka, T.O.; Uchegbu, U.J.; Alabuike, C.C.; Nnadi, C.O. Efficient Classification and Regression Models for the QSAR of Chloroquine Analogues Against Chloroquine-Sensitive and Chloroquine-Resistant Plasmodium Falciparum. *Lett. Appl. NanoBioSci.* **2024**, *13*, 90.
33. Filzmoser, P.; Maronna, R.; Werner, M. Outlier Detection in High-Dimensional Spaces. *Comput. Stat. Data Anal.* **2008**, *52*, 1694–1711. [CrossRef]

34. Vats, A.; Raja, R.; Jain, V.; Chadha, A. The Evolution of Mixture of Experts: A Survey from Basics to Breakthroughs. *Preprints* **2024**, 2024080583. [CrossRef]
35. Rauf, H.; Khalid, M.; Arshad, N. Machine Learning in State of Health and Remaining Useful Life Estimation: Theoretical and Technological Development in Battery Degradation Modelling. *Renew. Sustain. Energy Rev.* **2022**, *156*, 111903. [CrossRef]
36. Felser, T.; Trenti, M.; Sestini, L.; Gianelle, A.; Zuliani, D.; Lucchesi, D.; Montangero, S. Quantum-Inspired Machine Learning on High-Energy Physics Data. *NPJ Quantum Inf.* **2021**, *7*, 111. [CrossRef]

Journal of Marine Science and Engineering

Article

Long-Term (1979–2024) Variation Trend in Wave Power in the South China Sea

Yifeng Tong [1,2], Junmin Li [1,3,*], Wuyang Chen [1] and Bo Li [1,3,*]

1 State Key Laboratory of Tropical Oceanography, Key Laboratory of Science and Technology on Operational Oceanography, South China Sea Institute of Oceanology, Chinese Academy of Sciences, Guangzhou 511458, China; tongyifeng23@mails.ucas.ac.cn (Y.T.); chenwuyang@scsio.ac.cn (W.C.)
2 University of Chinese Academy of Sciences, Beijing 100049, China
3 Sanya Institute of Ocean Eco-Environmental Engineering, Sanya 572025, China
* Correspondence: jli@scsio.ac.cn (J.L.); libo@scsio.ac.cn (B.L.)

Abstract: Wave power (WP) is a strategic oceanic resource. Previous studies have extensively researched the long-term variations in WP in the South China Sea (SCS) for energy planning and utilization. This study extends the analysis of long-term trends to the last year based on ERA5 (European Centre for Medium-Range Weather Forecasts Reanalysis v5) reanalysis data from 1979 to 2024. Our results mainly indicate that the trends in WP after 2011 are significantly different from those before 2011. Before 2011, the WP in the SCS primarily showed an increasing trend, but, after 2011, it shifted to a decreasing trend. This trend has seasonal differences, manifested as being consistent with the annual trend in winter and spring while being inconsistent with the annual trend in summer and autumn. It indicates that the opposite trend in WP before and after 2011 was mainly the result of WP variations in winter and spring. To illustrate the driving factor for the WP's variations, the contemporary long-term trend of the wind fields is systematically analyzed. Analysis results reveal that, regardless of seasonal differences or spatial distribution, the two trends are consistent in most situations, indicating that wind fields are the dominant factor for the long-term variations in WP. Meanwhile, the effects of the wind fields on the WP variations can also be modulated by environmental factors such as oceanic swell propagation and local topography. This study contributes to the knowledge of the latest trends and driving factors regarding the WP in the SCS.

Keywords: wave power; wave energy resource; long-term trend; South China Sea; ERA5

1. Introduction

Wave power (WP) has essential strategic value in remote seas where laying power grids is costly. By utilizing the vast and largely untapped energy from ocean waves, WP can reduce reliance on traditional fossil fuels and provide a reliable and continuous power supply [1–5]. It can offer green energy for observation equipment, oil drilling platforms, ranches, and other offshore facilities. For example, WP can supplement the energy requirements of remote islands [6,7], where conventional energy infrastructure is often challenging to establish and maintain.

It is necessary to carry out systematic resource assessments before planning WP deployment projects and designing the wave energy converters [2–5]. Take the South China Sea (SCS), the largest marginal sea in the western Pacific, as an example; due to its unique geographical characteristics and rich marine resources, many studies have been performed to assess the richness and stability of WP resources, based on in situ observations, satellite data, and numerical models [6–16]. For example, numerical models reveal that the WP is richest in the northern deep basin area of the SCS [8,11,12]. Meanwhile, it can be influenced by shallow topography such as islands [6,12,13,15] and coastal regions [6,9,10,14,16]. As a result, the WP exhibits significant seasonal and regional variations under the combined effects of seasonal winds and shallow topography in the SCS, e.g., [14,15].

Because WP is a strategic oceanic resource, accessing the long-term development trends is particularly important. Therefore, recent studies have increasingly paid more attention to the long-term variations and their forcing driving mechanisms in the WP assessment studies for the SCS [17–22]. For example, Ching-Piao et al. quantitatively evaluated the variations in wave climate in the northwestern Pacific and Taiwan waters based on a long-term wave dataset [17]. Zheng et al. proposed that the China Seas exhibited a significant overall increasing trend in WP density for several decades, mainly before 2011 [18–20]. They point out that the rising trend in winter and spring is more substantial than that in summer and autumn in the SCS [18]. Sun et al. focused on the WP trend in the coastal regions of the China Seas, and their results emphasize the significantly increasing trend in the northern coastal SCS during winter [21,22]. Liu et al. evaluated the long-term variability in global WP and demonstrated the increasing WP results from the global climate change and intensification of the Antarctic Oscillation [23]. Although the existing studies have greatly enhanced our understanding of long-term characteristics and distribution patterns for the WP in the SCS, most of the analysis focuses on a monotonic trend within a limited period. Previous studies have pointed out that a WP peak appeared in 2011 for the SCS (e.g., [18,19]); however, the long-term trend after this peak, especially its difference compared to the trend before 2011, has still received limited attention.

Moreover, clarifying the driving factors behind the trends will help us understand the variation mechanism and further predict WP. The SCS has a complex topography [24] and a unique oceanographic environment [25], and the factors affecting WP variation should be comprehensively considered. Previous studies have shown that the seasonal distribution of and variation in the wind field are the main driving forces that cause the variance of waves and WP. For example, Zheng et al. conducted a regionalization analysis of wind and wave energy resources in the East China Sea and the SCS [26]; Wang et al. assessed wave and wind energy in the Weifang Sea area over 20 years [27]; Dong et al. simulated the wind and wave energy resources in the waters off the Yangtze River Delta [28]. Their results reveal a close relationship between wind and wave energy. However, for the SCS, in addition to wind forcing, the modulation of environmental factors such as topography and background swells on the WP may also need to be considered. This is because, although the direction of wind and waves changes seasonally with the monsoon, the swell energy from the deep ocean that propagates from the northeast to the southwest throughout the year always dominates [15,29]; in addition, complex topographic factors have a significant impact on the wave dynamics and energy in local areas [12,13].

Based on the above considerations, this study extends the WP long-term trend analysis to the most recent year. It systematically analyzes the spatial and seasonal distribution characteristics of the trend in the SCS from 1979 to 2024. The study focuses on the differences between the trends before and after 2011. Based on the results of the WP's long-term trend, the driving mechanisms of the trend are discussed in relation to the wind field's contemporary variations. Background environmental factors such as topography and swell are combined into the discussion for the situations where trends in WP and winds are not entirely consistent.

2. Data and Methods

2.1. Data

2.1.1. Reanalysis Data

The European Centre for Medium-Range Weather Forecasts Reanalysis v5 (ERA5) reanalysis data were employed to analyze the wave energy resources in the SCS. The data consist of the fifth generation of global meteorological reanalysis products released by the European Center for Medium-Range Weather Forecasts [30,31]. Parameters including significant wave height (*Hs*) and energy period (*Te*) with a spatial resolution of 0.5° from 1 January 1979 to 31 December 2024, with a time resolution of 1 h, were obtained from the product. The quality of ERA5 wave data has been thoroughly validated by different authors [32,33]. This dataset has also been applied in various aspects, such as observation data reconstruction [34], satellite data calibration [35], and wave energy resource analysis [15].

To discuss the dynamic reasons for the long-term trend in WP, the wind data from the ERA5 dataset were employed to compare the spatiotemporal characteristics of the wind fields with WP variations. There are many widely used wind field datasets provided by satellite remote sensing observations or model assimilation reanalysis results [36–39]. The reason for choosing the ERA5 wind data in this study is that these data have enough reliability and sufficient spatiotemporal coverage. Prior investigations from different global regions have shown that the ERA5 wind field data match the performance of other popular wind products, such as the NCEP version 2 coupled forecast system model (CFSv2) and the satellite altimeter data [38,39]. In the SCS, the accuracy of ERA5's wind field data is similar to that of the products provided by satellite remote sensing data [36] and the data assimilation system of the China Meteorological Administration [37]. More importantly, ERA5 data have global coverage, including the entire SCS, with a horizontal spatial resolution of 0.25°, and the data period can cover the whole analysis period from 1979 to 2024. It is vital to have sufficient time and space coverage for the wind data to match the WP assessment results in this study.

2.1.2. Bouy Observations

In this study, the accuracy of ERA5 reanalysis data in evaluating WP in the SCS was further verified using in situ observations from a buoy. The buoy is located in the middle of the southern SCS at a longitude of 130 °E and a latitude of 9.5 °N (Figure 1). It was deployed by the South China Sea Institute of Oceanology, Chinese Academy of Sciences, in 2020. Due to communication interruption, the buoy's data remained interrupted for a long time before 22 February 2021 and after 2 October 2021. For this reason, this study uses data from 22 February to 2 October 2021, totaling more than seven consecutive months. The results of comparing the observed data with the WP density calculated by ERA5 are detailed in Section 3.1.

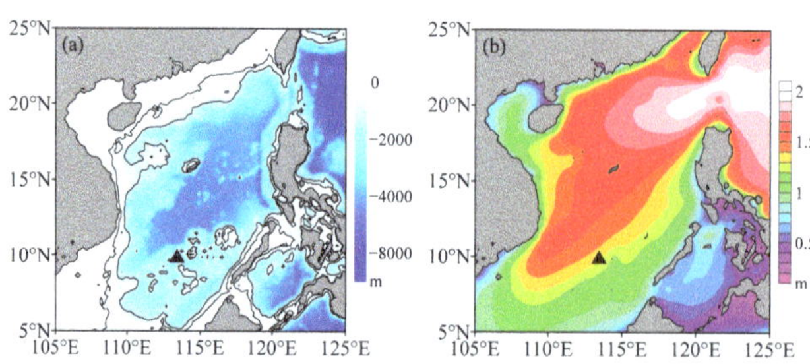

Figure 1. (**a**) Topography and (**b**) climatological mean (1979–2024) of significant wave height in the South China Sea (SCS), accompanied by the location of the buoy observation (black triangle) employed in this study. The contour lines in (**a**) represent the 100 and 1000 m isobaths.

2.2. Methods

2.2.1. Calculation of the Energy Density

Based on previous studies on WP assessments in different sea regions, e.g., [4,12,18], the following equation was used to calculate the WP density (Pw):

$$Pw = \rho g^2 Hs^2 Te/64\pi \quad (1)$$

where Hs is the significant wave height, Te is the wave energy period, g is the gravitational acceleration, and ρ is the seawater density, which equals 1025 kg/m^3 in this study.

Due to data resolution of only 0.5°, and considering the spatial continuity of the wave field, the Kriging method was used for interpolation when plotting the results. In the resulting graphs, the actual resolution of the plot is 0.2°. All the graphs displaying spatial distribution in this paper were made using the Surfer software version 11.0.642.

2.2.2. Determination of the Long-Term Trend

The annual and seasonal mean Pw of all spatial grids from 1979 to 2024 was calculated, and then linear fittings were performed relative to the annual and seasonal mean Pw. The slope obtained by the fitting was applied to represent the interannual variation trend in WP at the corresponding locations and during the corresponding seasons. Linear fitting methods offer substantial advantages in terms of computational simplicity and efficiency, making them ideal for large-scale datasets and long-term trend research [40,41]. In practice, the outcomes of linear fitting and other trend computations are generally identical [21]; nevertheless, it is a more straightforward computational process, making it a better choice in many scenarios [42].

At the same time, the reliability of the trends was evaluated through correlation analysis and p-value testing. The p-value was obtained by analyzing the correlation between the mean Pw and the year series, which can be used to evaluate the significance of the long-term trend.

Due to an impressive peak in the annual mean Pw that occurred in 2011 (see the results in Section 3.2 below), this study further divides the data into two periods, 1979–2011 and 2011–2024, with an emphasis on the analysis of the differences in the WP's interannual trend in the two periods.

3. Results

3.1. Validity of ERA5 Data Applied in This Study

Pw was calculated using ERA5 and buoy-measured data. The comparison results show that the Pw calculated using the ERA5 data agree with that calculated using the buoy observation data (Figure 2). The observed data and computed results are highly consistent regarding time series and scatter comparison. The matched scatters are close to both sides of the 1:1 line. In addition, the baseline of the quantile–quantile plots is close to the $y = x$ line. Moreover, the two sets of calculated Pw are highly consistent in terms of their histograms, probability density, and cumulative density. According to statistics, the bias, MAE (mean absolute error), RMSE (root means square error), and SI (scatter index) are only −0.36 kW/m, 0.95 kW/m, 1.44 kW/m, and 0.28, respectively. The correlation coefficient (R) is as high as 0.94. These results suggest that the ERA5 reanalysis data are reliable for calculating WP in the SCS in this study.

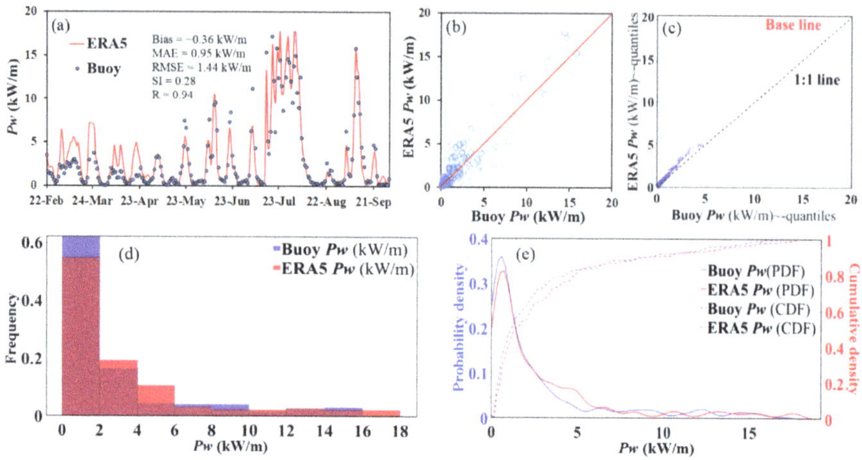

Figure 2. Comparison of wave power density (Pw) between buoy observations and ERA5 data in the form of (**a**) a time series, (**b**) a scatter diagram, (**c**) quantile–quantile plots, (**d**) a histogram, and (**e**) probability density function (PDF) and cumulative density function (CDF) graphs.

3.2. Overall Characteristics of Interannual WP Variations

Based on the Pw results from 1979 to 2024, it is found that the Pw in the SCS has significant annual and seasonal variations (Figure 3a). The WP is relatively high during winter and is relatively low during summer and spring. The peak of the monthly average Pw is about 20 kW/m during these years. By comparing the variations in the annual mean values, it is found that the WP appears to have experienced a generally increasing trend during the investigated 45 years (Figure 3b). As it can be seen from the figure, Pw reached its peak in 2011. Before 2011, Pw showed an increasing trend, with a growth rate of about 52.5 W/m/a. The significant ($p \leq 0.01$) upward annual trends from 1979 to 2011 and from 1979 to 2024 are also confirmed by correlation analysis. Moreover, the results of this study indicate that, during the past decade, from 2011 to 2024, the trend reversed, with a decline rate of about 52.6 W/m/a (Figure 3b). The reversal of this trend needs special attention in the future development planning of WP.

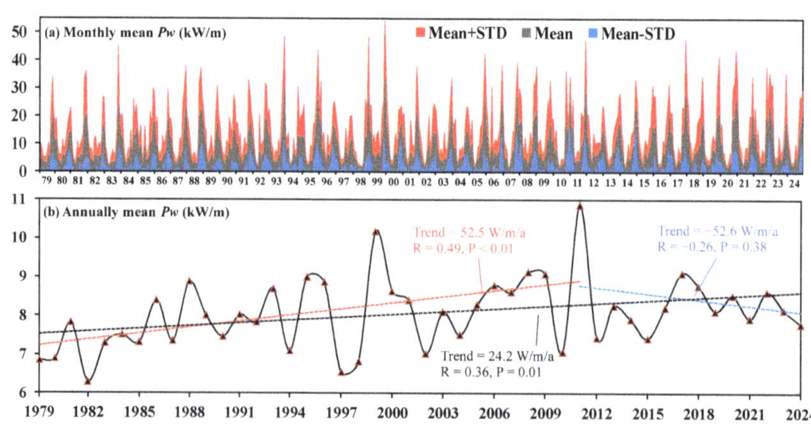

Figure 3. Variations in the monthly and annual mean Pw in the SCS during 1979–2024.

If we regard 2011 as a turning point and further analyze the spatial characteristics of the WP annual change rate, we can find that the spatial patterns of the WP's long-term change rate are consistent with the climatological mean WP intensity in the SCS (Figure 4). The spatial distributions in the figure reveal that the most apparent variation signal in the trends, no matter the strengthening trend before 2011 or the decreasing trend after 2011, mainly extends southwestward from the West Pacific and across the SCS along the deep-water basin.

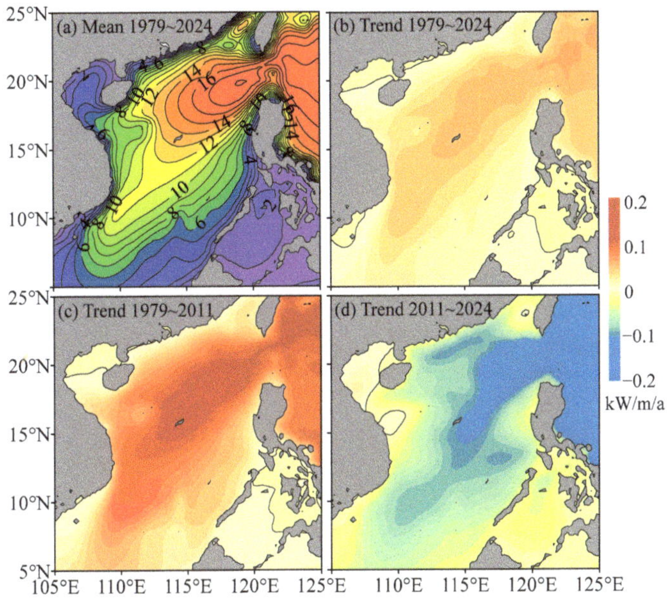

Figure 4. Spatial distribution of (**a**) the climatological mean (1979~2024) *Pw* in the SCS and the interannual variation trend in *Pw* during (**b**) 1979~2024, (**c**) 1979~2011, and (**d**) 2011~2024, respectively. The contour lines with numbers in (**a**) indicate the *Pw* values. The contour lines in (**b–d**) represent the trend equal to zero.

3.3. Seasonal Characteristics of WP Interannual Variations

The data were further divided into four seasons: spring (MAM), summer (JJA), autumn (SON), and winter (DJF), and then the interannual trend analysis from the previous section was further performed (Figure 5). The results show that the WP in spring and winter appears to have an upward trend before 2011 and a downward trend after 2011. The annual variation trend in WP in winter and spring is consistent with the yearly average variation trend of the SCS (Figure 2b). The upward trends in winter WP from 1979 to 2011 ($p < 0.01$) and from 1979 to 2024 ($p = 0.03$) and spring WP from 1979 to 2011 ($p < 0.01$) appear to be significant, with low p-values. The rising trend before 2011 and the falling trend after 2011 in winter are more potent than those recorded in other seasons. However, the WP trends in summer and autumn remain continuously downward and upward, respectively, from 1979 to 2024. Both trends after 2011 became more substantial than those before 2011 (Figure 4).

Further analysis of the spatial distribution of WP trends in the four seasons is presented in Figure 6. The figure shows that, for any statistical periods or seasons, the spatial patterns of the *Pw* trend are similar to those of the climatological mean *Pw* and the annual trends (Figure 4). The high-value areas of the trends always extend from the northeast to the southwest of the SCS (Figure 6). Section 3 presents the seasonal and spatial distribution of the long-term trend in WP. In the following Section 3, we focus on discussing the inner driving mechanisms behind these long-term trends.

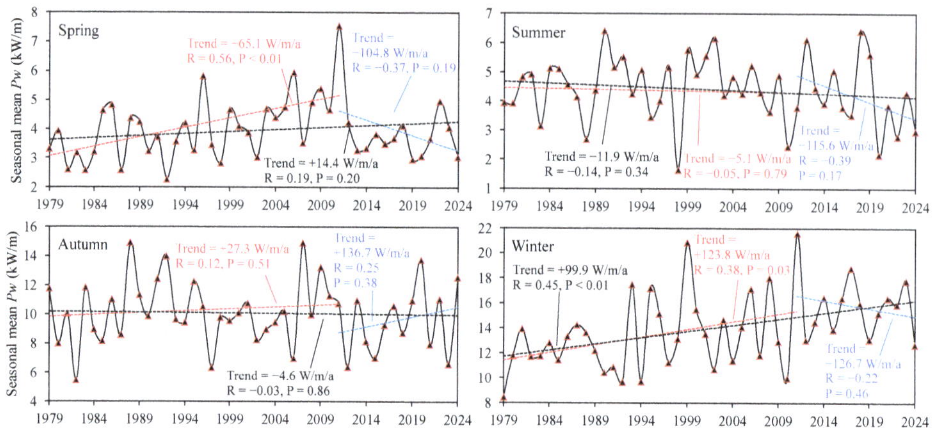

Figure 5. Annual variations and trends in the seasonal mean Pw in the SCS from 1979 to 2024.

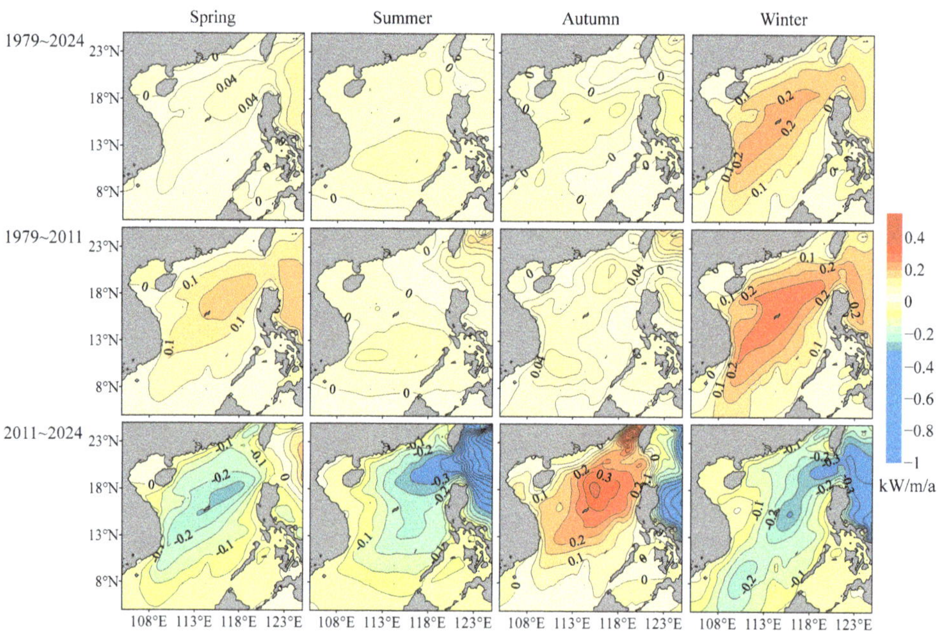

Figure 6. Spatial distribution of the interannual variation trend in Pw in the SCS in the four seasons during 1979–2024, 1979–2011, and 2011–2024, respectively.

4. Discussion

4.1. Effects of Seasonal Wind Fields on WP Variation

The above results reveal that the long-term trend in WP in the SCS from 1979 to 2024 can be divided into two parts: the increase from 1979 to 2011 and the decline from 2011 to 2024 (Figures 3 and 4). The increased trends before 2011 obtained in this study are consistent with previous studies with respect to magnitude [18–20] and spatial distribution characteristics [11,12,18] of the trends. The main difference between this study and previous ones is that we extend the trend analysis to the most recent years and point out that the long-term trend in WP from 2011 to 2024 is opposite to the trend before 2011.

In recent years, due to climate change, wind fields in the Western Pacific, and even in the rest of the world, have changed interannually [19,43–45]. Studies have shown that the increase in the frequency of strong winds is the main reason for the rising global wave height and WP trend [19,20,44]. Considering that the wind field is an essential driving factor for waves, the relationship between the variation trend in WP and the wind fields is further discussed in this section. Dominated by seasonal monsoons, the sea surface wind field is controlled by the strong northeasterly monsoon in winter and the northeasterly monsoon in summer (Figure 7). By analyzing the interannual variation of the wind field in the SCS, it can be found that the annual and seasonal variation trends in wind speed are generally consistent with WP variation. Figure 8 shows that the wind fields appear to have an increasing trend before 2011 and a decreasing trend after 2011 in different seasons. Whether before or after 2011, the variation in wind fields and WP is consistent (Figures 3b and 5). For example, wind speeds showed downward trends in summer from 1979 to 2011 and from 2022 to 2024; WP also exhibited such a trend.

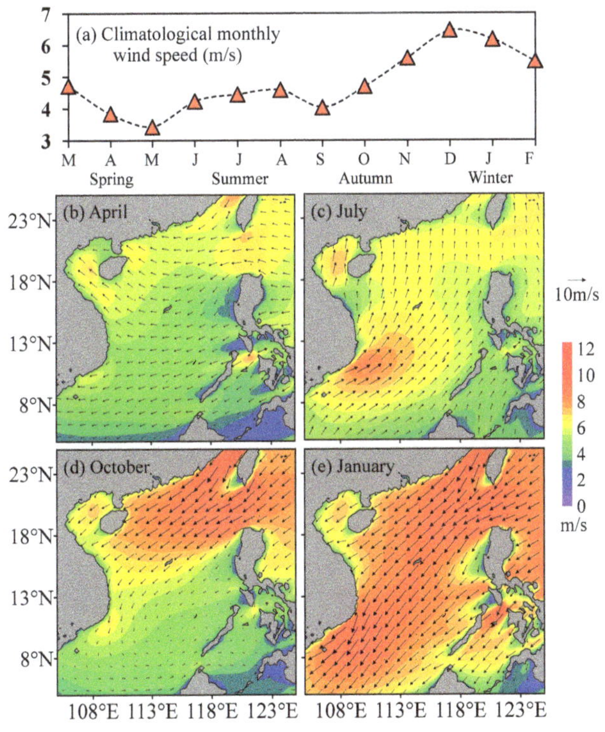

Figure 7. Climatological means (1979–2024) of (**a**) annual wind speed cycle and (**b**–**e**) monthly wind fields in the SCS in April, July, October, and January.

Further analysis of the spatial distribution of wind variations in the SCS is shown in Figure 9. By comparing this figure with Figure 6, it can be found that the WP and wind speed trends are in good agreement in terms of spatial distributions, regardless of the season and decade from which they were computed. For example, Figure 9 shows that the overall weakening trend in the autumn wind field in 2011–2024 (Figure 8) is mainly the result of the weakening wind field in the southern SCS. The wind field appears to have an increasing trend in the northern SCS, a phenomenon which is entirely consistent with the trend in WP (Figure 6). These consistencies further demonstrate that wind-forcing variations can be the direct factor behind the WP variations over the 45 years investigated in this study.

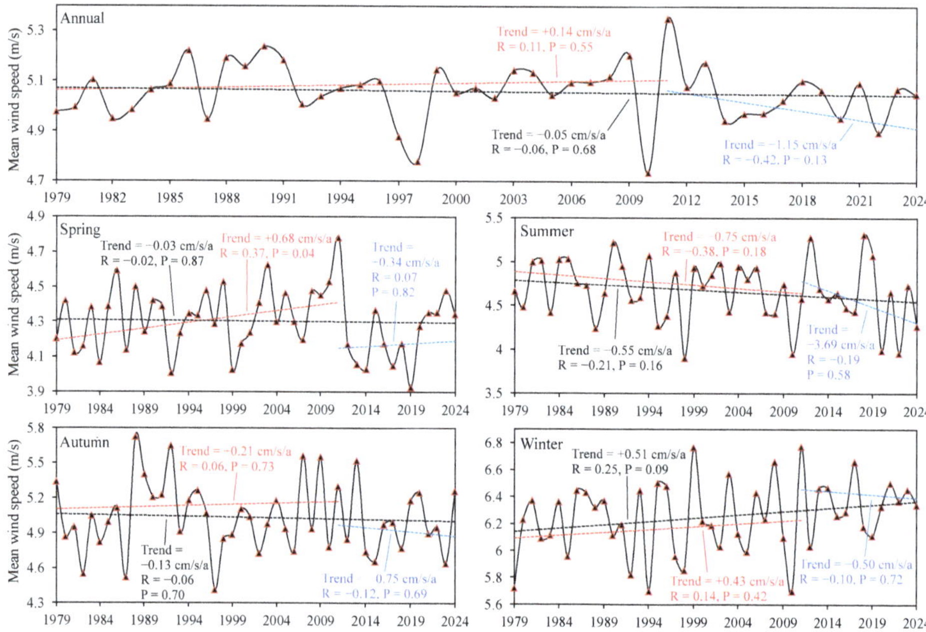

Figure 8. Variations and trends in the annual and seasonal mean wind speed in the SCS from 1979 to 2024.

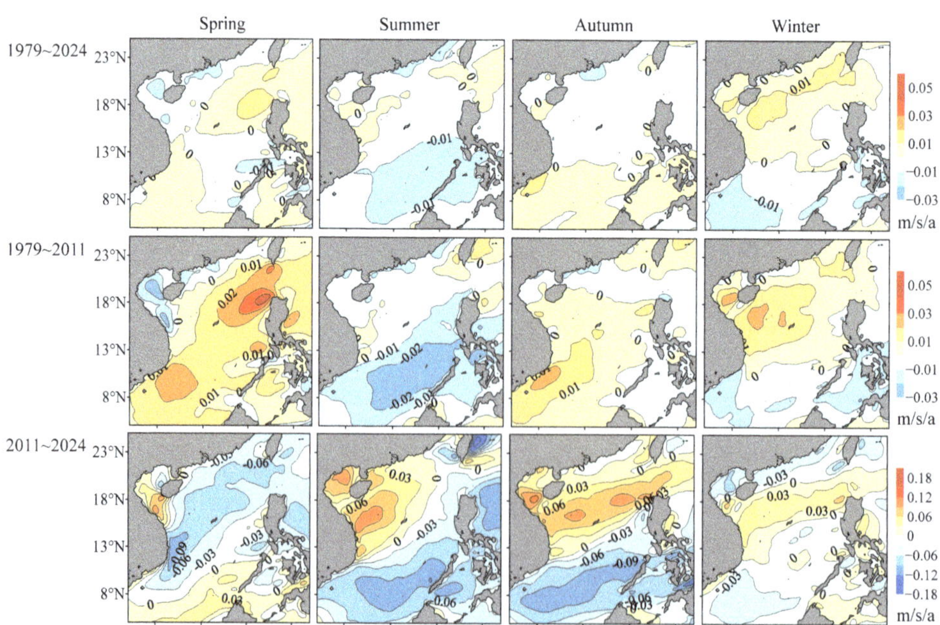

Figure 9. Spatial distribution of the interannual variation trend in the wind speed in the SCS in the four seasons during 1979–2024, 1979–2011, and 2011–2024, respectively.

4.2. Modulation of the Background Swell in Relation to the WP Variation

Although the wind fields in the SCS controlled by monsoons exhibit seasonal variations, the swells introduced from the Pacific always propagate from northeast to southwest throughout the year [12,29]. Our results also reflect the consistency between the long-term trend in WP and the propagation direction of swells (e.g., Figures 1b, 4a and 6). In this study, one notable phenomenon of the WP trends is that the high-value areas, regardless of the increasing trend during 1970–2011, 1979–2024, or the decreasing trend during 2011–2024, always extend from the northeast to the southwest of the SCS (Figures 4 and 6), such areas being aligned with the swell propagation pattern. In addition, the area with the highest trends appears to be located, in most cases, around the Luzon strait, where oceanic swells from the Western Pacific propagate into the SCS, in agreement with the results reported in previous studies, e.g., [12,18]. These phenomena mainly result from the regulatory effect of oceanic swells on the variation in WP in the SCS.

Another notable result is that the long-term trends in WP in winter and spring are consistent, but those in summer and autumn are inconsistent with the annual trend (Figure 3 vs. Figures 4 and 5 vs. Figure 6), indicating the vital contribution of these two seasons to the annual variations in WP. Note that, in winter and spring, the direction of wind vectors in most areas of the SCS is consistent with the direction of wave propagation, which is toward the southwest (Figure 7). In these circumstances, the variations in the wind field may form a combined effect with the swell, leading to a further increase in the impacts on the trends in WP.

Furthermore, it is worth noting that the long-term trend in the wind of 2011–2024 and the WP trend are inconsistent in their spatial distributions in the summer and winter. In both seasons, the wind fields in the northern SCS showed an increasing trend (Figure 9), while the WP showed a decreasing trend (Figure 6). The anomalies in the seasonal wind fields of 2011–2024 relative to their climatological seasonal means are illustrated in Figure 10 to explain the inconsistency. The figure reveals that it is probably due to the effects of the southwestward swells and local topography combined with the wind anomalies. For example, in the summer of 2011–2024, the abnormal wind field blowing toward the northeast was opposite in direction to that of the swells (Figure 10), so that the increase in wind speed may have weakened the WP. In the winter of 2011–2024, abnormal wind strengthening occurred around the northern coastal regions with shallow water (Figure 10), a phenomenon which may have attenuated wave energy [12,13]. Therefore, the effects of wind strengthening on waves may be limited. Previous studies have shown that, under specific environmental conditions, the interannual variations in WP are sensitive to the changes in speed and direction of winds [46,47]. Our results further confirm this sensitivity and indicate that the influence of swell and topography may be coupled with the effects of winds.

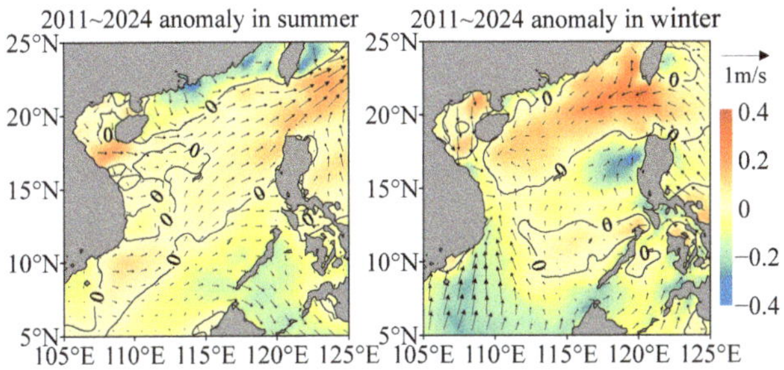

Figure 10. The 2011–2024 anomalous seasonal wind fields relative to the climatological seasonal means in summer and winter.

5. Conclusions

Based on the ERA5 (European Centre for Medium-Range Weather Forecasts Reanalysis v5) reanalysis data for 45 consecutive years from 1979 to 2024, this study systematically evaluates the interannual variation trend in wave power (WP) in the South China Sea (SCS). Based on the wind field data, the driving mechanism of the long-term WP trend is further discussed. The results can be summarized as the following points of conclusions.

(1) Although the WP experienced a general, long-term, increasing trend from 1979 to 2024, there was a remarkable turning point in 2011. Before 2011, the WP mainly exhibited an increasing trend, but such a trend reversed after 2011.

(2) The WP trend has remarkable seasonal and spatial variation characteristics. Seasonally, the trends in winter and spring are consistent, while the trends in summer and autumn are inconsistent with the annual trend. Spatially, the high-value area of the trend mainly extends from the northeast to the southwest over the deep basin.

(3) The variations in wind fields are the direct forcing factor leading to the long-term variation in WP. Meanwhile, the background swells propagating from the Western Pacific and the local shallow topography can also play essential roles in the modulation of the WP's variation trend.

This study contributes to the continuously updated research on wave energy resources and their long-term trends in the SCS by extending the trend analysis to the most recent year. The results emphasize the opposite long-term trend in WP before and after 2011, and the mechanism can be related to coupled effects combining dynamic and environmental factors. However, our study still has limitations regarding the mechanisms by which global climate change affects wind fields and swells. Therefore, the complexity of the long-term variation in WP should be fully considered, and the mechanism for the variations still needs to be further clarified in future studies.

Author Contributions: Conceptualization, J.L.; methodology, Y.T.; software, Y.T.; validation, J.L.; formal analysis, Y.T. and W.C.; investigation, W.C.; resources, J.L. and B.L.; data curation, W.C.; writing—original draft preparation, Y.T. and J.L.; writing—review and editing, J.L.; visualization, W.C.; supervision, J.L. and B.L.; project administration, J.L.; funding acquisition, J.L. and B.L. All authors have read and agreed to the published version of the manuscript.

Funding: This research was funded by the Guangdong Basic and Applied Basic Research Foundation (2023A1515011497 and 2024A1515010286), the Hainan Provincial Natural Science Foundation of China (422MS160), and the development fund of the South China Sea Institute of Oceanology of the Chinese Academy of Sciences (SCSIO202207), and the Administrative Bureau of Sanya Yazhou Bay Science and Technology City.

Institutional Review Board Statement: Not applicable.

Informed Consent Statement: Not applicable.

Data Availability Statement: The data will be available on request.

Acknowledgments: The analysis in this study was supported by the High-Performance Computing Division at the South China Sea Institute of Oceanology.

Conflicts of Interest: The authors declare no conflicts of interest.

Abbreviations

The following abbreviations are used in this manuscript:

WP	Wave power
SCS	South China Sea
ERA5	European Centre for Medium-Range Weather Forecasts Reanalysis v5
CFSv2	NCEP version 2 coupled forecast system model

NCEP	National Centers for Environmental Prediction
PDF	Probability density function
CDF	Cumulative density function
MAE	Mean absolute error
RMSE	Root means square error
SI	Scatter index
R	Correlation coefficient

References

1. Iglesias, G.; López, M.; Carballo, R.; Castro, A.; Fraguela, J.A.; Frigaard, P. Wave energy potential in Galicia (NW Spain). *Renew. Energy* **2009**, *34*, 2323–2333. [CrossRef]
2. Lehmann, M.; Karimpour, F.; Goudey, C.A.; Jacobson, P.T.; Alam, M.-R. Ocean wave energy in the United States: Current status and future perspectives. *Renew. Sustain. Energy Rev.* **2017**, *74*, 1300–1313. [CrossRef]
3. Kilcher, L.; García Medina, G.; Yang, Z. A scalable wave resource assessment methodology: Application to U.S. waters. *Renew. Energy* **2023**, *217*, 119094. [CrossRef]
4. Bouhrim, H.; El Marjani, A.; Nechad, R.; Hajjout, I. Ocean wave energy conversion: A review. *J. Mar. Sci. Eng.* **2024**, *12*, 1922. [CrossRef]
5. Pazhouhan, M.; Karimi Mazraeshahi, A.; Jahanbakht, M.; Rezanejad, K.; Rohban, M.H. Wave and tidal energy: A patent landscape study. *J. Mar. Sci. Eng.* **2024**, *12*, 1967. [CrossRef]
6. Li, B.; Chen, W.; Li, J.; Liu, J.; Shi, P. Integrated monitoring and assessments of marine energy for a small uninhabited island. *Energy Rep.* **2022**, *8*, 63–72. [CrossRef]
7. Li, B.; Li, J.; Chen, W.; Liu, J.; Shi, P. Meteo-climatic conditions of wind and wave in the perspective of joint energy exploitation: Case study of Dongluo Island, Hainan. *Atmosphere* **2022**, *13*, 1076. [CrossRef]
8. Zheng, C.W.; Pan, J.; Li, J.X. Assessing the China Sea wind energy and wave energy resources from 1988 to 2009. *Ocean Eng.* **2013**, *65*, 39–48. [CrossRef]
9. Zhou, G.; Huang, J.; Zhang, G. Evaluation of the wave energy conditions along the coastal waters of Beibu Gulf, China. *Energy* **2015**, *85*, 449–457. [CrossRef]
10. Chen, X.; Wang, K.; Zhang, Z.; Zeng, Y.; Zhang, Y.; O'Driscoll, K. An assessment of wind and wave climate as potential sources of renewable energy in the nearshore Shenzhen coastal zone of the South China Sea. *Energy* **2017**, *134*, 789–801. [CrossRef]
11. Wang, Z.; Duan, C.; Dong, S. Long-term wind and wave energy resource assessment in the South China Sea based on 30-year hindcast data. *Ocean Eng.* **2018**, *163*, 58–75. [CrossRef]
12. Sun, Z.; Zhang, H.; Xu, D.; Liu, X.; Ding, J. Assessment of wave power in the South China Sea based on 26-year high-resolution hindcast data. *Energy* **2020**, *197*, 117218. [CrossRef]
13. Sun, Z.; Zhang, H.; Liu, X.; Ding, J.; Cai, Z. Wave energy assessment of the Xisha Group Islands zone for the period 2010–2019. *Energy* **2021**, *220*, 119721. [CrossRef]
14. Chen, W.; Liu, J.; Li, J.; Sun, L.; Li, B.; Xing, H.; Shi, P. Wave energy assessment for the nearshore region of the northern South China Sea based on in situ observations. *Energy Rep.* **2022**, *8*, 149–158. [CrossRef]
15. Li, B.; Chen, W.; Li, J.; Liu, J.; Shi, P.; Xing, H. Wave energy assessment based on reanalysis data calibrated by buoy observations in the southern South China Sea. *Energy Rep.* **2022**, *8*, 5067–5079. [CrossRef]
16. Wen, Y.; Kamranzad, B.; Lin, P. Joint exploitation potential of offshore wind and wave energy along the south and southeast coasts of China. *Energy* **2022**, *249*, 123710. [CrossRef]
17. Ching-Piao, T.; Ching-Her, H.; Chien, H.; Hao-Yuan, C. Study on the wave climate variation to the renewable wave energy assessment. *Renew. Energy* **2012**, *38*, 50–61. [CrossRef]
18. Zheng, C.W.; Li, C.Y. Variation of the wave energy and significant wave height in the China Sea and adjacent waters. *Renew. Sustain. Energy Rev.* **2015**, *43*, 381–387. [CrossRef]
19. Zheng, C.; Zhang, R.; Shi, W.; Li, X.; Chen, X. Trends in significant wave height and surface wind speed in the China Seas between 1988 and 2011. *J. Ocean Univ. China* **2017**, *16*, 717–726. [CrossRef]
20. Zheng, C.-W. Global oceanic wave energy resource dataset—With the Maritime Silk Road as a case study. *Renew. Energy* **2021**, *169*, 843–854. [CrossRef]
21. Sun, P.; Xu, B.; Wang, J. Long-term trend analysis and wave energy assessment based on ERA5 wave reanalysis along the Chinese coastline. *Appl. Energy* **2022**, *324*, 119709. [CrossRef]
22. Sun, P.; Wang, J. Long-term variability analysis of wave energy resources and its impact on wave energy converters along the Chinese coastline. *Energy* **2024**, *288*, 129644. [CrossRef]
23. Liu, J.; Li, R.; Li, S.; Meucci, A.; Young, I.R. Increasing wave power due to global climate change and intensification of Antarctic Oscillation. *Appl. Energy* **2024**, *358*, 122572. [CrossRef]

24. Duan, Y.; Liu, Y.; Li, M.; Zhou, M.; Yang, Y. Survey of reefs based on Landsat 8 operational land imager (OLI) images in the Nansha Islands, South China Sea. *Acta Oceanol. Sin.* **2016**, *35*, 11–19. [CrossRef]
25. Shaw, P.-T. The seasonal variation of the intrusion of the Philippine sea water into the South China Sea. *J. Geophys. Res. Oceans* **1991**, *96*, 821–827. [CrossRef]
26. Zheng, C.W.; Zhuang, H.; Li, X.; Li, X.Q. Wind energy and wave energy resources assessment in the East China Sea and South China Sea. *Sci. China Technol. Sci.* **2012**, *55*, 163–173. [CrossRef]
27. Wang, Z.; Dong, S.; Dong, X.; Zhang, X. Assessment of wind energy and wave energy resources in Weifang sea area. *Int. J. Hydrogen Energy* **2016**, *41*, 15805–15811. [CrossRef]
28. Dong, S.; Gong, Y.J.; Wang, Z.F.; Incecik, A. Wind and wave energy resources assessment around the Yangtze River Delta. *Ocean Eng.* **2019**, *182*, 75–89. [CrossRef]
29. Su, H.; Wei, C.; Jiang, S.; Li, P.; Zhai, F. Revisiting the seasonal wave height variability in the South China Sea with merged satellite altimetry observations. *Acta Oceanol. Sin.* **2017**, *36*, 38–50. [CrossRef]
30. Molina, M.O.; Gutiérrez, C.; Sánchez, E. Comparison of ERA5 surface wind speed climatologies over Europe with observations from the HadISD dataset. *Int. J. Climatol.* **2021**, *41*, 4864–4878. [CrossRef]
31. Hersbach, H.; Bell, B.; Berrisford, P.; Biavati, G.; Horányi, A.; Muñoz Sabater, J.; Nicolas, J.; Peubey, C.; Radu, R.; Rozum, I.; et al. ERA5 hourly data on single levels from 1940 to present. *Copernic. Clim. Chang. Serv. (C3S) Clim. Data Store (CDS)* **2023**. [CrossRef]
32. Liu, J.; Li, B.; Chen, W.; Li, J.; Yan, J. Evaluation of ERA5 wave parameters with in situ data in the South China Sea. *Atmosphere* **2022**, *13*, 935. [CrossRef]
33. Wang, J.; Li, B.; Gao, Z.; Wang, J. Comparison of ECMWF significant wave height forecasts in the China Sea with buoy data. *Weather Forecast.* **2019**, *34*, 1693–1704. [CrossRef]
34. Li, J.; Tong, Y.; Xu, Y.; Chen, W.; Shi, P. Reconstruction of significant wave height for bottom-mounted acoustic profilers with pressure sensor failure: A case study. *Ocean Eng.* **2025**, *319*, 120270. [CrossRef]
35. Li, B.; Li, J.; Liu, J.; Tang, S.; Chen, W.; Shi, P.; Liu, Y. Calibration experiments of CFOSAT wavelength in the Southern South China Sea by artificial neural networks. *Remote Sens.* **2022**, *14*, 773. [CrossRef]
36. Liu, Y.; Lin, M.; Jiang, X.; Sun, X.; Song, X. A comparison of multiplatform wind products in the South China Sea during summer and autumn in 2019. *J. Oceanol. Limnol.* **2021**, *39*, 2181–2194. [CrossRef]
37. Jiang, Y.; Han, S.; Shi, C.; Gao, T.; Zhen, H.; Liu, X. Evaluation of HRCLDAS and ERA5 Datasets for Near-Surface Wind over Hainan Island and South China Sea. *Atmosphere* **2021**, *12*, 766. [CrossRef]
38. Silva, K.; Abreu, T.; Oliveira, T.C.A. Inter- and intra-annual variability of wave energy in Northern mainland Portugal: Application to the HiWave-5 project. *Energy Rep.* **2022**, *8*, 6411–6422. [CrossRef]
39. Zhang, W.; Zhao, H.; Chen, G.; Yang, J. Assessing the performance of SWAN model for wave simulations in the Bay of Bengal. *Ocean Eng.* **2023**, *285*, 115295. [CrossRef]
40. Schuster, U.; Watson, A.J.; Bates, N.R.; Corbiere, A.; Gonzalez-Davila, M.; Metzl, N.; Pierrot, D.; Santana-Casiano, M. Trends in North Atlantic sea-surface fCO2 from 1990 to 2006. *Deep Sea Res. Part II* **2009**, *56*, 620–629. [CrossRef]
41. Santos, F.; Gómez-Gesteira, M.; de Castro, M.; Álvarez, I. Upwelling along the western coast of the Iberian Peninsula: Dependence of trends on fitting strategy. *Clim. Res.* **2011**, *48*, 213–218. [CrossRef]
42. Kim, K.-Y.; Kim, Y. A comparison of sea level projections based on the observed and reconstructed sea level data around the Korean Peninsula. *Clim. Change* **2017**, *142*, 23–36. [CrossRef]
43. Li, C. Interaction between anomalous winter monsoon in East Asia and El Nino events. *Adv. Atmos. Sci.* **1990**, *7*, 36–46. [CrossRef]
44. Young, I.R.; Zieger, S.; Babanin, A.V. Global trends in wind speed and wave height. *Science* **2011**, *332*, 451–455. [CrossRef] [PubMed]
45. Bromirski, P.D.; Cayan, D.R.; Helly, J.; Wittmann, P. Wave power variability and trends across the North Pacific. *J. Geophys. Res. Oceans* **2013**, *118*, 6329–6348. [CrossRef]
46. Reeve, D.E.; Chen, Y.; Pan, S.; Magar, V.; Simmonds, D.J.; Zacharioudaki, A. An investigation of the impacts of climate change on wave energy generation: The Wave Hub, Cornwall, UK. *Renew. Energy* **2011**, *36*, 2404–2413. [CrossRef]
47. Kamranzad, B.; Etemad-Shahidi, A.; Chegini, V. Assessment of wave energy variation in the Persian Gulf. *Ocean Eng.* **2013**, *70*, 72–80. [CrossRef]

Journal of
Marine Science and Engineering

MDPI

Article

Analysis, Forecasting, and System Identification of a Floating Offshore Wind Turbine Using Dynamic Mode Decomposition

Giorgio Palma, Andrea Bardazzi, Alessia Lucarelli, Chiara Pilloton, Andrea Serani, Claudio Lugni and Matteo Diez *

CNR-INM, National Research Council-Institute of Marine Engineering, Via di Vallerano, 139, 00128 Rome, Italy; giorgio.palma@cnr.it (G.P.); andrea.bardazzi@cnr.it (A.B.); alessia.lucarelli@cnr.it (A.L.); chiara.pilloton@cnr.it (C.P.); andrea.serani@cnr.it (A.S.); claudio.lugni@cnr.it (C.L.)

* Correspondence: matteo.diez@cnr.it

Abstract: This article presents the data-driven equation-free modeling of the dynamics of a hexafloat floating offshore wind turbine based on the application of dynamic mode decomposition (DMD). The DMD has here been used (i) to extract knowledge from the dynamic system through its modal analysis, (ii) for short-term forecasting (nowcasting) from the knowledge of the immediate past of the system state, and (iii) for system identification and reduced-order modeling. All the analyses are performed on experimental data collected from an operating prototype. The nowcasting method for motions, accelerations, and forces acting on the floating system applies Hankel-DMD, a methodological extension that includes time-delayed copies of the states in an augmented state vector. The system identification task is performed by using Hankel-DMD with a control (Hankel-DMDc), which models the system as externally forced. The influence of the main hyperparameters of the methods is investigated with a full factorial analysis using error metrics analyzing complementary aspects of the prediction. A Bayesian extension of the Hankel-DMD and Hankel-DMDc is introduced by considering the hyperparameters as stochastic variables, enriching the predictions with uncertainty quantification. The results show the capability of the approaches for data-lean nowcasting and system identification, with computational costs being compatible with real-time applications. Accurate predictions are obtained up to 4 wave encounters for nowcasting and 20 wave encounters for system identification, suggesting the potential of the methods for real-time continuous-learning digital twinning and surrogate data-driven reduced-order modeling.

Keywords: floating offshore wind turbine; forecasting; system identification; dynamic mode decomposition; uncertainty quantification; data-driven; equation-free; reduced-order modeling

1. Introduction

In the efforts to contain the global temperature increase under 2 °C below pre-industrial levels, as set by the Paris Agreement [1], most countries have committed to reaching the goal of *net zero emissions* by 2050, meaning that all their greenhouse gas emissions must be counterbalanced by an equal amount of removals from the atmosphere. To reach this critical and ambitious task for sustainable growth, the decarbonization of our society is a key aspect that passes through the decarbonization of energy production [2,3]. The shift from fossil fuels to renewable sources for power production is considered the fundamental step in the process. Power generation is, in fact, responsible for 30% of the global carbon dioxide emissions at the moment. In 2018, the European Union (EU) set intermediate targets of 20% of energy obtained from renewable resources by 2020 and 32% by 2030, and the latter has been raised to 42.5% (with the aspiration of reaching 45%) by amending the Renewable Energy Directive in 2021 [4]. Reaching the mentioned targets means almost doubling the existing share of renewable energy in the EU.

Wind energy technology has been identified as one of the most promising ones, along with photovoltaic, for power production from renewable sources. Several growth scenarios predict a prominent role of wind power, exceeding the 35% share of the total electricity demand by 2050 [5] which represents a nearly nine-fold rise in the wind power share in the total generation mix compared to 2016 levels. Offshore wind energy production has a bigger growth potential compared to its onshore counterpart. The reasons are connected to fewer technical, logistic, and social restrictions of the former. Offshore installed turbines may exploit abundant and more consistent winds, which would be helped by the reduced friction of the sea surface and the absence of surrounding hills and buildings [6]. In addition, offshore wind farms benefit from greater social acceptance, a minor value of their occupied space, and the possibility of installing larger turbines with fewer transportation issues than onshore [7–9]. The 2023 Global Offshore Wind Report predicts the installation of more than 380 GW of offshore wind capacity worldwide in the next ten years [10].

The exponential growth of the sector passes through the possibility of realizing floating offshore plants, enabling the exploitation of sea areas with deeper water that make fixed-foundation turbines not a feasible/affordable solution (indicatively deeper than 60 m). The main advantage of exploiting deep offshore sea areas relies on the abundant and steady winds characterizing them. One of the main limiting factors in the reduction of the levelized cost of energy (LCOE) of advanced floating offshore wind turbines (FOWTs) is the current size and cost of their platforms. Its reduction, alongside the development of advanced moorings, improved control systems, and maintenance procedures, is among the most impacting technical goals research activities are focusing on.

The power production by FOWTs presents additional challenges compared to their fixed wind turbine counterpart (on- or offshore) which are inherent to their floating characteristic that adds six degrees of freedom to the structures. Nonlinear hydrodynamic loads, wave–current interactions, aero-hydrodynamics coupling producing negative aerodynamic damping, and wind-induced low-frequency rotations are among the main causes of large amplitude motions of the platform. These are in turn causes of reductions in the average power output of the power plant and increases in the fluctuations of the produced power. Both the quantity and quality of the power production are affected, and the structure and all the components (blades, cables, bearings, etc.) also suffer increased fatigue-induced wear from nonconstant loadings [11] (about 20% of operation and maintenance costs come from blade failures [12], and almost 70% of the gearbox downtime is due to bearing faults [13]). The floating wind turbine operations are considerably altered by the stochastic nature of the wind, waves, and currents in the sea environment, which excite platform motion, leading to uncertainties in structural loads and power extraction capability. As shown first in Jonkman [14], waves are responsible for a large part of the dynamic excitation of an FOWT. Rotor speed fluctuations are 60% larger when the same turbine is operated in a floating environment compared to onshore installation, and the difference has been shown to increase with increasing wave conditions. Therefore, it is essential to develop appropriate strategies to improve FOWTs' platform stability and maximize their turbines' energy conversion rate, achieving a better LCOE with higher power production and lower maintenance operation costs.

Both passive and active technologies have been studied and developed within this scope, such as tuned mass dampers [15–17] mounted on different floaters, ballasted buoyancy cans [18–20], gyro-stabilizers [21], and blade pitch and/or torque controllers [7–9,22,23].

Developing advanced control systems is a high-potential cost reduction strategy for offshore wind turbines that impacts multiple levels: effective control strategies may increase the energy production, which has a direct impact on the LCOE; a reduction in platform motions may help in reducing their sizes and costs; reduced vibratory loads on the turbine's components help increase their lifetime and reduce maintenance costs. A thorough comparison of various controllers designed for managing vibratory loads is provided in Awada et al. [24]. Both feedback [7,8,25–31] and feedforward [32–41] control systems have been successfully developed for the effective control of FOWTs. The two philosophies may also be effectively coupled, creating a feedforward control with a feedback loop such as in Al et al. [42], where real-time prediction of the free-surface elevation was exploited to compensate for the wave disturbances on the FOWT. Feedback algorithms may take advantage of accurate models of the controlled systems for improved performance; at the same time, feedforward controllers rely on forecasting techniques to estimate upcoming disturbances or changes in the state to be controlled. Hence, the predictive algorithm plays a primary role in the success of the control strategy.

Although white- and gray-box models for the FOWT dynamics can be obtained [43,44], the modeling process can be extremely complex, and clearly representing the operational status of the turbine and platform under random meteorological conditions is not trivial. Recently, data-driven methods have demonstrated to be a powerful alternative for the identification of dynamic systems and the forecasting of their response. In particular, advanced machine learning and deep learning algorithms have been successfully applied to predict FOWT motions and loads. Several examples can be found in the literature. A multilayer feedforward neural network was used in Wang et al. [45] to predict maximum blade and tower loadings and maximum mooring line tension using the wind speed, turbulence intensity, meaningful wave height, and spectral peak period as the model's input parameters. Zhang et al. [46] built a data-driven prediction model for the FOWT output power, the platform pitch angle, and the blades' flapwise moment at the root using wind speed, wave height, and blade pitch control variables as inputs by training a gated recurrent neural network (GRNN). The study in Barooni and Velioglu Sogut [47] adopted a convolutional neural network merged with a GRNN to forecast the dynamic behavior of FOWTs. Long short-term memory (LSTM) networks are the subject of the studies in Gräfe et al. [48], where the fairlead tension, surge, and pitch motions were predicted with a data-driven method, including onboard sensors measurements and lidar inflow data. A self-attention method was integrated with LSTM in Deng et al. [49] to improve the accuracy in predicting the motion response of an FOWT in wind–wave coupled environments. The hybridization of LSTM with empirical mode decomposition (EMD) was studied in Ye et al. [50], where the neural network was used to predict the subcomponents of the EMD process for the short-term prediction of the motions of a semi-submersible platform, and in Song et al. [51], where the authors studied FOWT motion response prediction under different sea states.

Albeit powerful, machine learning and deep learning methods typically require large training datasets, comprising a range of operating conditions needing to be as complete as possible to learn patterns that generalize to *new* situations. In addition, the training of such algorithms can be computationally expensive and typically not compatible with real-time learning and digital twinning [52], where the system characteristics and responses to external perturbations also change as the system ages.

Dynamic mode decomposition (DMD) offers an interesting alternative for data-driven and equation-free modeling [53–55]. The method is based on the Koopman operator theory, an alternative formulation of the dynamical systems theory that provides a versatile framework for the data-driven study of high-dimensional nonlinear systems [56]. DMD builds a reduced-order linear model of a dynamical system, approximating the Koopman operator. The approach requires no specific knowledge or assumption about the system's dynamics and can be applied to both empirical and simulated data. The model is obtained with a direct procedure from a small set of multidimensional input–output pairs, which constitutes, from a machine learning perspective, the training phase.

The literature features several methodological extensions of the original DMD algorithm aimed at improving the accuracy of the decomposition and, more generally, broadening the method's capabilities. Particularly relevant to this study are the Hankel-DMD [55–59], the DMD with control (DMDc) [60,61], and their combination in the Hankel-DMD with control (Hankel-DMDc) [62,63]. The Hankel-DMD, also referred to as Augmented-DMD [59], Time Delay Coordinates Extended DMD [62], and Time Delay DMD [64], has proven to be a powerful tool for enhancing the linear model's ability to capture significant features of nonlinear and chaotic dynamics. This is achieved by extending the system state with time-delayed copies, which, in the limit of infinite-time observations, yields the true Koopman eigenfunctions and eigenvalues [56]. For instance, it has been effectively used in Dylewsky et al. and Mohan et al. [64,65] to predict the short-term evolution of electric loads on the grid. The DMDc extends the DMD framework to handle externally forced systems, allowing for the separation of the system's free response from the effects of external inputs. Notable applications include Al-Jiboory [66], wherein they developed a novel real-time control technique for unmanned aerial quadrotors using DMDc, enabling the control system to adapt promptly to environmental or system behavior change. Another example is Dawson et al. [67], where DMDc was applied to simulation data to create a reduced-order model (ROM) of the forces acting on a rapidly pitching airfoil. In Brunton et al. [62], the algorithmic variant combining control and state augmentation with time-delayed copies is called Time Delay Coordinates DMDc, and it was introduced using the same number of delayed copies for both the state and the input. Similarly, Zawacki and Abed [63] introduced the DMD with Input-Delayed Control, which, as the name suggests, includes time-delayed copies of the inputs only.

The data-driven nature, noniterative training process, and data efficiency of DMD have contributed to its widespread adoption as a reduced-order modeling technique and real-time forecasting tool in various fields. These include fluid dynamics and aeroacoustics [53,68–71], epidemiology [72], neuroscience [73], and finance [74], among others. Several studies have demonstrated the effectiveness of DMD in forecasting complex system behaviors in the marine environment, such as Diez et al. [75], where DMD was applied for the forecasting of ship trajectories motions and forces. Serani et al. [59] conducted a statistical evaluation of DMD's predictive performance for naval applications, incorporating state augmentation techniques such as augmenting the system state with its derivatives and time-delayed copies. Diez et al. [76] provides a comparative analysis for naval application of DMD-based prediction algorithms and various neural network architectures, including standard and bidirectional long short-term memory networks, gated recurrent units, and feedforward neural networks. Furthermore, Diez et al. [77] studied the hybridization of DMD with artificial neural networks to enhance prediction accuracy.

The objective of this paper is to propose the use of DMD and its variants to extract knowledge and forecast motions and loads, as well as perform system identification of an FOWT from experimental data. In particular, Hankel-DMD is used as a data-lean forecasting method, producing short-term forecasting (nowcasting) from the immediate past history of the system state, with a continuously learning data-driven reduced-order model suitable for digital twinning and real-time predictions. On the other side, Hankel-DMDc is applied as an effective and efficient approach to model-free system identification, aiming to create an accurate ROM for the long-term prediction of the platform motions and loads from the knowledge of the wave elevation in the proximity of the platform and the wind speed. In this work, the nowcasting and system identification tasks are performed on experimentally measured data; however, the Hankel-DMD and Hankel-DMDc methods here developed also directly apply to different data sources such as simulations of various fidelity levels. The effect on the predictions of the main hyperparameters of the methods are studied with a full-factorial design of experiment, assessing the performances using three error metrics and identifying the most promising configurations. In addition, novel Bayesian extensions of Hankel-DMD and Hankel-DMDc are introduced to include uncertainty quantification in the methods' predictions by considering their hyperparameters as stochastic variables. The stochastic hyperparameter variation ranges are identified after deterministic analyses, and the results from the deterministic and Bayesian methods were compared using the same test sequences.

The two approaches, nowcasting and system identification, are of paramount relevance for developing advanced controllers and digital twins for the FOWT, combining accuracy, adaptivity, and reliability (through uncertainty quantification), with computational costs compatible with real-time execution.The efficiency of the DMD-based methods is provided by the small dimensionality of the relevant state variables and the low computational cost required for both the model construction (training) and exploitation (prediction) as opposed to more data- and resource-intensive machine learning methods.

The methods are applied to real-life measured data obtained by various sensors mounted on a scale prototype of a 5MW Hexafloat FOWT, which is the first of its type. The experimental activity has been conducted as part of the National Research Project *RdS-Electrical Energy from the Sea* funded by the Italian Ministry for the Environment (MaSE) and coordinated by CNR-INM.

The paper is organized as follows. Section 2 presents the wind turbine test case, details the DMD methods applied, and introduces the performance metrics used to assess the predictive performances of the algorithms. The numerical setup and the data preprocessing are described in Section 4. Section 5 collects the results from the modal analysis and the forecasting of the quantities of interest obtained with the deterministic Hankel-DMD and and its Bayesian version for nowcasting, and finally, conclusions about the conducted analyses are given in Section 6.

2. Material and Methods

2.1. Wind Turbine Test Case

The presented analyses are conducted on a set of experimental data collected on the prototype of an FOWT built and tested at the Interdisciplinary Marine Renewable Energy Sea Lab (In-MaRELab); see Figure 1a.

The tests were conducted offshore the Naples port, right in front of the breakwater Molo San Vincenzo. The prototype and the experimental activity at sea are part of the National Research Project *RdS-Electrical Energy from the Sea* funded by the MaSE and coordinated by CNR-INM.

The FOWT is a 1:6.8 scale prototype of a 5MW FOWT, which is the first one existing at sea for the Hexafloat concept. The floater is a Saipem patented lightweight semisub platform consisting of a hexagonal tubular steel structure around a central column and a deeper counterweight connected to the floater by six tendons (one for each corner of the hexagon) in synthetic material. The FOWT platform features a maximum outer diameter of 13 m, with a nondimensional draught-to-diameter ratio of 0.37.

(**a**) (**b**)

Figure 1. (**a**) Aerial view of In-MaRELab with the Hexafloat FOWT during the tests at sea in 2021. (**b**) View of the Hexafloat FOWT during the towing stage from the shipyard to the test site in 2024.

The floater hosts a Tozzi Nord TN535 10-kW wind turbine [78] originally designed for onshore application and, within the present research project, suitably modified in the electrical part for the specific aims of the offshore application (see Figure 1b). The turbine is characterized by a cut-in wind speed $v_{cut-in} = 2$ m/s, a rated wind speed $v_{rated} = 6.7$ m/s, and a cut-out wind speed $v_{cut-out} = 16$ m/s. Figure 2 shows the power curve of the TN535 10 kW wind turbine.

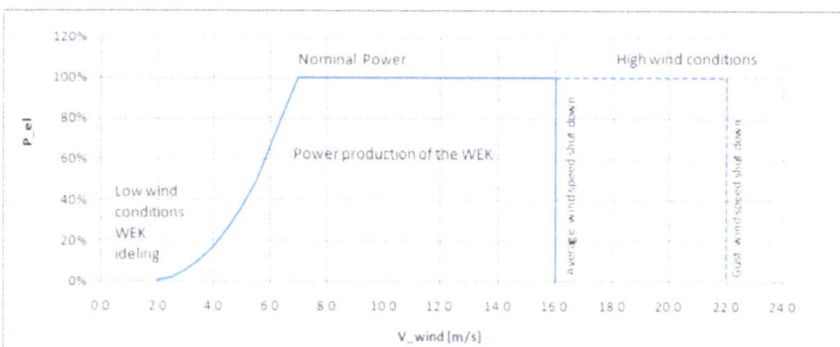

Figure 2. Tozzi Nord TN535 10 kW wind turbine power curve [78].

The FOWT was anchored with three drag anchors located at 30 m of water depth through three mooring lines, with ropes breaking load of about 3.3 tons, in catenary configuration at a relative angle of 120 degrees counterclockwise, with M_1 directed toward the breakwater and orthogonal to it. The whole structure, i.e., the floater and the turbine, weighs a total of approximately 11 tons.

The studied dataset includes 12-hour synchronized time histories of the following:

1. The loads applied to one of the three moorings of the platform (M_3) and three of the six tendons connecting the counterweight to the floater (T_1, T_5, and T_6), as measured by a system of underwater load cells LCM5404 with work limit load (WLL) of 2.3 tons and 4.5 tons.
2. The acceleration along three coordinate axes ($\dot{u}$, $\dot{v}$, $\dot{w}$), the pitch and roll angles (θ, ϕ), and the respective angular rates ($\dot{\theta}$, $\dot{\phi}$) collected by a Norwegian Subsea MRU 3000 inertial motion unit.
3. The power extracted by the wind turbine (P) estimated by a programmable logic controller (PLC) through a direct measure of the electrical quantities at the generator on board the nacelle of the wind turbine, the rotor angular velocity (Ω) measured by two sensors in continuous cross-check, and the relative wind speed (V_w) through

two different anemometers positioned on the nacelle, behind the rotor. All signals were collected by the PLC on the nacelle with a variable but well-known sample frequency of approximately 1 Hz.

4. The wave elevation (h_w) measured by a pressure transducer integrated into the Acoustic Doppler Current Profiler (ADCP) Teledyne Marine Sentinel V20, located at a distance of approximately 50 m from the FOWT in the southeast direction.

The observed state of the system is hence composed as $\mathbf{x} = \{T_1, T_5, T_6, M_3, \phi, \theta, \dot{\phi}, \dot{\theta}, \dot{u}, \dot{v}, \dot{w}, P, \Omega, V_w, h_w\}$.

The measured significant wave height in the considered time frame is in the order of $h_s = 1.25$ m, and the wave peak period is approximately $T_p = 6.9$ s. The data represent a period of continuous operation for the FOWT in extreme weather conditions for the Mediterranean Sea [79], which the FOWT is designed for: the full-scale significant wave height reaches approximately 8.75 m, and the full-scale wave peak period is about $T_p = 18$ s. The system may show induced strongly nonlinear physical dynamics in such weather conditions. In particular, the intense wind causes a nonlinear behavior in the extracted power and blades' rotating speed, showing a saturation to the maximum values supported by the machine. This poses the DMD-based methods in a challenging condition for modal analysis and prediction.

An average incoming wave period is identified from the peak in the wave elevation spectrum and used in the following as reference period $\hat{T} = 7.3143$ s ($\hat{f} = 0.1367$ Hz).

2.2. *Dynamic Mode Decomposition*

Dynamic mode decomposition was originally presented in Schmid and Sesterhenn [80] and Schmid [53] to identify spatiotemporal coherent structures from high-dimensional time series data, providing a linear reduced-order representation of possibly nonlinear system dynamics. Given a time series of data, the DMD computes a set of modes with their associated frequencies and decay/growth rates [62]. When the analyzed system is linear, the modes obtained by the DMD correspond to the system's linear normal modes. The potential of the DMD in the analysis of nonlinear systems comes from its close relation to the spectral analysis of the Koopman operator [68]. The Koopman operator theory is built upon the original work in Koopman [81], defining the possibility of transforming a nonlinear dynamical system into a possibly infinite-dimensional linear system [61,82]. DMD is an equation-free data-driven approach that was shown by Rowley et al. [68] to be a computation of the Koopman operator for linear observables [83].

Its state-of-the-art definition has been given by Tu et al. [82] and is resumed in the following. Consider a dynamical system described by the following:

$$\frac{\mathrm{d}\mathbf{x}}{\mathrm{d}t} = \mathbf{f}(\mathbf{x}, t, \gamma), \tag{1}$$

where $\mathbf{x}(t) \in \mathbb{R}^n$ represents the system's state at time t, γ contains the parameters of the system, and $\mathbf{f}(\cdot)$ represents its dynamics, possibly including nonlinearities. Equation (1) can represent various types of systems, including discretized partial differential equations at some discrete spatial points or the evolution of multivariable time series. The DMD analysis approximates the eigenmodes and eigenvalues of the infinite-dimensional linear Koopman operator associated with the system $\mathbf{f}(\mathbf{x}, t, \gamma)$, providing a locally (in time) linearized finite-dimensional representation of it ($\mathcal{A} \in \mathbb{R}^{n \times n}$) based on observed data [54]:

$$\frac{\mathrm{d}\mathbf{x}}{\mathrm{d}t} = \mathcal{A}\mathbf{x}. \tag{2}$$

DMD makes no assumption of the underlying physics, i.e., it does not require knowledge of the system governing equations and considers the system $\mathbf{f}(\mathbf{x}, t, \gamma)$ as an unknown when extracting its data-driven model $\mathcal{A}$.

Once obtained, the DMD model can be used to forecast the system behavior. The solution of the approximated system can be expressed in terms of n eigenvalues ω_k and eigenvectors φ_k of the matrix $\mathcal{A}$ [62]:

$$\mathbf{x}(t) = \sum_{k=1}^{n} \varphi_k q_k(t) = \sum_{k=1}^{n} \varphi_k b_k \exp(\omega_k t), \tag{3}$$

where the coefficients b_k define the coordinates of the initial condition $\mathbf{x}_0$ in the eigenvector basis, $\mathbf{b} = \mathbf{\Phi}^{-1}\mathbf{x}_0$, and $\mathbf{\Phi}$ is a matrix containing the φ_k eigenvectors columnwise.

In practical applications, the state of the system is measured at m discrete time steps $t_j = j\Delta t$ and can be expressed as $\mathbf{x}_j = \mathbf{x}(j\Delta t)$, with $j = 1, \ldots,$ m. Consequently, the approximation can be written as follows:

$$\mathbf{x}_{j+1} = \mathbf{A}\mathbf{x}_j, \qquad \text{with} \qquad \mathbf{A} = \exp(\mathcal{A}\Delta t). \tag{4}$$

For each time step j, a snapshot of the system is defined as the column vector collecting the measured full state of the system $\mathbf{x}_j$. Two matrices, $\mathbf{X}$ and $\mathbf{X}' \in \mathbb{R}^{n\times(m-1)}$, can be obtained by arranging the available snapshots as follows:

$$\mathbf{X} = \begin{bmatrix}\mathbf{x}_1 & \mathbf{x}_2 & \ldots & \mathbf{x}_{m-1}\end{bmatrix}, \qquad \mathbf{X}' = \begin{bmatrix}\mathbf{x}_2 & \mathbf{x}_3 & \ldots & \mathbf{x}_m\end{bmatrix} \tag{5}$$

such that Equation (4) may be written in terms of these data matrices:

$$\mathbf{X}' \approx \mathbf{A}\mathbf{X} \tag{6}$$

Hence, the matrix $\mathbf{A} \in \mathbb{R}^{n\times n}$ can be constructed using the following approximation

$$\mathbf{A} \approx \mathbf{X}'\mathbf{X}^{\dagger} \tag{7}$$

where $\mathbf{X}^{\dagger}$ is the Moore–Penrose pseudoinverse of $\mathbf{X}$, which minimize $||\mathbf{X}' - \mathbf{A}\mathbf{X}||_F$, where $||(\cdot)||_F$ is the Frobenius norm.

The evaluation of the matrix $\mathbf{A}$, drawing a parallel with other machine learning techniques, practically constitutes the *training* or *learning* phase of the method, which is performed in a fast and direct way, i.e., with no need for iterative processes.

In order to evaluate the DMD modes $\boldsymbol{\varphi}_k$ and frequencies ω_k, the exact DMD algorithm is applied as described in [82]. The pseudoinverse of $\mathbf{X}$ can be efficiently evaluated using singular value decomposition (SVD) as

$$\mathbf{X}^{\dagger} = \mathbf{V}\mathbf{\Sigma}^{-1}\mathbf{U}^*, \tag{8}$$

where * denotes the complex conjugate transpose. Due to the low dimensionality of data in the current context, Equation (8) is computed using full SVD decomposition, with no rank truncation. The matrix $\tilde{\mathbf{A}}$ is evaluated by projecting $\mathbf{A}$ onto the proper orthogonal decomposition (POD) modes in $\mathbf{U}$ as

$$\tilde{\mathbf{A}} = \mathbf{U}^*\mathbf{A}\mathbf{U}, \tag{9}$$

and its spectral decomposition can be evaluated as

$$\tilde{\mathbf{A}}\mathbf{W} = \mathbf{W}\mathbf{\Lambda} \tag{10}$$

The diagonal matrix $\mathbf{\Lambda}$ contains the DMD eigenvalues λ_k, while the DMD modes φ_k constituting the matrix $\mathbf{\Phi}$ are then reconstructed using the eigenvectors $\mathbf{W}$ and the time-shifted data matrix $\mathbf{X}'$:

$$\mathbf{\Phi} = \mathbf{X}'\mathbf{V}\mathbf{\Sigma}^{-1}\mathbf{W} \tag{11}$$

The state-variable evolution in time can be approximated by the modal expansion of Equation (3), where $\omega_k = \ln(\lambda_k)/\Delta t$, starting from an initial condition corresponding to the end of the measured data $\mathbf{b} = \mathbf{\Phi}^{-1}\mathbf{x}_m$.

2.3. Dynamic Mode Decomposition with Control

The original DMD characterizes naturally evolving dynamical systems. The DMDc aims at extending the algorithm to include in the analysis the influence of forcing inputs and disambiguate it from the unforced dynamics of the system [60]. While DMD is considered in this work for the nowcasting task, DMDc is considered more suitable for the system identification task, obtaining a reduced-order model for the prediction of FOWT platform motions and loads forced by two control variables, namely, wind velocity and wave elevation.

The DMDc formulation can be obtained from a forced dynamic system:

$$\mathbf{x}_{j+1} = \mathbf{f}(\mathbf{x}_j, j, \gamma, \mathbf{u}_\mathrm{j}), \tag{12}$$

similarly to Equation (1) and now including the forcing input $\mathbf{u} \in \mathbb{R}^l$ in the nonlinear mapping describing the evolution of the state. DMDc modeling approximates Equation (12) as

$$\mathbf{x}_{j+1} = \mathbf{A}\mathbf{x}_j + \mathbf{B}\mathbf{u}_j \tag{13}$$

where $\mathbf{B} \in \mathbb{R}^{n\times l}$, and the discrete time matrix $\mathbf{A} \in \mathbb{R}^{n\times n}$.

Introducing the vector $\mathbf{y}_j \in \mathbb{R}^{n+l}$ as

$$\mathbf{y}_j = \begin{bmatrix} \mathbf{x}_j \\ \mathbf{u}_j \end{bmatrix}, \tag{14}$$

Equation (13) can be rewritten in a form close to Equation (4):

$$\mathbf{x}_{j+1} = \mathbf{G}\mathbf{y}_j, \qquad \text{with} \qquad \mathbf{G} = \begin{bmatrix} \mathbf{A} & \mathbf{B} \end{bmatrix}. \tag{15}$$

The collected data are arranged in the matrices $\mathbf{Y} \in \mathbb{R}^{(n+l)\times(m-1)}$ and $\mathbf{X}' \in \mathbb{R}^{n\times(m-1)}$ as follows:

$$\begin{aligned} \mathbf{Y} &= \begin{bmatrix} \mathbf{y}_j & \mathbf{y}_{j+1} & \dots & \mathbf{y}_{m-1} \end{bmatrix}, \\ \mathbf{X}' &= \begin{bmatrix} \mathbf{x}_{j+1} & \mathbf{x}_{j+2} & \dots & \mathbf{x}_m \end{bmatrix}, \end{aligned} \tag{16}$$

and the DMD approximation of the matrix $\mathbf{G} \in \mathbb{R}^{n\times(n+l)}$ can be obtained from

$$\mathbf{G} \approx \mathbf{X}'\mathbf{Y}^\dagger, \tag{17}$$

where $\mathbf{Y}^\dagger$ is the Moore–Penrose pseudoinverse of $\mathbf{Y}$, which minimizes $\|\mathbf{X}' - \mathbf{G}\mathbf{Y}\|_F$. In this way, the matrices $\mathbf{A}$ and $\mathbf{B}$ are obtained as the ones providing the best fitting of the sampled data in the least squares sense. The pseudoinverse of $\mathbf{Y}$ can be again efficiently evaluated using the singular value decomposition (SVD)

$$\mathbf{G} = \mathbf{X}'\mathbf{V}\mathbf{\Sigma}^{-1}\mathbf{U}^*. \tag{18}$$

The DMD approximations of the matrices $\mathbf{A}$ and $\mathbf{B}$ are obtained by splitting the operator $\mathbf{U}$ in $\mathbf{U_1} \in \mathbb{C}^{n\times n}$ and $\mathbf{U_2} \in \mathbb{C}^{l\times n}$ such that $\mathbf{U} = [\mathbf{U}_1\ \mathbf{U}_2]^T$ becomes

$$\mathbf{A} = \mathbf{X}'\mathbf{V}\mathbf{\Sigma}^{-1}\mathbf{U_1^*}, \qquad \mathbf{B} = \mathbf{X}'\mathbf{V}\mathbf{\Sigma}^{-1}\mathbf{U_2^*}. \tag{19}$$

Due to the low dimensionality of the data in the current context, the pseudoinverse was computed using the full SVD decomposition with no rank truncation. Otherwise, truncating the SVD to rank p, one would have $\mathbf{U_1} \in \mathbb{C}^{n\times p}$ and $\mathbf{U_2} \in \mathbb{C}^{l\times p}$.

Once the DMDc approximations of $\mathbf{A}$ and $\mathbf{B}$ are obtained, the system dynamics can be predicted with Equation (13) with the given initial conditions and the sequence of inputs $\mathbf{u}_j$.

2.4. Hankel Extension to DMD and DMDc

The standard DMD and DMDc formulations approximate the Koopman operator based on linear measurements, creating a best-fit linear model linking sequential data snapshots [53,54,84]. In this way, DMD provides a locally linear representation of the dynamics that is unable to capture many essential features of nonlinear systems. The augmentation of the system state is thus the subject of several DMD algorithmic variants [62,85–87], aiming to find a coordinate system (or *embedding*) that spans a Koopman-invariant subspace to search for an approximation of the Koopman operator that is valid also far from fixed points and periodic orbits in a larger space. The need for state augmentation through additional observables is even more critical for applications in which the number of states in the system is small, typically smaller than the number of available snapshots, such as the case at hand. However, there is no general rule for defining these observables and guaranteeing they will form a closed subspace under the Koopman operator [88].

The Hankel-DMD [56] is a specific version of the DMD algorithm that has been developed to deal with the cases of nonlinear systems in which only partial observations are available such that there are *latent* variables [62]. The state vector is thus augmented, embedding s time-delayed copies of the original variables. The Hankel-DMD with control (Hankel-DMDc) involves, in addition, the augmentation of the input vector with z time-delayed copies of the original forcing inputs. This results in an intrinsic coordinate system that forms an invariant subspace of the Koopman operator (the time delays form a set of observable functions that span a finite-dimensional subspace of Hilbert space, in which the Koopman operator preserves the structure of the system Brunton et al. [57], Pan and Duraisamy [89]). The use of time-delayed copies as additional observables in the DMD has been connected to the Koopman operator as a universal linearizing basis [57], yielding the true Koopman eigenfunctions and eigenvalues in the limit of infinite-time observations [56].

Incorporating time-lagged information in the data used to learn the model, Hankel-DMD and Hankel-DMDc increase the dimensionality of the system, allowing the algorithm to represent a richer phase space of the system, which is essential for capturing nonlinear dynamics of the original variables, even though the underlying DMD algorithm remains linear. In other words, including time-delayed data in the analysis, the Hankel-DMD and Hankel-DMDc can extract linear modes spanning a space of augmented dimensionality that are able to reflect the nonlinearities in the time evolution of the original system through complex relations between present and past states. Hence, the Hankel augmented DMD variants can better represent the underlying dynamics of the systems allowing the capture of their important nonlinear features.

The formulation of the Hankel-DMD can be obtained starting from the DMD presented in Section 2.2. The dynamical system is approximated by Hankel-DMD as

$$\hat{\mathbf{x}}_{j+1} = \hat{\mathbf{A}}\hat{\mathbf{x}}_j, \tag{20}$$

where the augmented state vector is defined as $\hat{\mathbf{x}}_j = [\mathbf{x}_j, \mathbf{x}_{j-1}, \dots, \mathbf{x}_{j-s}]^T \in \mathbb{R}^{n(s+1)}$. Two augmented data matrices $\widehat{\mathbf{X}}$ and $\widehat{\mathbf{X}}' \in \mathbb{R}^{n(s+1)\times(m-1)}$ are built as follows:

$$\widehat{\mathbf{X}} = \begin{bmatrix} \mathbf{X} \\ \mathbf{S} \end{bmatrix}, \qquad \widehat{\mathbf{X}}' = \begin{bmatrix} \mathbf{X}' \\ \mathbf{S}' \end{bmatrix}. \tag{21}$$

where the Hankel matrices $\mathbf{S}$ and $\mathbf{S}'$ are

$$\mathbf{S} = \begin{bmatrix} \mathbf{x}_{j-1} & \mathbf{x}_j & \cdots & \mathbf{x}_{m-2} \\ \mathbf{x}_{j-2} & \mathbf{x}_{j-1} & \cdots & \mathbf{x}_{m-3} \\ \vdots & \vdots & \vdots & \vdots \\ \mathbf{x}_{j-s-1} & \mathbf{x}_{j-s} & \cdots & \mathbf{x}_{m-s-1} \end{bmatrix}, \quad \mathbf{S}' = \begin{bmatrix} \mathbf{x}_j & \mathbf{x}_{j+1} & \cdots & \mathbf{x}_{m-1} \\ \mathbf{x}_{j-1} & \mathbf{x}_j & \cdots & \mathbf{x}_{m-2} \\ \vdots & \vdots & \vdots & \vdots \\ \mathbf{x}_{j-s} & \mathbf{x}_{j-s+1} & \cdots & \mathbf{x}_{m-s} \end{bmatrix}. \tag{22}$$

In this way, the augmented system matrix $\widehat{\mathbf{A}} \in \mathbb{R}^{n(s+1)\times n(s+1)}$ is approximated with

$$\widehat{\mathbf{A}} \approx \widehat{\mathbf{X}}'\widehat{\mathbf{X}}^{\dagger} \tag{23}$$

Following the exact DMD procedure [82] as described in Section 2.2, in order to evaluate the Hankel-DMD modes $\hat{\boldsymbol{\varphi}}_k$ and frequencies $\hat{\omega}_k$, the pseudoinverse of $\widehat{\mathbf{X}}$ is obtained with SVD as

$$\widehat{\mathbf{X}}^{\dagger} = \widehat{\mathbf{V}}\widehat{\boldsymbol{\Sigma}}^{-1}\widehat{\mathbf{U}}^*, \tag{24}$$

and a matrix $\tilde{\widehat{\mathbf{A}}}$ is calculated as

$$\tilde{\widehat{\mathbf{A}}} = \widehat{\mathbf{U}}^*\widehat{\mathbf{A}}\widehat{\mathbf{U}}, \tag{25}$$

The spectral decomposition of $\tilde{\widehat{\mathbf{A}}}$ is evaluated as follows:

$$\tilde{\widehat{\mathbf{A}}}\widehat{\mathbf{W}} = \widehat{\mathbf{W}}\widehat{\boldsymbol{\Lambda}}. \tag{26}$$

The diagonal matrix $\widehat{\boldsymbol{\Lambda}}$ contains the Hankel-DMD eigenvalues $\hat{\lambda}_k$, while the Hankel-DMD eigenvectors $\hat{\boldsymbol{\varphi}}_k$ constituting the matrix $\widehat{\boldsymbol{\Phi}}$ are then reconstructed using the eigenvectors $\widehat{\mathbf{W}}$ of the matrix $\tilde{\widehat{\mathbf{A}}}$ and the time-shifted data matrix $\widehat{\mathbf{X}}'$:

$$\widehat{\boldsymbol{\Phi}} = \widehat{\mathbf{X}}'\widehat{\mathbf{V}}\widehat{\boldsymbol{\Sigma}}^{-1}\widehat{\mathbf{W}}. \tag{27}$$

The time evolution of the augmented state variables can be finally evaluated by the following modal expansion:

$$\hat{\mathbf{x}}(t) = \sum_{k=1}^{n(s+1)} \hat{\boldsymbol{\varphi}}_k \hat{q}_k(t) = \sum_{k=1}^{n(s+1)} \hat{\boldsymbol{\varphi}}_k \hat{b}_k \exp(\hat{\omega}_k t), \tag{28}$$

where $\hat{\omega}_k = \ln(\hat{\lambda}_k)/\Delta t$, and the coefficients $\hat{b}_k$ are the coordinates of the augmented initial condition for the prediction $\hat{\mathbf{x}}_m$ in the eigenvector basis $\hat{\mathbf{b}} = \widehat{\boldsymbol{\Phi}}^{-1}\hat{\mathbf{x}}_m$.

The prediction of the time evolution of the original state variables $\tilde{\mathbf{x}}(t)$ is finally extracted by the augmented state vector isolating its first n components.

The augmentation of the system state with its delayed copies can be similarly applied to DMDc, modifying the formulation presented in Section 2.3. In this case, not only the state but also the input vector is extended with time-shifted copies, leading to the following representation of the dynamic system:

$$\hat{\mathbf{x}}_{j+1} = \widehat{\mathbf{A}}\hat{\mathbf{x}}_j + \widehat{\mathbf{B}}\hat{\mathbf{u}}_j \tag{29}$$

where $\hat{\mathbf{x}}_j$ follows the definition given for the Hankel-DMD, and $\hat{\mathbf{u}}_j = [\mathbf{u}_j, \mathbf{u}_{j-1}, \ldots, \mathbf{u}_{j-z}]^T \in \mathbb{R}^{l(z+1)}$ is the extended input vector, including the z delayed copies, and $\widehat{\mathbf{B}}$ is the augmented system input matrix. In addition to $\widehat{\mathbf{X}}'$, the augmented data matrix $\widehat{\mathbf{Y}} \in \mathbb{R}^{(n(s+1)+l(z+1))\times(m-1)}$ is defined as

$$\widehat{\mathbf{Y}} = \begin{bmatrix} \mathbf{X} \\ \mathbf{S} \\ \mathbf{U} \\ \mathbf{Z} \end{bmatrix} \tag{30}$$

with the matrix $\mathbf{Z}$ showing a Hankel structure defined as

$$\mathbf{Z} = \begin{bmatrix} \mathbf{u}_{j-1} & \mathbf{u}_j & \cdots & \mathbf{u}_{m-2} \\ \mathbf{u}_{j-2} & \mathbf{u}_{j-1} & \cdots & \mathbf{u}_{m-3} \\ \vdots & \vdots & \vdots & \vdots \\ \mathbf{u}_{j-z-1} & \mathbf{u}_{j-z} & \cdots & \mathbf{u}_{m-z-1} \end{bmatrix}. \tag{31}$$

The augmented matrix $\widehat{\mathbf{G}} = [\widehat{\mathbf{A}}, \ \widehat{\mathbf{B}}] \in \mathbb{R}^{ns\times(ns+lz)}$ is approximated in Hankel-DMDc as

$$\widehat{\mathbf{G}} \approx \widehat{\mathbf{X}}'\widehat{\mathbf{Y}}^{\dagger}, \tag{32}$$

The pseudoinverse of $\widehat{\mathbf{Y}}$ is evaluated by SVD as $\widehat{\mathbf{Y}}^{\dagger} = \widehat{\mathbf{V}}\widehat{\mathbf{\Sigma}}^{-1}\widehat{\mathbf{U}}^*$, leading to

$$\widehat{\mathbf{G}} = \widehat{\mathbf{X}}'\widehat{\mathbf{V}}\widehat{\mathbf{\Sigma}}^{-1}\widehat{\mathbf{U}}^*. \tag{33}$$

The Hankel-DMDc approximations of the matrices $\widehat{\mathbf{A}}$ and $\widehat{\mathbf{B}}$ are obtained by splitting the operator $\widehat{\mathbf{U}}$ in $\widehat{\mathbf{U}}_1 \in \mathbb{C}^{n(s+1)\times(n(s+1)+l(z+1))}$ and $\widehat{\mathbf{U}}_2 \in \mathbb{C}^{l(z+1)\times(n(s+1)+l(z+1))}$ such that $\widehat{\mathbf{U}} = [\widehat{\mathbf{U}}_1 \ \widehat{\mathbf{U}}_2]^T$. Equation (29) is hence used to obtain the time evolution of the augmented state vector, and finally, by isolating its first n components, the predicted time evolution of the original state variables $\tilde{\mathbf{x}}(t)$ are extracted.

2.5. Bayesian Extension to Hankel-DMD and Hankel-DMDc

The Bayesian extension is introduced to incorporate uncertainty quantification in the analyses, adding confidence intervals to the predictions coming from the numerical methods. Its definition starts by noting that the dimensions and the values within matrices $\widehat{\mathbf{A}} \in \mathbb{R}^{n(s+1)\times n(s+1)}$ and $\widehat{\mathbf{B}} \in \mathbb{R}^{n(s+1)\times l(z+1)}$ depend on three hyperparameters of the algorithms: the observation time length, $l_{tr} = t_m - t_1$ and the maximum delay time in the augmented state $l_{d_x} = t_{j-1} - t_{j-s-1}$ for Hankel-DMD, with the addition of the maximum delay time in the augmented input $l_{d_u} = t_{j-1} - t_{j-z-1}$ for Hankel-DMDc.

These dependencies can be denoted as follows:

$$\begin{aligned} &\text{Hankel}-\text{DMD}: \quad \widehat{\mathbf{A}} = \widehat{\mathbf{A}}(l_{tr}, l_{d_x}) \\ &\text{Hankel}-\text{DMDc}: \quad \widehat{\mathbf{A}} = \widehat{\mathbf{A}}(l_{tr}, l_{d_x}, l_{d_u}), \qquad \widehat{\mathbf{B}} = \widehat{\mathbf{B}}(l_{tr}, l_{d_x}, l_{d_u}). \end{aligned} \tag{34}$$

In the Bayesian formulations, the hyperparameters are considered stochastic variables with given probability density functions $p(l_{tr})$, $p(l_{d_x})$, and $p(l_{d_u})$, introducing uncertainty in the process. Through uncertainty propagation, the solution $\mathbf{x}(t)$ also depends on l_{tr}, l_{d_x}, and, in Bayesian Hankel-DMDc, l_{d_u}. At a given time t, the expected value of the solution and its standard deviation can be expressed for the Bayesian Hankel-DMD as

$$\mu_{\mathbf{x}}(t) = \int_{l_{tr}^l}^{l_{tr}^u} \int_{l_{d_x}^l}^{l_{d_x}^u} \mathbf{x}(t, l_{tr}, l_{d_x}) p(l_{tr}) p(l_{d_x}) dl_{tr} dl_{d_x}, \tag{35}$$

$$\sigma_{\mathbf{x}}(t) = \left\{ \int_{l_{tr}^l}^{l_{tr}^u} \int_{l_{d_x}^l}^{l_{d_x}^u} [\mathbf{x}(t, l_{tr}, l_{d_x}) - \mu_{\mathbf{x}}(t)]^2 p(l_{tr}) p(l_{d_x}) dl_{tr} dl_{d_x} \right\}^{\frac{1}{2}}, \tag{36}$$

and, for the Bayesian Hankel-DMDc, as

$$\mu_{\mathbf{x}}(t) = \int_{l_{d_u}^l}^{l_{d_u}^u} \int_{l_{d_x}^l}^{l_{d_x}^u} \int_{l_{tr}^l}^{l_{tr}^u} \mathbf{x}(t, l_{tr}, l_{d_x}, l_{d_u}) p(l_{tr}) p(l_{d_x}) p(l_{d_u}) dl_{tr} dl_{d_x} dl_{d_u}, \tag{37}$$

$$\sigma_{\mathbf{x}}(t) = \left\{ \int_{l_{d_u}^l}^{l_{d_u}^u} \int_{l_{d_x}^l}^{l_{d_x}^u} \int_{l_{tr}^l}^{l_{tr}^u} [\mathbf{x}(t, l_{tr}, l_{d_x}) - \mu_{\mathbf{x}}(t)]^2 p(l_{tr}) p(l_{d_x}) p(l_{d_u}) dl_{tr} dl_{d_x} dl_{d_u} \right\}^{\frac{1}{2}}, \tag{38}$$

where l_{tr}^l, $l_{d_x}^l$, and $l_{d_u}^l$ and l_{tr}^u, $l_{d_x}^u$, and $l_{d_u}^u$ are lower and upper bounds for l_{tr}, l_{d_x}, and l_{d_u}.

In practice, a uniform probability density function is assigned to the hyperparameters, and a set of realizations is obtained through a Monte Carlo sampling. Accordingly, for each realization of the hyperparameters, the solution $\mathbf{x}(t, l_{tr}, l_{d_x})$ or $\mathbf{x}(t, l_{tr}, l_{d_x}, l_{d_u})$ is computed, and at a given time t, the expected value and standard deviation of the solution are then evaluated.

3. Performance Metrics

To evaluate the predictions made by the models and to compare the effectiveness of different configurations, three error indices are employed: the normalized mean square error (NRMSE) [76], the normalized average minimum/maximum absolute error (NAMMAE) [76], and the Jensen-Shannon divergence (JSD) [90]. All the metrics are averaged over the variables that constitute the system's state, providing a holistic assessment of the prediction accuracy. This comprehensive evaluation considers aspects such as overall error, the range, and the statistical similarity of predicted versus measured values.

The NRMSE quantifies the average root mean square error between the predicted values $\tilde{\mathbf{x}}_t$ and the measured (test) values $\mathbf{x}_t$ at different time steps. It is calculated by taking the square root of the average squared differences, which is normalized by k times the standard deviation of the measured values:

$$\text{NRMSE} = \frac{1}{N} \sum_{i=1}^{N} \frac{1}{k\sigma_{x_i}} \sqrt{\frac{1}{\mathcal{T}} \sum_{j=1}^{\mathcal{T}} (\tilde{x}_{ij} - x_{ij})^2}, \tag{39}$$

where N is the number of variables in the predicted state, $\mathcal{T}$ is the number of considered time instants, and σ_{x_i} is the standard deviation of the measured values in the considered time window for the variable x_i.

The NAMMAE metric, introduced in Diez et al. [76,77], provides an engineering-oriented assessment of the prediction accuracy. It measures the absolute difference between the minimum and maximum values of the predicted and measured time series that is normalized by k times the standard deviation of the measured values as follows:

$$\text{NAMMAE} = \frac{1}{2N} \sum_{i=1}^{N} \frac{1}{k\sigma_{x_i}} \left(\left| \min_j(\tilde{x}_{ij}) - \min_j(x_{ij}) \right| + \left| \max_j(\tilde{x}_{ij}) - \max_j(x_{ij}) \right| \right), \tag{40}$$

Lastly, the JSD measures the similarity between the probability distributions of the predicted and reference signal [90]. For each variable, it estimates the entropy of the predicted time series probability density function Q relative to the probability density function of the measured time series R, where M is the average of the two [91].

$$\text{JSD} = \frac{1}{N}\sum_{i=1}^{N}\left(\frac{1}{2}D(Q_i\,||\,M_i) + \frac{1}{2}D(R_i\,||\,M_i)\right), \tag{41}$$

$$\text{with} \quad M = \frac{1}{2}(Q+R), \tag{42}$$

$$\text{and} \quad D(K\,||\,H) = \sum_{y\in\chi} K(y)\ln\left(\frac{K(y)}{H(y)}\right). \tag{43}$$

The JSD is based on the Kullback–Leibler divergence D, given by Equation (43), which is the expectation of the logarithmic difference between the probabilities K and H that are both defined over the domain χ, where the expectation is taken using the probabilities K [92]. The similarity between the distributions is higher when the Jensen–Shannon distance is closer to zero. The JSD is upper bounded by $\ln(2)$.

Each of the three indices contributes to the error assessment with its peculiarity, providing a holistic assessment of prediction accuracy:

- The NRMSE evidences phase, frequency, and amplitude errors between the reference and the predicted signal, evaluating a pointwise difference between the two. However, it is not possible to discern between the three types of error and to what extent each type contributes to the overall value.
- The NAMMAE indicates if the prediction varies in the same range of the original signal, but it does not give any hint about the phase or frequency similarity of the two.
- The JSD index is ineffective in detecting phase errors between the predicted and the reference signals and is scarcely able to detect infrequent but large amplitude errors. Instead, it highlights whether the compared time histories assume each value in their range of variation a similar number of times. Hence, it is sensitive to errors in the frequency and trend of the predicted signal.

An example of synergic use of the three is given for the case of a prediction that rapidly goes to zero and evolves with an overly small amplitude. In this case, the NRMSE has a subtle behavior that may mislead the interpretation of the results if used alone: using the definition in Equation (39), the NRMSE would be close to an eighth of the standard deviation of the observed signal. This may be lower than or comparable to the error obtained with a prediction that captures the trend of the observed time history but with a small phase shift, and it may be misleading regarding the real capability of the algorithm at hand. Assessment of the NAMMAE and JSD would help to discriminate the mentioned situation, as those metrics tackle different aspects of the prediction.

An additional time-resolved error index is considered, evaluating the time evolution of the squared root difference between the reference and predicted signal averaged among the variables and normalized by k times the standard deviation of the measured values:

$$\varepsilon(t) = \frac{1}{N}\sum_{i=1}^{N}\frac{1}{k\sigma_{x_i}}\sqrt{(\tilde{x}_i(t) - x_i(t))^2} \tag{44}$$

The index $\varepsilon(t)$ is used to investigate the progression of the prediction error in the test time frame and identify possible trends.

The value of k in Equations (39), (40) and (44) is set to 10, indicating a normalizing interval of $\pm 5\sigma$ that corresponds to a coverage percentage equal to 96% using Chebishev's inequality.

4. Numerical Setup

This section presents the numerical setup of the DMD for the nowcasting and system identification tasks, along with the preprocessing applied to the data. In this work, the analyses are performed on experimentally measured data, but it is worth noting that the methods also directly apply to other data sources such as simulations of various fidelity levels. All DMD analyses are based on normalized data using the Z-score standardization. Specifically, time histories are shifted and scaled, with the average and variance evaluated on the training set.

A lexicon borrowed from machine learning can be used to describe the workflow for the DMD analyses due to their data-driven nature, even though the peculiarities of the method will cause some differences in the meaning of some terms. Calling *present instant* the DMD prediction starting point, the observed data lie in the past. Hence, the Hankel-DMD models the matrices $\widehat{\mathbf{A}}$ and $\widehat{\mathbf{B}}$, which are built using such past time histories that constitute the *training data*. The *test data*, conversely, lie in the future, and test sequences are used to assess the predictive performances of the models.

In the nowcasting approach, the (Bayesian) Hankel-DMD models are trained with sequences from the near past, i.e., ending just before the present instant, and used to forecast short sequences in the future in the order of few wave encounter periods (referring to the time between the passage of two consecutive waves relative to a fixed point on the floating platform). A new training is performed for each test sequence in a sliding window fashion, as sketched in Figure 3.

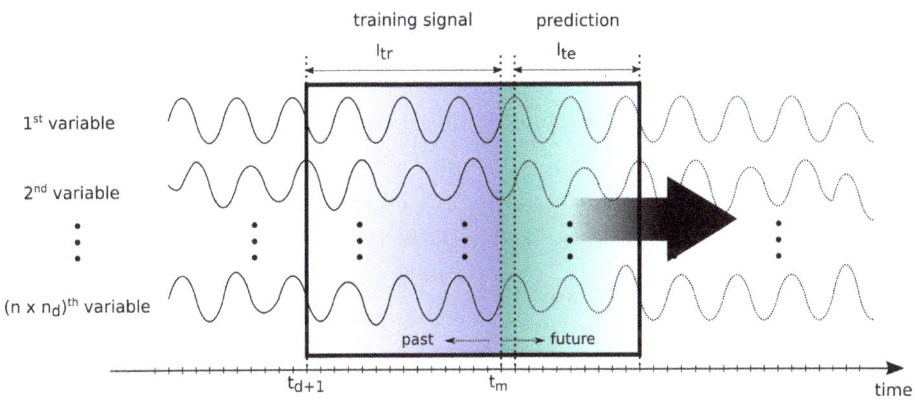

Figure 3. Sketch of the Hankel-DMD modeling approach for short-term forecasting (nowcasting).

In the system identification task, the training and the test phases are independent such that a (Bayesian) Hankel-DMDc model is trained on a dedicated sequence only once and taken as a representative ROM for the FOWT. Hence, its performances are tested against multiple test sequences with no changes in the $\widehat{\mathbf{A}}$ and $\widehat{\mathbf{B}}$ matrices, as suggested by the sketch in Figure 4.

It is worth stressing that, differently from most machine learning methods, training a DMD/DMDc model is not an iterative procedure. In fact, the model is built, i.e., trained, with a direct procedure as described in Section 2.4, identifying the Hankel-DMD modes, the matrix $\widehat{\mathbf{A}}$ and, for DMDc, the matrix $\widehat{\mathbf{B}}$.

Figure 5 offers a view of the workflow of the Hankel-DMD (Figure 5a) and Hankel-DMDc (Figure 5b) analyses. The first operation is the collection of the training data to be processed, which are in this work extracted from the existent dataset. This is strictly dependent on the prediction time instant only for the nowcasting using Hankel-DMD. Then, data are fed to the preprocessing step: To provide a common baseline for processing by DMD, time sequences are resampled using a sampling rate $\Delta t = \hat{T}/32$ s. The wave encounter frequency $\hat{f} = 1/\hat{T}$ is expected to be relevant in the platform dynamics, which will have, however, relevant energetic content also at higher frequencies. The sampling rate has been hence selected to ensure at least six samples per wavelength up to $5\hat{f}$, avoiding aliasing. Data are then organized into the matrices $\hat{\mathbf{X}}$ and $\hat{\mathbf{X}}'$ based on the hyperparameter values of the DMD method at hand.

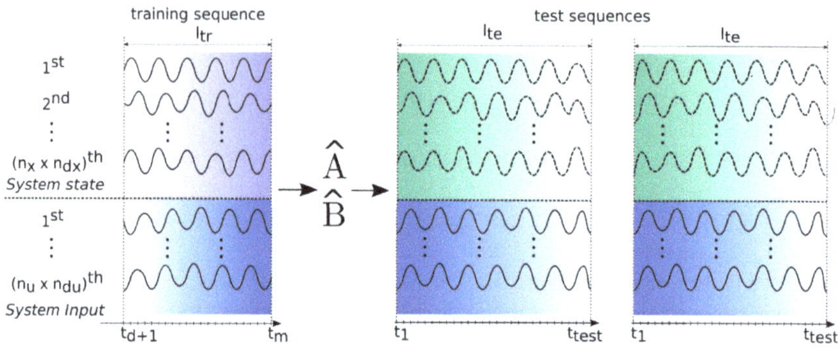

Figure 4. Sketch of the Hankel-DMD modeling approach for system identification.

The Hankel-DMD/DMDc algorithm is thus applied, obtaining the eigenvalues and eigenvectors of the $\widehat{\mathbf{A}}$ matrix and the vector $\hat{\mathbf{b}}$ of the initial conditions for Hankel-DMD in nowcasting or the matrices $\widehat{\mathbf{A}}$ and $\widehat{\mathbf{B}}$ for Hankel-DMDc in system identification.

The output of the Hankel-DMD or Hankel-DMDc is used to calculate the predicted time series $\tilde{\mathbf{x}}(t)$ of the states, which are then compared with the test signals to evaluate the error metrics for performance assessment.

The nowcasting by Hankel-DMD only requires past histories of the variables under analysis, in contrast to the system identification in which the Hankel-DMDc needs the current value of the input time series at each time step to advance with the prediction. In particular, in this study, the wind speed V_w and the wave elevation h_w as measured by the PLC on the nacelle and the ACDP, respectively, are included in the vector $\mathbf{u}$. The mentioned characteristics make the two approaches very different from each other. The nowcasting is more suitable for short-term predictions, in the range of a few characteristic periods, and appropriate for being applied in real-time digital twins or to model predictive controllers, also exploiting the possibility of continuous learning of the method during the system evolution. The system identification approach is more suited to produce a reduced-order model of the system as a surrogate of the original one that produced the data used for training. Once trained, the ROM can be applied for fast and reliable predictions of the system's response to given operational conditions of possibly undefined time extension at a reduced computational cost, with potentially useful applications in control, design, life-cycle cost assessment, maintenance, and operational planning, as an alternative to high-fidelity simulations or experiments.

A full-factorial design of experiment is conducted to investigate the influence of the two main hyperparameters of the Hankel-DMD on the nowcasting performances. Five levels of variation are used for $l_{tr} = \hat{T}, 2\hat{T}, 4\hat{T}, 8\hat{T}, 16\hat{T}$ and six for $l_{d_x} = 0.5\hat{T}, \hat{T}, 2\hat{T}, 4\hat{T}, 8\hat{T}, 16\hat{T}$, as also outlined in Table 1 in terms of training time steps n_{tr} and number of delayed time histories embedded n_d with the current time sampling.

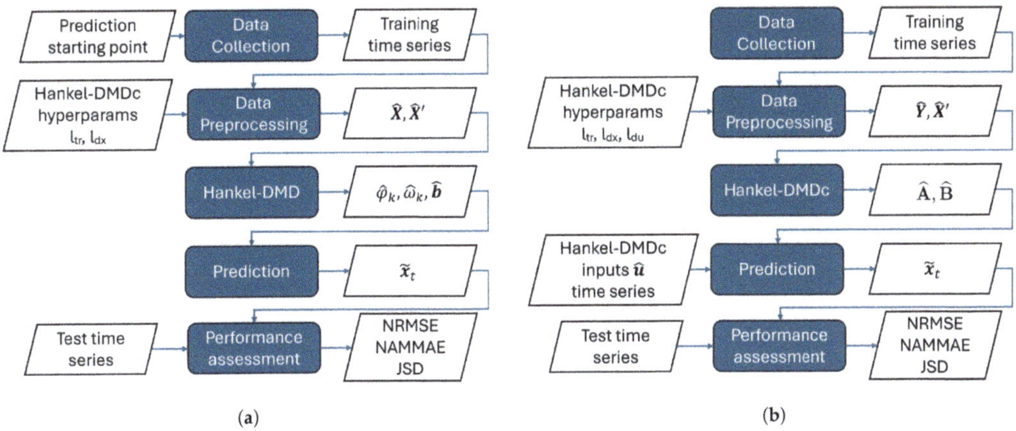

Figure 5. Hankel-DMD for nowcasting (**a**) and Hankel-DMDc for system identification (**b**) learning–prediction–assessment flowchart.

Table 1. List of the hyperparameter settings tested for Hankel-DMD nowcasting.

l_{tr}	[-]		$\hat{T}$	$2\hat{T}$	$4\hat{T}$	$8\hat{T}$	$16\hat{T}$
l_{d_x}	[-]	$0.5\hat{T}$	$\hat{T}$	$2\hat{T}$	$4\hat{T}$	$8\hat{T}$	$16\hat{T}$
n_{tr}	[-]	16	32	64	128	256	512
n_{d_x}	[-]	16	32	64	128	256	512

The prediction performance of each configuration is assessed through the NRMSE, NAMMAE, and JSD metrics introduced in Section 3 on a statistical basis using 100 random starting instants as validation cases for prediction inside the 12-hour considered time frame. A forecasting horizon of $l_{te} = 4\hat{T}$ is considered, corresponding to approximately 30 s.

The statistical assessment of the system identification procedure shall also include the choice of the training sequence as an influencing parameter. For this reason, the dataset is subdivided into training, validation, and test portions that are completely separated from each other. Ten different training sets are identified inside the data portion dedicated to training. For each one of them, the effect of the three hyperparameters of Hankel-DMDc on the system identification is analyzed with a full-factorial design of experiment using seven levels for l_{tr} and six levels for l_{d_x} and l_{d_u}, with the values in Table 2 used.

Table 2. List of the hyperparameter settings tested for Hankel-DMDc system identification algorithm.

l_{tr}	[-]	$50\hat{T}$	$75\hat{T}$	$100\hat{T}$	$125\hat{T}$	$150\hat{T}$	$175\hat{T}$	$200\hat{T}$
l_{d_x}	[-]	$0.5\hat{T}$	$\hat{T}$	$2\hat{T}$	$3\hat{T}$	$4\hat{T}$	$5\hat{T}$	
l_{d_u}	[-]	$5\hat{T}$	$10\hat{T}$	$20\hat{T}$	$30\hat{T}$	$40\hat{T}$	$50\hat{T}$	
n_{tr}	[-]	1600	2400	3200	4000	4800	5600	6400
n_{d_x}	[-]	16	32	64	96	128	160	
n_{d_u}	[-]	160	320	640	960	1280	1600	

The prediction performance of each of the 252 configurations is assessed through the NRMSE, NAMMAE, and JSD metrics on a statistical basis using 10 random validation signals extracted from the validation set for a total of 100 evaluations of each error metric per hyperparameters configuration. The prediction time window considered has a length of $l_{te} = 20\hat{T}$, or approximately 146 s.

The results from the deterministic Hankel-DMD and Hankel-DMDc analyses are used to identify suitable ranges for the hyperparameter values to be used with their Bayesian extensions.

5. Results

This section discusses the DMD analysis of the system dynamics in terms of complex modal frequencies, modal participation, and most energetic modes, and it assesses the results of the DMD-based forecasting method for the prediction of the state evolution.

5.1. Modal Analysis

Figure 6 presents the DMD results for the FOWT system dynamics. Specifically, Figure 6a shows the complex modal frequencies identified by DMD with no state augmentation. These were ranked in Figure 6b based on the normalized energy of the respective modal coordinate signal:

$$\left\langle \hat{q}_k^2 \right\rangle = \frac{\left\langle q_k^2 \right\rangle}{\sum_{k=1}^{n} \left\langle q_k^2 \right\rangle}, \quad \text{with} \quad \left\langle q_k^2 \right\rangle = \langle q_k, q_k \rangle = \int_{t_i}^{t_f} q_k^2(t) dt. \tag{45}$$

As can be seen in Figure 6c, the dynamic is dominated by four couples of complex conjugate modes. Their components' magnitudes are presented in Figure 6d. Modes (1,2) and (7,8) show a slow (frequency around 0.0237 Hz, period around 42.3 s) and a faster (frequency around 0.0745 Hz, period around 13.5 s) coupling between the loads on tendons (and weakly on moorings) and the platform motion. Mode (3,4)'s variable participation suggests that the mode describes a slow wave height oscillation (frequency 0.00022 Hz, with a period of almost 1 h and 15 min) influencing the platform motion variables, both angular and linear. Finally, mode (5,6) identifies a subsystem describing the variation in extracted power and turbine rotational speed with wind speed (frequency 0.039 Hz, period around 25.4 s). The power extracted by the wind turbine and the rpm of its blades are almost not involved in the description of the floating motions and scarcely influenced by them, despite the extreme operating conditions that could have a coupling effect through large motions, as well as hydro- and aerodynamic nonlinearities.

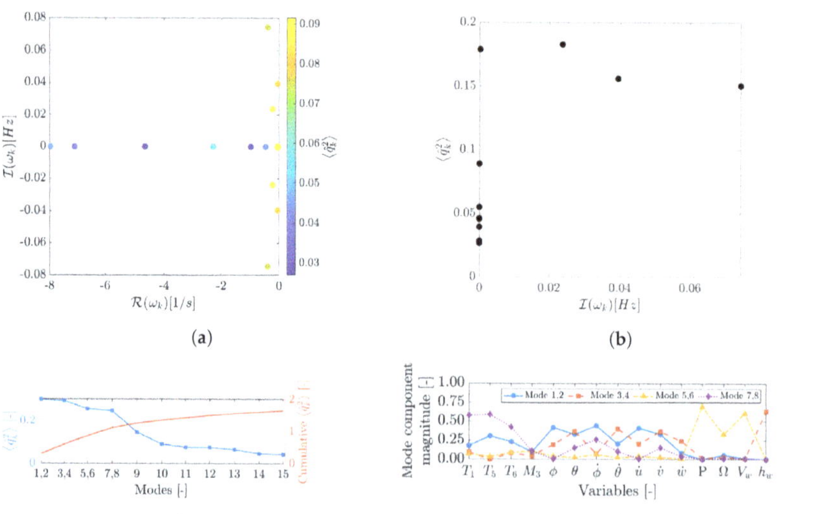

Figure 6. DMD complex modal frequencies (**a**), modal participation spectrum (**b**) and cumulative values (**c**), and first modes shapes (**d**).

5.2. Nowcasting via Hankel-DMD

As anticipated in Section 4, a full-factorial combination of settings of the Hankel-DMD hyperparameters was tested to investigate their influence on the forecasting capability of the method. The results, gathering the outcomes from all the algorithm setups and test cases, are outlined in Figure 7 as boxplots for the NRMSE, NAMMAE, and JSD, focusing on a length of the test signal $l_{te} = 4\hat{T}$. The boxplots show the first, second (equivalent to the median value), and third quartiles, while the whiskers extend from the box to the farthest data point lying within 1.5 times the inter-quartile range, which is defined as the difference between the third and the first quartiles from the box. The diamonds indicate the average of the results for each combination. Outliers are not shown to improve the readability of the plot.

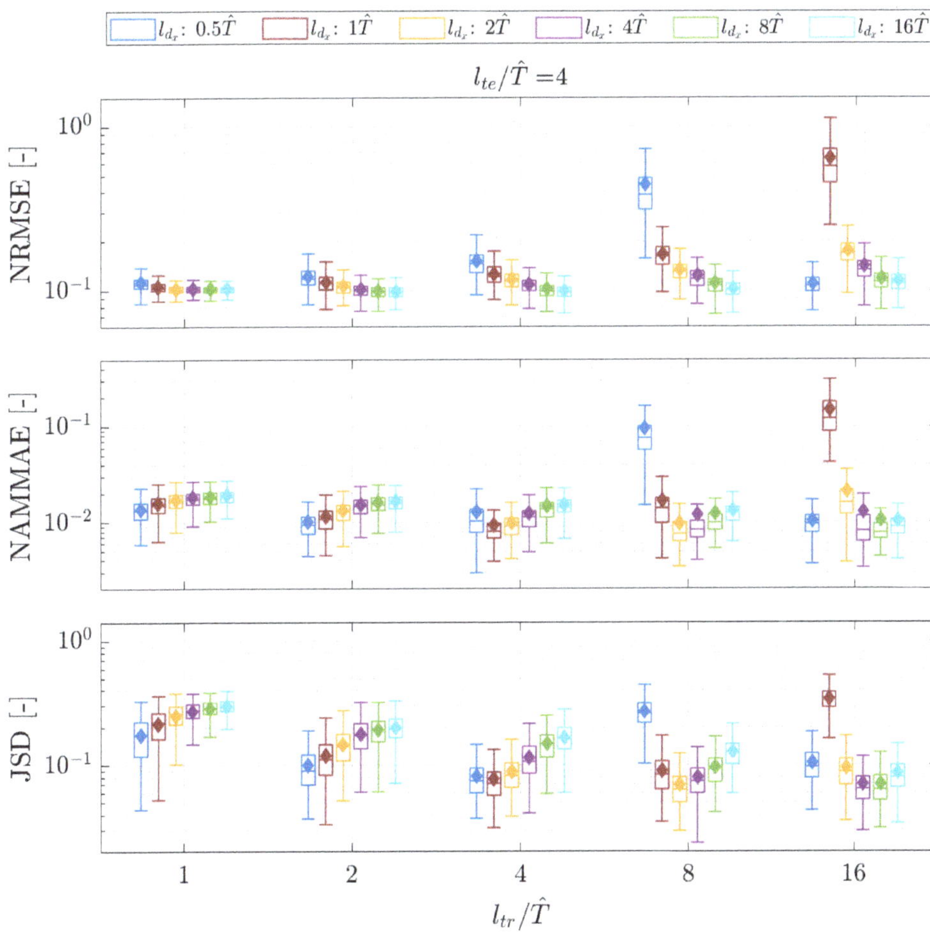

Figure 7. Hankel-DMD boxplot of error metrics over the validation set for tested l_{tr} and l_{d_x}, $l_{te} = 4\hat{T}$ (∼30 s). Diamonds indicate the average value of the respective configuration.

It can be noted that the three metrics indicate different *best* hyperparameter settings. Their values are reported in Table 3. However, the different types of errors targeted by the three metrics help to interpret the results and gain some insight:

(a) Long training signals with few delayed copies in the augmented state showed poor prediction capabilities, as confirmed by all the metrics for both the short-term and mid-term time windows. The effect is notable for $\frac{l_{d_x}}{l_{tr}} < 1/8$.

(b) A high number of embedded time-delayed signals with insufficiently long training lengths was prone to producing NRMSEs, progressively reducing the metric's dispersion around the value of an eighth of the standard deviation of the observed signals. This happens, with the explored values of l_{d_x}, particularly for $l_{tr} = \hat{T}, 2\hat{T}$, and, to a lesser extent, $4\hat{T}$ when $\frac{l_{d_x}}{l_{tr}}$ exceeded 1. At the same time, the NAMMAE and JSD values for the same settings are progressively increasing their values; this indicates that the predicted signals are not able to catch the maximum and minimum values of the reference sequences and that the distribution of the predicted data is not adherent to the true data advancing in time. The combination of those two behaviors is due to the method generating numerous rapidly decaying predictions, whose signals become highly damped after a short observation time.

A suitable range for the hyperparameter settings to obtain accurate results can be inferred by combining the above considerations. The best deterministic results were obtained when $4 \leq l_{tr}/\hat{T} \leq 16$ and $l_{d_x}/l_{tr} = 1/4$.

Figures 8–11 show the forecast by the Hankel-DMD for random test sequences taken as representative nowcasting examples. The figures show the last part of the training sequence with a solid black line, the test sequence in a dashed black line, and the prediction obtained with the $\text{Best}_{\text{NRMSE}}$, $\text{Best}_{\text{NAMMAE}}$, and Best_{JSD} hyperparameters, as reported in Table 3, with an orange dash-dotted, yellow dotted, and purple dashed line, respectively.

The forecast data are in fairly good agreement with the measurements, particularly for the $\text{Best}_{\text{NAMMAE}}$ and Best_{JSD} lines. Confirming the previous statement, some predictions of the $\text{Best}_{\text{NRMSE}}$ show a rapidly decaying amplitude not following the ground truth; see, e.g., T_1, T_5, θ, $\dot{\phi}$, $\dot{v}$, $\dot{w}$, and h_w in Figure 10 or $\dot{\phi}$ and $\dot{\theta}$ in Figure 8.

As expected from the nowcasting algorithm, the forecasting accuracy is higher at the beginning of the prediction, see the ϵ trend in Figures 8–11, but in most cases is satisfactory for the entire window. The variables reproduced with the highest errors are the extracted power P, the blade rotational speed Ω, and the wind speed V_w. Their time histories estimated by the PLC on the nacelle do not show strong periodicity in the observed time frame and, moreover, show strong nonlinearities: the turbine control algorithms limit the maximum power extracted by the turbine and its blades' rotational speed for example, acting as a saturator when the wind is too strong. In addition, and partially as a consequence of the above, these variables are seen to form an almost separate subsystem in the modal analysis; hence, a limited portion of the data could be actually used by the DMD to extract related modal content and produce their forecast, putting the method in a very challenging situation.

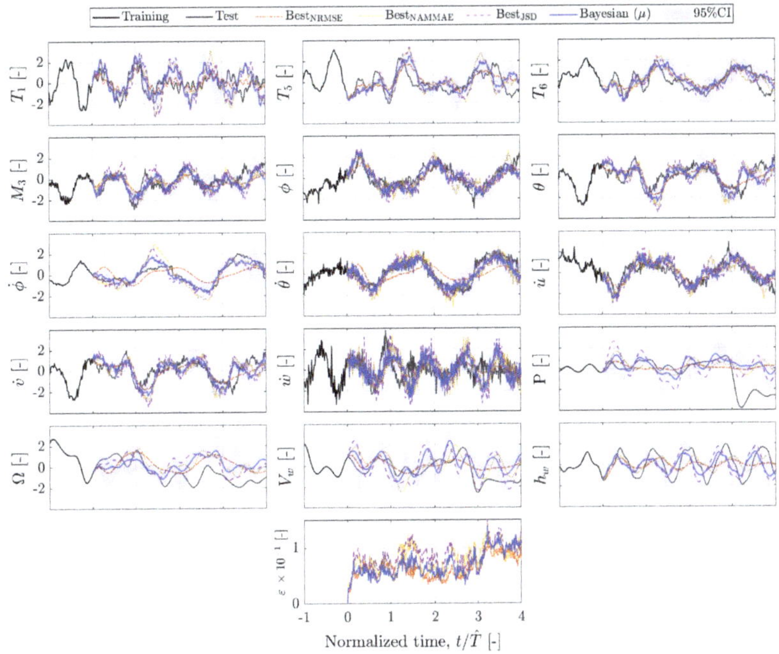

Figure 8. Standardized time series nowcasting by deterministic (hyperparameters for best average metrics) and Bayesian Hankel-DMD. Selected sequence 1.

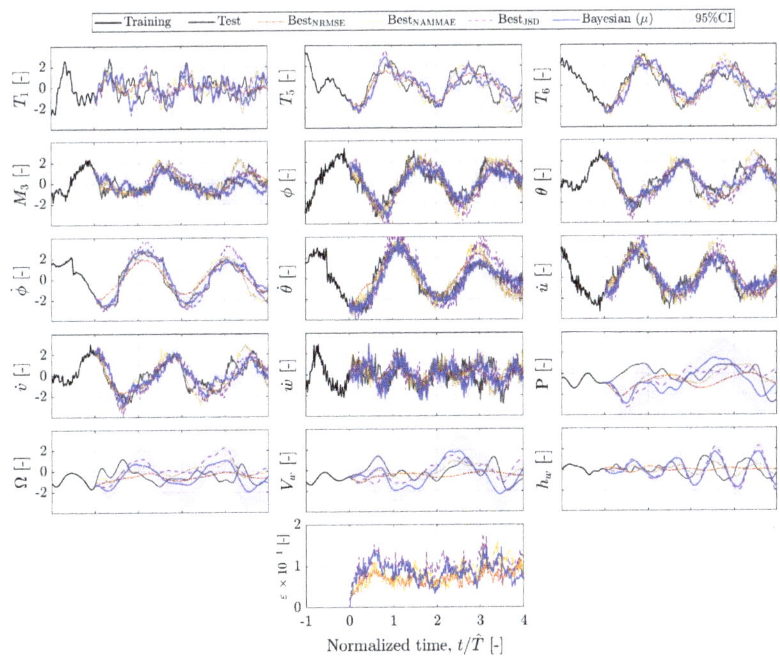

Figure 9. Standardized time series nowcasting by deterministic (hyperparameters for best average metrics) and Bayesian Hankel-DMD. Selected sequence 2.

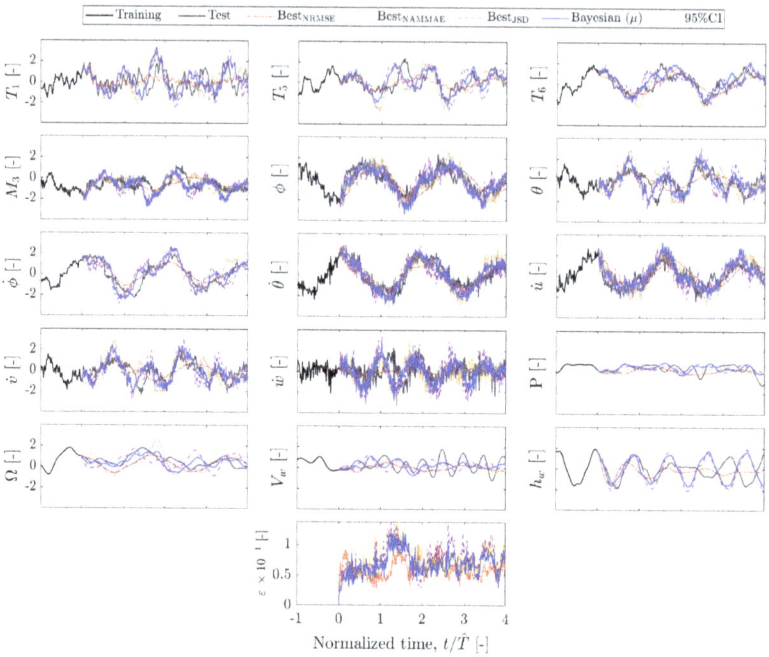

Figure 10. Standardized time series nowcasting by deterministic (hyperparameters for best average metrics) and Bayesian Hankel-DMD. Selected sequence 3.

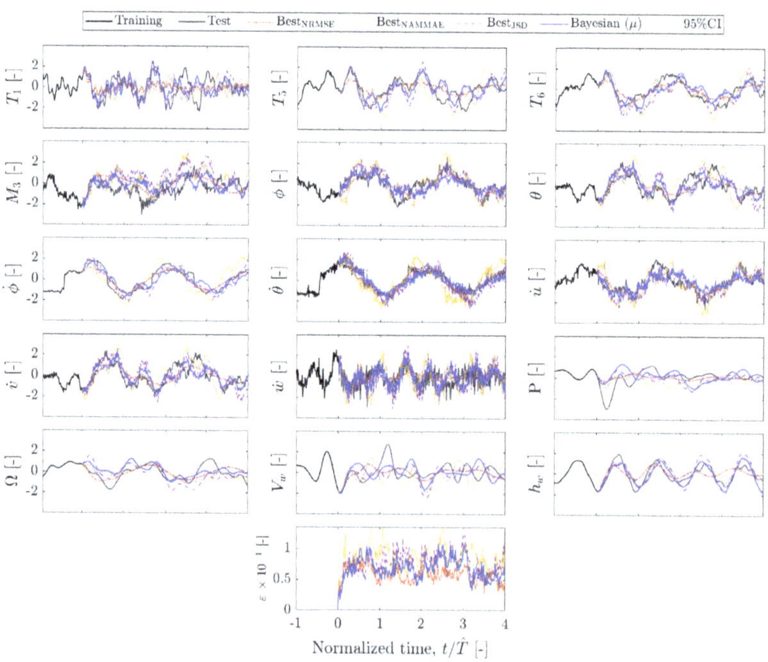

Figure 11. Standardized time series nowcasting by deterministic (hyperparameters for best average metrics) and Bayesian Hankel-DMD. Selected sequence 4.

5.3. Nowcasting via Bayesian Hankel-DMD

As highlighted by the authors in previous works [59,76,77,93], the final prediction from DMD-based models may strongly vary for different hyperparameters settings, and no general rule is given for the determination of their optimal values. Aiming at including uncertainty quantification in the prediction and making the prediction more robust, the Bayesian extension of the Hankel-DMD considers the hyperparameters of the method as stochastic variables with uniform probability density functions.

The insights gained in the deterministic analysis are applied to determine suitable variation ranges for l_{tr} and l_{d_x}. In particular, a probabilistic length of the training time history is considered, uniformly distributed between 4 to 16 incoming wave periods as $l_{tr}/\hat{T} \sim \mathcal{U}(4, 16)$. Moreover, for each realization of l_{tr}, l_{d_x} is also taken as a probabilistic variable, being uniformly distributed in the interval $l_{d_x} \sim \mathcal{U}\left(\frac{l_{tr}}{8}, l_{tr}\right)$ (each actual n_d is taken as its respective integer part).

The solid blue lines in Figures 8–11 show the expected value of the Bayesian predictions on representative test set sequences obtained using 100 uniformly distributed Monte Carlo realizations; the blue shadowed areas indicate the 95% confidence interval of the uncertain predictions. The Bayesian Hankel-DMD provides fairly good forecasting of the measured quantities and the same considerations made in the deterministic analysis hold. The biggest discrepancies are noted in the prediction of P, Ω, and V_w, which also show the largest uncertainty bands, suggesting poor accuracy.

Figure 12 compares the error metrics from the Bayesian Hankel-DMD and the $\text{Best}_{\text{NRMSE}}$, $\text{Best}_{\text{NAMMAE}}$, and Best_{JSD} configurations of the deterministic analysis for $l_{te}/\hat{T} = 4$. The mean values of the metrics are summarized in Table 3. The boxplots indicate that Bayesian nowcasting achieved results comparable to the best deterministic configurations for NAMMAE and JSD, slightly improving their NRMSEs. This appears remarkable considering the poor NAMMAE and JSD performance of the $\text{Best}_{\text{NRMSE}}$ configuration.

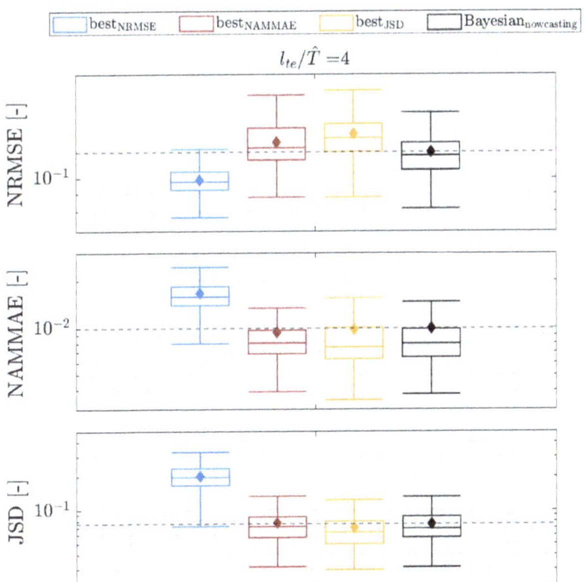

Figure 12. Error metrics comparison, Hankel-DMD vs. Bayesian Hankel-DMD nowcasting, $l_{te} = 4\hat{T}$ (∼30 s).

Table 3. Summary of the best hyperparameter configurations for nowcasting as identified by the deterministic design of experiment and Bayesian setup, where $l_{te} = 4\hat{T}$.

	NRMSE (avg)	NAMMAE (avg)	JSD (avg)	l_{tr}	l_{d_x}
$\text{Best}_{\text{NRMSE}}$	0.124	0.026	0.200	$2\hat{T}$	$16\hat{T}$
$\text{Best}_{\text{NAMMAE}}$	0.159	0.015	0.077	$4\hat{T}$	$\hat{T}$
Best_{JSD}	0.168	0.015	0.070	$8\hat{T}$	$2\hat{T}$
Bayesian	0.148	0.015	0.075	$[4\text{–}16]\hat{T}$	$l_{tr}/4$

The forecasting time window here considered, i.e., $l_{te} = 4\hat{T}$ ($\sim$30 s), can be assumed satisfactory from the perspective of the design of a model predictive or feedforward controller according to Ma et al. [39], where a five-second horizon was considered and found to be sufficient. Moreover, the nowcasting algorithm is inherently suitable for continuous learning and digital twinning, adapting the model and predictions along with the incoming data from an evolving changing system and environment.

It shall be noted that the evaluation time for a single Hankel-DMD training, averaged over 10 realizations using 100 different hyperparameter values in the intervals of the Bayesian analysis, ranged from $\mu_t = 0.029$ s, $\sigma_t = 0.0041$ s to $\mu_t = 1.225$ s, $\sigma_t = 0.0159$ s on a mid-end laptop with an Intel Core i5-1235U CPU and 16 Gb of memory using a noncompiled MATLAB 2023a code, depending on the algorithm setup (longer training signals with more delays require more time). The computational cost for obtaining a Bayesian Hankel-DMD prediction linearly depends on the number of Monte Carlo samples used in the hyperparameters sampling: for each hyperparameter combination, a different Hankel-DMD model has to be evaluated. However, the task is embarrassingly parallel, and, with a sufficient number of computational units, the actual computational time can be kept as low as a single deterministic evaluation. The one-shot and fast training phase, related to the direct linear algebra operations detailed in Section 2.2, makes the Hankel-DMD and Bayesian Hankel-DMD algorithms very promising in the context of real-time forecasting and nowcasting.

5.4. System Identification via Hankel-DMDc

The results from the design of experiment on system identification via the deterministic Hankel-DMDc are reported in terms of boxplots graphs in Figures 13–18 combining the outcomes of the 100 training/validation sequences combinations for each hyperparameter configuration. The metrics are evaluated using a prediction timeframe of $l_{te} = 20\hat{T}$ ($\sim$146 s).

Analyzing the boxplots, it can be noted that some configurations of the hyperparameters are characterized by very high values of all the metrics. The $\mathbf{A}$ matrices of the pertaining Hankel-DMDc models have been noted to have eigenvalues with positive real parts, causing the predictions to be unstable. As pointed out by Rains et al. [94], DMDc algorithms are particularly susceptible to the choice of the model dimensions and prone to identify spurious unstable eigenvalues. In the nowcasting approach with Hankel-DMD, this phenomenon can be effectively mitigated by projecting the unstable discrete time eigenvalues onto the unit circle, i.e., stabilizing them. However, in system identification with Hankel-DMDc, the $\mathbf{B}$ matrix is also affected by the identification of unstable eigenvalues, and no simple stabilization procedure is available.

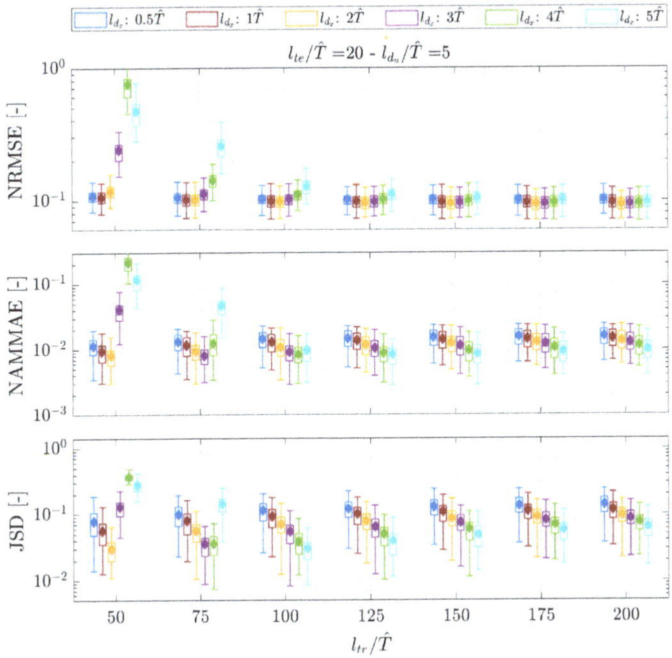

Figure 13. Hankel-DMDc boxplot of error metrics over the validation set for tested l_{tr} and l_{d_x}, with $l_{d_u}/\hat{T} = 5$. Diamonds indicate the average value of the respective configuration. $l_{te} = 20\hat{T}$ (~146 s).

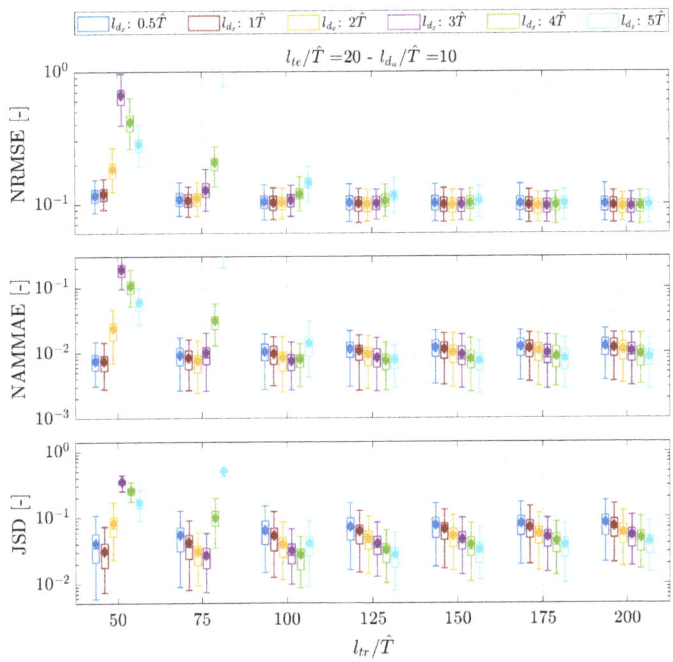

Figure 14. Hankel-DMDc boxplot of error metrics over the validation set for tested l_{tr} and l_{d_x}, with $l_{d_u}/\hat{T} = 10$. Diamonds indicate the average value of the respective configuration. $l_{te} = 20\hat{T}$ (~146 s).

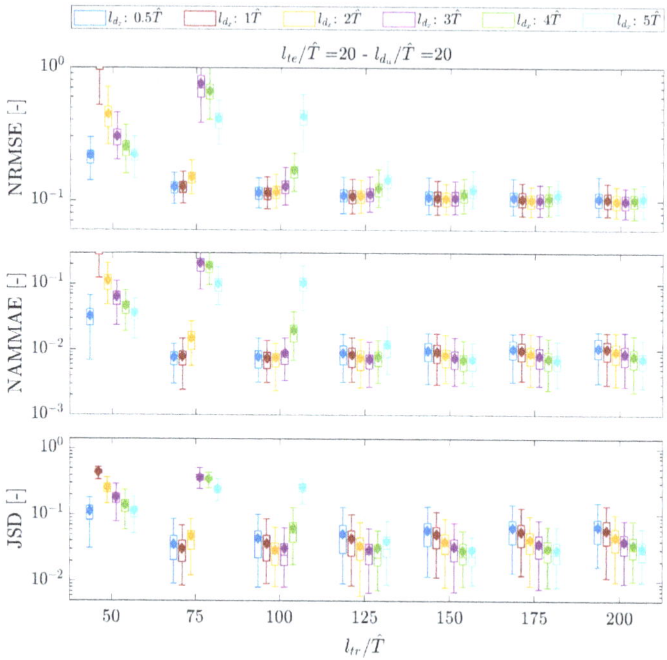

Figure 15. Hankel-DMDc boxplot of error metrics over the validation set for tested l_{tr} and l_{d_x}, with $l_{d_u}/\hat{T} = 20$. Diamonds indicate the average value of the respective configuration. $l_{te} = 20\hat{T}$ (∼146 s).

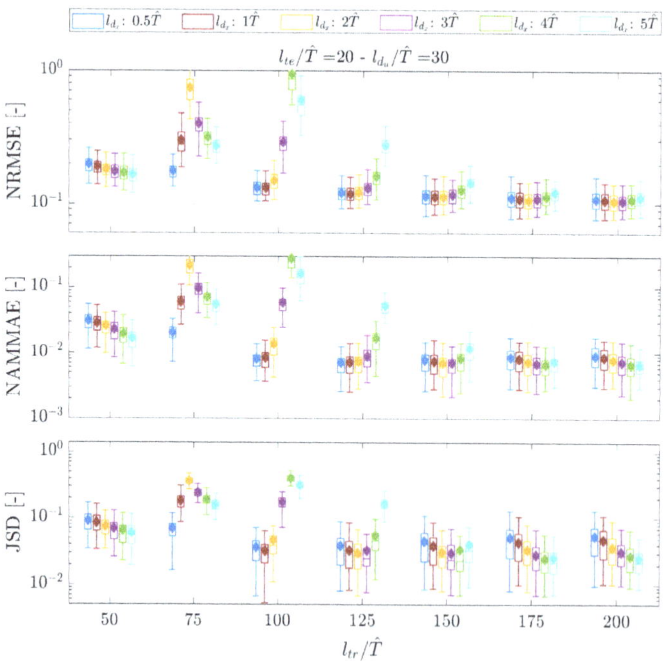

Figure 16. Hankel-DMDc boxplot of error metrics over the validation set for tested l_{tr} and l_{d_x}, with $l_{d_u}/\hat{T} = 30$. Diamonds indicate the average value of the respective configuration. $l_{te} = 20\hat{T}$ (∼146 s).

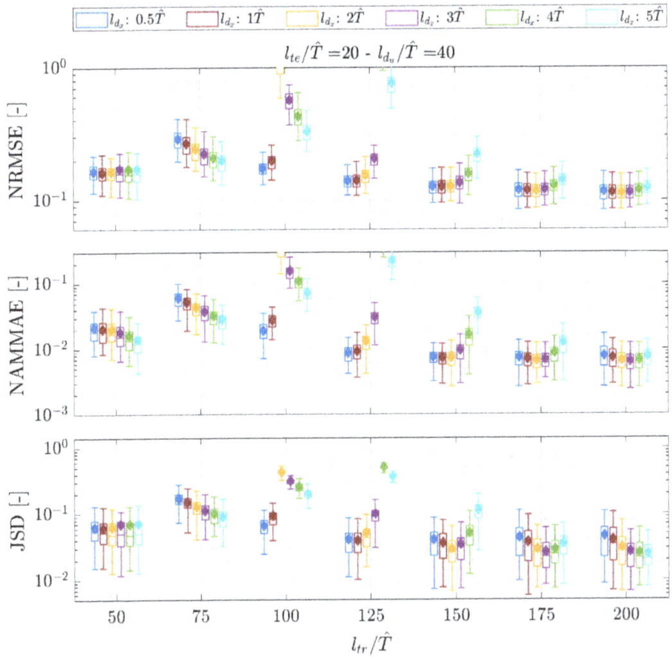

Figure 17. Hankel-DMDc boxplot of error metrics over the validation set for tested l_{tr} and l_{d_x}, with $l_{d_u}/\hat{T} = 40$. Diamonds indicate the average value of the respective configuration. $l_{te} = 20\hat{T}$ (~146 s).

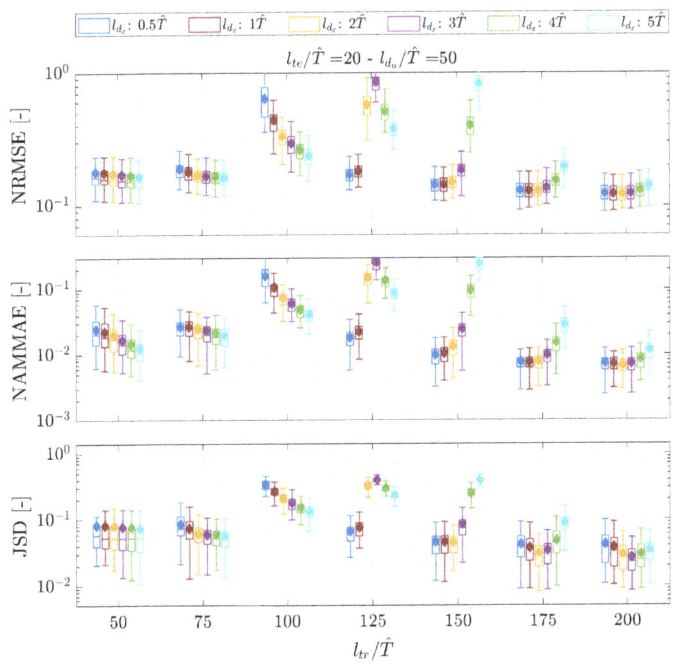

Figure 18. Hankel-DMDc boxplot of error metrics over the validation set for tested l_{tr} and l_{d_x}, with $l_{d_u}/\hat{T} = 50$. Diamonds indicate the average value of the respective configuration. $l_{te} = 20\hat{T}$ (~146 s).

Table 4 reports the value of the hyperparameters for the configurations producing the best average value of the NRMSE, NAMME, and JSD. It emerges that the most accurate predictions are obtained with high values of training length of $l_{tr} < 175\hat{T}$. The noisy nature of the experimental measures and the variability of operational conditions encountered by the FOWT during the acquisitions can partially explain this result. A large l_{tr} implies a training signal that extends over a broader set of operative situations, allowing the Hankel-DMDc to capture the system's relevant features with increased effectiveness and, hence, to obtain good predictions for unseen input sequences. A subdomain of the explored range for the hyperparameters value, defined as $175\hat{T} \leq l_{tr} \leq 200\hat{T}$, $2\hat{T} \leq l_{d_x} \leq 4\hat{T}$, and $20\hat{T} \leq l_{d_u} \leq 40\hat{T}$, includes configurations with low values of all the metrics. The $\text{Best}_{\text{NAMMAE}}$ and Best_{JSD} configurations are similar and lay in this range for which also the NRMSE showed small values (although not the best one). On the contrary, the $\text{Best}_{\text{NRMSE}}$ setup is characterized by a small value of l_{d_u} in a range that showed higher NAMMAE and JSD errors.

Figures 19–22 show the predictions by the Hankel-DMDc for random test sequences taken as representatives. The figures show the input variables with a solid black line, the test sequence in a dashed black line, and the prediction obtained with the $\text{Best}_{\text{NRMSE}}$, $\text{Best}_{\text{NAMMAE}}$, and Best_{JSD} hyperparameters, as reported in Table 4, with an orange dash-dotted, yellow dotted, and purple dashed line, respectively. $\text{Best}_{\text{NAMMAE}}$ and Best_{JSD} produces similar predictions, following their similarity in hyperparameters values. The $\text{Best}_{\text{NRMSE}}$ line behaves slightly differently from the other two and seems to capture less high-frequency oscillations of the test sequence.

As a general consideration, even though a phase-resolved agreement is not always obtained, the predictions show a strong statistical similarity with the test signals, as testified both qualitatively by Figures 19–22 and quantitatively by the JSD boxplots. It can be noted that, for all the plotted configurations, the value of ε does not show a monotonically increasing trend as the prediction time progresses, or in other words, the prediction accuracy is not negatively proportional to the prediction horizon. This suggests that the systems identified by the Hankel-DMDc may keep the shown level of accuracy indefinitely in time. This characteristic is fundamental for the proposed usages of the method.

5.5. System Identification via Bayesian Hankel-DMDc

As it was done for the nowcasting, the Bayesian extension of the Hankel-DMDc algorithm for system identification is obtained by exploiting the insights on the hyperparameters derived from the deterministic analysis, in particular for the identification of a suitable range of variation of l_{tr}, l_{d_x}, and l_{d_u}. The three hyperparameters are treated as probabilistic variables uniformly distributed in $l_{tr}/\hat{T} \sim \mathcal{U}(175, 200)$, $l_{d_x}/\hat{T} \sim \mathcal{U}(2, 4)$, and $l_{d_u}/\hat{T} \sim \mathcal{U}(20, 40)$ (the actual n_{d_x} and n_{d_u} are taken as the nearest integers from the calculated values).

Figures 19–22 show a comparison between the prediction by the Bayesian system identification and the deterministic best configurations, with the blue shadowed area representing the 95% confidence interval of the stochastic prediction. As observed for the deterministic analysis, no accuracy degradation trend with the prediction time is noted for the Bayesian prediction. The Bayesian expectation is very close to the $\text{Best}_{\text{NAMMAE}}$ and Best_{JSD} lines, with small uncertainty. This reflects a general *robustness* of the deterministic predictions in the range of variation of the stochastic parameters, which has been already noted in the similarity between the $\text{Best}_{\text{NAMMAE}}$ and Best_{JSD} solutions.

A comparison between the best deterministic configurations and the Bayesian system identification in terms of the NRMSE, NAMMAE, and JSD metrics is presented in Figure 23 for $l_{te} = 20\hat{T}$. The Bayesian approach improves the NRMSE compared to the deterministic solutions, preserving the NAMMAE and JSD results that are only slightly degraded.

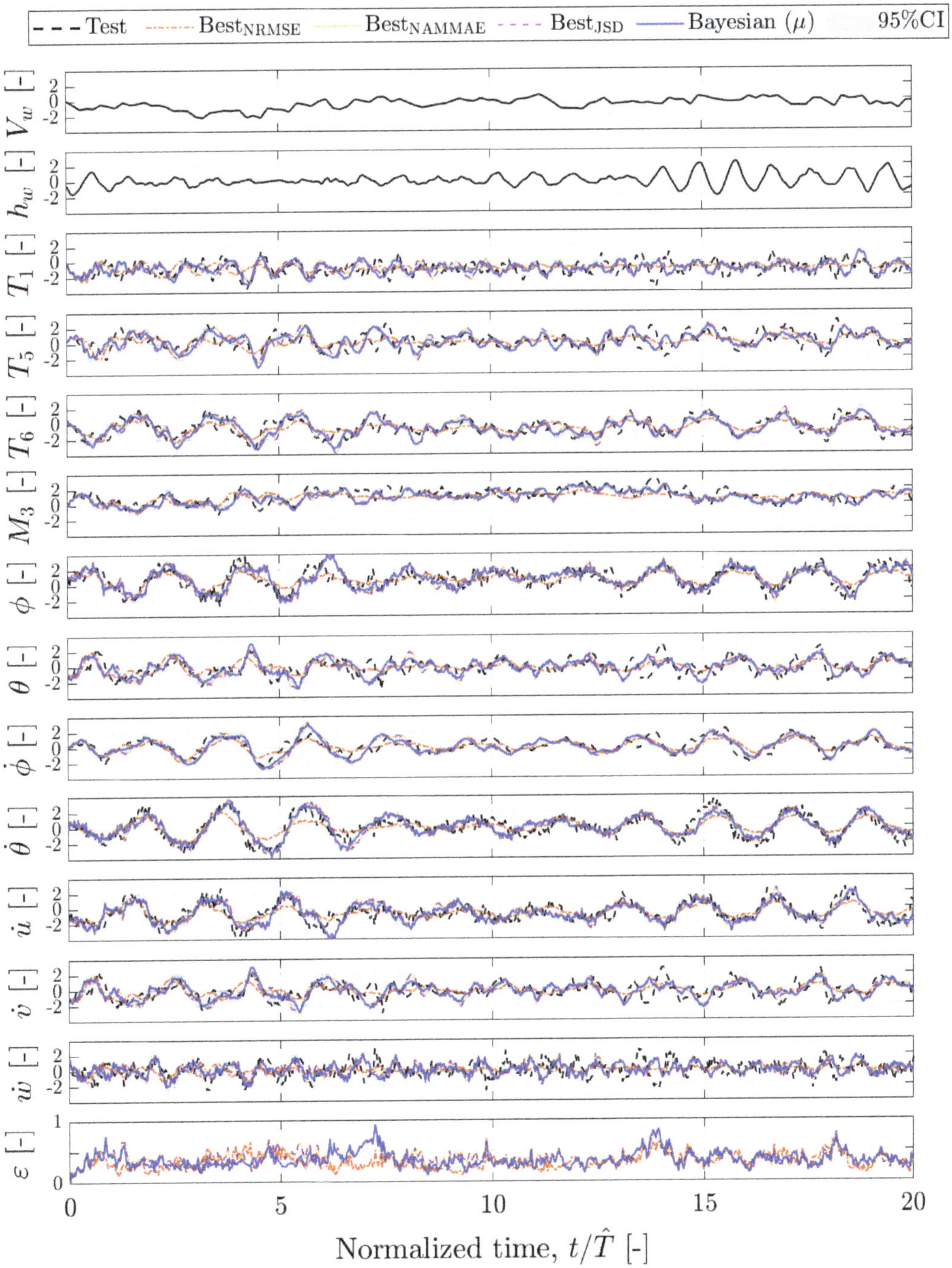

Figure 19. Standardized time series prediction by deterministic (hyperparameters for best average metrics) and Bayesian Hankel-DMDc. Selected sequence 1.

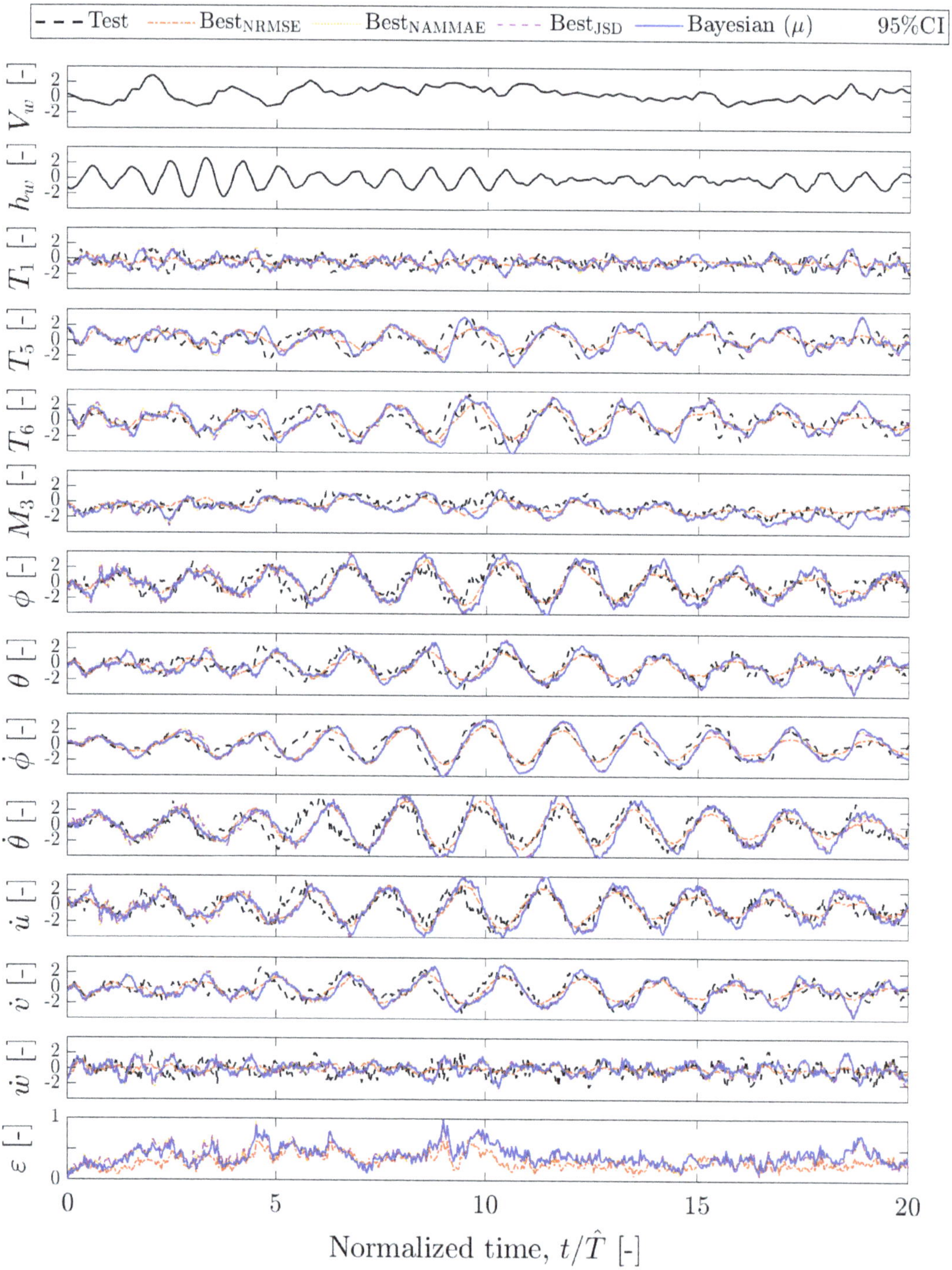

Figure 20. Standardized time series prediction by deterministic (hyperparameters for best average metrics) and Bayesian Hankel-DMDc. Selected sequence 2.

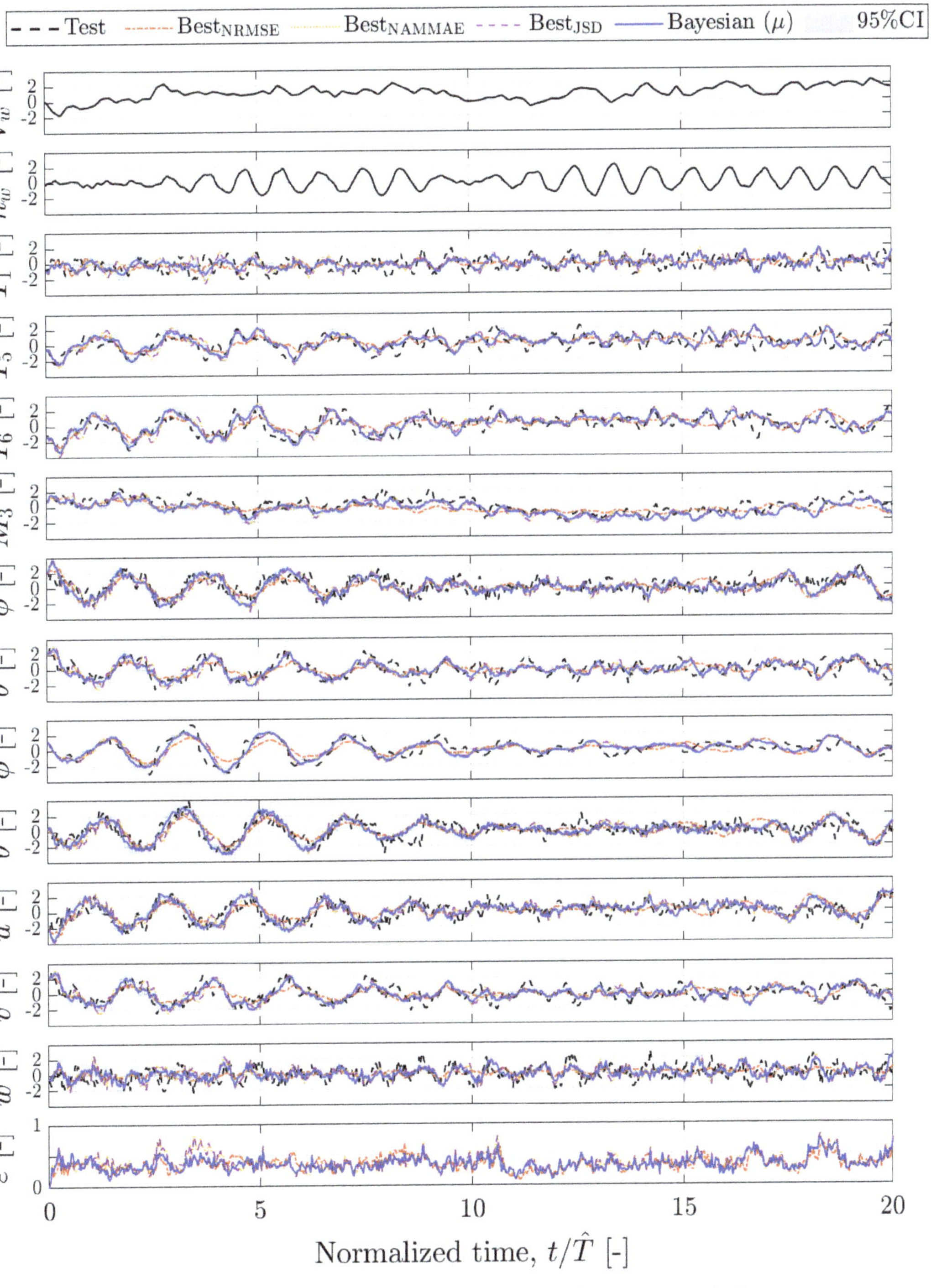

Figure 21. Standardized time series prediction by deterministic (hyperparameters for best average metrics) and Bayesian Hankel-DMDc. Selected sequence 3.

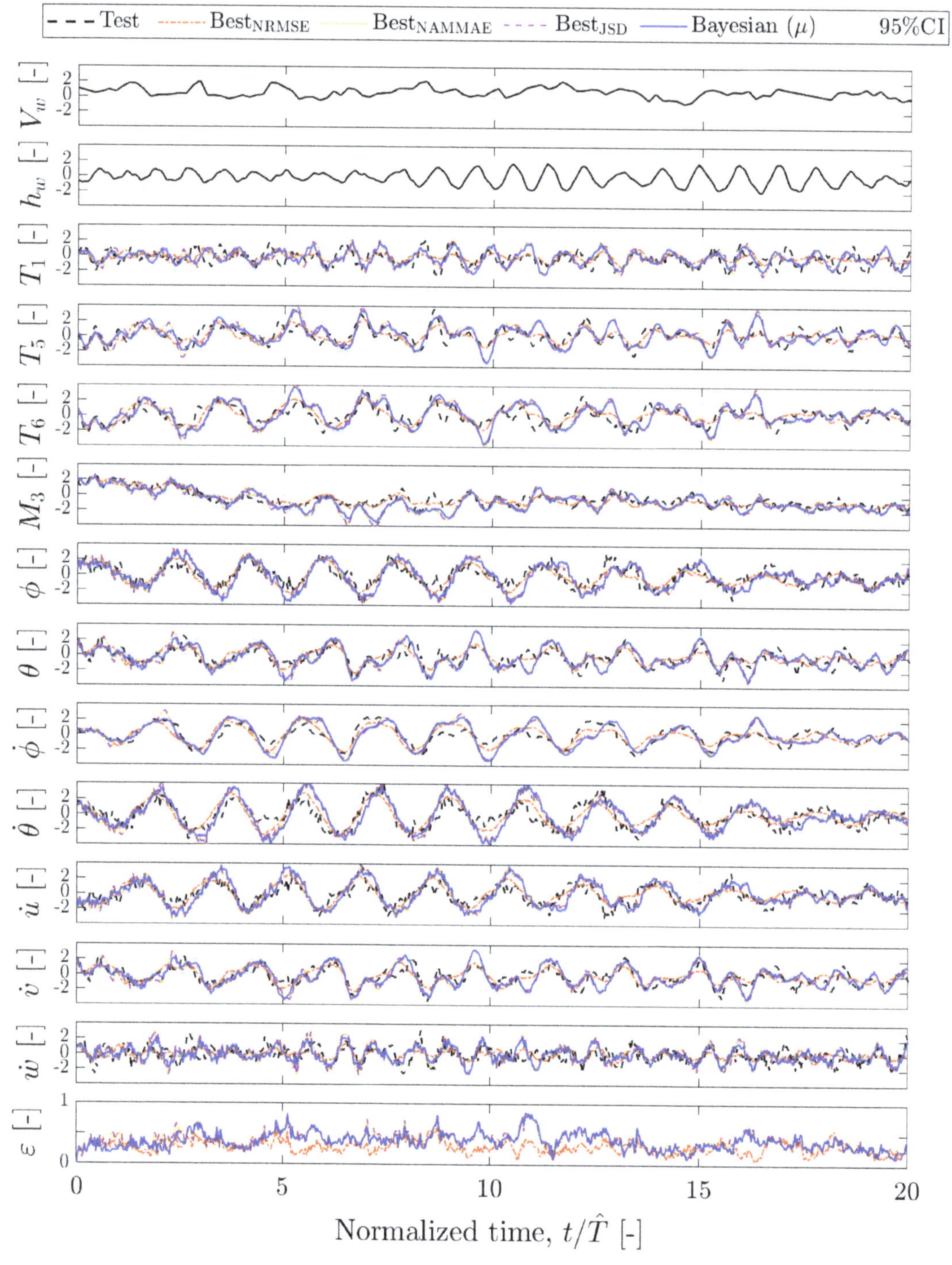

Figure 22. Standardized time series prediction by deterministic (hyperparameters for best average metrics) and Bayesian Hankel-DMDc. Selected sequence 4.

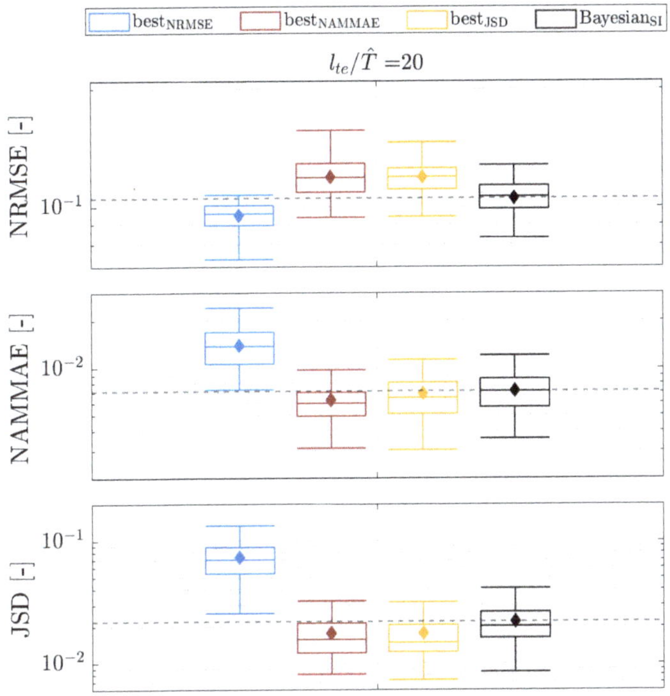

Figure 23. Error metrics comparison, Hankel-DMDc vs. Bayesian Hankel-DMDc system identification, $l_{te} = 20\hat{T}$ ($\sim$146 s).

Table 4. Summary of the best hyperparameter configurations for system identification as identified by the deterministic design of experiment, $l_{te} = 20\hat{T}$, and Bayesian setup.

	NRMSE (avg)	NAMMAE (avg)	JSD (avg)	l_{tr}	l_{d_x}	l_{d_u}
Best$_{\text{NRMSE}}$	0.118	0.022	0.073	$200\hat{T}$	$2\hat{T}$	$5\hat{T}$
Best$_{\text{NAMMAE}}$	0.149	0.010	0.018	$200\hat{T}$	$3\hat{T}$	$40\hat{T}$
Best$_{\text{JSD}}$	0.149	0.011	0.017	$175\hat{T}$	$4\hat{T}$	$30\hat{T}$
Bayesian	0.131	0.011	0.021	$[175–200]\hat{T}$	$[2–4]\hat{T}$	$[20–40]\hat{T}$

The effectiveness of the Bayesian Hankel-DMDc ROM as a surrogate model is further assessed by statistically comparing the probability density functions (PDFs) of each variable as obtained from the experimental measurements and the Bayesian system identification time series. In particular, a moving block bootstrap (MBB) method is employed to define 100 time series for the analysis, following [95]. The PDF of each time series, for both the experimental data and expected value of ROM predictions, are obtained using kernel density estimation [96] as follows:

$$\text{PDF}(x, y) = \frac{1}{\mathcal{T}h} \sum_{i=1}^{\mathcal{T}} K\left(\frac{y - x_i}{h}\right). \tag{46}$$

Here, K is a normal kernel function defined as

$$K(\xi) = \frac{1}{\sqrt{2\pi}} \exp\left(-\frac{\xi^2}{2}\right), \tag{47}$$

where $h = \sigma_x \mathcal{T}^{-1/5}$ is the bandwidth [97]. In this way, a set of 100 PDFs is obtained for each variable of the system state $\mathbf{x}$, introducing uncertainty in their estimation. Hence, an expected value and a confidence interval are calculated for the PDF of each variable for both the experimental data and expected value of ROM predictions. The quantile function q is evaluated at probabilities $p = 0.025$ and 0.975, defining the lower and upper bounds of the 95% confidence interval as $U_{PDF(\xi,y)} = PDF(\xi, y)_{q=0.95} - PDF(\xi, y)_{q=0.025}$. Figure 24 shows, per each variable, the expected value of the PDFs over the bootstrapped series as solid lines, with the 95% confidence interval shown as shaded areas.

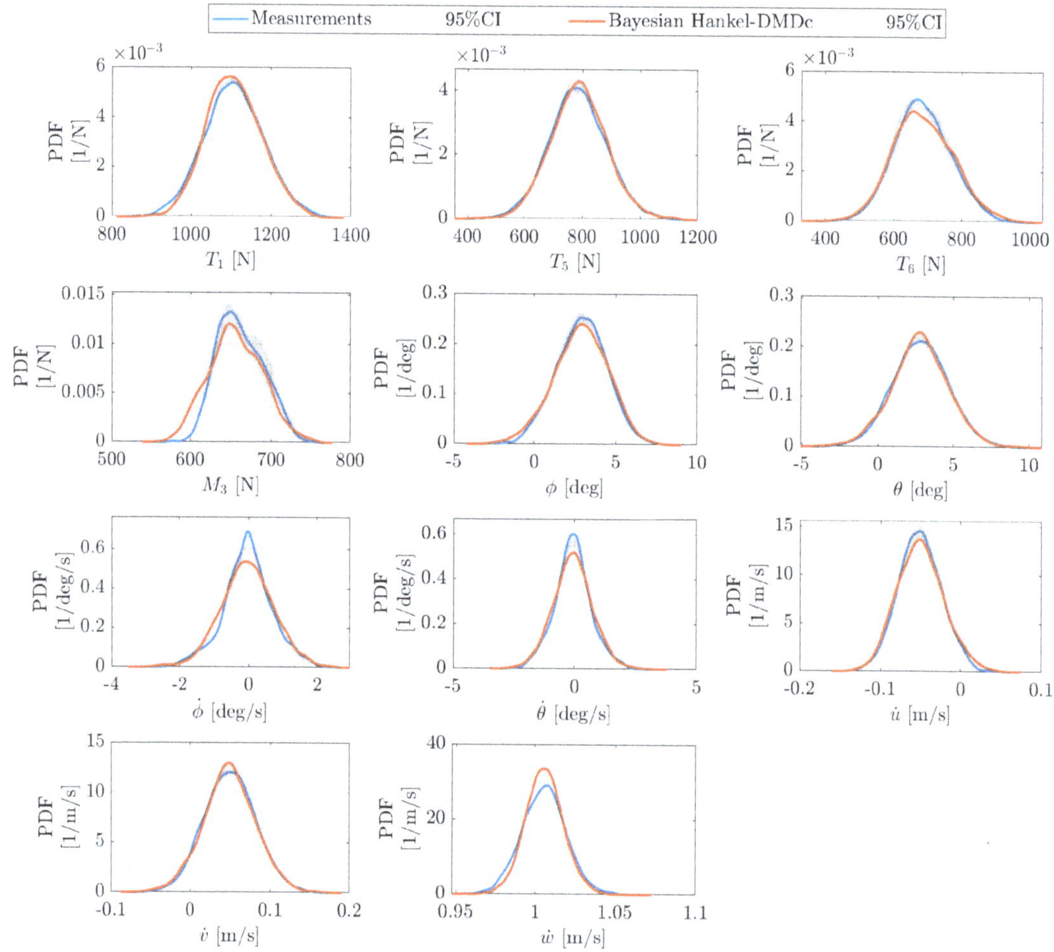

Figure 24. Probability density function comparison between measured data and the expected value of the Bayesian Hankel-DMDc prediction on bootstrapped sequences for each variable. Shaded areas indicate the 95% confidence interval of the two PDFs.

The results show a good overall agreement between the distributions obtained from the ROM and experimental measurements for all the system variables. In other words, the statistics of motion and loads emerging from the real data are effectively captured over the bootstrapped histories by the Bayesian Hankel-DMDc ROM. It may be noted that the tails of the measured PDFs, representing large amplitudes, are particularly well matched by the predictions for motion variables. The largest differences are observed for the derivative of the pitch and roll angles in the small values range. The confidence intervals of the Bayesian Hankel-DMDc predictions adequately cover the PDF of the measured data, indicating that the predictions are accurate and reliable. The statistics of the JSD metrics, in terms of the expected value and confidence interval as evaluated on the bootstrapped time series for the eleven variables, are reported in Table 5 to quantify the differences between the experimental and DMD distributions in Figure 24. The analysis confirms the similarity between the probability distributions of Bayesian Hankel-DMDc and real data sequences, as JSD showed small expected values and uncertainty. The adherence between the experimental and predicted PDF for the system variables confirms that the ROM identified by the Hankel-DMDc can be effectively applied in unseen scenarios, providing accurate and reliable predictions from the knowledge of the input variables V_w and h_w. The statistical accuracy of the system identification is of paramount importance for the application of the method in lifecycle assessment and maintenance planning.

Table 5. Expected value and 95% confidence lower bound, upper bound, and interval of JSD of bootstrapped time series.

ξ	**JSD (ξ) EV**	**q = 0.025**	**q = 0.975**	**U**
T_1	0.0039	0.0018	0.0072	0.0054
T_5	0.0021	0.0009	0.0043	0.0034
T_6	0.0042	0.0011	0.0107	0.0096
M_3	0.0218	0.0100	0.0376	0.0276
ϕ	0.0021	0.0009	0.0041	0.0032
θ	0.0037	0.0009	0.0086	0.0077
$\dot{\phi}$	0.0040	0.0011	0.0091	0.0080
$\dot{\theta}$	0.0021	0.0009	0.0040	0.0032
$\dot{u}$	0.0068	0.0036	0.0110	0.0074
$\dot{v}$	0.0079	0.0033	0.0176	0.0144
$\dot{w}$	0.0047	0.0013	0.0113	0.0100
avg	0.0058	0.0024	0.0114	0.0091

The training time for the system identification is investigated as in Section 5.3 on the same mid-end laptop, averaging over 10 realizations using 100 different hyperparameter values in the intervals of the Bayesian analysis. The larger sizes of data managed compared to the nowcasting task results in larger matrices and longer times, ranging from $\mu_t = 21.512$ s, $\sigma_t = 1.493$ s to $\mu_t = 41.116$ s, $\sigma_t = 3.027$ s, though these results are still computationally cheaper compared to high-fidelity simulations or typical training of deep learning methods, as well as more data-lean compared to the latter ones. The computational cost of the Bayesian system identification is linearly dependent on the number of Monte Carlo realizations used in the sampling of the hyperparameters combinations, as a different Hankel-DMDc model is evaluated for each combination. However, as mentioned for nowcasting, the task is embarrassingly parallel, and the actual time required to obtain a Bayesian prediction can be kept close to the single deterministic evaluation time by using multiple computational units.

6. Conclusions

To the best of the authors' knowledge, this work represents the first use of DMD and its variants to extract knowledge, as well as forecast and identify the system dynamics of a real-life FOWT using experimental field data. The approach also applies to other data sources such as simulations of various fidelity levels with no modifications.

Modal analysis revealed strong couplings between floater motions, tendons/moorings loads, and wave elevation, demonstrating the method's ability to capture complex system interactions.

Hankel-DMD successfully demonstrated data-driven, equation-free, and data-lean short-term forecasting (nowcasting) of FOWT motions and loads, achieving accurate predictions up to four wave encounters with a computational cost compatible with real-time execution and the needed accuracy for applications such as model predictive control and digital twinning. Spanning an augmented coordinate system by incorporating time-delayed variables in the system state, Hankel-DMD effectively captures the essential nonlinear features of FOWT dynamics within a linear framework. Uncertainty quantification is introduced through a novel Bayesian extension of the Hankel-DMD by considering the hyperparameters of the method as stochastic variables, with prior distribution identified from a full-factorial deterministic analysis. A systematic difficulty was encountered in predicting the turbine extracted power P and blades RPM Ω, which is partially explained by the very weak coupling observed in the modal analysis between the mentioned variables and the FOWT motions and loads: this dramatically reduced the size of data explaining the dynamics of P and Ω that is available to the Hankel-DMD method to extract a meaningful data-driven model for them. An additional challenge for the DMD-based method is represented by the large nonlinear characteristics of the power and RPM signals due to the intervention of the turbine control system.

The system identification task is performed by applying the Hankel-DMDc method, which models the FOWT as an externally forced dynamical system considering wave elevation and wind speed as inputs. This approach yielded data-driven equation-free reduced-order models capable of extended prediction horizons using small data, providing continuous knowledge of the input variables. Such models provide statistically accurate predictions with significant computational efficiency, making them valuable for applications in control systems, life-cycle assessments, and maintenance planning. A novel Bayesian extension is obtained for incorporating uncertainty quantification in the Hankel-DMDc by using the same rationale of the Bayesian Hankel-DMD.

Despite challenges posed by noisy data and strong nonlinearities from extreme conditions, the DMD-based methods showed promising results for both nowcasting and system identification. The complexity and variety of operational conditions in the experimental data have been, on one side, precious to test the DMD-based system identification in a realistic environment; on the other side, they posed a significant challenge for system identification, requiring long training signals and numerous delayed variables.

Future work will explore hybridizing DMD methods with machine learning-based approaches to further improve noise rejection and nonlinear feature capturing while preserving the DMD's inherent characteristics. In addition, a different approach for the system identification task shall also be tested for model parametrization and generalization: firstly applying the Hankel-DMDc to data collected in more specific conditions/excitations (such as single wave headings, specific magnitude ranges, wind direction, etc.) and secondly using parametric reduced-order models interpolation [98,99]. Enhancements to the experimental setup, such as multiple wave elevation measurements and additional load cells, would also provide more comprehensive data for improved system identification, adding, for example, meaningful information about waves and wind directions.

Author Contributions: G.P.: Methodology, Software, Investigation, Validation, Formal analysis, Writing—Original Draft, Visualization. A.B.: Investigation, Data curation, Resources. A.L.: Investigation, Data curation, Resources. C.P.: Investigation, Data curation, Resources. A.S.: Methodology, Writing—Review and Editing. C.L.: Investigation, Data curation, Resources, Project administration,

Funding acquisition. M.D.: Conceptualization, Methodology, Resources, Writing—Review and Editing, Supervision. All authors have read and agreed to the published version of the manuscript.

Funding: This research is supported thorugh the "Ricerca di Sistema" project (RSE, 1.8 "Energia elettrica dal mare") by the Italian Ministry of the Environment and Energy Safety (Ministero dell'Ambiente e della Sicurezza Energetica, MASE), CUP B53C22008560001, and through "Network 4 Energy Sustainable Transition–NEST", Project code PE0000021, Concession Decree No. 1561 of 11.10.2022, by the Italian Ministry of University and Research (Ministero dell'Università e della Ricerca, MUR), CUP B53C22004060006.

Institutional Review Board Statement: Not applicable.

Informed Consent Statement: Not applicable.

Data Availability Statement: The original data presented in the study are openly available at https://cnrsc-my.sharepoint.com/:f:/g/personal/giorgio_palma_cnr_it/EvegVNzuvytGpPio8gj8IJwBAdSfNIfYJ7dniapE0G98bA?e=AvrcRj accessed on 21 March 2025.

Conflicts of Interest: The authors declare no conflicts of interest.

List of Symbols and Abbreviations

Abbreviations

ADCP	acoustic doppler current profiler
DMDc	dynamic mode decomposition with control
DMD	dynamic mode decomposition
EMD	empirical mode decomposition
EU	European Union
FOWT	floating offshore wind turbine
GRNN	gated recurrent neural network
JSD	Jensen-Shannon divergence
LCOE	levelized cost of energy
LSTM	long short-term memory
MBB	moving block bootstrap
NAMMAE	normalized average minimum/maximum absolute error
NRMSE	normalized mean square error
PDF	probability density function
PLC	programmable logic controller
POD	proper orthogonal decomposition
ROM	reduced order model
SVD	singular value decomposition

Greek symbols

$\mu_x(t)$	time history of the expected value of the components of the vector $\mathbf{x}(t)$
$\sigma_x(t)$	time history of the standard deviation of the components of the vector $\mathbf{x}(t)$
Δt	time step for discretization
$\dot{\phi}$	floater roll velocity
$\dot{\theta}$	floater pitch velocity
$\mu_{(\cdot)}$	expected value of $(\cdot)$
Ω	wind turbine rotor angular velocity
ω_k	k-th eigenvalue of $\mathcal{A}$, $k = 1, \dots, n$
ϕ	floater roll angle
$\sigma_{(\cdot)}$	standard deviation of $(\cdot)$
θ	floater pitch angle

φ_k	k-th eigenvector of $\mathcal{A}$
Symbols	
$(\cdot)^*$	Hermitian transpose operator on $(\cdot)$
$(\cdot)^T$	non conjugate transpose operator on $(\cdot)$
$(\cdot)^\dagger$	Moore-Penrose pseudoinverse of $(\cdot)$
$(\cdot)_j$	j-th time snapshot of $(\cdot)$, $j = 1, \ldots, m$
$\dot{u}$	floater acceleration along x direction
$\dot{v}$	floater acceleration along y direction
$\dot{w}$	floater acceleration along z direction
$\hat{\mathbf{x}}$	augmented system state vector
$\hat{\mathbf{x}}_j$	snapshot of the augmented system state vector
$\hat{f}$	floater wave encounter frequency
$\hat{T}$	floater wave encounter period. reference period for non-dimensional time
$\langle \cdot, \cdot \rangle$	inner product
$\mathbf{A}$	discrete time system state matrix
$\mathbf{B}$	discrete time system input matrix
$\mathbf{S}'$	matrix collecting delayed system state vector snapshots excluding the first
$\mathbf{S}$	matrix collecting delayed system state vector snapshots excluding the last
$\mathbf{u}$	augmented system input vector
$\mathbf{u}$	system input vector
$\mathbf{X}'$	matrix collecting system state vector snapshots excluding the first
$\mathbf{X}$	matrix collecting system state vector snapshots excluding the last
$\mathbf{x}$	system state vector
$\mathbf{x}_0$	initial condition of the system state vector
$\mathbf{Z}$	matrix collecting delayed system input vector snapshots excluding the last
$\mathcal{A}$	continuous time system matrix
$\widehat{\mathbf{A}}$	augmented discrete time system state matrix
$\widehat{\mathbf{B}}$	augmented discrete time system input matrix
b_i	i-th coordinate of the initial condition in the eigenvector basis
h_w	wave elevation
l_{d_u}	maximum delay time in augmented input
l_{d_x}	maximum delay time in augmented state
l_{te}	test signal time length
l_{tr}	training signal time length
n_{d_u}	number of maximum delay samples in augmented input
n_{d_x}	number of maximum delay samples in augmented state
n_{tr}	number of samples in training signal
P	power extracted by the wind turbine
t	time
V_w	relative wind speed at the wind turbine rotor
M_i	load at the i-th mooring of the FOWT platform
T_i	load at the i-th tendon of the floater counterweight

References

1. Falkner, R. The Paris Agreement and the new logic of international climate politics. *Int. Aff.* **2016**, 92, 1107–1125. [CrossRef]
2. Nastasi, B.; Markovska, N.; Puksec, T.; Duić, N.; Foley, A. Renewable and sustainable energy challenges to face for the achievement of Sustainable Development Goals. *Renew. Sustain. Energy Rev.* **2022**, 157, 112071. [CrossRef]

3. International Energy Agency (IEA). *Net Zero by 2050*; IEA: Paris, France, 2021.
4. The European Parliament and Council. *Directive (EU) 2018/2001 of the European Parliament and of the Council of 11 December 2018 on the Promotion of the Use of Energy from Renewable Sources*; The European Parliament and Council: Brussels, Belgium , 2018.
5. Prakash, G.; Anuta, H.; Wagner, N.; Gallina, G.; Gielen, D.; Gorini, R. *Future of Wind-Deployment, Investment, Technology, Grid Integration and Socio-Economic Aspects*; International Renewable Energy Agency (IRENA): Masdar City, Abu Dhabi, 2019.
6. Konstantinidis, E.I.; Botsaris, P.N. Wind turbines: Current status, obstacles, trends and technologies. *IOP Conf. Ser. Mater. Sci. Eng.* **2016**, *161*, 012079. [CrossRef]
7. Pustina, L.; Lugni, C.; Bernardini, G.; Serafini, J.; Gennaretti, M. Control of power generated by a floating offshore wind turbine perturbed by sea waves. *Renew. Sustain. Energy Rev.* **2020**, *132*, 109984. [CrossRef]
8. Pustina, L.; Serafini, J.; Pasquali, C.; Solero, L.; Lidozzi, A.; Gennaretti, M. A novel resonant controller for sea-induced rotor blade vibratory loads reduction on floating offshore wind turbines. *Renew. Sustain. Energy Rev.* **2023**, *173*, 113073. [CrossRef]
9. López-Queija, J.; Robles, E.; Jugo, J.; Alonso-Quesada, S. Review of control technologies for floating offshore wind turbines. *Renew. Sustain. Energy Rev.* **2022**, *167*, 112787. [CrossRef]
10. Global Wind Energy Council (GWEC). *Global Offshore Wind Report 2020*; GWEC: Brussels, Belgium, 2020; Volume 19, pp. 10–12.
11. McMorland, J.; Collu, M.; McMillan, D.; Carroll, J. Operation and maintenance for floating wind turbines: A review. *Renew. Sustain. Energy Rev.* **2022**, *163*, 112499. [CrossRef]
12. Florian, M.; Sørensen, J.D. Wind Turbine Blade Life-Time Assessment Model for Preventive Planning of Operation and Maintenance. *J. Mar. Sci. Eng.* **2015**, *3*, 1027–1040. [CrossRef]
13. de Azevedo, H.D.M.; Araújo, A.M.; Bouchonneau, N. A review of wind turbine bearing condition monitoring: State of the art and challenges. *Renew. Sustain. Energy Rev.* **2016**, *56*, 368–379. [CrossRef]
14. Jonkman, J. *Dynamics Modeling and Loads Analysis of an Offshore Floating Wind Turbine*; University of Colorado at Boulder: Boulder, CO, USA, 2007. [CrossRef]
15. Si, Y.; Karimi, H.R.; Gao, H. Modelling and optimization of a passive structural control design for a spar-type floating wind turbine. *Eng. Struct.* **2014**, *69*, 168–182. [CrossRef]
16. Li, X.; Gao, H. Load Mitigation for a Floating Wind Turbine via Generalized H_∞ Structural Control. *IEEE Trans. Ind. Electron.* **2016**, *63*, 332–342. [CrossRef]
17. Dong, H.; Edrah, M.; Zhao, X.; Collu, M.; Xu, X.; K A, A.; Lin, Z. Model-Free Semi-Active Structural Control of Floating Wind Turbines. In Proceedings of the 2020 Chinese Automation Congress (CAC), Shanghai, China, 6–8 November 2020; pp. 4216–4220. [CrossRef]
18. Tetteh, E.Y.; Fletcher, K.; Qin, C.; Loth, E.; Damiani, R. Active Ballasting Actuation for the SpiderFLOAT Offshore Wind Turbine Platform. In Proceedings of the AIAA SCITECH 2022 Forum, San Diego, CA, USA, 3–7 January 2022. [CrossRef]
19. Galván, J.; Sánchez-Lara, M.J.; Mendikoa, I.; Pérez-Morán, G.; Nava, V.; Rodríguez-Arias, R. NAUTILUS-DTU10 MW Floating Offshore Wind Turbine at Gulf of Maine: Public numerical models of an actively ballasted semisubmersible. *J. Phys. Conf. Ser.* **2018**, *1102*, 012015. [CrossRef]
20. Grant, E.; Johnson, K.; Damiani, R.; Phadnis, M.; Pao, L. Buoyancy can ballast control for increased power generation of a floating offshore wind turbine with a light-weight semi-submersible platform. *Appl. Energy* **2023**, *330*, 120287. [CrossRef]
21. Palraj, M.; Rajamanickam, P. Motion control studies of a barge mounted offshore dynamic wind turbine using gyrostabilizer. *Ocean. Eng.* **2021**, *237*, 109578. [CrossRef]
22. Salic, T.; Charpentier, J.F.; Benbouzid, M.; Le Boulluec, M. Control Strategies for Floating Offshore Wind Turbine: Challenges and Trends. *Electronics* **2019**, *8*, 1185. [CrossRef]
23. Tiwari, R.; Babu, N.R. Recent developments of control strategies for wind energy conversion system. *Renew. Sustain. Energy Rev.* **2016**, *66*, 268–285. [CrossRef]
24. Awada, A.; Younes, R.; Ilinca, A. Review of Vibration Control Methods for Wind Turbines. *Energies* **2021**, *14*, 3058. [CrossRef]
25. Larsen, T.J.; Hanson, T.D. A method to avoid negative damped low frequent tower vibrations for a floating, pitch controlled wind turbine. *J. Phys. Conf. Ser.* **2007**, *75*, 012073. [CrossRef]
26. Jonkman, J. Influence of Control on the Pitch Damping of a Floating Wind Turbine. In Proceedings of the 46th AIAA Aerospace Sciences Meeting and Exhibit, Reno, NV, USA, 7–10 January 2008. [CrossRef]
27. Yu, W.; Lemmer, F.; Schlipf, D.; Cheng, P.W.; Visser, B.; Links, H.; Gupta, N.; Dankemann, S.; Counago, B.; Serna, J. Evaluation of control methods for floating offshore wind turbines. *J. Phys. Conf. Ser.* **2018**, *1104*, 012033. [CrossRef]
28. Bakka, T.; Karimi, H. Robust $\mathcal{H}_\infty$ Dynamic Output Feedback Control Synthesis with Pole Placement Constraints for Offshore Wind Turbine Systems. *Math. Probl. Eng.* **2012**, *2012*, 616507. [CrossRef]
29. Betti, G.; Farina, M.; Marzorati, A.; Scattolini, R.; Guagliardi, G.A. Modeling and control of a floating wind turbine with spar buoy platform. In Proceedings of the 2012 IEEE International Energy Conference and Exhibition (ENERGYCON), Florence, Italy, 9–12 September 2012; pp. 189–194. [CrossRef]

30. Lemmer (né Sandner), F.; Yu, W.; Schlipf, D.; Cheng, P.W. Robust gain scheduling baseline controller for floating offshore wind turbines. *Wind. Energy* **2020**, *23*, 17–30. [CrossRef]
31. Sarkar, S.; Fitzgerald, B.; Basu, B. Individual Blade Pitch Control of Floating Offshore Wind Turbines for Load Mitigation and Power Regulation. *IEEE Trans. Control Syst. Technol.* **2021**, *29*, 305–315. [CrossRef]
32. Harris, M.; Hand, M.; Wright, A. *Lidar for Turbine Control: March 1, 2005-November 30, 2005*; Technical Report; NREL—National Wind Technology Center: Boulder, CO, USA, 2006. [CrossRef]
33. Laks, J.; Pao, L.; Wright, A.; Kelley, N.; Jonkman, B. Blade Pitch Control with Preview Wind Measurements. In Proceedings of the 48th AIAA Aerospace Sciences Meeting Including the New Horizons Forum and Aerospace Exposition, Orlando, FL, USA, 4–7 January 2010; American Institute of Aeronautics and Astronautics: Reston, VA, USA, 2010; Chapter 2010-251, pp. 1–24. [CrossRef]
34. Dunne, F.; Pao, L.; Wright, A.; Jonkman, B.; Kelley, N. Combining Standard Feedback Controllers with Feedforward Blade Pitch Control for Load Mitigation in Wind Turbines. In Proceedings of the 48th AIAA Aerospace Sciences Meeting Including the New Horizons Forum and Aerospace Exposition, Orlando, FL, USA, 4–7 January 2010; American Institute of Aeronautics and Astronautics: Reston, VA, USA, 2010; Chapter AIAA 2010-250, pp. 1–18. [CrossRef]
35. Dunne, F.; Pao, L.; Wright, A.; Jonkman, B.; Kelley, N.; Simley, E. Adding Feedforward Blade Pitch Control for Load Mitigation in Wind Turbines: Non-Causal Series Expansion, Preview Control, and Optimized FIR Filter Methods. In Proceedings of the 49th AIAA Aerospace Sciences Meeting including the New Horizons Forum and Aerospace Exposition, Orlando, FL, USA, 4–7 January 2011 ; American Institute of Aeronautics and Astronautics: Reston, VA, USA, 2011; Chapter 2011-819, pp. 1–17. [CrossRef]
36. Dunne, F.; Schlipf, D.; Pao, L.; Wright, A.; Jonkman, B.; Kelley, N.; Simley, E. Comparison of Two Independent Lidar-Based Pitch Control Designs. In Proceedings of the 50th AIAA Aerospace Sciences Meeting including the New Horizons Forum and Aerospace Exposition, Nashville, TN, USA, 9–12 January 2012; American Institute of Aeronautics and Astronautics: Reston, VA, USA, 2012; Chapter 2012-1151, pp. 1–19. [CrossRef]
37. Raach, S.; Schlipf, D.; Sandner, F.; Matha, D.; Cheng, P.W. Nonlinear model predictive control of floating wind turbines with individual pitch control. In Proceedings of the 2014 American Control Conference, Portland, OR, USA, 4–6 June 2014; pp. 4434–4439. [CrossRef]
38. Schlipf, D.; Simley, E.; Lemmer, F.; Pao, L.; Cheng, P.W. Collective Pitch Feedforward Control of Floating Wind Turbines Using Lidar. *J. Ocean. Wind. Energy* **2015**, *2*. [CrossRef]
39. Ma, Y.; Sclavounos, P.D.; Cross-Whiter, J.; Arora, D. Wave forecast and its application to the optimal control of offshore floating wind turbine for load mitigation. *Renew. Energy* **2018**, *128*, 163–176. [CrossRef]
40. Simley, E.; Bortolotti, P.; Scholbrock, A.; Schlipf, D.; Dykes, K. IEA Wind Task 32 and Task 37: Optimizing Wind Turbines with Lidar-Assisted Control Using Systems Engineering. *J. Phys. Conf. Ser.* **2020**, *1618*, 042029. [CrossRef]
41. Fontanella, A.; Al, M.; van Wingerden, J.W.; Belloli, M. Model-based design of a wave-feedforward control strategy in floating wind turbines. *Wind. Energy Sci.* **2021**, *6*, 885–901. [CrossRef]
42. Al, M.; Fontanella, A.; van der Hoek, D.; Liu, Y.; Belloli, M.; van Wingerden, J.W. Feedforward control for wave disturbance rejection on floating offshore wind turbines. *J. Phys. Conf. Ser.* **2020**, *1618*, 022048. [CrossRef]
43. Otter, A.; Murphy, J.; Pakrashi, V.; Robertson, A.; Desmond, C. A review of modelling techniques for floating offshore wind turbines. *Wind. Energy* **2022**, *25*, 831–857. [CrossRef]
44. Høeg, C.E.; Zhang, Z. A semi-analytical hydrodynamic model for floating offshore wind turbines (FOWT) with application to a FOWT heave plate tuned mass damper. *Ocean. Eng.* **2023**, *287*, 115756. [CrossRef]
45. Wang, K.; Gaidai, O.; Wang, F.; Xu, X.; Zhang, T.; Deng, H. Artificial Neural Network-Based Prediction of the Extreme Response of Floating Offshore Wind Turbines under Operating Conditions. *J. Mar. Sci. Eng.* **2023**, *11*, 1807. [CrossRef]
46. Zhang, Y.; Yang, X.; Liu, S. Data-driven predictive control for floating offshore wind turbines based on deep learning and multi-objective optimization. *Ocean. Eng.* **2022**, *266*, 112820. [CrossRef]
47. Barooni, M.; Velioglu Sogut, D. Forecasting Pitch Response of Floating Offshore Wind Turbines with a Deep Learning Model. *Clean Technol.* **2024**, *6*, 418–431. [CrossRef]
48. Gräfe, M.; Pettas, V.; Cheng, P.W. Data-driven forecasting of FOWT dynamics and load time series using lidar inflow measurements. *J. Phys. Conf. Ser.* **2024**, *2767*, 032025. [CrossRef]
49. Deng, S.; Ning, D.; Mayon, R. The motion forecasting study of floating offshore wind turbine using self-attention long short-term memory method. *Ocean. Eng.* **2024**, *310*, 118709. [CrossRef]
50. Ye, Y.; Wang, L.; Wang, Y.; Qin, L. An EMD-LSTM-SVR model for the short-term roll and sway predictions of semi-submersible. *Ocean. Eng.* **2022**, *256*, 111460. [CrossRef]
51. Song, B.; Zhou, Q.; Chang, R. Short-term motion prediction of FOWT based on time-frequency feature fusion LSTM combined with signal decomposition methods. *Ocean. Eng.* **2025**, *317*, 120046. [CrossRef]
52. Mainini, L.; Diez, M. Digital Twins and their Mathematical Souls. In Proceedings of the STO-MP-AVT 369 Research Symposium on Digital Twin Technology Development and Application for Tri-Service Platforms and Systems, NATO Science and Technology Organization, Båstad, Sweden, 10–12 October 2023.

53. Schmid, P.J. Dynamic mode decomposition of numerical and experimental data. *J. Fluid Mech.* **2010**, *656*, 5–28. [CrossRef]
54. Kutz, J.; Brunton, S.; Brunton, B.; Proctor, J. *Dynamic Mode Decomposition: Data-Driven Modeling of Complex Systems*; SIAM—Society for Industrial and Applied Mathematics: Philadelphia, PA, USA, 2016.
55. Mezić, I. Koopman Operator, Geometry, and Learning of Dynamical Systems. *Not. Am. Math. Soc.* **2021**, *68*, 1087–1105. [CrossRef]
56. Arbabi, H.; Mezić, I. Ergodic Theory, Dynamic Mode Decomposition, and Computation of Spectral Properties of the Koopman Operator. *SIAM J. Appl. Dyn. Syst.* **2017**, *16*, 2096–2126. [CrossRef]
57. Brunton, S.L.; Brunton, B.W.; Proctor, J.L.; Kaiser, E.; Kutz, J.N. Chaos as an intermittently forced linear system. *Nat. Commun.* **2017**, *8*, 19. [CrossRef]
58. Kamb, M.; Kaiser, E.; Brunton, S.L.; Kutz, J.N. Time-Delay Observables for Koopman: Theory and Applications. *SIAM J. Appl. Dyn. Syst.* **2020**, *19*, 886–917. [CrossRef]
59. Serani, A.; Dragone, P.; Stern, F.; Diez, M. On the use of dynamic mode decomposition for time-series forecasting of ships operating in waves. *Ocean. Eng.* **2023**, *267*, 113235. [CrossRef]
60. Proctor, J.L.; Brunton, S.L.; Kutz, J.N. Dynamic mode decomposition with control. *SIAM J. Appl. Dyn. Syst.* **2016**, *15*, 142–161.
61. Proctor, J.L.; Brunton, S.L.; Kutz, J.N. Generalizing Koopman Theory to Allow for Inputs and Control. *SIAM J. Appl. Dyn. Syst.* **2018**, *17*, 909–930.
62. Brunton, S.L.; Budišić, M.; Kaiser, E.; Kutz, J.N. Modern Koopman Theory for Dynamical Systems. *SIAM Rev.* **2022**, *64*, 229–340. [CrossRef]
63. Zawacki, C.C.; Abed, E.H. Dynamic Mode Decomposition for Control Systems with Input Delays. *IFAC-PapersOnLine* **2023**, *56*, 97–102. [CrossRef]
64. Dylewsky, D.; Barajas-Solano, D.; Ma, T.; Tartakovsky, A.M.; Kutz, J.N. Stochastically Forced Ensemble Dynamic Mode Decomposition for Forecasting and Analysis of Near-Periodic Systems. *IEEE Access* **2022**, *10*, 33440–33448. [CrossRef]
65. Mohan, N.; Soman, K.; Kumar, S.S. A data-driven strategy for short-term electric load forecasting using dynamic mode decomposition model. *Appl. Energy* **2018**, *232*, 229–244.
66. Al-Jiboory, A.K. Adaptive quadrotor control using online dynamic mode decomposition. *Eur. J. Control* **2024**, *80*, 101117. [CrossRef]
67. Dawson, S.T.; Schiavone, N.K.; Rowley, C.W.; Williams, D.R. A Data-Driven Modeling Framework for Predicting Forces and Pressures on a Rapidly Pitching Airfoil. In Proceedings of the 45th AIAA Fluid Dynamics Conference, Dallas, TX, USA, 22–26 June 2015; American Institute of Aeronautics and Astronautics: Reston, VA, USA, 2015; Chapter AIAA 2015-2767, pp. 1–14. [CrossRef]
68. Rowley, C.W.; Mezić, I.; Bagheri, S.; Schlatter, P.; Hennigson, D.S. Spectral analysis of nonlinear flows. *J. Fluid Mech.* **2009**, *641*, 115–127. [CrossRef]
69. Tang, Z.; Jiang, N. Dynamic mode decomposition of hairpin vortices generated by a hemisphere protuberance. *Sci. China Phys. Mech. Astron.* **2012**, *55*, 118–124. [CrossRef]
70. Semeraro, O.; Bellani, G.; Lundell, F. Analysis of time-resolved PIV measurements of a confined turbulent jet using POD and Koopman modes. *Exp. Fluids* **2012**, *53*, 1203–1220. [CrossRef]
71. Song, G.; Alizard, F.; Robinet, J.C.; Gloerfelt, X. Global and Koopman modes analysis of sound generation in mixing layers. *Phys. Fluids* **2013**, *25*, 124101. [CrossRef]
72. Proctor, J.L.; Eckhoff, P.A. Discovering dynamic patterns from infectious disease data using dynamic mode decomposition. *Int. Health* **2015**, *7*, 139–145. [CrossRef]
73. Brunton, B.W.; Johnson, L.A.; Ojemann, J.G.; Kutz, J.N. Extracting spatial—Temporal coherent patterns in large-scale neural recordings using dynamic mode decomposition. *J. Neurosci. Methods* **2016**, *258*, 1–15. [CrossRef]
74. Mann, J.; Kutz, J.N. Dynamic mode decomposition for financial trading strategies. *Quant. Financ.* **2016**, *16*, 1643–1655. [CrossRef]
75. Diez, M.; Serani, A.; Campana, E.F.; Stern, F. Time-series forecasting of ships maneuvering in waves via dynamic mode decomposition. *J. Ocean. Eng. Mar. Energy* **2022**, *8*, 471–478. [CrossRef]
76. Diez, M.; Gaggero, M.; Serani, A. Data-driven forecasting of ship motions in waves using machine learning and dynamic mode decomposition. *Int. J. Adapt. Control Signal Process.* **2024**. [CrossRef]
77. Diez, M.; Serani, A.; Gaggero, M.; Campana, E.F. Improving Knowledge and Forecasting of Ship Performance in Waves via Hybrid Machine Learning Methods. In Proceedings of the 34th Symposium on Naval Hydrodynamics, Washington, DC, USA, 26 June–1 July 2022.
78. Rialti, M.; Cimatti, G. *Aerogeneratore Mod. TN535 Descrizione Generale*; Tozzi Green: Mezzano, Italy, 2016.
79. Copernicus Marine Service. *Mediterranean Sea Significant Wave Height extreme from Reanalysis*; Copernicus Marine Service: Ramonville-Saint-Agne, France, 2021. [CrossRef]
80. Schmid, P.; Sesterhenn, J. Dynamic Mode Decomposition of Numerical and Experimental Data. In *Sixty-First Annual Meeting of the APS Division of Fluid Dynamics, San Antonio, TX, USA, 23–25 November 2008*; Cambridge University Press: San Antonio, TX, USA, 2008.

81. Koopman, B.O. Hamiltonian Systems and Transformation in Hilbert Space. *Proc. Natl. Acad. Sci. USA* **1931**, *17*, 315–318. [CrossRef]
82. Tu, J.H.; Rowley, C.W.; Luchtenburg, D.M.; Brunton, S.L.; Kutz, J.N. On dynamic mode decomposition: Theory and applications. *J. Comput. Dyn.* **2014**, *1*, 391–421. [CrossRef]
83. Marusic, I. Dynamic mode decomposition for analysis of time-series data. *J. Fluid Mech.* **2024**, *1000*, F7. [CrossRef]
84. Mezić, I. On Numerical Approximations of the Koopman Operator. *Mathematics* **2022**, *10*, 1180. [CrossRef]
85. Otto, S.E.; Rowley, C.W. Linearly Recurrent Autoencoder Networks for Learning Dynamics. *SIAM J. Appl. Dyn. Syst.* **2019**, *18*, 558–593. [CrossRef]
86. Takeishi, N.; Kawahara, Y.; Yairi, T. Learning Koopman invariant subspaces for dynamic mode decomposition. In Proceedings of the 31st International Conference on Neural Information Processing Systems, Red Hook, NY, USA, 4–9 December 2017; NIPS'17; pp. 1130–1140.
87. Lusch, B.; Kutz, J.N.; Brunton, S.L. Deep learning for universal linear embeddings of nonlinear dynamics. *Nat. Commun.* **2018**, *9*, 4950. [CrossRef]
88. Brunton, S.L.; Brunton, B.W.; Proctor, J.L.; Kutz, J.N. Koopman Invariant Subspaces and Finite Linear Representations of Nonlinear Dynamical Systems for Control. *PLoS ONE* **2016**, *11*, e0150171. [CrossRef]
89. Pan, S.; Duraisamy, K. On the structure of time-delay embedding in linear models of non-linear dynamical systems. *Chaos Interdiscip. J. Nonlinear Sci.* **2020**, *30*, 073135. [CrossRef]
90. Marlantes, K.E.; Bandyk, P.J.; Maki, K.J. Predicting ship responses in different seaways using a generalizable force correcting machine learning method. *Ocean. Eng.* **2024**, *312*, 119110. [CrossRef]
91. Lin, J. Divergence measures based on the Shannon entropy. *IEEE Trans. Inf. Theory* **1991**, *37*, 145–151. [CrossRef]
92. Kullback, S.; Leibler, R.A. On Information and Sufficiency. *Ann. Math. Stat.* **1951**, *22*, 79–86.
93. Serani, A.; Diez, M.; Aram, S.; Wundrow, D.; Drazen, D.; McTaggart, K. Model Order Reduction of 5415M in Irregular Waves via Dynamic Mode Decomposition: Computational Models' Diagnostics, Forecasting, and System Identification Capabilities. In Proceedings of the 35th Symposium on Naval Hydrodynamics, Nantes, France, 8–12 July 2024.
94. Rains, J.; Wang, Y.; House, A.; Kaminsky, A.L.; Tison, N.A.; Korivi, V.M. Constrained optimized dynamic mode decomposition with control for physically stable systems with exogeneous inputs. *J. Comput. Phys.* **2024**, *496*, 112604. [CrossRef]
95. Serani, A.; Diez, M.; van Walree, F.; Stern, F. URANS analysis of a free-running destroyer sailing in irregular stern-quartering waves at sea state 7. *Ocean. Eng.* **2021**, *237*, 109600. [CrossRef]
96. Jeffrey, C. Miecznikowski, D.W.; Hutson, A. Bootstrap MISE Estimators to Obtain Bandwidth for Kernel Density Estimation. *Commun. Stat. Simul. Comput.* **2010**, *39*, 1455–1469. [CrossRef]
97. Silverman, B.W. *Density Estimation for Statistics and Data Analysis*; Routledge: London, UK, 2018. [CrossRef]
98. Amsallem, D.; Farhat, C. Interpolation Method for Adapting Reduced-Order Models and Application to Aeroelasticity. *AIAA J.* **2008**, *46*, 1803–1813. [CrossRef]
99. Amsallem, D.; Farhat, C. An Online Method for Interpolating Linear Parametric Reduced-Order Models. *SIAM J. Sci. Comput.* **2011**, *33*, 2169–2198. [CrossRef]

MDPI AG
Grosspeteranlage 5
4052 Basel
Switzerland
Tel.: +41 61 683 77 34

Journal of Marine Science and Engineering Editorial Office
E-mail: jmse@mdpi.com
www.mdpi.com/journal/jmse

www.ingramcontent.com/pod-product-compliance
Lightning Source LLC
Chambersburg PA
CBHW041018270926
51850CB00024B/1486
* 9 7 8 3 7 2 5 8 6 5 6 0 4 *